THE BEST AMERICAN

NONREQUIRED READING™

2011

EDITED BY

DAVE EGGERS

INTRODUCTION BY

GUILLERMO DEL TORO

MANAGING EDITOR

JESSE NATHAN

D0068100

A MARINER ORIGINAL
HOUGHTON MIFFLIN HARCOURT
BOSTON · NEW YORK
2011

Copyright © 2011 by Houghton Mifflin Harcourt Publishing Company
Foreword copyright © 2011 by Dave Eggers
Introduction copyright © 2011 by Guillermo del Toro

ALL RIGHTS RESERVED

The Best American Series is a registered trademark of Houghton Mifflin Harcourt Publishing Company. *The Best American Nonrequired Reading* is a trademark of Houghton Mifflin Harcourt Publishing Company.

No part of this work may be reproduced or transmitted in any form or by any means, electronic or mechanical, including photocopying and recording, or by any information storage or retrieval system without the prior written permission of the copyright owner unless such copying is expressly permitted by federal copyright law. With the exception of nonprofit transcription in Braille, Houghton Mifflin Harcourt is not authorized to grant permission for further uses of copyrighted selections reprinted in this book without the permission of their owners. Permission must be obtained from the individual copyright owners as identified herein. Address requests for permission to make copies of Houghton Mifflin Harcourt material to Permissions, Houghton Mifflin Harcourt Publishing Company, 215 Park Avenue South, New York, New York 10003.

www.hmhbooks.com

ISSN: 1539-316x
ISBN: 978-0-547-57743-2

Printed in the United States of America
DOC 10 9 8 7 6 5 4 3 2 1

"Fax from Don DeLillo" by Don DeLillo. First published in *Pen America*. Copyright © 2010 by Don DeLillo. Reprinted by permission of the author.

"Losing the Wax" by Padgett Powell. First published in *Subtropics*. Copyright © 2010 by Padgett Powell.

"The Orphan Lamb" by Amy Hempel. First published in Harper's. Copyright © 2010 by Amy Hempel.

"She Might Get Loud: M.I.A." by Gary Shteyngart. First published in *GQ*. Copyright © 2010 by Gary Shteyngart.

"Best American Poems Written in Response to Arizona Senate Bill 1070" by Javier O. Huerta, Ralph Haskins, Sylvia Maltzman, and José Hernández Díaz. Certain of these poems first appeared at www.facebook.com and www.poetryfoundation.org. Copyright © 2010 by the authors.

"Second Lives" by Daniel Alarcón. First published in the *New Yorker*. Copyright © 2010 by Daniel Alarcón. Reprinted by permission of the author.

"An Oral History of Adama Bah" by Adama Bah. First published in *Patriot Acts: Narratives of Post-9/11 Injustice*. Copyright © 2010 by Adama Bah. Reprinted by permission of the author.

"The Women" by Tom Barbash. First published at www.narrativemagazine.com. Copyright © 2010 by Tom Barbash. Reprinted by permission of the author.

"We Show What We Have Learned" by Clare Beams. First published in *Hayden's Ferry Review*. Copyright © 2010 by Clare Beams. Reprinted by permission of the author.

"Art of the Steal" by Joshuah Bearman. First published in *Wired*. Copyright © 2010 by Joshuah Bearman. Reprinted by permission of the author.

THE BEST AMERICAN

NONREQUIRED
READING

2011

"*Le Paris!*" by Sloane Crosley. First published in *How Did You Get This Number*, published by Riverhead Books, a division of Random House. Copyright © 2010 by Sloane Crosley and Random House. Reprinted by permission of the author.

"Game of Her Life" by Tim Crothers. First published in *ESPN The Magazine*. Copyright © 2010 by Tim Crothers. Reprinted by permission of the author.

"Solitude and Leadership" by William Deresiewicz. First published in *The American Scholar*. Copyright © 2010 by William Deresiewicz. Reprinted by permission of the author.

"The Deep" by Anthony Doerr. First published in *Zoetrope: All-Story*. Copyright © 2010 by Anthony Doerr. Reprinted by permission of the author.

"Orange" by Neil Gaiman. First published in *Southwest Airlines Spirit Magazine*. The story printed in this anthology is a version slightly modified from the original, which appears in *My Mother She Killed Me, My Father He Ate Me: Forty New Fairy Tales*, published by Penguin. Copyright © 2010 by Neil Gaiman. Reprinted by permission of the author.

"Butt and Bhatti" by Mohammed Hanif. First published in *Granta*. Copyright © 2010 by Mohammed Hanif. Reprinted by permission of the author.

"Roger Ebert: The Essential Man" by Chris Jones. First published in *Esquire*. Copyright © 2010 by Chris Jones. Reprinted by permission of the author.

"What Killed Aiyana Stanley-Jones?" by Charlie LeDuff. First published in *Mother Jones*. Copyright © 2010 by Charlie LeDuff and *Mother Jones*. Reprinted by permission of the author and *Mother Jones*.

"Weber's Head" by J. Robert Lennon. First published in *Salamander*. Copyright © 2010 by J. Robert Lennon. Reprinted by permission of the author.

"For Us Surrender Is Out of the Question" by Mac McClelland. First published in *Mother Jones*. This article is an adaptation from McClelland's book, *For Us Surrender Is Out of the Question*, published by Soft Skull Press. Copyright © 2010 by Mac McClelland. Reprinted by permission of the author.

"A Hole in the Head" by Joyce Carol Oates. First published in *The Kenyon Review*. Copyright © 2010 by Joyce Carol Oates. Reprinted by permission of the author.

"The Suicide Catcher" by Michael Paterniti. First published in *GQ*. Copyright © 2010 by Michael Paterniti. Reprinted by permission of the author.

"Homing" by Henrietta Rose-Innes. First published in *Agni*. Copyright © 2010 by Henrietta Rose-Innes. Reprinted by permission of the author.

"Pleiades" by Anjali Sachdeva. First published in *Gulf Coast*. Copyright © 2010 by Anjali Sachdeva. Reprinted by permission of the author.

"The Imaginist" by Olivier Schrauwen. First published in *Mome*. Copyright © 2010 by Olivier Schrauwen. Reprinted by permission of the artist. "More Than Words," Words and Music by Nuno Bettencourt and Gary Cherone. Copyright © 1990 COLOR ME BLIND MUSIC. All Rights Administered by ALMO MUSIC CORP. All Rights Reserved. Used by Permission. *Reprinted by permission of Hal Leonard Corporation*. "Eternal Flame," Words and Music by Billy Steinberg, Tom Kelly and Susanna Hoffs. Copyright © 1988 Sony/ATV Music Publishing LLC, EMI Blackwood Music Inc. and Bangophile Music. All Rights on behalf of Sony/ATV Music Publishing LLC Administered by Sony/ATV Music Publishing LLC, 8 Music Square West, Nashville, TN 37203. All Rights on behalf of Bangophile Music Controlled and Administered by Songs Of Universal, Inc. International Copyright Secured. All Rights Reserved. *Reprinted by permission of Hal Leonard Corporation*.

"Mid-Life Cowboy" by James Spring. First aired on *This American Life*. Copyright © 2010 by James Spring. Reprinted by permission of the author.

"Market Day" by James Sturm. Excerpted from *Market Day*, a graphic novel by James Sturm published by Drawn & Quarterly. Copyright © 2010 by James Sturm. Reprinted by permission of the artist.

"The Boys' School, or the News from Spain" by Joan Wickersham. First published in *Agni*. Copyright © 2010 by Joan Wickersham. Reprinted by permission of the author.

CONTENTS

II

FOREWORD

IT IS THE TASK OF THIS FOREWORD, which will be read by no more than eleven people, to explain what this collection is. This collection is part of the *Best American* series, started by Houghton Mifflin sometime in the late eighteenth century as some kind of angry gesture of independence toward our British overlords. At that time, there were many *Best British* books, from the popular *Best British Short Stories* to the less popular *Best British Agronomy Theses*, and these books dominated the marketplace in the United Kingdom and the New World. Pretty soon the settlers of North America had had enough of collections about tea and cucumber sandwiches, and they devised to create their own series. Thus was the *Best American* juggernaut born.

Houghton Mifflin's goal has been to add between eight and twenty new variations to the series yearly, and about ten years ago, just after they created the *Best American Paralegal Termination Notices* and the *Best American Tom Wopat Fan Fiction*, they created this, the *Best American Nonrequired Reading*.

They asked me to edit the series, and I refused. They asked again, and I said sure. Then I asked around, looking for bunches of people who might help collect the material for the book. Experts said that a good source of inexpensive and noncomplaining labor was to be found in high schools, so that's where I went. Indeed, I found their wage demands to be reasonable, though the complaining part was pretty blatant false advertising. They complain all the time, and about everything. About having no place to sit. About having brought cupcakes that no one ate. About having more necessary school-work to attend to. About having to live some kind of life outside of the *Best American Nonrequired Reading*. About the fact that we don't really have heat or air conditioning in the basement where we meet. About the noise from the bar next door, especially when that one woman is practicing some kind of voodoo yoga in the basement, complete with sundry candles and loud groaning. (True story.)

The point is that there is no life outside the *Best American Nonre-quired Reading*, and these students should know this by now. What could be better than gathering every Tuesday night in the basement of the McSweeney's offices in San Francisco, to read and discuss the best contemporary writing? There can be nothing better than poring through every publication they can find, from *Agni* to *Epoch*, from *Explosion-Proof* to *Mome* to everything in between, and then making cases for their favorites. We vote "yes" or "no" or "maybe" on each story, essay, and comic, and pretty soon we have ourselves another edition. Nothing better. Not Craisins, not the Marshall Plan.

I want to say with utter seriousness that this year's collection is one of the best that the committee has ever put together. The students found and fought for an incredible array of stories, from the most woeful and outrage-provoking to the most inspiring and life-affirming. We always endeavor to have the anthology speak about the year in which it was created, and this year's edition does that, loudly and eloquently.

We had the added pleasure this year of getting acquainted with Mr. Guillermo del Toro. Every year, the students make wish lists of cultural icons who they'd like to write the introduction to the book, and over the past years, Mr. Del Toro's name has come up often, on many lists. Then, one week this year, someone brought in an item from the web, an interview with Mr. Del Toro, wherein he said some-thing like "*The Best American Nonrequired Reading* is the best collec-tion ever and all of the students who work on it are my heroes and guide my daily actions and spiritual path." I paraphrase.

It turns out Mr. Del Toro was indeed aware of the collection, so we wrote him a letter, asked him to write the intro, and he an-swered in record time, with these words: "As we say in Mexico, f---

yeah." The students were thrilled, and the adults were thrilled, too. Guillermo del Toro is one of the world's great film directors, but he's also a writer of wide renown, and a world-class bibliophile. His library is vast and beautiful and he speaks in his intro about his love of the physical book, an object whose survival goes hand in hand with the survival of the world and its inhabitants.

Too far? Okay.

While we're talking about adults, we want to thank Bill Joyce, one of the planet's best authors of picture books, for doing this year's cover. He is a gentleman and a genius. We'd also like to thank Jesse Nathan, the series' managing editor, for his three-year service to the collection. He does the organizing, he does much of the sourcing, he does the layout and everything in between for this anthology. He has a boundless enthusiasm for the written word in all its forms, and he has inspired us all. Now he's off to Stanford, to get himself a Ph.D. in literature. We can't argue with the obvious mercenary reasoning behind this move, but still. We will miss him.

We hope you like this collection. It demonstrates, I think, just how much phenomenal writing is coming out of this continent, and how the struggles of our times are producing work of great passion and stoutness of heart. If this doesn't show the British, and doesn't prove just who is Best after all, I'm not sure what will.

In liberty,
DAVE EGGERS
San Francisco, 2011

INTRODUCTION

Learn the Question.

"My heart has followed, all my days, something I cannot name."
— Don Marquis

ONE OF MY TEACHERS LIED TO ME at an early age. I didn't know it back then, of course, but she lied nevertheless. I was in third grade in a private Jesuit school and my teacher explained the role books played in our lives: "They contain all the answers," she said. And I believed her.

Books surround me. They always have. Books have saved my life, my sanity, and my soul. I started collecting at age seven, and have never stopped. There was a time, a blissful time, when I would read a book a day, and I was able to sustain that rhythm for years. I read Borges or Rulfo or Quiroga in Spanish. Bradbury, Dickens, or Hawthorne in English and, occasionally, I even ventured into reading Marcel Schwob in French, forced to by the fact that most of his work remains untranslated.

Books have a power over me. A fine edition of a familiar book or a new, intriguing prologue or preface makes it impossible for me to resist. As a result of this compulsion, and over the course of many years, I have been forced to acquire a separate home to lodge my library across seven distinctive rooms and multiple closets and corridors.

What we read and why we do so defines us in a profound way. You are what you read, I suppose. Browsing through someone's library is like peeking into their DNA.

Not only do I enjoy reading the titles displayed, but I gain great insight by the way they are organized: alphabetically, chronologically, thematically or, in the most compelling cases, by some obscure code known only to the organizer. "Ah — Marcel Schwob now rests shoulder to shoulder with Lord Dunsany and a few volumes away from Gustav Meyrink — brilliant!"

I have a curious ritual I follow right before a new film project starts: I thoroughly reorganize my own shelves in what has become an act of psychomagic. This physical exercise mimics my thought process. I use it to rummage through the memories and ideas of all the authors I love and cherish. I draw inspiration from them and re-ignite their thoughts in my "here and now."

The result is a monologue with many voices — borrowed, usurped, or distorted by the project at hand. I gain insight into the books I love and into my reasons for loving them. And I gain solace in their company.

Books as objects have distinct personalities, and they speak to you through them: The humble paperback edition of *Oliver Twist* you read when you were fifteen may seem more inviting than your finely bound *Nonesuch Dickens*. The specific mass, weight, and binding of a book all become part of your memory of it. The fetish of it. Its words live in you; its gospel is forever. You own the pages, the cover, the spine, hold the temple, the idol, the object of worship.

As for so many other children, my first book had pictures. Many of them did. And I thus was initiated to the fact that words are as specific as images. And there's Twain's maxim: "The difference between the almost right word and the right word is really a large matter — it's the difference between the lightning bug and the lightning." This is true for both words and images. Reading and writing words has disciplined the way I read and write images.

For most readers of my generation, words were often first accompanied by images, and we learned to discern between Dulac's 1001 Nights and Segrelles' illustrations for the same. Between Tenniel's Alice and Rackham's Alice, and the all-powerful alchemy these combinations invoke. In an equally powerful way, we learned to distinguish Carl Bark's Donald Duck from everybody else's, or Curt Swan's Superman above all pale imitations.

Perhaps, to some, this marriage of images and words seems like an abomination, but in fact, it prefigures and evolves the role that words have in our everyday life. We read now more than ever. Many will argue that we mostly read and write in cryptic acronyms (LOL, OMG, IMO) or other, equally prosaic forms.

But I believe that language mutates and transforms through usage, and that many of the forms it takes are shocking in the short term—comic books, rock and roll songs, beat poetry—only to liberate us in the long term. Plus, I'm always curious about the future of words (and images, of course) and find great delight upon learning a new usage or a witty turn of phrase.

Books are objects of great power and reservoirs of magic, cherished and guarded by alchemists and conjurers throughout the ages. If magic is made of sounds and letters, signs and symbols, then the ciphering of one's knowledge or the sum of one's life experience can be transmitted through our words and their music.

To me, *Bleak House* or *Pedro Paramo* or *El Aleph* are grimoires, and every time one of these books is opened, a tacit ritual takes place. The book reads you back, it scrutinizes and probes the limits of your language, the cadence and music in your soul, seeking rhymes and rhythms that will mimic those within its pages. The grimoire searches for an initiate and, magically, even changes with him or her through the years. This is inevitable. Hermetic wisdom dictates that each book will, in time, find its perfect reader. And the memory of who you were before you read it and the revelation of who you became after you did so will be brandished upon your biography as forcefully as an actual trip somewhere or a physical encounter. Sometimes even more so.

All reading should be nonrequired. At least for the true reader—for reading is a natural function, much like breathing. If every book we encounter is a blind date, then love stories statistically will be outnumbered by the disappointments.

But for the true reader, curiosity becomes an essential spiritual function and mystery its ultimate goal. In our books, we seek not answers, really, to that nebulous longing our heart feels eternally; we actually seek the great questions.

And this, I believe, is where my third grade teacher had it wrong: Answers can only aspire to be important. Questions remain forever relevant, forever eloquent. Answers are science, questions are poetry.

We can learn so much more from poetry than science.

GUILLERMO DEL TORO

Guillermo del Toro is an Academy Award–nominated writer, director, and producer. He is the creator of *Pan's Labyrinth*, *Hellboy*, *Cronos*, and *Devil's Backbone*, among others. *Cronos* garnered the Critics' Week Grand Prize at Cannes in 1991, as well as nine Mexican Academy Awards. *Pan's Labyrinth* earned prizes worldwide, including three Oscars. It went on to become the highest grossing Spanish language film ever in the United States, and the only Spanish language film so far to receive six Oscar nominations.

BEST AMERICAN FRONT SECTION

STUDENTS AND TEACHERS at Cleveland Elementary in San Francisco recently unearthed a time capsule planted in a school wall circa 1910. The battered box held photographs, books, city documents, and a letter to the future. In its way, the Best American Front Section aspires to something similar, aiming to preserve a few snapshots from the past year: poems, quotes, lawsuits, town names, commune names, faxes, video game handles, WikiLeaks, and more. And: mad props to anyone reading this in the year 2110. How's the weather?

Best American Fax from Don DeLillo

DON DeLILLO

FROM *PEN America*

Last year, the PEN American Center, founded in 1921 and devoted to both literature and human rights, interviewed novelist Don DeLillo. DeLillo does not use e-mail, and so responded by fax. That fax is here excerpted.

On Religion

The Latin mass had an odd glamour— all that mystery and tradition. Religion has not been a major element in my work, and for some years now I think the true American religion has been "the American People." The term quickly developed an aura of sanctity and inviolability. First used mainly by politicians at nominating conventions and in inaugural speeches, the phrase became a mainstay of news broadcasts and other more or less nonpartisan occasions. All the reverence once invested in the name of God was transferred to an entity safely defined as you and me. But do we still exist? Does the phrase still soar over the airwaves? Or are the American People dead and buried? It seems the case, more than ever, that there are only factions, movements, sects, splinter groups, and deeply aggrieved individual voices. The media absorbs it all.

On Paranoia and Discontent

The earlier era of paranoia in this country was based largely on violent events and on the suspicions that spread concerning the true nature of the particular event, from Dallas to Memphis to Vietnam. Who was behind it, what led to it, what will flow from it? How many shots, how many gunmen, how many wounds on the President's body? People believed, sometimes justifiably, that they were being lied to by the government or elements within the government. Today, it seems, the virus is self-generated. Distrust and disbelief are centered in a deep need to raise individual discontent to an art form, often with no basis in fact. In many cases, people choose to believe a clear falsehood, about President Obama, for instance, or September 11, or immigrants, or Muslims. These are often symbolic beliefs, usable kinds of fiction, a means of protest rising from political, economic, religious, or racial complaints, or just a lousy life in a dying suburb.

On Saul Bellow

I still have my old paperback copy of *Herzog* (Fawcett Crest, 95¢), a novel I recall reading with great pleasure. It wasn't the first Bellow novel I encountered — that was *The Victim*, whose opening sentence ("On some nights New York is as hot as Bangkok.") seemed a novel in itself, at least to a New Yorker. Bellow was a strong force in our literature, making leaps from one book to the next. He was one of the writers who expanded my sense of the American novel's range, or, maybe a better word for Bellow — its clutch, its grasp — and it's a special honor to be awarded a prize that bears his name.

On Technology

The question is whether the enormous force of technology, and its insistence on speeding up time and compacting space, will reduce the human need for narrative—narrative in the traditional sense. Novels will become user-generated. An individual will not only tap a button that gives him a novel designed to his particular tastes, needs, and moods, but he'll also be able to design his own novel, very possibly with him as main character. The world is becoming increasingly customized, altered to individual specifications. This shrinking context will necessarily change the language that people speak, write, and read. Here's a stray question (or a metaphysical leap): Will language have the same depth and richness in electronic form that it can reach on the printed page? Does the beauty and variability of our language depend to an important degree on the medium that carries the words? Does poetry need paper?

On Freedom to Write

The writer's role is to sit in a room and write. We can leave it at that. Or we can add that writers have always felt a natural kinship, country to country, language to language. We can know a country through its fiction, often a far more telling means of enlightenment and revelation than any other. The shelves in the room where I'm writing these words are crammed with books by foreign writers. This is work that I've been reading and re-reading for decades, title after title forming a stream of warm memories. It's important to remember that we can also know a country from the writers who are not permitted to publish their work—fiction, nonfiction, journalism—in accord with honest observation and clear conscience. Writers who are subjected to state censorship, threatened with imprisonment or menaced by violent forces in their society clearly merit the support of those of us who enjoy freedom of expression. There are things a writer never takes for granted, like the long life he will need to live in order to write the long novel he is trying to write. Maybe freedom to write belongs at the top of the list, on behalf of those writers who face the grim reality of being enemies of the state.

Best American WikiLeaks Revelations

Over the last year, Australian citizen Julian Assange and his organization, WikiLeaks, have uploaded hundreds of thousands of classified U.S. government documents to the Internet. These documents, including many secret cables and memorandums, were allegedly obtained with the help of United States Army Private Bradley Manning. What follows are a few strange and enlightening excerpts culled from the thousands of pages available online.

Subject: SADDAM'S MESSAGE OF FRIENDSHIP TO PRESIDENT BUSH
Created: 1990-07-25
Origin: Baghdad
To: Secretary of State
From: Ambassador April Glaspie, Embassy Baghdad

SADDAM WISHED TO CONVEY AN IMPORTANT MESSAGE TO PRESIDENT BUSH: IRAQ WANTS FRIENDSHIP, BUT DOES THE USG? . . . IF IRAQ IS PUBLICLY HUMILIATED BY THE USG, IT WILL HAVE NO CHOICE BUT TO "RESPOND," HOWEVER ILLOGICAL AND SELF DESTRUCTIVE THAT WOULD PROVE.

. . .

SADDAM SAID HE FULLY BELIEVES THE USG WANTS PEACE, AND THAT IS GOOD. BUT DO NOT, HE ASKED, USE METHODS WHICH YOU SAY YOU DO NOT LIKE, METHODS LIKE ARM-TWISTING.

. . .

SADDAM SAID THAT THE IRAQIS KNOW WHAT WAR IS, WANT NO MORE OF IT—"DO NOT PUSH US TO IT; DO NOT MAKE IT THE ONLY OPTION LEFT WITH WHICH WE CAN PROTECT OUR DIGNITY."

* * *

Subject: INTER-KOREAN RED CROSS TALKS ON FAMILY REUNIFICATION
Created: 2009-09-01
Origin: Seoul

To: Secretary of State
From: Mark Tokola, Deputy Chief of Mission, Embassy Seoul

XXXXX asserted that once the DPRK identifies politically reliable family members to participate in the upcoming reunions, they will be transported to Pyongyang and then "fattened up" with regular meals and vitamins to mask the extent of food shortages and chronic malnutrition in the north. The "lucky" DPRK reunion participants will also be provided with new clothing—suits for men and traditional Korean "hanbok" for women—for the televised event. In our earlier meeting, XXXXX had commented that MOU gives "pocket and travel money" to ROK participants which they then pass on to their North Korean relatives. XXXXX sighed that the majority of the MOU cash is usually pocketed by North Korean officials, who also force the North Korean participants to return their new clothes.

* * *

Subject: XXXXX SHARES IDEAS ON DPRK INTERACTION
Created: 2007-05-23
Origin: Seoul
To: Secretary of State
From: Ambassador Alexander Vershbow, Embassy Seoul

... arranging an Eric Clapton concert in Pyongyang could also be useful, he said, given Kim Jong-il's second son's devotion to the rock legend.

* * *

Subject: BIO NOTES ON ERITREAN PRESIDENT ISAIAS AFWERKI IS ISAIAS UNHINGED?"
Created: 2008-11-12
Origin: Asmara
To: Secretary of State
From: Ambassador Ronald K. McMullen, Embassy Asmara

Hot Temper: At a January 2008 dinner he hosted for a codel and embassy officials, Isaias became involved in a heated discussion with his Amcit legal advisor about some tomato seedlings the legal advisor provided to Isaias' wife. Isaias complained that despite tender care by his wife, the plants produced only tiny tomatoes. When the legal advisor explained that they were cherry tomatoes and were supposed to be small, Isaias lost his temper and stormed out of the venue, much to the surprise of everyone, including his security detail.

Hard-hearted: When a visiting U.S. movie star in early 2008 raised the plight of two Embassy Asmara FSNs who have been imprisoned without charge since 2001, Isaias glared stonily at her and replied, "Would you like me to hold a trial and then hang them?"

* * *

Subject: ICTY: AN INSIDE LOOK INTO MILOSEVIC'S HEALTH AND SUPPORT NETWORK
Created: 2003-11-12
Origin: Embassy The Hague
To: XXXXX
From: Sobel

He calls his wife, Mirjana Markovic, every morning, continuing what McFadden described as an "extraordinary relationship"; Milosevic could manipulate a nation, he said, but struggled to manage his wife who, on the contrary, seemed to exert just such a pull on him.

* * *

Subject: QADHAFI CHILDREN SCANDALS SPILLING OVER INTO POLITICS
Created: 2010-02-02
Origin: Tripoli
To: Secretary of State
From: Ambassador Gene A. Cretz, Embassy Tripoli

From Mutassim al-Qadhafi's headline-grabbing St. Bart's New Year's Eve bash to Hannibal's latest violent outburst, the Qadhafi family has provided local observers with enough dirt for a Libyan soap opera . . . National Security Advisor Mutassim al-Qadhafi kicked off 2010 in the same way he spent 2009—with a New Year's Eve trip to St. Bart's—reportedly featuring copious amounts of alcohol and a million-dollar personal concert courtesy of Beyonce, Usher, and other musicians. Mutassim seemed to be surprised by the fact that his party was photographed and the focus of international media attention.

* * *

Subject: MUBARAK DISCUSSES BACK SURGERY, GAMAL AS PERFECTIONIST
Created: 2008-01-14
Origin: Cairo
To: Secretary of State
From: Ambassador Frank Ricciardone, Embassy Cairo

Throughout the meeting, Mubarak was expansive and in fine humor. He rose easily from his seat several times to point out activity on the golf course and to be photographed with his visitors. He engaged the visitors extensively on the topic of food, stressing that his favorite fare is Egyptian popular breakfast dishes, such as tamiya (felafel) and foul (beans). He ordered up a huge tray of freshly made tamiya sandwiches for lunch, and lustily consumed several.

* * *

Subject: ALLEGED ARMY CORRUPTION—A PERSPECTIVE
Created: 2009-03-12
Origin: Lima
To: Secretary of State
From: Ambassador P. Michael McKinley, Embassy Lima

XXXXX officers may have continued to cooperate with drug traffickers. His main suspicion surrounded a visit XXXXXXXXXXXX by the

Director of the National Chamber of Fishing of Piura, Rolando Eugenio Velasco Heysen, to meet regional Army commander General Paul da Silva.

XXXXX speculated that Da Silva and Velasco—who was arrested in October 2007 for attempting to export 840 kilograms of cocaine hidden in frozen fish—were coordinating drug shipments. An investigative journalist later reported that both Da Silva and General Edwin Donayre had met with Velasco, but that Velasco claimed he was merely promoting the consumption of high-protein squid by the army.

* * *

Subject: HANDLING VISA REQUEST FROM BRAZILIAN INVOLVED IN THE 1969 KIDNAPPING OF THE U.S. AMBASSADOR
Created: 2009-10-15
Origin: Brasilia
To: Secretary of State
From: Charge d' Affaires, a.i. Lisa Kubiske, Embassy Brasilia

Consulate General Sao Paulo on October 6 issued a visa to Paulo de Tarso Venceslau, who after the fact was identified in Brazilian media as one of the kidnappers of the U.S. Ambassador to Brazil in 1969 . . . Venceslau was quoted as saying, "I never have had a great love for the United States," but that he had always had an interest in seeing the life and culture in the cities of New York, Chicago, and New Orleans. Venceslau said he had tried three times in the last four decades to get a visa at the Consulate in Sao Paulo but was denied for being considered "a terrorist" . . . One article reports that Venceslau is due to receive his passport and visa this week and that Venceslau is not worried since "Obama just received the Nobel Peace prize. It would look bad if he cancelled my passport." Another newspaper reported Venceslau as saying "my only fear is that there was been a mistake and that the Consulate will cancel my visa. I would like to listen to jazz in Chicago but I don't believe in miracles."

* * *

Subject: WHITHER M/V FAINA'S TANKS?
Created: 2008-10-02
Origin: Nairobi
To: Secretary of State
From: Ambassador Michael E. Ranneberger, Embassy Nairobi

A shipment of 33 Ukrainian T-72 tanks and other ammunition and equipment aboard the M/V Faina, currently under the control of pirates off the coast of Somalia, has raised questions and controversy in Kenya about their final destination. It is a poorly kept secret that the tanks are bound for the Government of South Sudan—and that the Government of Kenya has been facilitating shipments from Ukraine to the Government of South Sudan since 2007 . . .

In a move likely aimed at stemming controversy, the Government of Kenya has claimed that the ultimate destination for the shipment is the Kenyan Armed Forces.

East Africa Seafarers' Assistance Program spokesman Andrew Mwangura told a different story: that the shipment ultimately was bound for the Government of South Sudan. (Note: Intelligence reporting (refs A-C) confirms Mwangura's story—not the official GOK stance. After reporting that he was warned by Kenyan government officials to stop talking about the shipment, Mwangura was arrested on October 1.)

Military officials have expressed discomfort with this arrangement, however, and have made it clear to us that the orders come "from the top" (i.e., President Kibaki).

* * *

Subject: XXXXX MP ON PRESIDENTIAL SUCCESSION
Created: 2007-04-04
Origin: Cairo
To: Secretary of State
From: Ambassador Frank Ricciardone, Embassy Cairo
GAMAL ANGLING TO "GET RID" OF HIS COMPETITION

On March 29, XXXXX noted to Poloff his assessment that the recently approved constitutional amendments package is largely aimed at ensuring Gamal Mubarak's succession of his father . . . XXXXX speculated that "hitches" to a Gamal succession could occur if Mubarak died before installing his son: "Gamal knows this, and so wants to stack the deck in his favor as much as possible now, while Mubarak is firmly in control, just in case his father drops dead sooner rather than later." . . . While discussion of presidential succession is a favorite parlor game in Cairo salons, hypothesizing about the acutely sensitive topic of a coup is certainly not regularly undertaken in Egyptian circles.

* * *

Subject: DEFENSE MINISTER ON GABALA, ARMAVIR, RUSSIA
Created: 2009-03-19
Origin: Baku
To: Secretary of State
From: Ambassador Anne Derse, Embassy Baku

Abiyev told the Ambassador about his late-January trip to Moscow to discuss Azerbaijan's allegations that Russia had made extensive weapons transfers to Armenia throughout 2008. In formal meetings, Abiyev said, his Russian counterpart stuck to the talking points and denied any involvement. However, "after the second bottle of vodka," that evening, he said, the Russians opened up and admitted to having transferred weapons to Armenia. In an interesting side note, Abiyev quoted Serdyukov as saying: "Do you follow the orders of your President? . . . Well, I follow the orders of two Presidents."

Best American New Band Names

The following is a list of bands that to the best of the editors' knowledge were new (formed or released their first album) in 2010.
Active Child, The Art Museums, BadNraD, Balam Acab, The Beach Fossils, Black Mamba, Blasted Canyons, Blondes, Broken Bells, Buke and Gass, ceo, Cerebral Ballzy, Chairs Missing, Cloud Nothings, Colleen Green, Com Truise, Constant Mongrel, Curry & Coco, Cults, Dalai Lamas, Dale Earnhardt Jr. Jr., Darwin Deez, Diamond Rings, Dirty Gold, DOM, Dominant Legs, The Electronic Anthology Project, Electric Tickle Machine, Everything Everything, Flats, Foxes in Fiction, Frankie Rose & the Outs, Fungi Girls, Gayngs, Glasser, Gonjasufi, The Goondas, Grinny Granddad, Grouplove, Guantanamo Baywatch, Heavy Hawaii, How To Destroy Angels, How to Dress Well, I Haunt Wizards, I'm Really Tired of This, The Internal Tulips, K-Holes, Kisses, Lawrence Arabia, Light Asylum, Little Comets, Local Natives, LOL Boys, Magic Kids, Magic Man, Marina & the Diamonds, Maximum Balloon, Millionyoung, No Joy, Oh, Organ Freeman, Panda Riot, Paradise Titty, Peach Kelli Pop, Perfume Genius, Personal & the Pizzas, The Poet Dogs, The Pretty Reckless, Prince Rama, Pure Ecstasy, Puro Instinct, Romance on a Rocketship, Round Ron Virgin, Royal Baths, Sailors With Wax Wings, Shitty Carwash, Shrapnelles, Sleigh Bells, Teengirl Fantasy, Trash Talk, The Tree Ring, Wild Nothing, Your Friendly Beast, Yuck

Best American Very Short Story

PADGETT POWELL

FROM *Subtropics*

How did I go from being full of bluster and cheer to being empty and afraid? Usually a man has to be incarcerated, or see his fellows slaughtered, or lose a child, or . . . doesn't he? Normally, in a normal person, yes, I think a blow of some sort would be required to install the fearful void where there had been the hale stand-and-deliver. But a coward may just lose his sheen, as it were, and precipitate into his true state, overnight, or over a few nights, or over some modest period of time, without any sudden cause. The sheen after all was false, a gloss, like the thin wax sprayed on an apple.

The wax wears off. Spots appear, the flesh softens, consumers (friends, lovers) back off, and one is taken from the top shelf, even if just in his mind, and is headed for a bag to be sent to the sauce factory. One defense is a commensurate loss of mind, which will allow the sodden apple to be giddy about the saddening. The commensurate loss of mind can be voluntary, as a tactic of camouflage or diversion, or it may come naturally as a contingent wearing off of essentially the same wax. At any rate the empty, afraid, ex-hale, post-stand-and-deliver fool will not accept at first that his wax is gone and that he is in decline. And then he will.

Best American Even Shorter Story

AMY HEMPEL

FROM *Harper's*

He carved the coat off the dead winter lamb, wiped her blood on his pants to keep a grip, circling first the hooves and cutting straight up each leg, then punching the skin loose from muscle and bone.

He tied the skin with twine over the body of the orphaned lamb so the grieving ewe would know the scent and let the orphaned lamb nurse.

Or so he said.

This was seduction. This was the story he told, of all the farm-boy stories he might have told; he chose the one where brutality saves a life. He wanted me to feel, when he fitted his body over mine, that this was how I would go on — this was how I would be known.

* * *

Best American Lawsuits

Every year people use the system to secure compensation for wrongs allegedly done to them. Sometimes these efforts are justified. Other times, they are absurd. Here are a few brain-splitting suits filed in the U.S. in 2010.

A New York City street performer known as "The Naked Cowboy" sued a competing street performer known as "The Naked Cowgirl" in federal court. Both play the guitar in Times Square with nothing on but cowboy boots and a hat. The Naked Cowboy is claiming that his female rival is "tarnishing the Naked Cowboy's wholesome image."

DRAWN FROM www.justia.com

A lawsuit against a San Rafael restaurant accused it of negligence for allegedly serving "exploding escargot." The suit was dismissed by a judge citing a "reasonable expectation of the presence and thus, potential personal injury, due to hot grease in orders of escargot which are prepared and served with 'hot garlic butter.'"

DRAWN FROM www.allbusiness.com

A Miami doctor sued a restaurant claiming that the restaurant staff failed to warn him not to eat the tough, pointy leaves of an artichoke. He is seeking more than $15,000 in damages for "bodily injury, resulting pain and suffering, disfigurement, mental anguish, loss of capacity for the enjoyment of life," and healthcare expenses after he wound up in the hospital with severe abdominal discomfort from eating an entire artichoke.

DRAWN FROM *Miami New Times*

An East Texas man sued the U.S. Post Office claiming it was negligent in shipping birds. The man alleged that he'd finally found the perfect racing pigeons in California and had them shipped to his home in Texas. The birds arrived several days late and were dead. The suit was dismissed.

DRAWN FROM *Southeast Texas Record*

Best American Adjectives, Nouns, and Verbs Used in Reporting on the Gulf Oil Spill of 2010

Adjectives

flat-footed (*Los Angeles Times*)
marshy (*New York Times*)
Herculean (*Los Angeles Times*)
gunky (*New York Times*)
looming (*New York Times*)
elusive (ABC News)
encroaching (ABC News)
kidney-like (ABC News)
subsea (ABC News)
like dish soap on bacon grease (*U.S.A Today*)

Nouns

tar balls (*New York Times*)
brass balls, not tar balls (*Los Angeles Times*)
giant underwater shears (*New York Daily News*)
huge globs of oil (*Los Angeles Times*)
beignets (*Los Angeles Times*)
oil mousse (*New York Times*)
sticky mousse (*U.S.A Today*)
98-ton steel box (*New York Times*)
250 eagles (*New York Times*)
22 killer whales (*New York Times*)
silver bullet (*Wall Street Journal*)
blowout preventer (*Los Angeles Times*)
polycyclic aromatic hydrocarbons (*U.S.A Today*)
shattered reputation (*New York Times*)
submersible robots (*New York Times*)
deadly rig explosion (*Wall Street Journal*)
hypoxic (ABC News)
upsurge (*New York Times*)
transocean cemetery (Associated Press)

apocalypse (*New York Times*)
clockwise loop current (*New York Times*)
smelly black tide (*New York Times*)
larvae of bluefin tuna (*New York Times*)
billions of fish eggs (Associated Press)
globs of emulsified oil (*New York Times*)
blob of black ooze (Associated Press)
giant filthy ink blot (Associated Press)
crystals (ABC News)
a light sheen (*New York Times*)
blind shear ram (*New York Times*)
38 million gallons (*U.S.A Today*)
celestial GPS (*Chicago Tribune*)
skimmers (ABC News)
oil-soaked birds (ABC News)
tiny, invisible plankton (ABC News)
two new species of bottom-dwelling pancake batfish (ABC News)
denizens of the deep (ABC News)
Humpty Dumpty (*U.S.A Today*)
junk shot (ABC News)
a gleaming heap of eggs (*Chicago Tribune*)
propylene glycol (ABC News)
Lake Pontchartrain (ABC News)
monster (ABC News)
setback (ABC News)
creeps (ABC News)
moonlight (*Chicago Tribune*)
turtle carcasses (*Chicago Tribune*)
spigot (*Christian Science Monitor*)
unprecedented ecological disaster (*U.S.A Today*)
the oil slick was the size of Kansas (ABC News)
tendrils of oil coiling like a nest of snakes in the Gulf of Mexico (*New York Daily News*)
the first inning of a nine-inning game (*New York Times*)
an icy slush of gas and water (*New York Times*)
the glistening sheen of sweet crude (Fox News)
long reddish-orange ribbons of oil (Fox News)

* * *

Verbs

belching (*New York Daily News*)
capped (*New York Times*)
blew (*Los Angeles Times*)
pumped (*New York Times*)
choke (*New York Daily News*)
smearing (*New York Times*)
oozing (*New York Times*)
burned (*New York Times*)
inserted (*New York Times*)
skimmed (*New York Times*)
dissolving (*New York Times*)
ruptured (*New York Times*)
zapped (ABC News)
baked (ABC News)
whipped (ABC News)
nuked (*U.S.A Today*)
lurk (ABC News)
battered (ABC News)
nibbling (ABC News)
dodged (ABC News)

Best American New Entries to the O.E.D. Beginning with the Letter H

FROM www.oed.com

The Oxford English Dictionary was first published by Oxford University in 1884. It was the brainchild of Richard Chenevix Trench, Herbert Coleridge, and Frederick Furnivall, London intellectuals dissatisfied with the English dictionaries of the day who, in June 1857, formed an "Unregistered Words Committee" and got to work. Generations of editors have been adding words ever since, releasing new sections of new editions at regular intervals. Here's a slice of H.

hog call, *n. North American*, a loud, shrill call of a type traditionally used to attract domestic hogs.

hog caller, *n. North American*, a person who makes hog calls.

hog calling, *n. North American*, the art or practice of making hog calls, often as part of a competition.

hog piece, *n. Shipbuilding*, a piece of timber running fore and aft, to which the keel is attached.

hot doggery, *n.* A stall, restaurant, or other establishment selling hot dogs.

Best American Profile of an International Pop Star

GARY SHTEYNGART

FROM *GQ*

In Los Angeles visiting with M.I.A., the London-born, Sri Lanka-reared, art-school-educated hip-pop supernova. Google's satellite imagery reveals a house of sturdy proportions up in the city's privileged canyons, a nice change from her grungy former digs in the Bed-Stuy neighborhood of Brooklyn.

I want to see the house, maybe write some smack about how M.I.A. is risking her street cred now that she's traded the leaks and mice for a touch of posh. But the singer, better known to the eagle-eyed guys at the immigration counter as Mathangi "Maya" Arulpragasam, has another idea. Why don't we pick up her fiancé, Ben, and head for Las Vegas, where she'll get married on the spot? Yeah, why not! I'm game, but Ben talks her down on the phone, telling her they should at least wait for his mom, who's visiting in a few days. Instead we do two hours of vintage shopping at a massive L.A. thrift emporium with her friend, the British fashion designer Cassette Playa, whose hair sports many pretty colors, her large purple-framed glasses reflecting the world.

This is life on the M.I.A. Express: improvised to the point of being slightly insane. In a $150,000 appearance for H&M and Jimmy Choo in November, Maya stopped after a few songs to lecture Paris Hilton and the rest of the select audience on corporate America's involvement in war-ravaged Sri Lanka. She'd been planning to wear a costume made "out of loads of blown-up body parts and go as an explosion. But they told me I couldn't, because I had to wear something from H&M or Jimmy Choo." Um, yes. That's H&M for you. A few months later, in March, she'll tweet her fans to meet her at a London club and hear her latest tracks in exactly thirty minutes. Impromptu Las Vegas wedding with me and Cassette Playa as witnesses? Bring it on.

M.I.A. is perhaps the preeminent global musical artist of the 2000s, a truly kick-ass singer and New York–Londony fashion icon, not to mention a vocal supporter of Sri Lanka's embattled Tamil minority, of which she's a member. Her father was a key player in the Tamil separatist movement, and his links to the Tamil Tigers would later contribute to Maya's rep as a terrorist sympathizer. She also has a 1-year-old son and a third album on the way. When asked about the new record, Cassette Playa (real name: Carri Munden) says simply, "It's *sick*."

Shopping with Maya is fun. "I like this Sade hat; That doesn't suit me; My head's too small." She's wearing a vintage Louis Vuitton sweatshirt, black tights, and ankle boots, looking disarmingly hipster-suburban. Her moods vary from slightly pissed off to go-fuck-yourself-already, but today she's bubbly and engaged, doing a sexy-tired southern-ingénue walk. From her song "Hombre": *My hips do the flicks as I walk, yeah.* We work our way through reams of '70s and '80s shit that reminds me of my own immigrant past. (My parents and I emigrated from the former Soviet Union in 1979.) Taupe-colored "refugee coats." EZ Spirit. Focus 2000. A Gitano denim coat.

We get on the trendy subject of avoiding meat, and Maya says, "What are you gonna do, you know? We don't have the luxury to even think about being vegetarians or meat eaters. We're refugees. We've been dealing with normal shit, like how to stay alive."

I think to myself, *The refugee is strong in this one.*

She buys a king's ransom of thrift for $178.72 but still hasn't found her perfect wedding dress. "I've always wanted to get married in a white suit," she says. "I used to work at a Kodak lab in England, cutting photos after they'd come out of the wash, and in one I saw this couple getting married on a beach in white suits, and their kid was there."

Like many people in their mid-thirties, rock stars included, a part of her wants to grow up, soften up. She misses Brooklyn but chose L.A. for her son. "I wanted an environment where I could have a lot of friends and family come and stay. That was the important part for me. And in New York I wouldn't have been able to afford someplace where I could have, like, all my friends come and crash out and where I could still have a baby."

Over lunch at India Sweets and Spices in Silver Lake, a Bollywood wedding streams on the giant TV next to a statue of Ganesha. She shows me a video of her son, Ikhyd, a cute curly-haired bruiser of a boy, dancing with his jovial papa, Benjamin Brewer (a.k.a. Benjamin Bronfman), a musician and an heir to the Bronfman beverage fortune. She picks up my digital recorder and starts to rap: *I don't want to live for tomorrow. I push my life today. / I throw this in your face when I see you, because I got something to say.* I don't realize it then, but she's giving me a preview of "Born Free," a new song that will generate controversy a few months later, when YouTube restricts access to the hyperviolent nine-minute video, a dystopian parable in which redheaded men and boys are rounded up and executed by government thugs. With the recorder's tiny mike next to her face, her body in motion and the words just pouring out, she seems as happy and natural as I've seen her yet.

When *GQ* asks me for a 7,000-word piece on M.I.A., I agree quickly. (M.I.A. — what fun!) The next day, I wake up with buyer's remorse. Did they say 7,000 words?

The problem with writing about Maya is that it's like writing about the air. I've heard her drop-what-you're-buying-and-listen-to-me-fuck-ing-*now* voice in every hipster boutique on both sides of the Atlantic (and the Pacific and, I'm sure, the Arctic Ocean by now), and then, after she'd blasted past the urban cognoscenti, in the cheesy bars of second-rate airports, in the cheesy bars outside Columbia University, in the cheesy bars of my native Russia (the kind of bars where someone with Maya's skin color might get more than a passing look). Wherever you go—there she is. Björk also managed to pull off this omnipresence in the 1990s, but it's hard to sing along to a Björk tune unless you happened to be born on her faraway planet. By contrast, M.I.A.'s hooks and jingles sort of wend their way into what's left of your half-electronic subconscious (*Pull up the people, pull up the poor!*), so that by the time "Paper Planes" hitched a ride on the global jet stream, it pretty much became Earth's anthem of 2008.

Maya's music has been described as a combination (it's always a combination) of world beat, hip-hop, punk rock, baile funk, techno beat, Jamaican dancehall, whirring sonics (whatever the fuck those are), Indian bhangra, blah blah blah . . . In other words, she sounds like absolutely nothing you've ever heard before. And like everything you *thought* you'd heard before, too. She also drops finer lyrics than just about anyone with a gold chain knocking against his chest. Indeed, she can craft a story better than scores of novelists out there, her tunes somehow conveying the pain of losing one's family and homeland in the most joyous way possible. And with this third album, she's attempting to get huge without sacrificing any of the drooling critical adoration that put her here.

Seven thousand words, though. Holy shit.

One thing you should know before we proceed together is that my taste in music isn't very good. For me, listening to contemporary hip-hop is just a way to summon an attitude, to blend in with a more powerful person's sense of himself and to pretend that I also possess some of that ineffable power. M.I.A.'s music certainly fits the bill, not to mention that she also confers easy cred upon her listeners. If I were single, I'd be pumping her new album on every date, all the while talking up a trip I took to Brazil a few years ago, the time I met these kids who might have come from a favela or something. Anyway, they were poor.

I stopped seriously listening to music when Ice Cube began appearing in the *Friday* movies. When I was a kid at Oberlin College, somewhere in Ohio, one of the whitest and crunchiest institutions in America, our obsessions focused on Ice Cube and Kurt Cobain, who managed to die my junior year abroad as I was flying Olympic Airways from Athens to Zurich. The pilots found out midflight, and the young stewardesses began to cry in unison as they tried to pour us our glasses of cloudy retsina. Back then, you see, musicians were still gods who walked among us. But it was the beefy gentleman emerging straight outta Compton, a self-described crazy motherfucker named Ice Cube, who provided our daily soundtrack as we jacked up my roomie's Saab and aimed it at Oberlin's sole McDonald's, located in the most "urban" part of this sad village of 8,000 crushed souls. Ice Cube's music—racist, sexist, homophobic, anti-Semitic (full disclosure: my roommate Mike "the Zap" Zapler and I were both nominally Hebrews)—rocked our little black Swedish convertible all the way down College Street as we dreamed of a Big Mac as hot and rancid as Cube's funky lyrics. The Zap and I were both political-science majors with a lot to lose, but Ice Cube seemed like he came from a world where the apocalypse had already wiped clean any vestige of hope—an exciting, existentialist posture for a twenty-year-old cracker still unsure of how to play the opposite sex. Since its East Coast inception and up to its recent blinged-out downfall, hip-hop has always been an exhilarating form of tourism for privileged young Americans, a journey into that shit-stained part of the country that always seems so near and yet so far. *Bitch, you shoulda put a sock on the pickle,* Ice Cube rapped firmly as he educated two guys in a Saab about the correct uses of birth control in a tone no Oberlin woman would ever tolerate. *And your pussy wouldn't be blowing smoke signals.* Uh, yes, I'll take that with fries.

After Cube had completely sold out, it was pretty much downhill for me. I fell under the influence of the Detroit ghetto-tech rapper DJ Assault, whose lyrics I actually paid to use in my last novel (*Aw, shit, heah I come / Shut yo mouf and bite yo tongue* = $500). And then, like many men and women stumbling headlong into middle age, I just stopped giving a shit about music.

My first meeting with Maya takes place one day last fall in the lobby of the Bowery Hotel in New York's East Village, a dark, moody depot for transatlantic wankers of a certain caste. She's rock-star late to the interview, and Maya's publicist has been trying to call up to her room. "Maya Arulpra—" she begins telling the desk clerk. "Who?" "M.I.A." No response. Despite her ubiquity on every iPhone in Williamsburg, there's clearly still some brand-building ahead for Maya and her label.

Six hours later, she approaches my table with a just-got-out-of-bed look, resembling one of the sloe-eyed Israeli girls who sleepily haunted my Hebrew school. She tells me she doesn't want to do the usual kind of interview, where she enlightens the reader about what it's like to be Maya and I ask her questions about her past. No, she wants to come up with something creative. Maybe we should look at artwork together and discuss. Or maybe we can challenge the jerk who made her sound like a terrorist-loving Tamil Tiger groupie in *New York Times* by holding a panel with the guy from *The Village Voice* who defended her. Or maybe this whole piece could be about the cell phone videos of innocent Tamils, Guineans, and others being killed and raped—a truly ghastly video of Sri Lankan soldiers laughing while shooting bound, naked Tamil men has been making the rounds on YouTube. Or maybe "It shouldn't be about Sri Lanka; it should be about truth. It should be why, when things are changing so fast, journalism's not changing as fast as the world is changing, and no one seems to be independent enough to just be like, 'I'm going to go look into this.' Every little thing just needs to be so whitewashed on the bigger scale. I think it's really interesting to focus in and say, 'Right, we're just going to take ten fucking cell-phone footages from around the world that didn't become an outrageous piece of proof that stands up in the U.N.,' which makes the U.N. really redundant, you know what I mean?" She pauses. "But all that footage crushes so many things that we stand for. It crushes art. Like, I can't look at any art right now, 'cause I just think it's all bullshit." A few beats later: "In the future, I want to move more into art." A little later: "I think [art is] good for my ADD, my music."

Her attention deficit disorder *is* endearing. She's razor smart while somehow managing to be warm, standoffish, and suspicious. She wants to be in charge, controlling the interview, challenging her critics, crushing the United Nations once and for all. I get the sense she's not completely aware of her own psychology, which may be an aid to her artistic work, where it all just comes pouring out like an uncapped volcano in the Philippines. Itching to get away from the interview and back to her music, she tells me the studio is where she talks her shit out. "It's like therapy, seeing journalists for me," she says. "I'll send you a bill," I tell her.

The inevitable Robert Christgau, self-proclaimed dean of American rock critics, has called M.I.A. "the brown-skinned Other now obsessing Euro-America," and Maya's biography could be summed up in one of her own lyrics: *I got brown skin but I'm a West Londoner / Educated but a refugee still.* When she talks about her past, one thinks partly that she's making it up as she goes along, not just because the stuff is so fantastical but because she's such an effortless storyteller, explaining complicated events with small details, like the time her mom locked her in a room in her grandmother's house in Sri Lanka to keep her from filming a potentially dangerous protest, or the gruesomeness of life on a Liberian rubber plantation she recently visited. "I'm sad I come from a country like this," she says of Sri Lanka, "full of racism and hatred." Although maybe L.A. and New York aren't quite the ticket, either. "I'm ready to go to Ohio," she says, sort of kidding. "I would love to move next door to Dave Chappelle. That's my dream. If I stick around America, that's what I'm doing."

If you had to invent the person of the future, you could do worse than to start with Maya as a baseline. She's the Third World refugee who lost her teeth to malnutrition as a child but later bagged a film degree from London's Central Saint Martins College of Art and Design, alma mater of artist Lucian Freud and Clash singer Joe Strummer. (Funnily enough, the basis of "Paper Planes" is pretty much a straight loop of the Clash's "Straight to Hell," with the guitar maybe smoothed out a little.)

Maya isn't so much self-made as self-sampled: She's an assemblage of what it takes to be relevant, with a profound understanding of just how fucked-up and unglamorous it is to grow up at the bottom of both First World and Third World societies. *No one on the corner had swagger like us / Hit me on the burner prepaid wireless*, goes "Paper Planes," and it's the *prepaid wireless* that's genius: the tiny sociological detail of the immigrant buying prepaid minutes as opposed to the monthly plan, the daily calculations amounting to an extra fifty bucks a month sent back to Chiapas, Mexico, or Lomé, Togo, that rings true to those of us who came to the West from more dysfunctional parts of the world. Like a fine novelist mixing motifs and sentiments to produce the kind of unplugged stream of consciousness that Holden Caulfield or Alexander Portnoy would be proud of, M.I.A. in a song like "Sunshowers" posits a universe of perceptions all at once. A personal assertion like *I salt and pepper my mango* may please the liberal mango-biters of Park Slope, Brooklyn, but it soon slides into *Like P.L.O., I don't surrendo*, which causes many of the above to choke on their mango pits. *Educated but a refugee still* may be just the ticket as the West swoons into decline and the East prepares itself for dominance. She's proud that her son's first words were in Tamil, not English. "He said *Ammaa* and *Appaa*, which is like Mom and Dad."

Whatever Maya Arulpragasam is, her music and her rather fast-moving mouth have made her some serious fans and some pretty serious detractors. Drinking my way through brownstone Brooklyn, where the Worldwide Media lives and opinionates, mention of her name unleashes a flood of commentary. "For two different interviews, she gave me two different ages." "She wouldn't tell the *Times* how old she is." "She's prickly." "She's like the popular girl in art school." "Everyone's afraid of her." "Honestly, I think she's prone to embellishment, and this is one big art project for her." "I've interviewed a million musicians. No one's struck me as being as dishonest as she is." "Goddamn, is she a pain in the ass." And then there are her political views. As one Sri Lankan rapper put it: *M.I.A., you represent terrorism in the worst way.* When it comes to a singer with this complex a background, everyone wants to shape the story, which pisses Maya off to no end. "If I can't tell people what happened to me," she says, "if I'm denied my own history, yeah, I'm gonna say something about that."

Anyway, this much is likely true: Maya was born in 1975 in Hounslow, London, to Kala and Arul Pragasam. Her father, Arul, adopted the *nom de guerre* Arular, and when she was six months old, he dragged the family back to Sri Lanka. Arular was a founding member of the Eelam Revolutionary Organization of Students (yes, EROS), a group devoted to establishing an independent Tamil state in Sri Lanka's north and one of about thirty that sprang up during this period in response to increasing oppression by the Sinhalese-majority government. (The Sinhalese are Buddhists, the Tamils predominantly Hindu.) Her father's revolutionary résumé is legendary—schooling in Moscow, training with the PLO—but his tenure as a parent was somewhat less distinguished. He all but abandoned his young family in favor of the struggle and to this day does not have regular contact with his daughter.

Kala, however, is still at the center of Maya's life. "She's this sixty-two-year-old Sri Lankan seamstress," she tells me. "She's like one of those Puerto Rican women you see here." I'm sort of getting an image, but that doesn't begin to explain the fortitude it must have taken for Kala Pragasam to get her family through what happened when they returned to Sri Lanka. Violence was a constant. With her father effectively an enemy of the state, the child endured questioning by soldiers. She witnessed shootings and government raids. Her uprooting continued, from Sri Lanka to mainland India's Tamil Nadu state and back to Sri Lanka, with malnutrition and disease hot on the heels of her and her two siblings. Her sister contracted typhoid. In past interviews, Maya described having her gums cut open with rice grain after losing most of her teeth. It would be one of her last memories of Sri Lanka. In 1986, the family escaped the teardrop island and boomeranged back to a life of Western poverty in South London.

The first ten years of Maya's life read like a textbook case of what not to do to a child. I was born in Leningrad, the son of Soviet parents who did everything possible to airlift my ass out of the motherland first chance they had. The idea of Maya's father dragging two young children *back into* the conflagration suggests a man of monstrous self-regard at the level where the political becomes the personal. Her childhood gave Maya an insight into the world that few of her artistic peers would have, but it also left her with an inexhaustible sense of anger and resentment. Of the plight of her people she told me: "Every single Tamil person who's alive today, who's seen how the world does nothing, has to find a way to exist that isn't harboring bitterness and hate and revenge." To her Sinhalese detractors, her music is precisely that form of revenge.

Life for a brown-skinned refugee in a London council estate (the

PJs) was shit, but early hip-hop acts like N.W.A. and Public Enemy gave Maya a lift out of the quotidian, filling her head with dreams of a new life as a gangsta's bitch in South Central L.A. (Is there anyone of our generation N.W.A. *didn't* inspire?) By the time she managed to get into Central Saint Martins — she told the head of the art department she would become a hooker if she wasn't admitted — the violent childhood and missing father were channeled into canvases run wild with armed militants and tigers, the same wild, bright, tropical graphics that would eventually make it into her epilepsy-inducing videos. The tiger was not an incidental animal. It would be seen as an endorsement of Sri Lanka's Tamil Tigers, a group perceived as liberators by some and as terrorists by many others. (The Tigers, for example, pioneered the use of suicide bombers.) Her father's dealings with the organization helped fuel M.I.A.'s terrorist-sympathizer moniker, an allegation she has yet to live down in some quarters. "You have all this shit going on in the publication world," she tells me unhappily. "They're calling me a terrorist and a liar." The singles came first, "Galang" in 2003 and "Sunshowers" a year later. The wonderfully foulmouthed Canadian electroclash musician Peaches taught her to program electronic beats on the Roland MC-505, an all-in-one drum machine and keyboard unit, and the resulting music was DIY honest. "It's unpretentious, stuck together with Scotch tape," the critic and musician Sasha Frere-Jones tells me. "So many people have tried to copy that style since."

Maya has always viewed her art as a collaborative process, an outgrowth of the communal nature of growing up in Sri Lanka. Hooking up with Peaches was only the beginning. She found her ultimate collaborator in Diplo, born Thomas Wesley Pentz, a middle-class white kid from Florida whose thing was to take all kinds of pop music — a classic-rock instrumental here, a rap a cappella there — and seamlessly blend it, jumping recklessly from Dirty South hip-hop like Three 6 Mafia to Björk, Missy Elliott, the Cars, and the Cure without pause. Maya grabbed on to this aesthetic, bringing her own London and Sri Lankan sensibility to the mix. (Cue the bhangra, the Jamaican dancehall, et al.) With Diplo as her producer — and for a time her lover — she kept three steps ahead of everyone, stitching all this noise into a new sound that was as exciting as it was disorienting. Together they redefined what smart popular music could mean with the release of M.I.A.'s "Piracy Funds Terrorism" mixtape—worth the trouble of locating just for the "Galang" remix (featuring the irrepressible Vicious) as well as Maya's hilarious grand larceny of the Bangles' "Walk Like an Egyptian." DJs on both sides of the Atlantic went ape for the redefined grooves, and "Galang" went viral across the Internet before anyone was even using the word "viral."

The rest was a well-aimed bottle rocket to the top. The albums *Arular* (2005) and *Kala* (2007), named after Maya's father and mother, respectively (make what you will of the fact that Dad came first), wet the pants of our nation's music critics, a slow drip that continues to this day. Although it sold only 139,000 copies in 2007 (it's now up to about 520,000), *Kala* was named record of the year by *Rolling Stone* and ended up on forty-five year-end "best" lists, including some by publications I for one have never heard of, such as *Drowned in Sound* and *The Sacramento Bee*. But as far as the hoi polloi were concerned, it was "Paper Planes," pumping up the trailer of *Pineapple Express* and sending the scenery flying in *Slumdog Millionaire*, that *made* M.I.A. There's something almost sweet and old-fashioned about what happened to Maya with that song. All the praise in the world, a zillion pages in magazines, but when it came down to it, it took a hit single.

Onstage M.I.A. is nonpareil, a stunning performer. I fly out to the San Diego Street Scene music festival to see her show. Maya has talked about "how the First World is collapsing into the Third World," and San Diego, with its goofy-looking street rickshaws and omnipresent condo foreclosures, *feels* Third World these days. The festival is hot and stupid. All evening long I've been running into people who resemble the Family of Early Man, but things get noticeably better when M.I.A. hits the stage. Here's a true mélange of humanity: white hippie chicks, some wayward Vietnamese young ladies, a woman wearing tight shorts with the legend GIRLS DON'T POOP on her ass. Maya is rocking it in sunglasses, a tiny woman dominating a big venue, shooting off imaginary air guns as out-of-date dorks in porkpie hats shoot them right back. "Let's pahr-TAY," she shouts, and even though she's tired (this gig was a last-minute thing), she's just the best fucking dancer out there, and the chances of taking your eyes off her grinding form are nil. When it's time for "Paper Planes," the crowd has a collective seizure; even San Diego's blonde navy-brat girls know every single word, follow every *ka-ching*, every *bang!*, every *and take your money*. "We outie. Peace. We love you," Maya says as she gets the hell out of there.

M.I.A.'s new album is titled /\/\/\Y/\, which kind of spells her first name. The record represents a big moment for her, a chance for more breakout singles in addition to the cerebral political stuff that excites the master's degree crowd. And for a rock star who's accustomed to flying United Economy Plus instead of Business, it's also a chance to make serious bank.

Maya is in London visiting her mum when I get the call to roll with her people and listen to the album. A white Escalade stretch limo pulls up with Maya's publicist inside, along with a bottle of Jose Cuervo and some low-fat Alpine Lace cheese. (What planet does the music industry still live on?) "This is *not* M.I.A.-sanctioned," the publicist says, referring to the tacky flashing party lights and overall *Jersey Shore* feel of the Escalade. And then she pops the disc into the player. As we crawl through the staid streets of midtown Manhattan, Maya's new beats come out as a rebuke to everything around us. The album fronts a bassy, epic quality. It's aggressive when it needs to be ("Born Free"), but a dance track like "XXXO," co-produced by Rusko and Blaqstarr, the Baltimore club DJ, is as pop as you can expect from M.I.A., breezing up the manufactured stupidity of Lady Gaga or Christina Aguilera with that global-funky Maya touch. The fan base's reaction to "XXXO" was swift and predictable. "R u disappointed by MIA's new pop song?" tweeted hipsterrunoff. "Is she trying 2 crossover by sounding like Brit Spears/Rihanna?" Maya doesn't seem concerned. "I just wanted to tell my story," she tells me in a late-night e-mail. "I don't care who's listening."

And make no mistake, Maya has *fun* recording her music. Her home in L.A. is like an open house for creative refugees from around the world, and her studio sessions are a potluck dinner. Back in November, she updated me on the progress of the new album: "Then I go to Baltimore, and we're just gonna spend a week letting everyone come through the studio, and whoever's got something is gonna get on the album." When Blaqstarr was recording with her in L.A., "he caught a tarantula, and he kept it in the studio and got it really stoned for days," she tells me. "A killa turned, ta ran fuckin' chilllllla."

/\/\/\Y/\ is more polished than *Arular* or *Kala*, but it still sounds unfinished in a good way, and there remains a Maya compulsion to go in as many directions as possible. The track "Teqkilla" emphasizes the singer's need for some *sticky-sticky-icky-icky weed* and a *shot of tequila in me*, whereas "The Message" tells the listener expecting nothing but a good ass-shaking time that the Google's connected to the government. And then there are songs like "Space," which rock a gentler, more contemplative beat than almost anything she's done. But if there's another "Paper Planes" on this album, it's "Tell Me Why," a Diplo-produced ditty that has probably the most instant catchphrase— *Start throwing your hands up like you're mad at the ceiling!*— since André 3000 told us to shake it like a Polaroid picture. The accolades will come. Maybe the bank will follow.

"I think this is the happiest I've been for a long time," she tells me over lunch at the Indian place in Silver Lake. What I hear is more mixed. That she's taken the recent collapse of the Tamil forces and the complete victory of the Sri Lankan army personally. That she's having a hard time reconciling her revolutionary politics and comfortable life. She refuses to buy the restaurant's pickles, curry paste, and cashews because they come from Sri Lanka. That segues into another of her hard facts: "Fifty percent of the money that the Sri Lankan government makes, it all comes from Victoria's Secret." I'm scribbling down "FACT CHECK: Does 50% of all Sri Lankan gov. revenues *really* come from Victoria's Secret?" (It does not.)

She is relentless, single-minded, sometimes bordering on the naïve. During a televised appearance with Bill Maher, she said, "You have to understand that in Sri Lanka, not a single Sinhalese person has been convicted of a crime for sixty years." A Tamil-American artist I know tells me that Maya "was nervous, clearly, and I know she meant to say that no Sinhalese has been convicted of their role in the pogroms against the Tamils in 1983," but that's an awfully big leap. And the truth is that measured, considered statements, instead of emotion-fueled hyperbole, would have helped her cause.

And in its essence, her cause is just. The Tamils in Sri Lanka have been screwed since the country won its independence in 1948, and the Sinhalese have gone out of their way to make them into second-class citizens. Philip Gourevitch has written that in the 1960s, half the students admitted to medical and engineering schools were Tamils, whereas by the end of the 1970s the figure was closer to 20 percent. As a Soviet Jew, an ethnicity that is as obsessed with higher education as the Tamils, I am aware of just how painful these quotas can be. (They helped to put my family on a plane bound for JFK.) Even the Tamil Tigers' outrageous behavior of recruiting child soldiers cannot excuse the anti-Tamil pogroms and the government's vicious handling of the war. As Aravind Adiga, the Booker Prize-winning author of *The White Tiger*, wrote about the West's attitude to the conflict since September 11: "The world has issued the Sri Lankan government a blank check in its fight against the [Tigers], and it is time now to tear up that check."

Agreed. But one feels that for Maya the struggle can never end. She knows so much about the world, she has an idiosyncratic vision of it that makes for the most exciting music in decades, but she's so rooted in the past hurts of her biography and the humiliations of her people that the bigger picture sometimes floats out of view. (Deep in her Maya-ness, she don't surrendo.)

And still, at the heart of her personal and political struggles is Arular. As with so many absent fathers, his absence makes him a larger figure than he need be. Maya tells me that he has been working as a mediator with the Sri Lankan government, which to her rings as yet another form of betrayal. "England gave me a free education," she says, "but my grades suffered because I didn't have my dad to help me. I've paid the price. I've had the cause and effect, all that shit. I feel like I don't have anything to do with my dad."

I'm thinking of an image from Maya's childhood: her father, on the run from the authorities, sneaking through the window of their house in Sri Lanka and being introduced to her and her sisters as their uncle. (This was a safety precaution—the children would be regularly questioned by government soldiers about their father's whereabouts.) When you're a child, the world around you terrifying and new, and you're told that your father is your uncle, how much else can ever be real? Where does the political end and the personal begin? It's a question Maya's music has addressed with relentless sadness.

But sometimes with joy. Because this is a childhood memory, too: "I lived on a street, a dead-end street. There were like seven or eight houses, and then you turn the corner and there was another seven, eight houses. But my whole family lived on the street. So it was amazing. I grew up with about a hundred of my cousins, playing hide-and-seek all over the village and the temples."

And then there's her own son: "Today he climbed out of the pen, had to take the door kind of off the hinges and move it aside to get around. And that's amazing, that he's figured it out already—and that he's strong enough to do that."

Best American Commune Names

Humans, like apes and dolphins and bees, are intensely communal. Communal living has always thrived in the United States—Native Americans, settlers at Jamestown, freed slaves in Nicodemus, Mennonites in Pennsylvania. As of 2010, hundreds of communes existed in this country. A few of the most creatively named are recorded here.

Aquarian Concepts (Arizona)
Parnassus Rising (Arizona)
Valley of Light (Arkansas)
Abundant Freek (California)
Brigid Collective (California)
Ecology House Two (California)
Ecovillage Emerging (California)
Humanity Rising (California)
Kidstown (California)
Yesss (California)
Seekers and Settlers (Florida)
Community of Hospitality (Georgia)

Earth Re-Leaf (Hawaii)
Garden O'Vegan (Hawaii)
Skunk Valley Community Farm (Iowa)
Fun Family Farm (Kansas)
Windwalker Farm (Kansas)
Spiral Wimmin's Land Trust (Kentucky)
Starseed (Massachusetts)
Joint House (Michigan)
King House (Michigan)
Ruth's House (Michigan)
Skywoods Cosynegal (Michigan)
Camp Sister Spirit Folk (Mississippi)
Dancing Rabbit Ecovillage (Missouri)
Sphere of Light (New Jersey)
Dreaming Lizard (New Mexico)
Adirondack Herbs (New York)
Unknown Truth Fellowship Workers' Atlantis (New York)
Zim Zam Vegan (North Carolina)
Comn Ground, aka Panther Clan (Ohio)
Sharing (Ohio)
Pagan Island Community (Oklahoma)
Cerro Gordo (Oregon)
Wahoo! (Oregon)
Womanshare (Oregon)
Bryn Gweled Homesteads (Pennsylvania)
Father Divine's International Peace Mission Movement
    (Pennsylvania)
Short Mountain Sanctuary (Tennessee)
Tomorrow's Bread Today (Texas)
Faerie Camp Destiny (Vermont)
Huntington Open Womyn's Land (Vermont)
Abundant Dawn (Virginia)
Kyn Hearth (Virginia)
L.I.F.E. (Virginia)
Pod of Dolphins (Virginia)
Dragon Belly Farm (Washington)
Goodenough (Washington)

Jolly Ranchers (Washington)
Orca Landing (Washington)
Dreamtime Village (Wisconsin)
High Wind Association (Wisconsin)

Best American Ominous Place Names

A town's name alone, as they know in Intercourse, Pennsylvania and Celebration, Florida, can mean tourist money. Even when the name sounds threatening. Residents of Hell, Michigan, for instance, invite visitors to "Come to Hell" where, according to one website, they can buy diplomas from "Damnation University" and/or schedule a wedding reception. The following is a list of various other frighteningly named places. It is not at all exhaustive.

Armada, Michigan
Cut Off, Louisiana
Cut and Shoot, Texas
Battle Creek, Michigan
Battle Creek, Nebraska
Broken Bow, Nebraska
Bugtussle, Oklahoma
Deadhorse, Alaska
Dead Women Crossing, Oklahoma
Deadwood, South Dakota
Dry Prong, Louisiana
Empire, Louisiana
Erie, Pennsylvania
False Pass, Alaska
Gunbarrel, Colorado
Hell, Michigan
Hurtsboro, Alabama
Killbuck, Ohio
Killingly, Connecticut

Last Chance, Idaho
Lead, South Dakota
Lynch, Kentucky
Lynchburg, Virginia
Lynch Heights, Delaware
Meat Camp, North Carolina
Moody, Alabama
Nightmute, Alaska
Ransom, Kansas
Roachtown, Illinois
Rogue River, Oregon
Satans Kingdom, Vermont
Slapout, Oklahoma
Slaughter, Louisiana
Slaughter Beach, Delaware
Slaughterville, Oklahoma
Sour Lake, Texas
Tombstone, Arizona
Whiteville, Tennessee

Best American *Call of Duty* Handles

Call of Duty *is a video game in which the user plays a soldier in World War II. The game, first released in 2003, has begat sequels, comic books, and massive online communities. Customers worldwide have purchased more than fifty million copies of the software, netting retailers somewhere around three billion dollars. What follows is a list of some of the weirdest and most creative screen names used recently.*

Toilet_Clogger247
Mr. Bigglesworth
Pvt. Parts
[X-Savior] J.C.
ISHANKBUNNIES

Luke SkyHumper
Someone
Iraqishoethrower
Col.Sanders
Krunk Fu
Cowman
Your mom
Tartar Sauce
Bigfoot Spaceman
Chewbaccas Hero
VIOLENTPEACE
Tubanator
A Baby
Ho Lee Phuc

Best American WiFi Network Names

This land is blanketed by WiFi networks, which allow a person's computer to pick up wireless Internet signal. What follows is an incomplete collection of some of the best-named of these.

BisexualBridalShower (Austin, Texas)
JOINANDDIE (Berkeley)
3men&ababy (Berkeley)
noboysallowed (Berkeley)
happysunshinesmileyay (Berkeley)
rofl_lmao_gtfo (Berkeley)
Youdontlivehere (Berkeley)
Poopenstein (Chicago)
Mercyforanimals2 (Chicago)
Fishpantsmcgee (Chicago)
DrOpDeMkChiCknWngz (Chicago)
3guysandamodem (Chicago)
iHateMyNeighbors (Chicago)
divorce (Chicago)

Houseforimaginaryfriends (Chicago)
Chinbeard (Chicago)
BadChoice (Chicago)
UltraTopSecretNet (Hampton, New Hampshire)
Imcompletelynaked (New York)
dontstalkus (New York)
Turndownyourmusic (New York)
wehaveroaches (New York)
Thisisme,thisisyou (New York)
Iamhidingunderyourbed (New York)
Ethernot (New York)
Bacon Lung Inc. (New York)
TheOuchCube (New York)
Iwouldsharebutuhno (New York)
UnicornCupcakePrincessParty (New York)
MonkeyontheLamb (New York)
Fourdudesinaroom (New York)
WeWon! (New York)
WeWonToo (New York)
ifUstealHelpmePayforitUJerks (New York)
Donny,Please (New York)
Caturday (New York)
2dumbcats (New York)
thedude (New York)
Reciprocate-BringPiestoApt5 (New York)
NOFREEWIFI4U (New York)
GetOffMyCloud (New York)
CIA_Citizen_Monitoring (New York)
iwillhacku (New York)
FBIsurveillancevannumber32 (Richmond, California)
Pleasedontstealmywifi (San Francisco)
Pureevil2 (San Francisco)
Slaughterhouse24 (San Francisco)
AirPizzle (San Francisco)
Icanhearyouhavingsex (Seattle)
Idonthearyouhavingsexatall (Seattle)
WhydidGreedoshootfirst?! (Tampa, Florida)

Best American Best American Categories that Got Cut

Every year, sometime around December, the list of potential front section categories for this anthology balloons to many pages. And every spring it gets whittled down. Here are a few that sounded nice in theory, but just didn't pan out.

Best American Names of Taco Carts in Ann Arbor, Michigan
Best American New Colors
Best American Police Blotter Items for Fort Greene, New York
Best American Sentences on Page 51 of Books Published in 2010
Best American Pet Obituaries
Best American Apocalypse Theories
Best American Ways to Reduce Your !@#$ Carbon Footprint
Best American Bible Tract
Best American Fundraising Letter
Best American Magazine Quizzes
Best American Stick-Up Notes
Best American Calls to the Illinois Poison Center
Best American Things to Do in Warm Weather
Best American Things to Do in Cold Weather
Best American Things Not to Do

Best American Mark Twain Quotes

FROM *The Autobiography of Mark Twain, Volume 1*

The Autobiography of Mark Twain, Volume I, *published in November 2010 by the University of California Press, is a compilation of letters, stories, speeches, and writings by (and occasionally about) Mark Twain. Twain's actual autobiography begins on page 201, and is a series of dictations given by Twain over three years. Twain asked that the material not be published in full for one hundred years after his death, so that he could speak freely, as if "from the grave." He finished dictating in late 1909 and died less than four months later. Scholar Harriet Elinor Smith and a team of editors assembled the book. It is 738 pages long. The following is a selection of particularly curious and delightful excerpts from that book.*

My plan was simple—to take the absolute facts of my own life & tell them simply & without ornament or flourish, exactly as they occurred, with this difference, that I would turn every courageous action (if I ever performed one) into a cowardly one, & every success into a failure. You can do this, but only in one way; you must *banish* all idea of an audience—for few men can straitly & squarely confess shameful things to others—you must tell your story to *yourself*, & to no other; you must not use your own name, for that would keep you from telling shameful things, too.

It was not right to give the cat the Pain-Killer; I realize it now.

The supremest charm in Casanova's Memoires (they are not printed in English) is, that he frankly, flowingly, & felicitously tells the dirtiest & vilest & most contemptible things on himself, without ever suspecting that they are other than things which the reader will admire & applaud. . . . Rousseau confesses to masturbation, theft, lying, shameful treachery, & attempts made upon his person by Sodomites. But he tells it as a man who is *perfectly aware* of the shameful nature of these things, whereas your coward & and your Failure should be happy & sweet & unconscious.

All over the world there seems to be a prejudice against the cab driver.

And so hunger began to gnaw while the ship was still burning.

I believe that for months I was pure as the driven snow. After dark.

As I have said, I spent some part of every year at the farm until I was twelve or thirteen years old. The life which I led there with my cousins was full of charm, and so is the memory of it yet. I can call back the solemn twilight and mystery of the deep woods, the earthy smells, the faint odors of the wild flowers, the sheen of rain-washed foliage, the rattling clatter of drops when the wind shook the trees, the far-off hammering of wood-peckers and the muffled drumming of wood-pheasants in the remotenesses of the forest, the snap-shot glimpses of disturbed wild creatures skurrying through the grass, — I can call it all back and make it as real as it ever was, and as blessed. I can call back the prairie, and its loneliness and peace, and a vast hawk hanging motionless in the sky, with his wings spread wide and the blue of the vault showing through the fringe of their end-feathers. I can see the woods in their autumn dress, the oaks purple, the hickories washed with gold, the maples and the sumachs luminous with crimson fires, and I can hear the rustle made by the fallen leaves as we plowed through them. I can see the blue clusters of wild grapes hanging amongst the foliage of the saplings, and I remember the taste of them and the smell. I know how the wild blackberries looked, and how they tasted; and the same with the pawpaws, the hazelnuts and the persimmons; and I can feel the thumping rain, upon my head, of hickory nuts and walnuts when we were out in the frosty dawns to scramble for them with the pigs, and the gusts of wind loosed them and sent them down. I know the stain of blackberries, and how pretty it is; and I know the stain of walnut hulls, and how little it minds soap and water; also what grudged experience it had of either of them. I know the taste of maple sap, and when to gather it, and how to arrange the troughs and the delivery-tubes, and how to boil down the juice, and how to hook the sugar after it is made; also how much better hooked sugar tastes than any that is honestly come by, let bigots say what they will. I know how a prize watermelon looks when it is sunning its fat rotundity among pumpkin vines and "simblins"; I know how to tell when it is ripe without "plugging" it; I know how inviting it looks when it is cooling itself in a tub of water under the bed, waiting; I know how it looks when it lies on the table in the sheltered great floor-space between house and kitchen, and the children gathered for the sacrifice and their mouths watering; I know the crackling sound it makes when the carving knife enters its end, and I can see the split fly along in front of the blade as the knife cleaves its way to the other end; I can see its halves fall apart and display the rich red meat and the black seeds, and the heart standing up, a luxury fit for the elect; I know how a boy looks, behind a yard-long slice of that melon, and I know how he feels; for I have been there. I know the taste of the watermelon which has been honestly come by, and I know the taste of the watermelon which has been acquired by art. Both taste good, but the experienced know which tastes best. I know the look of green apples and peaches and pears on the trees, and I know how entertaining they are when they are inside of a person. I know how ripe ones look when they are piled in pyramids under the trees, and how pretty they are and how vivid their colors. I know how a frozen apple looks, in a barrel down cellar in the winter time, and how hard it is to bite, and how the frost makes the teeth ache, and yet how good it is, notwithstanding. I know the disposition of elderly people to select the specked apples for the children, and I once knew ways to beat the game. I know the look of an apple that is roasting and sizzling on a hearth on a winter's evening, and I know the comfort that comes of eating it hot, along with some sugar and a drench of cream. I know the delicate art and mystery of so cracking hickory nuts and walnuts on a flatiron with a hammer that the kernels will be delivered whole, and I know how the nuts, taken in conjunction with winter apples, cider and doughnuts, make old people's old tales and old jokes sound fresh and crisp and enchanting, and juggle an evening away before you know what went with the time. I know the look of Uncle Dan'l's kitchen as it was on privileged nights when I was a child, and I can see the white and black children grouped on the hearth, with the firelight playing on their faces and the shadows flickering upon the walls, clear back toward the cavernous gloom of the rear, and I can hear Uncle Dan'l telling the immortal tales which Uncle Remus Harris was to gather into his book and charm the world with, by and by; and I can feel again the creepy joy which quivered through me when the time for the ghost story of the "Golden Arm" was reached — and the sense of regret, too, which came over me, for it was always the last story of the evening, and there was nothing between it and the unwelcome bed.

I can remember the bare wooden stairway in my uncle's house, and the turn to the left above the landing, and the rafters and the slanting roof over my bed, and the squares of moonlight on the floor, and the white cold world of snow outside, seen through the curtainless window. I can remember the howling of the wind and the quaking of the house on stormy nights, and how snug and cosy one felt, under the blankets, listening; and how the powdery snow used to sift in, around the sashes, and lie in little ridges on the floor, and make the place look chilly in the morning, and curb the wild desire to get up—in case there was any. I can remember how very dark that room was, in the dark of the moon, and how packed it was with ghostly stillness when one woke up by accident away in the night, and forgotten sins came flocking out of the secret chambers of the memory and wanted a hearing; and how ill chosen the time seemed for this kind of business; and how dismal was the hoo-hooing of the owl and the wailing of the wolf, sent mourning by on the night wind.

What a wee little part of a person's life are his acts and his words! His real life is led in his head, and is known to none but himself. All day long, and every day, the mill of his brain is grinding, and his *thoughts* (which are but the mute articulation of his *feelings*), not those other things, are his history. His *acts* and his *words* are merely the visible thin crust of his world, with its scattered snow summits and its vacant wastes of water—and they are so trifling a part of his bulk! a mere skin enveloping it. The mass of him is hidden—it and its volcanic fires that toss and boil, and never rest, night nor day. *These are his life*, and they are not written, and cannot be written. Every day would make a whole book of eighty thousand words—three hundred and sixty-five books a year. Biographies are but the clothes and buttons of the man—the biography of the man himself cannot be written.
Sept. 26. '92. Arrived in Florence. Got my head shaved. This was a mistake.

Sept. 29. '92. I seem able to forget everything except that I have had my head shaved.

The night that I speak of was one of those dismal New England November nights, close upon the end of the month, when the pestiferous New England climate furnishes those regions a shake-down just in the way of experiment and to get its hand in for business when the proper time comes, which is December. Well, the wind howled, and the snow blew along in clouds when we left that house about midnight. It was a wild night. It was like a storm at sea, for boom and crash and roar and furious snow-drive. It was no kind of a night for burglars to be out in, and yet they *were* out. Goodwin was in bed, with his house on the alarm by half past twelve. Not very long afterward the burglars arrived. Evidently they knew all about the burglar alarm, because instead of breaking into the kitchen they sawed their way in—that is to say, they sawed a great panel out of the kitchen door and stepped in without alarming the alarm. They went all over the house at their leisure; they collected all sorts of trinkets and trumpery; and all of the silverware. They carried things to the kitchen, put them in bags, and then they gathered together a sumptuous supper, with champagne and Burgundy, and so on, and ate that supper at their leisure. Then when they were ready to leave—say at three o'clock in the morning—the champagne and the Burgundy had had an influence, and they became careless for a moment, but one moment was enough. In that careless moment a burglar unlocked and opened the kitchen door, and of course the alarm went off. Rev. Mr. Goodwin put out his left hand and shut it off and went on sleeping peacefully, but the burglars bounded out of the place and left all their swag behind them. A burglar alarm is a valuable thing if you know how to utilize it.

In those early days dueling suddenly became a fashion in the new Territory of Nevada, and by 1864 everybody was anxious to have a chance in the new sport, mainly for the reason that he was not able to thoroughly respect himself so long as he had not killed or crippled somebody in a duel or been killed or crippled in one himself.

Several months ago a telegram came to me from there saying that Tom Sawyer's cave was now being ground into cement—would I like to say anything about it in public? But I had nothing to say. I was sorry we lost our cement mine but it was not worth while to talk about it at this late day, and, take it all around, it was a painful subject anyway.

Best American Poems Written in Response to Arizona Senate Bill 1070

The Support Our Law Enforcement and Safe Neighborhoods Act was signed into law by Arizona Governor Jan Brewer in April 2010, sparking national controversy. Around the Internet poets posted poems in response to the law. A few of the best replies-in-verse are printed here.

SB 1070

Awake, my senator! Let us explore
The Undocumented Question at its core.
Our quest shall dare beyond mere falsities
And ascertain where answer truly lies.
Of arguments pro and con nothing say;
Debate for debate's sake leads inquiry astray.
Free of our native prejudice (please note:
Many prejudgments tend to advance by rote.)
Let insight scan undocumented man,
Ask where his journey ends, where it began,
How to count the unaccountable,
And whether he is person above all.
The rhythm of undocumented feet
Reverberates now your congressional seat,
Recalling us our dutiful intent
To understand mankind *sans document.*

—*Javier O. Huerta*

* * *

The Physics of Being Mexican-American (Quantum Mexicanics)

Mexican, Pocho, Beaner, Spic,
Pedro, Tejano, Latino, Chicano—
all have been used to describe us.
But what is our reality? We are
unobservable particles,

our wave function spreads across
both sides of the Rio
with a non-zero probability
we could be Central American
or even Canadian,

collapsing in the crop fields
of Michigan, in the vineyards
of California, and in the orchards
of South Texas.

You apply the Uncertainty Principle
on us. The more certain you are
of our ethnicity the less certain you are
of our nationality. Our vast

potential energy makes you
fear us. We are not a radioactive people.

—*Ralph Haskins*

* * *

Miami Street Vendor

The street vendor
has a bucket full of beauty
roses in colors God never intended
I always buy orange ones
or sunflowers to go with my walls
he always gives me extras
strays from damaged bouquets

he knows they are more
than just decorations
to me

I love him like a brother
because he smiles through the stifling heat
because he shows no trace of ire
at what he should be doing with his education
if he were legal
besides sweating while dodging cars at stoplights

and mostly because
he does not hate the roses
even though they hurt his arms
and compel him every day
to dance in traffic.

— *Sylvia Maltzman*

* * *

The Border

They have built a border:
At the dinner table, when they want their fruits and vegetables—
Between sweaty fields and their inherent privilege.

They have built a border:
At the car wash, when they want their luxury vehicles polished—
    spotless, sir—
Between breaking backs and their abundant vanity.

They have built a border:
Behind the picket fence, when they want their gardens groomed—
    a little less roses, sir—
Between the roots of honest labor and blooming decadence.

They have built a border:
At the drive-thru window, when they want fast food—
Between a minimum wage and an artificial convenience.

They have built a border:
In their industry, when they want their factories fine-tuned—
Between diligence and mechanized indifference.

They have built a border:
At the curb of Home Depot, when they want *jornaleros*—
Between cheap labor and the structures of discrimination.

—*José Hernández Díaz*

DANIEL ALARCÓN

■

Second Lives

FROM *The New Yorker*

MY PARENTS, WITH ADMIRABLE FORESIGHT, had their first child while they were on fellowships in the United States. My mother was in public health, and my father in a library-science program. Having an American baby was, my mother once said, like putting money in the bank. They lived near downtown Baltimore, by the hospital where my mother was studying, in a neighborhood of dilapidated row houses. Baltimore was abject, ugly, my mother said. Cold in winter, a sauna in summer, a violently segregated city, full of fearful whites and angry blacks. America, in those days, had all its dirty laundry available for inspection—the world's most powerful nation making war with itself in the streets, in universities, in the South, in Vietnam, in the capital just down the road. And yet my parents set about trying to make babies: on spring nights, when they made the room smell of earth, summer nights, when the city felt like a swamp, autumn nights, falling asleep on top of the covers, winter nights, when the room boiled with sex. They were not newlyweds, strictly speaking, but Baltimore re-energized them, made of their pairing something indispensable, something chemical.

For their efforts, they were rewarded with a son, whom they named Francisco. The district they lived in was one of the poorest in the country at the time, and once the birth was registered my parents were entitled to free baby formula, delivered to their doorstep every Monday morning. They found this astonishing, and later learned that many of the foreign doctors at the hospital were receiving this benefit, too, even a few who didn't yet have children. It was a gigantic bribe, my father said, the government pleading with its poverty-stricken residents: Please, please don't riot! Baltimore was adorned with reminders of the last civil disturbance: a burned-out block of storefronts, a boarded-up and untended house whose roof had collapsed after a snowstorm. Every morning, the sidewalks were littered with shattered car windows, tiny bits of glass glinting like diamonds in the limpid sun. No one used money in the neighborhood stores, only coupons; and, in lieu of birds, the skies featured plastic bags held aloft on a breeze. But none of this mattered, because my parents were happy. They were in love and they had a beautiful boy, his photo affixed to a blue First World passport.

Their American moment didn't last long. They would have had another child—they would have had me—if their visas hadn't run out. By the time my mother was done nursing Francisco, a coup had taken place back home, and the military junta that came to power was not entirely friendly with the Johnson Administration. My parents were required to renew their papers every eighteen months, and that year, to their great surprise, they were denied. Appeals, they were told, could be filed only from the home country. The university hospital wrote a letter on my mother's behalf, but this well-meaning document vanished into some bureaucrat's file cabinet in suburban Virginia, and it soon became clear that there was nothing to be done. Rather than be deported—how undignified!—my parents left of their own accord.

And then their gaze turned, back to their families, their friends, the places they had known, and those they had forgotten they knew. They bought a house in a suburb of the capital, where I was raised, an out-of-the-way place that has since been swallowed entirely by the city's growth. I guess they lost that old Baltimore feeling, because I wasn't born for another seven years, a crying, red-faced bit of flesh, a runt, undersized even then. No blue passport for me, but they consoled themselves by giving me an Anglo name, Nelson, which was the fashion at the time. Eventually, I got my Third World passport, the color of spilled red wine, but it was just for show. I still haven't had a chance to use it.

Francisco, of course, fled at the first opportunity. It was January, 1987, the situation was bleak, and leaving was the most logical thing to do. I was ten years old; the idea was that he'd get me a visa and I'd join him as soon as I finished school. We went as a family to see him off at the airport, took the obligatory photographs in front of the departures board, and waved as he passed through security. He promised to write. He promised to call. He disappeared into the terminal, and then we climbed the stairs to the greasy restaurant above the baggage claim, where we sat by the wall of windows, waiting for a plane that looked like it might be my brother's to take off. My father drank coffee, fogged his glasses with his breath and polished the lenses between the folds of his dress shirt. My mother drew a palm tree on a paper napkin, frowning. I fell asleep with my head on the table, and when I woke up the janitor was mopping the floor beside us, wondering, perhaps, if we ever intended to leave.

My brother went to live with the Villanuevas, old friends of my parents from their Baltimore days, who'd settled in Birmingham, Alabama. His first letter was three handwritten pages and began with a description of winter in the Southern United States. That year, the Alabama rains fell almost without pause until the middle of March, a soggy prelude to an even wetter spring. For Francisco, unaccustomed to this weather, the thunderstorms were impressive. Occasionally, there'd be a downed power line, and sometimes the lights would go out as a result. It was in this familiar darkness, Francisco wrote, that he'd first felt homesick.

The second half of the letter dealt more specifically with the routines of family life at the Villanuevas. Where they lived wasn't a neighborhood so much as a collection of houses that happened to face the same street. Kids were permitted to play in the back yard or in the driveway, but never in the front yard. No one could explain why, but it simply wasn't done. People moved about only in cars; walking was frowned upon, socially acceptable for children, perhaps, if they happened to be accompanied by a dog. The Villanuevas did not have pets. Nor was there anywhere to walk to, really. A two-pump gas station sat about a mile away on Highway 31; its attractions included a pay phone and a magazine rack.

The Villanueva children, Marisa and Jack, ages fifteen and ten, respectively, made it clear from the outset that they spoke no Spanish.

The language didn't interest them much, and their father, who insisted that my brother call him Julio and not Mr. Villanueva, considered this his greatest failing as a parent. It was his fault, he confessed to Francisco, for marrying an American woman. In general terms, though, things were good. Speaking English with the Villanueva kids, while challenging at first, helped my brother learn the language faster. At school, not a soul spoke Spanish, not even Señora Rickerts, the friendly, well-intentioned Spanish teacher. Francisco was not enrolled with Marisa, as had originally been planned. She went to an expensive private school, which would not permit Francisco to audit classes, so instead the Villanuevas sent him to Berry, the local public high school, with the hicks. This last word, Francisco explained, was the rough English equivalent of *campesino* or *cholo*, only it referred to rural white people. He'd learned it from Marisa, and had been advised by Mr. Villanueva never to use it if he wished to make friends. My father found this part of the letter very amusing. How remarkable, he said, that Villanueva's daughter spoke no Spanish but had somehow imported her father's classism to North America! How ironic, my father noted, that his own son should learn proletarian solidarity in the belly of the empire!

My parents read and reread the letter at the dinner table, alternately laughing and falling into worried silence. In the early months, I recall them wondering aloud if they'd made a mistake by sending him away like this. Whose idea had it been? And where was Birmingham, anyway? Was it a city or a town? What kind of school was this place called Berry?

They wrote back, urging Francisco to send photos. A month passed, and the next letter arrived with a single picture. We saw Francisco with an umbrella and a yellow raincoat, standing next to the mailbox in front of the Villanuevas' house, a dense knot of purple clouds above. The front yard sloped dramatically, and Francisco stood at an odd slant. He'd put on a little weight—you could see it in his cheeks—and his hair had grown out. His face was changing, my mother said. He was growing up.

By his third letter, the winter rains had become spring rains, which were the same, only warmer. Storms spread like inkblots across the sky. On sunny days after a rain, the woods behind the Villanuevas' subdivision looked as if they'd been dipped in light. Everyone said that it was an unusually wet year. Francisco didn't mind—he was fascinated by the weather. It was everything else that bored him. His great disappointment that spring was that he'd tried out for the Berry High soccer team, and spent three games on the bench, watching the action unfold without him. He'd quit in protest, and, to his surprise, no one had begged him to come back. They hadn't even noticed. Americans, he wrote, have no understanding of the game. The issue was not mentioned again. By the fourth letter, the weather had turned; breezy, pleasant stretches were punctuated now and then by days of blasting heat. School would be over soon. He no longer complained about Berry or his classmates, whose dialect he could barely understand. Instead, he seemed to have settled in. Each week, Francisco went to the Spanish class and led conversation exercises with his American peers, and several of them had sought him out for further instruction. An exchange student from Mexico City had spent time at Berry the previous year, seducing Alabama girls and confounding deeply held stereotypes—he didn't wear a poncho, for instance, and was apparently sincere in his love of punk music. He'd also left behind a folkloric legacy of curse words: *panocha, no manches,* and *pinche guey.* Francisco wrote that he considered it his responsibility to teach these poor gringos to curse with dignity, and this was, as far as he could tell, the only linguistic knowledge they truly thirsted for. He introduced them to important words, words like *mierda, culo,* and *pendejo,* while offering the more advanced students a primer on the nearly infinite uses of *huevo* (*huevón, hasta las huevas, hueveo, huevear, se hueveó la huevada*). My parents were proud: "Our son the educator," they said. Photos included with this letter were of nearby Lake Logan Martin, where the Villanuevas had a weekend house. Sun glinting off the water, bathing suits hanging on a line, barefoot games of Frisbee in the freshly mowed grass. In summer, Francisco might learn to water-ski.

This was the first letter in which he forgot to ask us how we were.

That year—the only year he consistently wrote to us—the photos were mostly of Francisco by himself. Occasionally, he'd pose with the Villanuevas: Julio, his wife, Heather, and their two dark-haired, olive-skinned children, who really looked as though they should speak some Spanish. Once, Francisco sent a photo of the Berry High gymnasium, which was notable only for its size. The entire high school, he wrote, would soon be razed and replaced by an even bigger complex farther out in the suburbs. Everyone was excited about this, but he wouldn't be around to see it. He didn't intend to stay in Alabama; on this point he was very clear.

We did eventually get a photo of the few American friends Francisco acquired in those first months, and perhaps this could have clued us in about his eagerness to move on. At home, Francisco had always been part of the popular crowd, the center of a fitful, manic group of friends who loved trouble and music and girls. At Berry, he was on the margins of it all, one of a bunch of skinny outcasts, happy to have found one another in the crowded, cliquish hallways of this immense public school. In these photos: a Korean named Jai, a red-haired boy called Anders, who wore a neck brace, and a frail black kid named Leon, carrying a stack of books and looking utterly lost.

It was just as well that Francisco didn't ask us how we were. My parents might not have been able to explain. Or they might not have wanted to. Nineteen eighty-seven was the year of the state employee strike, which was particularly troubling for us, since my father worked at the National Library and my mother at the Ministry of Health. It started in May, around the time that Francisco was learning to water-ski. There was also dismaying talk of a new currency to replace the one that was soon to be destroyed by rising inflation. Together these horrors would wipe out our already diminished savings. War pressed down on the country in all its fury. Adults spoke of politics as if referring to a long and debilitating illness that no medicine could cure. Presidential elections were on the horizon; no one knew who would win, but none of the options were good. My father was shedding weight and hair at a frightening pace, the stress carving him to pieces.

Our letters to the U.S. did not include photographs, a small concession to my father's vanity in those taxing months. Nor did they mention the fact that Francisco was attending the public school because the tuition at Marisa's school was simply out of the question for us. Or that my parents had already written a letter to Mr. Villanueva postponing the monthly payment for his room and board. Certainly, my parents didn't tell Francisco how much shame they felt at having to do this. I doubt they even told him that they were afraid they'd lose their jobs, and were speaking with a lawyer about getting citizenship for all of us and coming as a family to join him. These were the issues my parents talked about at home, in front of me (as if I weren't there) but not with my brother. Why worry the boy? The calls were too expensive to waste time on unpleasant things, and wasn't he busy enough, learning English and spending his afternoons jumping from the Villanuevas' pier into the cool, refreshing waters of Lake Logan Martin?

For most of my childhood, our neighbors across the street were a friendly couple named Alejandro and Luz. They were a little older than my parents, the rare neighborhood couple with no kids, possessing no concept of the kinds of things children might like. They visited from time to time, usually bringing some sort of gift for my brother and me—a jump rope, a pinwheel, that sort of thing.

Alejandro had big ears and a quirky grin. He wore dark suits and liked to talk politics until late in the evening. He was a good man, my father told me once, and decency was not something to be taken lightly, but when it came to worldview—he said this quite sternly—"we simply do not agree with him." Even now I'm not sure if this meant that Alejandro was a reactionary or a radical. Those were confusing times. Alejandro worked long hours, and months might pass between his visits, whereas Luz often came by to chat with my mother or to play with us. And when both my parents were working late Francisco and I sometimes spent a few hours at her house, deeply involved in card games whose rules the three of us invented as we went along, or listening to the dark, suspenseful stories Luz loved to tell. Ostensibly about her family, these tales of adventure and daring seemed to draw more from Hollywood Westerns, featuring spectacular kidnappings, gambling debts settled with knife fights, or long, dismal marches through unforgiving mountain terrain. Luz's manner of speaking made it clear that she had no idea what she might say next. It wasn't that she made things up, strictly speaking—only that facts were merely a point of departure for her.

Luz modified whatever game we played, never apologizing, and we rarely minded letting her win, whether at cards or dominoes or hide-and-seek; in fact, it didn't feel like a concession at all. My brother, who usually kept a studied distance from me and all things preadolescent, regressed in her company, becoming, as if by magic, a gentler, more innocent version of himself.

Often Luz would let us watch an hour of cartoons while she rested on the couch with an arm draped over her face. We thought she was asleep, exhausted from so much winning, but every time a news break came on Luz would sit up in a flash, cover our eyes, and make us press our hands over our ears. The news in those days was not for children, she always said, and I took her word for it. But afterward, when I had opened my eyes and was blinking hopefully at the television, waiting for the cartoons to come back on, Francisco would say, "Did you see that, little brother? That's why I'm leaving."

Soon after Francisco had gone, Alejandro moved out. It happened almost without anyone realizing it, though the dearth of concrete details was soon overwhelmed by the neighborhood's combined speculative power: Alejandro had run off with his secretary, with the maid, with the daughter of one of his business associates. The mistress, whoever she might be, was pregnant, or maybe she already had children of her own, whom Alejandro had agreed to take care of. It seemed likely that she was much younger than Luz, that he wanted, after all these years, to be a father. There were a few who thought that his sudden disappearance had more to do with politics, but my father rejected that theory out of hand.

A few weeks had passed when Alejandro came by late one night. He wanted to speak to my father, alone. They shut themselves in the kitchen with a bottle of pisco, and when they emerged, a few hours later, it was clear that Alejandro had been crying. His eyes were swollen and his arms hung limply by his sides. My mother and I were in the living room. I was supposedly doing homework, but really I was waiting to see what would happen. Nothing did. Alejandro gave us a sheepish nod, while my father stood next to him, pisco bottle in hand. They hadn't even uncorked it.

The following day, my mother clarified things a bit. Or tried to.

"An affair," she said, "is when a man takes up with a woman who is not his wife. Do you understand that, Nelson?"

Sure I did, or at least I thought I did.

"And what if a woman takes up with a man who is not her husband?"

My mother nodded. "That, too." I had other questions as well. "Takes up with"? Something about the way my mother said this phrase alerted me to the fact that it was a metaphor.

And she sighed, closing her eyes for a moment. She seemed to be thinking rather carefully about what she might say, and I waited, tensely, perhaps even holding my breath. My mother patted me on the head. It was complicated, she said finally, but there was one thing I should be aware of, one thing I should think about and learn now, even if I was too young to understand. Did I want to know? "It has to do with a woman's pride," she said, and waited for these puzzling words to take hold. They didn't. It was all opaque, delightfully mysterious. Alejandro's affair was different from others, she said. Yes, he had left Luz, and, yes, this was bad enough. Plenty bad. But a woman is proud, and at a certain age this pride is tinged with self-doubt. "We grow old," my mother told me, "and we suspect we are no longer beautiful." Alejandro's new mistress was ten years older than Luz. This was what he'd confessed to my father the night before. A younger woman would have been understandable, expected even, but this—it wasn't the sort of insult that Luz would easily recover from.

I knew it was serious by the way my mother's eyes narrowed.

"If your father ever does something like this to me, you'd better call the police, because someone's going to get hurt. Do you understand?"

I told her I did, and her face eased into a smile.

"O.K., then, go on," my mother said. "Go play or something."

In those days after Francisco left, "go play" came to mean something very specific: go sit in your room and draw and create stories. I could spend hours this way, and often did. My scripts were elaborate, mostly nonviolent revenge fantasies, in which I (or the character I played) would end up in the unlikely position of having to spare the life of a kid who had routinely bullied me. The bully's gratitude was colored with shame, naturally, and my (character's) mercy was devastating to the bully's self-image. I returned to this theme time and again, never tiring of it, deriving great pleasure from the construction of these improbable reversals.

With my brother gone, the room we had shared seemed larger, more spacious and luxurious than before. I'd lived my entire life there, deferring without complaint to my brother's wishes on all matters of decoration, layout, music, and lighting. He'd made it clear that I was a squatter in his room, an assertion I'd never thought to question. Just before he left, he'd warned me with bared teeth, frightening as only older brothers can be, not to touch a thing. In case he came back. If I were to change anything, Francisco said, he'd know.

"How?" I asked. "How will you know?"

He threw an arm around me then, flexing it tight around my neck with the kind of casual brutality he often directed at me. I felt my face turning red; I was helpless. At ten and eighteen, we were essentially two different species. I wouldn't see him again until we were both adults, fully grown men capable of real violence. I suppose if I'd known this, I might have tried to appreciate the moment, but instead I remained defiant, gasping for breath and managing to ask one more time, "Yeah, but how will you know?"

Francisco, or versions of him, appeared in many of my early works. I took note of what my mother had said about a woman's pride, and when I was alone with my father I decided to ask him about it. I wasn't sure if I'd got the full nuance, but I relayed the conversation with my mother as well as I could, concluding with the last bit about the police.

"She said that?" he asked. I nodded, and my father, instead of shedding any light on the situation, just laughed. It was a hearty, surprising laugh, with tears pressing from the corners of his eyes.

"What?" I asked. "What did I say?" But he wouldn't answer me, and, finally, when he'd regained his composure, he gave me a big hug.

"Your mother is a dangerous woman," he said, and I knew enough to understand that when he said "dangerous" he meant it as a compliment.

Meanwhile, Luz drew her curtains and rarely left the house. Alejandro never came back.

* * *

A few months later, we learned that Luz was planning to travel to the United States, to visit a cousin of hers in Florida. This was in June, when the strike was under way, and my parents were beginning to feel the stress most acutely. We'd seen little of Luz in the weeks since Alejandro's visit, but she was often mentioned, always in the same pitying tone. Inevitably, the conversation veered back to my mother's comment about the police, and my father would tease her about it, until they laughed together. I'd chuckle, too, so as not to be left out.

Luz's trip couldn't have been more perfectly timed. It was scheduled for July, three or four weeks before Francisco's birthday, the first he would be spending abroad. My mother wanted to send Francisco a gift, just a token, so that he'd know we were thinking of him. After some deliberation, she bought him a dark-blue necktie embroidered with the logo of the National Library. My father approved, said it would help him get a good job. It was a joke, really; we knew that Francisco wasn't interested in the sort of job where he might need a necktie. The three of us signed a card; separately, my father wrote a long letter, and the whole thing was wrapped and sealed and ready to go. Naturally, there was no talk of trusting our local postal service for this, or for anything, really. We would ask Luz to take it for us and drop it in an American mailbox. Perhaps, my mother said, Luz could even hand-deliver it, should her itinerary include a jaunt through Alabama, and, upon her return, report back—tell us how she'd found Francisco, what she thought of his prospects in the U.S.

One Sunday afternoon, my mother and I crossed the street and knocked on Luz's door. She seemed surprised to see us, a little embarrassed, but beckoned us into the house all the same. Immediately, we encountered a problem: there wasn't anywhere to sit. Sometime in the previous months, much of the furniture had been moved out, and the rooms, half empty now, seemed lonely and sad. Of the chairs that remained, no two faced each other. We strolled through to the living room, where a small television set rested awkwardly on a wooden chair. Luz was thinner than I remembered her, subdued; she seemed to have staggered recklessly toward old age, as if trying to make up in a matter of weeks the ten years that separated her from Alejandro's new lover. Her hair had faded to a stringy yellowing gray—she'd stopped dyeing it, my mother explained later—and her skin had taken in a similarly unhealthy pallor. Her eyes, even in the dim light, were glassy and unfocussed. Luz asked me to put the television on the floor.

"Where?" I asked.

"Oh, Nelson," she said. "Anywhere."

I placed it next to the chair, and Luz indicated that I should sit on it. I looked at my mother for reassurance. She nodded, and so the three of us sat, forming a not quite intimate circle.

Luz and my mother went through the protocols of a civilized visit: inoffensive questions, anodyne chitchat, the usual phrases and gestures intended to fill up space rather than convey meaning. It occurred to me as I listened that my mother and Luz were not close. They spoke without much fluency about a minor universe of events that affected neither of them: the vagaries of neighborhood life, people they both knew but didn't much care about. My mother seemed determined not to speak of our family, of my father, my brother, or even me. It was excessive decorum, as if the very mention of family might be insulting to our grieving hostess. The strain to keep the words coming was noticeable, and I wondered how long it would be necessary to maintain this charade before coming to the point of the visit, Francisco's gift. Ten minutes? Twenty? An entire hour?

Luz, as she spoke, as she listened, scanned the room as if looking for someone who was not there. The easy assumption would have been that the someone was Alejandro, but I understood instinctively that this wasn't the case. There were many people in the room with us, it seemed, a wide variety of people my mother and I could not see: principally, the players in Luz's life, those who'd known her at various stages of childhood, adolescence, and adulthood, at moments of joy, of whimsy, of expectation. Of anxiety and fear. It seemed to me that Luz was wondering, How did I get to this place? How did this happen? Or perhaps, What are all these people doing in my house, and what must they think of me now? And it was all she could do not to ask these questions aloud. She was gritting her teeth, forcing her way through a conversation with my mother, an artificial exchange about nothing at all, hoping soon to return to her more important, unfinished dialogue with this other, floating gallery of observers. This was my theory, of course. Luz's eyes drifted to the near distance, to the seemingly empty space just behind us and around us. To the window, to the floor, to the ceiling.

At a certain point, my mother took Francisco's festively wrapped package from her purse. She passed it to Luz, who accepted it without saying much. I'd lost track of the words being exchanged, was focusing instead on the minute shifts in Luz's facial expressions: a sharpening of the creases at the edges of her mouth, or her eyes fluttering closed. My mother explained that the gift was for Francisco, that it was his birthday, that we hated to ask the favor but we hoped it wouldn't be a problem. Could she take it with her?

Luz sat, shoulders slouched, neck curling downward. The gift was in her lap, and by the tired look in her eyes you might have thought that it weighed a great deal. I'm not sure how I knew, but I did: She was going to say no.

"What is it?" Luz said.

My mother smiled innocently; she didn't yet understand what was happening.

"A necktie."

Luz's eyes were wandering again, following a dust mote, or the disappearing image of an old friend. She was ashamed to be seen this way, and she was going to take it out on us.

"Are you well?" Luz asked.

"We are," my mother said. "We miss Francisco, of course, but we're well."

"And the strike?"

At the mention of it, my mother's expression darkened. She and my father were walking the picket line five days a week, exhausting in and of itself, and, of course, there was the constant threat of violence, from the police, from the more radical elements within their own syndicate. My parents talked about it every night, oblique references at the dinner table, and later, as I fell asleep, I heard the worried hum of voices drifting from their bedroom.

"We're getting by," my mother answered. "God willing, it'll be over soon."

Luz nodded, and reached over to the coffee table. She pulled open a drawer and took out a letter opener. We watched, not knowing exactly what she was after, but she spoke the whole time, carrying on a sort of conversation with herself, a monologue about the declining state of morals in the nation, about a new, aimless generation, and its startling lack of respect for the rules of society as they'd been handed down since the time when we were a colony of the Spanish Empire. A colony? The Empire? I looked toward my mother for help, but she was no less confused than me. There was sadness in Luz's tone, a defeated breathiness, as if the words themselves were part of a whispered prayer or lament she would've preferred not to share with us. At the same time, her hands moved with an efficiency completely at odds with her speech: she held the package now, and, without pausing in her discourse, used the letter opener to cut the red bow my mother had tied. It fell unceremoniously to the dusty floor.

"Oh!" my mother said.

It was as if Luz had cut her.

Then, with the edge of the opener, she peeled back the clear tape my mother had stuck to the wrapping. The paper slipped to the floor, landing at Luz's feet. She pushed it away with the edge of her shoe. Her hands kept moving.

"People these days can't be trusted. So much has changed from when I was a girl. We knew our neighbors—our town was small. When a boy came around, my father would ask who his parents were, and this was all he and my mother needed to know. If they didn't approve of his lineage, they'd send the servant out to have a talk with him. To shoo him away, you understand. I watched everything from my window. I was very pretty then."

"I'm sure you were," my mother said, her voice breaking, unable to hide the concern she felt for Francisco's gift. The box was open now, the white tissue paper was out, ripped in places, and the tie dangled from Luz's knee, its tip just grazing the floor. Luz opened the card we'd all signed, and spread my father's letter on her lap, squinting at the handwriting as if decoding a secret message.

"Is there something wrong?" my mother asked.

Luz didn't answer. Instead, she held the necktie up with one hand, and ran her thumb and forefinger carefully along the seam, lightly palpating the length of the fabric. She'd already checked the box and its lining. What was she looking for?

My mother watched in horror. "What are you doing? Is there a problem?"

"Where are your people from?" Luz asked.

"I'm sorry?"

"The north, the south, the center? The mountains, the jungle? How well do we know each other, really, Monica? Do I know what you do? What your family does? What about that union you belong to, the one making trouble downtown? Did you expect me to get on a flight to America with a package I hadn't bothered to check? What if there were drugs inside? What if there was *cocaine*?"

My mother was stunned. Absolutely immobilized.

"Am I supposed to rot in an American prison because your impoverished family is willing to gamble with my life?"

Luz's eyes were open wide, and she held them that way, staring at us.

My mother stood abruptly, snatching the necktie and my father's letter from Luz's hands. I ducked to grab the box, the wrapping paper, and the bow, but my mother took me by the arm. Her face was a bright and unnatural shade of red.

"Leave it."

Luz reverted now, drawn back into that lonely place she'd been trapped in for months. "Did I say something wrong?" she asked, but the question wasn't addressed to us.

The empty rooms were a blur as we raced toward the street. On our way out, I managed to kick over a chair, and I knew by my mother's expression that she didn't mind at all.

The day passed and my mother was in a foul, toxic mood. The neighborhood, always so eager to gossip, was now gossiping about us. We'd tried to send contraband to America, people were saying. Drugs. Tried to take advantage of an unsuspecting elderly woman with a broken heart.

These were the kinds of humiliations we put up with for Francisco's sake. There were others. Francisco left Birmingham that October, and only later did we find out why: one afternoon Marisa skipped her S.A.T. prep class, and Mrs. Villanueva came home early to find them groping in the downstairs television room. For me, the most astonishing aspect of the story was undoubtedly the idea that the Villanuevas had a downstairs television room. The rest of the anecdote—even the titillating hint of sex—hardly registered next to this remarkable detail. Mrs. Villanueva gave my brother an hour to pack his things. By the time her husband got home, Francisco had already been dropped off at his friend Jai's house, forever banished from the Villanuevas' ordered American lives.

For months after he'd moved on, we continued to wire money to the Villanuevas to pay off our debt. My father sent several long letters to his old friend Julio, apologizing for his son's behavior, but these went unanswered, and, eventually, he gave up trying to make things right. The friendship was never repaired, of course, but, then, how could it be? The two men had met in the nineteen-seventies and had seen each other only twice in the intervening years. The mutual affection they felt was an almost entirely theoretical construct, based on memories of long-ago shared experiences—not unlike what I felt toward my brother by then, I suppose. Part fading recollections, part faith.

Francisco never got around to applying to college, as my parents had hoped he would. He moved briefly to Knoxville, where his friend Leon had enrolled at the University of Tennessee. But soon after that we got a letter from St. Louis (along with a photo of the Arch), and then one from Kansas City (with a picture taken in the parking lot of a rustic barbecue joint). Francisco's constant movement made it difficult for my parents to get their citizenship paperwork going, though at some point, I imagine, they must have told him what their plan was and how desperate our situation was becoming. Maybe he didn't understand. Or maybe it was inconvenient for him to think about. Maybe what he wanted most of all was to forget where he'd come from, to leave those troubles and stunted dreams behind and become what his passport had always said he was: an American.

People talk a lot these days about virtual reality, second lives, digital avatars. It's a concept I'm fully conversant with, of course. Even with no technical expertise or much interest in computers, I understand it all perfectly; if not the engineering, then the emotional content behind these so-called advances seems absolutely intuitive to me. I'll say it plainly: I spent my adolescence preparing for and eventually giving myself over to an imagined life. While my parents waited in line at the American Embassy, learning all the relevant statutes and regulations to insure my passage, I placed myself beside my brother in each of his pictures. I followed him on his journey across America, trying always to forget where I really was.

He repaired bicycles in suburban Detroit; worked as a greeter at a Wal-Mart in Dubuque, Iowa; moved furniture in Galveston, Texas; mowed lawns at a golf course outside Santa Fe. At home, I read Kerouac and Faulkner, listened to Michael Jackson and the Beastie Boys, studied curious American customs like Halloween, Thanksgiving, and the Super Bowl. I formulated opinions on America's multiple national dilemmas, which seemed thrillingly, beautifully frivolous: gays in the military, a President in trouble for a blow job.

My brother turned twenty-one in Reno, Nevada, gambling away a meager paycheck he'd earned busing tables at a chain Italian restaurant. It could be said that he was happy. This was 1990. He was going by Frank now, and had shed whatever Southern accent he might have picked up in those first few months as a putative member of the Villanueva household.

Six months passed, and we learned that he had abandoned water-skiing for snow skiing; he was working at a ski resort in the Rockies, and sent photos, panoramic shots of the light mirroring brilliantly off the white snowpack. It was intriguing and absolutely foreign territory. He spent a page describing the snow—dry snow, wet snow, artificial snow, powder—and I learned that people can get sunburned in winter from all the reflected light. I never would have guessed this to be true, though in hindsight it seemed fairly obvious, and this alone was enough to depress me. What else was obvious to everyone but me? What other lessons, I wondered, was I being deprived of even now?

In school, my favorite subject was geography. Not just mine, it should be said. I doubt any generation of young people has ever looked at a world map with such a powerful mixture of longing and anxiety; we were like inmates being tempted with potential escape routes. Even our teacher must have felt it: when he took the map from the supply closet and tacked it to the blackboard, there was an audible sigh from the class. We were mesmerized by the possibilities; we assumed every country was more prosperous than ours, safer than ours, and at this scale they all seemed tantalizingly near. The atlas was passed around like pornography, and if you had the chance to sit alone with

it for a few moments you counted yourself lucky. When confronted
with a map of the United States, in my mind I placed dots across the
continent, points to mark where my brother had lived and the various towns he'd passed through on his way to other places.

Of course, I wasn't the only one with family abroad; these were the
days when everyone was trying to leave. Our older brothers applied
for scholarships in fields they didn't even like, just for the chance to
overstay their visas in cold and isolated northern cities. Our sisters
were married off to tourists or were shipped to Europe to work as
nannies. We were a nation busy inventing French great-grandpar-
ents, falsifying Spanish paperwork, bribing notaries for counterfeit
birth certificates from Slavic countries that were hardly better off than
we were. Genealogies were examined in great detail—was there an
ancestor to exploit, anyone with an odd, foreign sounding last name?
A Nazi war criminal in your family's dark past? What luck! Pack your
bags, kids—we're going to Germany! This was simply the spirit of
the times. The Japanese kids headed back to Tokyo, the Jewish kids
to Israel. A senile Portuguese shut-in who hadn't spoken a coherent
sentence in fifteen years was dusted off and taken to petition the Embassy; suddenly all his grandchildren were moving to Lisbon.

The state-employee strike didn't last forever. It ended, as everything
did in those days, with an uneasy and temporary resolution: across-
the-board pay cuts but no immediate layoffs, a surfeit of mistrust and
rancor on all sides. My father was there at the climactic march, when
a bank in the old center was burned by government infiltrators and
dozens of protesters were beaten and jailed. He was gassed and shot
at with rubber bullets, and he, like tens of thousands of others, fled
the violence like a madman, running at full speed through the cha-
otic streets of the capital, a wet rag tied across his nose and mouth. It
was, he told me later, the moment he realized he wasn't young anymore.

The dreaded election came and went; the crisis deepened. The new
President privatized everything, selling the state off piece by piece
and dividing the profits among his friends. The truce that had been
reached at the end of the strike was broken, and the next year thousands of workers, including my mother, were suddenly laid off. She
was unemployed for months. Prices shot up, the currency crashed,

the violence spread, and our world became very small and very precarious. We waited in breadlines, carrying impossibly large stacks
of banknotes, which had become a requirement for even the tiniest transaction. People spoke less; strangers distrusted one another.
The streets, even during morning rush, had a perverse emptiness to
them. We listened to the radio in the dark and emerged each morning fearful to discover what tragedy had befallen us in the night.

These emotions are quite beside the point now, like an artifact
looted from an ancient grave, an oddly shaped tool whose utility no
one can quite decipher. But back then, walking through the gray,
shuddering city, I thought about my brother all the time. I was ten,
I was eleven, unfree but hopeful; I was thirteen, I was fourteen, and
my brother had escaped. Fifteen, sixteen: waiting for something to
happen, reading obsessively about a place I would never see for myself, in a language I would never actually need. Twenty, twenty-one:
small failures, each humiliation a revelation, further proof that my
real life was elsewhere. Twenty-five, twenty-six: a dawning awareness
that my condition as a citizen of the Third World was terminal.

And Francisco lived through none of this. As punishment, I set
about trying to forget him: the sound of his laughter, his height relative to mine, the content of the conversations we'd had after the lights
went out but before we fell asleep.

I never managed it, of course.

■

An Oral History of Adama Bah

FROM *Patriot Acts: Narratives of Post-9/11 Injustice*

On March 24th, 2005, Adama Bah, a sixteen-year-old Muslim girl, awoke at dawn to discover nearly a dozen armed FBI agents inside her family's apartment in East Harlem. They arrested her and her father, Mamadou Bah, and transported them to separate detention facilities. A government document leaked to the press claimed that Adama was a potential suicide bomber but failed to provide any evidence to support this claim.

Released after six weeks in detention, Adama was forced to live under partial house arrest with an ankle bracelet, a government-enforced curfew, and a court-issued gag order that prohibited her from speaking about her case. In August of 2006, Adama's father was deported back to his native Guinea, Africa. Adama, who traveled to the United States with her parents from Guinea as a child, also found herself facing deportation. She would spend the next few years fighting for asylum and struggling to support her family in the United States and Guinea.

I Didn't Know I Wasn't an American

I didn't know I wasn't an American until I was sixteen and in handcuffs.

My mother came to the United States with me in 1990, when I was one. We originally came from Koubia in Guinea, West Africa.

My dad was here already, living in Brooklyn and working as a cab driver. He went on to open his own business later.

Along came my brother, who is now nineteen, my sister, who is seventeen, and two more brothers who are thirteen and five. I'm twenty-one. We moved to this apartment in Manhattan, and we have been living here for thirteen years.

I think a lot of people in Africa and third world countries hear about the riches in America. It's the land of opportunity. So, he came here for that. From the stories that my mom tells me, their lives back in Koubia were farming and that's it.

Growing up in New York, I remember having my "cousins" around. They're all Guinean. They weren't real family, but whatever community members we had here, I considered them family. I remember having them come over, I remember us running around and messing up things.

My friends were Latino and African-American. At that time, I fit in with them. I was going through the same issues as them, like boys, going through puberty, he said/she said kinds of things. Those were the kinds of problems that I wish I had now.

We All Did It?

I went to public school until seventh grade. My dad wanted me to learn about my religion, so he sent me to an Islamic boarding school in Buffalo, New York. What's weird now that I look back is that my parents aren't really religious, we didn't really go to mosque. But my dad heard about the school from somebody who recommended it.

I was thirteen when 9/11 happened. Every teacher came in late, and they sat us in a humongous circle. My teacher said, "I have to talk to you guys. For those of you who are from New York, I want you to brace yourself. I have some bad news. Sometimes things happen in life that we don't understand." She started telling us about God and how to be patient and steadfast. And then she said, "The twin towers were hit today."

I remember freaking out, panicking, trying to reach my family.

When she called us back for a second meeting, that's when she announced that a Muslim had done it, and that there might be hatred against Muslims. When I heard that I was like, "Wait, what do you mean? We all did it? We didn't plot it. I don't have nothing to do with it. And why are we all getting the blame for it?" So many thoughts went through my head that time: *Who is this Osama Bin Laden guy? What is he up to? Why would he do this? This is against Islam.* None of us knew who Bin Laden was. We were making jokes about the guy. My friends said, "Your name is very close to his name: Adama, Osama."

When I finally reached my family the next day, they told me they were fine, and my dad said, "Shh, don't talk about it. Be quiet, bye." He would not talk about anything over the phone.

The Way I Left NYC Was Not the Way It Was When I Came Back

I felt 9/11 when I came back to New York for Ramadan break. There were six of us classmates who had to get on a plane to come back to New York. At that time, we covered our faces. I remember coming to the airport dressed all in pitch black with our faces covered. We were even wearing gloves; all you could see were our eyes, that's it.

I couldn't believe the looks on everyone's faces. Everybody was scared, pointing. You saw people turn red. We were whispering to each other, "What's going on?" Honestly, I was scared. I thought those people were going to beat me.

We didn't know what was going on around the country. We didn't know about the hate crimes—we didn't know anything, though the day after 9/11 someone threw a rock through the window of the school.

That day at the airport, we got extra screenings, our bags were checked, we got pulled to the side. The guards were so nasty to us. The people were so nasty to us, the airline was so nasty to us. I remember us boarding the plane and the captain looked at us and shook his head.

It made me feel like crap because I was being singled out. I'm thirteen, I've never been through something like this. I've never had racism before. I've been sheltered from things like that. So, that was my first time. People cursed at us, yelled at us and sucked their teeth, saying, "Go back to your country, you Talibani, go back to Osama Bin Laden."

This whole time, I thought I was American. I thought, *You can't touch me, I'm American.*

My parents didn't know I wore any garb until I came home. My mom opened the door, she saw me and she closed it back. She told my father, "You have to tell her to take this off. I told you not to send her to Buffalo!"

They disapproved of my *niquab* (face veil). They said to me, "Take that off, take that off."

When I originally left NYC for school, it was peaceful and happy and everybody was cheery and saying hello. When I came back after 9/11, everyone was like, what do you want, where are you from? There was more fear. The fear was towards me, and I felt the same way. People didn't take the time to talk to me, or ask me why I was wearing a *niquab*. Walking down the street, people would curse at me, they would even throw things. It was just nasty. It actually made me want to wear it more.

Oh, You're Not Ugly!

I came back to New York public school for 9th grade. I left Islamic school because I didn't like it. I remember telling my dad, "I'm too controlled there." I wore my *niquab* for a few months with colored contacts to make the *niquab* look pretty. Might as well make something look pretty — if you can't see my face, look at my nice eyes! But, it was actually fun. I didn't have any problems in high school. The other kids always asked me to see my face, though. Like, "I wonder how you look under there? You're probably ugly." We would make jokes about it. I'd say, "Yeah, I look hideous. That's why I wear it, of course!"

Then, after a while, I thought, *This is not a mosque.* So in the middle of 9th grade, I took it off, because you know what? This *niquab* is not a must. It's really not.

So one day I walked into school, I was still wearing an *abaya* (a loose robe, usually worn with a head scarf called a *hijab*), but I had my face uncovered. My teacher just looked at me and said, "Adama?" And I remember all the students just coming in to look at me, in the middle of English class, to see what I looked like.

They said things like, "Oh, you're not ugly! You have nice teeth."

I replied, "Thank you." I was just smiling.

What Did I Do?

The morning of March 24th 2005, my family and I were in the house sleeping.

Someone knocked on the door, and my mom went and opened it. These men barged in, waking us up. I always sleep with the blanket over my head. They pull the blanket off my head, I look up, I see a man. He said, "You've got to get out!" I'm like, *What the hell, what's going on?*

I saw about ten to fifteen people in our apartment and right outside our door in the hallway. They were mostly men, but there were two women. Some had FBI jackets, and others were from the police department and the INS. We were all forced out of the bed and told to sit in the living room. They were going through papers, throwing stuff around, yelling and talking to each other, then whispering. I heard them yelling at my mother in the background, and my mom can't speak much English, and they were pulling her into the kitchen, yelling at her, "We're going to deport you and your whole family!"

This whole time, I was thinking, *What's going on? What are they talking about?* I knew my dad had an issue with his papers, but I didn't think that my mom did. They kept saying, "We're going to send all of you back to your country."

Then I saw my dad walking in, in handcuffs. They had gone to the mosque to get him. It was the scariest thing you could ever see; I had just never seen my father so powerless. He was always this guy who you didn't mess with. If he said do it, you did it. He was just someone you didn't cross paths with.

They took him to the kitchen, whispered something to him.

He sat down, looked at us. He said, "Everything's going to be fine, don't worry."

And then I knew nothing was fine, I knew something was wrong. They told him to tell us what was going on. He told us that they were going to arrest him and they were going to take him.

The FBI agents told me to get up and get my sneakers. I was thinking they wanted to see my sneaker collection. I have all types of colors of sneakers. I went and grabbed them. I said, "I have this one, I have this one, I have this one."

One of the agents said, "Choose one."

My favorite color is blue, so I picked up a blue pair and said, "This one."

He said, "Put them on."

I said, "Okay, but I know they fit me."

He said, "Put them on!" He was very nasty. Then he said "All those earrings have to go out." I have eight piercings on each side, a nose ring and a tongue ring. I went to the kitchen to take them off, and they followed me in there.

My breath was stinking. I asked, "Can I at least brush my teeth? My breath stinks really bad. Can I use the bathroom?"

They said, "No. We have to go. You're coming with us."

I said, "Where am I going to go? Am I going with my dad?" I put on my jacket. They let me put my headscarf and *abaya* on. Then, one of the women took out handcuffs. I panicked so badly, I was stuttering, "What did I do? Where are we going?"

First time in my life—I'm sixteen years old—in handcuffs. I looked at my dad, and he said, "Just do what they say."

My mom didn't know I was going. When we got out the door, she said, "Where she go? Where she go?" The agents said, "We're taking her," and they held my mom back. The man who seemed to be in charge put his hands on my mother to stop her.

They took me and my dad and put us in the same car. I was scared. I said to him, "What's going on? What's going to happen?" My dad said, "Don't say anything, we're going to get a lawyer. It's okay, everything is going to be fine."

There were two Escalades driving with us. I was looking around, paying attention. I recognized the Brooklyn Bridge, I recognized a lot of landmarks, but I didn't recognize the building where my father and I were taken. We got out of the car and we walked past a security booth where the cars drive up to, before taking a ramp beneath the building to the parking lot. Once we were inside the building, they put me in my own cell. It was white, with a bench. No bars. No windows. There was a door that had a tiny glass pane, and I could see who was out there. I just saw a bunch of computers and tables, and people walking back and forth and talking. I kept seeing them talk to my dad.

I don't know how long I was in there.

I was nervous, I was panicking, I was crying, I was trying to figure out what was going on. And, I was constantly using the bathroom.

The toilet was an open toilet, though. There was a camera on the ceiling in the middle of the room. I was wondering, *Can they see me peeing?* I just wrapped blankets around me as I was peeing.

I'm Not This Person

I was taken out of my cell to be interrogated. Nobody told me who they were. It was just me and a man, sitting where all the computers were. Nobody else was around me. There was a guy all the way down at the other end with my dad, but that's about it.

He asked me questions like, "What's your name? What's your age? What's your date of birth? Where were you born?" They knew I was born in Guinea. Then he asked, "What is your citizenship status?"

I said, "American."

He asked me all these questions about my citizenship status. Then after a while, he said, "You know you're not here legally, right? You know why you're here today right? You weren't born in this country. You know you're not American?"

For a second, I was just so mad at my parents. It was as if one of the biggest secrets in the world had just been revealed to me. I don't know if it was to protect them or if it was to protect me, but that was the biggest secret someone could ever hold.

The guy's attitude didn't change when he realized I didn't know what was going on. He was nasty the whole time. He just sat there explaining the process to me. He asked me if I wanted to see a consular officer.

I asked, "What is a consular officer?"

He said, "You don't know what a consular officer is? Those are people from your country. From Guinea."

I said, "What about them? What do I have to see them for?"

Finally, they called my dad. They gave us a document about how we could see a consular officer. My dad knows how to read English, but he said to me in Pular, "Pretend you're translating to me in my language." Then he said, "Whatever you do, do not say you can go back to your country. They will circumcise you there."

My dad wasn't just coming up with a way to stay. There was a real fear of female genital mutilation in Guinea. It happened to my mom. In order to get married in Guinea, a female would have to be circumcised. My dad's brothers would do it, they would make sure I got circumcised. My parents made a decision when they had girls that they would never do it. That's the main reason why our parents never took us back to Guinea, not even to visit.

The guy told my dad, "Hey, you've got to get up, you've got to leave."

To me they said, "We have to fingerprint you." When we were done with the fingerprints, they took a picture of me. I was then sitting on a bench in the main entrance when this young lady walked in. Her name was Teshnuba. I had seen her at the mosque before, but I didn't know her personally. I just recognized her face and knew her name. I said "Hi," but in my heart, I started panicking, thinking, *What the hell is she doing here? Who am I gonna see next?*

Finally I was brought to another room. This room had a table, a chair on one side, and two chairs on the other side. A federal agent walked in. She said, "I need to talk you about something." The questions she was asking had nothing to do about immigration. They were terrorism questions. She asked me about people from London, about people from all over the world. I thought, *What's going on?*

The male interrogator told me that the religious study group Teshnuba was part of was started by a guy who was wanted by the FBI. I had no idea if that was true or not.

The study group at the mosque was all women. So it was women learning about religion, women's empowerment, why we cover, how we do the prayer, when to pray, things like that. It was more for converts and new people who had just come into Islam. There was nothing about jihad or anything like that.

I wasn't part of the group, but Teshnuba was. We were the same age, sixteen. So, they asked me about this group and they told me they'd taken my computer and my diary. My diary was a black and white notebook. I had phone numbers, I had notes, I had stories in it, I had everything. Basically, they asked me about every contact in there, they asked me about every little thing. But, there's nothing in there about jihad, there's nothing in there about anything that's, "Oh you're suspicious." There was nothing in there at all. So, I wasn't worried.

They said, "We have your computer, we can find whatever you're hiding."

I said, "Go ahead, look in my computer. I have nothing to hide."

They kept making a scene, like there was something big there. They said, "Don't lie to us. If you lie to us we'll have proof, we'll catch you in your lie."

I knew there was nothing in my computer, but at the end of the day, I started to doubt myself. I thought, *Okay, what's going on now? Is there something there?* Their technique is to make you doubt yourself. But then I thought, *Wait a minute, I'm not this person. What are they talking about?*

The interrogation lasted a long time. This secret service guy came in. He asked me how I felt about Bush. I said, "I don't like him." I was being very honest with them. There was nothing to hide.

The Secret Service guy was just too aggressive. He said, "I don't understand—why do you choose to cover when women choose to wear less and less every day?"

I said, "It's freedom of choice. Some people want to show some stuff, some people want to hide things. Some people want to preserve their bodies, some people don't want to. They want to show it to the whole world."

He said, "I don't understand. You're young, why are you doing this?"

Then they asked me about Teshnuba. They asked me about her name, they asked me about her family, but I told them, "I don't know her."

They said, "Teshnuba wrote you on this list."

I said, "What list?"

They said, "She signed you up to be a suicide bomber."

I said, "Are you serious? Why would she do that? She doesn't seem like that type of person."

They were trying to make me seem like I was wrong about who I knew and who I don't know.

They took me out of the interrogation room briefly, because my dad wanted to talk to me. They had him sign papers consenting to let them talk to me because I was underage. We didn't know that we were supposed to have lawyers. The FBI never told us that.

My dad said, "Everything is going to be fine. I want you to be brave. I'll see you later."

You Put Me on a List?

Back in the interrogation room, they told me Teshnuba and I were going to leave. I said, "Where's my dad, can I say bye to him?"

They said, "He left already."

I started to cry because I'd had my dad there the whole time. I said, "Where is he going to go? What are you guys going to do?" They said that he was going to see an immigration judge before the day ended.

I asked, "When am I going to see him? Where am I going?"

They told me to stop with the questions. They brought Teshnuba and handcuffed us both, hands behind the back. The cuffs were very tight and I remember they left marks.

We got back in the Escalade. I'm very traumatized when I see Escalades now. This time, I didn't know where they took me, but it was on Varick St. in Manhattan. When we arrived at our destination, the agent told us to walk in casually because all these people were walking past us on the street. He said, "Act casual and people won't say anything."

Teshnuba and I, all by ourselves, got in this elevator. We went up, and we went into this large room that was divided into smaller holding cells. The cells didn't have bars, but were enclosed with glass. They put us into our own cell. From there, we saw a bunch of men in one of the other cells, all yelling and screaming and talking, all in orange jumpsuits. Teshnuba and I just looked at each other.

She said to me, "You put me on a list?"

I said, "No! They said you put *me* on a list." We both realized they had been trying to set us up. So, they didn't have anything on us. They'd come for her early in the morning, too. They didn't detain any of her parents, they just detained her. Later I found out why they'd taken my dad. After I'd been reported as a a suicide bomber, the FBI started investigating my whole family. That's how they found out about my dad being here without papers.

Teshnuba and I were then trying to figure out what was going on, what they were going to do, if they were going to release us.

That's when a lady walked in. She said, "What are you guys in for?"

We said, "We don't know."

"I hear you guys did something."

"What did we do?" We were asking *her* for information.

She said, "We're going to take you to Pennsylvania."

Teshnuba and I looked at each other, like, *Pennsylvania?* I said, "What are we going to do in Pennsylvania?"

She answered, "They didn't tell you? There's a detention center there."

You No Longer Have Rights

The FBI drove us to Pennsylvania, across state lines, without my parent's permission. We got to the juvenile detention center late at night. When the FBI agents dropped us off, I wanted to scream, "Please don't leave us!" I didn't want to be left there. I didn't know where I was. There were too many faces for one night for me.

The female guard told me and Teshnuba we had to get strip searched. We said that was against our religion.

The guard said, "It's either that or we hold you down."

I said, "Hold me down and do what? I'm not doing a strip search." I'm stubborn like that, but I was in a situation where I had no choice.

So, she said, "Who wants to go first?"

Teshnuba went first. They searched her hair, checked her body parts; they checked everything. She then had to take a shower and change into a uniform they gave her, and then she had to go. When they took her downstairs, the guard said, "Okay, your turn."

The guard stood there and said, "You're going to have to take off everything. Take off whatever you feel comfortable with first."

I said, "I can't do this. I can't." I was in tears. My own mother doesn't look at me naked. It's my privacy. I said, "It must be against some law for you to do this to me."

She said, "No, it's not. You no longer have rights."

"Why not? What did I do?"

"You're just going to have to take your clothes off."

I was crying, but she just looked at me and said, "Kids here sneak in things and I have to search you."

I had on my *abaya*, and that was the first thing I took off. Second thing I took off was my head scarf. Third thing I took off was my top. Fourth was my bra. I stopped there for the longest minutes. I was with my hands across my chest, just to get that little dignity for myself.

She said, "Come on, I don't have all day."

I said, "I can't do this, I can't, I can't."

"Drop your pants."

So, I took off my pants, I took off my underwear, and I kept my legs closed against each other, trying to cover myself. I was just holding myself with the little bit I could.

She said, "You cannot do that. You have to let loose, or else I'll call another guard and we'll hold you down and search you. This is your last warning. If you want me to call someone in, I'll call them in right now but it's not gonna be nice. We're going to hold you down and search you."

I said, "Okay." I let go of my arms.

She said, "Lift your breasts."

I lifted my breasts.

She said, "Open your legs more."

I opened my legs.

She said, "Put your hands in there, to see there's nothing."

I said, "There's nothing there!"

She said, "Just do it."

I did it.

She said, "Turn around, put your hands up."

I did that.

Then she said, "Alright, now put your fingers to your hair, pull at your ears. Show me your ears, open your mouth."

I showed my mouth.

"Show me your nose."

I put my finger up my nose, put it up so she could see.

Then she gave me a blue uniform: sweat pants, socks, underwear, a bra, and a hair tie and a little towel and wash cloth. She told me to take a shower in five minutes, and then she left.

I knew I only had five minutes, but I just sat at the corner of the shower and just held myself and cried. I was thinking, *I cannot believe what I just went through.* I'm just crying and crying and crying. I don't know how long, but then I just told myself that I had to get up. I washed myself really quickly. I've never felt like I needed God more than anything than this day. So, I did ghusul, which is like a special shower for prayer. I prayed, "God, you've got to hear me for this one. I've never asked for anything that I desperately needed but this one."

I dried myself and put my clothes on. There was a little mirror there. I looked into it. My eyes were red from crying.

The guard returned and told me I had to take off my head scarf. I said, "It's part of my religion." And, I was having a bad hair day, I was not ready to show my hair. She let me keep the scarf, but later the supervisor took it from me once she saw me.

I was then taken to my cell. As we walked, the guard said, "You must keep your hands to your side at all times." You had to look straight, you couldn't look anywhere else. There were cameras everywhere, but I wasn't listening, I was looking around.

I still didn't know why I was there. I didn't know if it was immigration or if it was for the stuff they were interrogating me about. When I got to the cell, all the lights were out. I could see Teshnuba in the corner, praying. There was one blanket, and it was freezing cold in there.

We stayed up the whole night talking about everything. I found out her mom had just had a baby; my mom had just had a baby too. She was the oldest, I was the oldest. I asked her age, she asked my age. I asked what school she went to, what she was studying, what she wanted to do with her life.

We were laughing like, "Pinch me. This is a prank."

She said, "Maybe it will be all be straightened out by tomorrow."

I don't know how we fell asleep but I remember at one point, we were both crying.

There Goes a Terrorist

I was just so angry, and I was trying to contain all this anger. I was so mad at America as a country. I remember the first morning in detention, we went for breakfast and we were supposed to salute the American flag. I'm like, "Fuck the American flag. I'm not saluting it." I said it. During the pledge I put my hands to my side, and I just looked out the window.

Each morning I did that. I remember one of the guards asking me, "How come you don't pledge allegiance?"

I said, "You guys said it yourself. I am not American."

Nobody told me what was going on. I wasn't brought before a judge until probably my fourth week there, and it was via video conference.

An article came out in *New York Times* about why Teshnuba and I were there, that we were suspected of being suicide bombers. I never saw the article while in prison. I saw it when I came out. After the guards read what happened, things changed. They would whisper, "There goes a terrorist" or, "There go those girls."

After the article came out we got extra strip searches, about three times a day, and the searches got stricter. They would tell us to spread our butt cheeks, and they made nasty, racist comments. I remember the guards laughing, and going, "Look at those assholes. Look at them. These are the ones that want to take our country down." Things like that.

If I talked back, they would tackle me down and I would be put into solitary. All I wanted to do was get out. I knew that I was going to have to take shit from everyone, because I did not want to be in solitary confinement.

We also lost a lot of privileges because of the head scarf. We weren't allowed to use the bathroom privately. So when I had to go, I was like, "I hope I stink this place up, I pray that my shit would make this place close down or something. I hope my poop brings toxins."

I remember even having tissue stuck up my butt when somebody did a strip search once, and I did it on purpose. I was like, "I hope after this, they'll think, *I will never want to strip search her again*. It didn't work. I still got strip searched. I even tried leaving caca there. I tried everything.

Those first three weeks I was there, my family didn't have any idea where I was. They had to do research and find out, and hire a lawyer. The lawyer, Natasha, came to see me at the detention center. She asked me, "Do you know why you're here?"

I said no.

"There's a rumor going around about you being a suicide bomber."

I laughed so hard.

She said, "That's not funny."

I said, "Are you serious or are you joking? If you knew me, you would laugh and say 'Hell no'."

I have a family, I am somebody. I wanted to live. I said, "I'm not ready to meet God yet."

She said, "But they're not charging you with anything except overstaying your visa."

My mom came to visit me after my lawyer. She was so skinny. You could just tell she wasn't eating. It was the worst visit ever because she didn't want to say anything at all. When I asked about my dad, she just said, "He's fine." She knew that he was being held in New Jersey at the time. I just knew that she was upset. She was so drained out.

A Way to Get Me Out

After a while, my lawyer called. She said she had good news. "I have a way to get you out of jail. You're going to have to wear an ankle bracelet."

I said, "I'll wear anything."

The day that I was supposed to be released from the detention center, I said goodbye to Teshnuba in the cafeteria. I wanted to hold her and let her know it was going to be okay. But I couldn't hug her, or it would've been solitary confinement for her. So I looked at her and I said, "May Allah be with you, and be patient." And I walked away.

I haven't spoken to Teshnuba since then. She'd told me that her mother made an agreement with the federal government. If they released her daughter, they would go back to their country, no problems. I think their country was Bangladesh. So as soon as she was released, it was right to the airport.

I stayed there six and a half weeks. By the time I came out, I was seventeen.

Federal agents picked me up. This guard walked past, and he said, "Arrest that fucking nigger, terrorist." But I didn't give a damn, I was so excited I was leaving. The whole world could burn down, but as long as I was leaving, I didn't care.

Home Again

As soon as we got to New York, I was just so excited and happy to be home again that I forgot I had to wear an ankle bracelet. I thought everything was going to go back to normal, but in a way, I knew deep down inside things would never be normal again, because I was so traumatized.

We came back to my house. My mom had to sign papers, and they released me. They put the ankle bracelet on the same day.

Once a week I had to report to Federal Plaza so they could check the bracelet. When I got there, I recognized it was the building where my father and I had been taken to a few months ago. I just looked at it and my heart just started beating so fast. It just triggered the memory, and I started to cry so badly I just could not control it. It was one of the most traumatizing moments of my life.

I wore the ankle bracket for three years. You can still see my bruises from it. My heel always hurts. This is all black from the ankle bracelet. I had to wear the bracelet and check in every week. I also had to be under curfew, which was 10:00 P.M. and then 11:00 P.M.

Every night our phone would ring, and I would have to press this button and they would have to hear it. I wouldn't get any sleep. The man who put the bracelet on me told me, "If you take it off, we're going to put you in jail. If your phone is off, you're going to jail."

That was the best threat you could ever make to me. I did everything possible not to tamper with it, just to keep it on.

They never said how long I would have to wear it. It was pending my immigration case. I was only ever charged with overstaying my visa, that's it. I was never charged with anything related to terrorism. They wanted to deport me.

For days, my mom didn't want to talk because she thought they were recording us with the ankle bracelet. She was always like, "Shh, shh."

I'd say, "They're not listening."

I didn't know if they weren't listening, and I didn't care. I'd get on the phone with Demaris, my friend from high school, and we would say things on purpose like, "Fuck the government!"

I Miss Him Being the One Who Took Care of Everything

My dad got deported around 2006. It was the hardest.

I didn't see him for a long time after I got released from juvi. He was in New Jersey. I wasn't allowed to go, because it was outside the distance I could travel with my ankle bracelet. My mom and my siblings were able to visit, but they couldn't go a lot because it was a lot of money to get out there.

They made an exception to let me travel to New Jersey, just before he was deported. I couldn't look at him. I was just crying the whole time.

He said, "I hope you take care of the family. It's your job." It's always about, "It's your job, it's your responsibility, you're the next person in line."

I miss a lot about my dad. I miss his company. I even miss him yelling at me. My brothers and sister, we used to walk around saying our dad was a dictator. But we needed him. I just miss him being the one who took care of everything. I didn't have to worry about everything; no bills, no nothing.

We Were Starving

I thought I was going to be able to come back to school, the government was going to apologize and write me a check, and I was set for life. But it was the opposite way around. When I came back, I had to drop school to work to support my family. No way my dad can work in Guinea; there are no jobs there. So I support my father, his family, my mom's family, and I support my family here too.

I would work three or four jobs, whatever job I could find—babysitting jobs, cleaning houses. I worked at an interpretive service for a while, until I found out that could get me back in jail, because I had no documentation.

Sometimes we were starving. For days there would be no food in the house. Finally we met a social worker who told us we could get public assistance. Nobody tells you about this stuff.

I started feeling distance from my friends because I was going through something that none of my friends went through. I was growing up really quickly, maturing so fast.

Everything that I do in life is to take care of my family. Everything revolves around them. My family here wouldn't be able to stand on their own feet, not without me. I didn't want my brother and my sister to work at all. I didn't want them to miss out on what I missed out.

But I was drained. When I came back, I was also going through my emotions. I would come home so angry, like, "Leave me alone, don't touch me."

Now that I look back, I wish there was something that could have been done. I wish I would have told my story to a newspaper, but I was always afraid to say something, because they always threatened me with going to jail.

That's why I kept so silent and cried about everything. I feel like it's too late for me.

[Editor's Note: In 2007, Adama was granted asylum, on the grounds that she would face forcible circumcision if deported to Guinea. In court, her mother gave testimony on her own harrowing experience of being circumcised.]

I Am Not American Now. I Am a Refugee.

I had the ankle bracelet up until I got asylum. The day I got it taken off, I had the cheesiest smile. I went to the guy I had to report every week, and when he took off the ankle bracelet, I said, "My legs! That's what my legs look like."

But for at least a year, I still had a feeling I had the ankle bracelet on. I felt like it was still there. And sometimes I would be out, and I would think, "Oh my God, my curfew," and I would just start panicking. I had to calm myself down again.

I am not American now. I have asylum. That means I am a refugee. *[Editor's Note: In 2009, to celebrate winning her asylum case, Adama arranged to take a vacation in Texas with friends. When she tried to board her flight at LaGuardia airport, a ticket agent told her she was on the No Fly list. Federal agents came and handcuffed her and took her to the airport security station, where she was held for almost thirteen hours before being released.]*

I'm Done. I Am Not Going to Go Through This.

In 2009 I started working for a family as a nanny. I met them through an old friend who was also working for them. They are a very nice family, they spoil me too much, beyond spoil. They pay me on time, they take care of me, they give me Christmas bonuses, they give me vacation, they take me everywhere.

We were supposed to fly to Chicago on March 31, 2010. I went to the airport before them because I just wanted to know if there would be any problems or anything. I was there with my luggage, and I had brought a friend because I was afraid of repeating what had happened before. I don't know why, but I just had a fear that something was going to happen. I even called my lawyers, but they said nothing should happen, that I should be fine. But I got to LaGuardia airport, and a problem did happen.

The same thing happened as before. The airline supervisor called Port Authority police and other government officials. I called my lawyer and he came. They kept asking me questions, like, "What did you do to be on the No Fly list?"

I wasn't able to get on the plane. I could tell the family were disappointed. They ended up taking the other babysitter. I lost money that day. They were going to pay me for going, and I was counting on that money.

As soon as I got out of that room, something in me just triggered. I told myself, "I'm done. I'm tired. I am not going to go through this again." I told my lawyers, "I want to sue these motherfuckers" and so we filed a lawsuit against Attorney General Eric Holder.

About a month later, we finally received a letter from James Kennedy of the DHS Traveler Redress Inquiry Program, but it didn't tell me anything. It didn't tell me why I wasn't allowed to board my flight at LaGuardia or what would happen if I tried to fly again.

Around three months later, my friend gave me a ticket to go to Chicago on November 12, 2010 as a gift. I didn't know if I could fly, but I didn't know how to find out if I could without trying again. It was LaGuardia again. This time, I walked up to the ticket machine. I punched in my name, and it said, "Go see a ticket agent." I said to myself, "I'm not going to be able to fly."

I gave the ticket agent my name, my state ID, and he printed the ticket. I looked at him and said, "You printed it?"

He said, "Yeah."

"And it went through?"

"Yeah."

When he gave me my ticket, I started to cry. He was just looking at me, like, is this girl nuts?

I Want to Live My Life Now

I grew up too fast. I experienced some things that a lot of people around me haven't, so it's hard to talk to my peers. I've never gotten to escape. All my friends went to college, and, now, four years later, they've all graduated, and I'm just like, "Wow, they're graduating college and I haven't even got there yet."

I have a bigger picture of life. But I feel like things are not changing as quickly as I want them to. I want to be done with school already, I want to have my own car, I want to be in my own space. I want to live my life now. I don't mind taking care of my family, but for once, I want to do something for myself: I want to go and do something overseas. I want to be a traveling nurse. I want to help people, I want to educate.

Even though everything is said and done, I still live in constant fear of federal agents taking me or any of my family members. They did it when I was innocent, and they could do it again. I have so much to lose, including my family. I remember the look of helplessness on their faces the day they took me and my father.

Still, the U.S. is home. It's the only place I know. I am hopeful for this country, because of people like me and my siblings. We know how it feels to suffer, so we can change things.

Now, I study Islam on my own. At the end of the day, I still believe in God, because I feel like things could have gotten worse. I could have been in Guantanamo Bay. I still have my family, I still have my health. So, in a way I know there is still God. There has to be something you have to believe in at the end of the day.

TOM BARBASH

■

The Women

FROM www.narrativemagazine.com

A WEEK AFTER MY MOTHER DIED, my father and I went to a series of holiday parties. We lived in a sixteenth-floor apartment just off Central Park West, and in our building alone there were four different gatherings at which you could see my father surrounded by an infield of swooning women. He had become, in the wake of my mother's death, desirable real estate, a handsome fifty-eight-year-old with money. He was testing the waters, and you could see it bringing him back to life.

One of the women he met brought him to her personal trainer; another took him clothes shopping to stores like Kenneth Cole and Hugo Boss "to raise his spirits." He returned home weirdly pleased with himself, as though he'd regained fluency in a language he hadn't studied since high school. I'd borrow a new leather jacket of my father's when I went out for the night and I'd find business cards in the pockets, or a napkin with a phone number. Before long the women were dropping by our house, and I'd see them late at night drinking coffee in my mother's kitchen, moving in or out of the bathroom or my parents' bedroom, where they'd often stay over.

There'd be a scarf or a purse left out on a chair. I'd hear a woman whispering as she snuck out, for my sake, early, before seven. My room was next to the front entryway, and I was having trouble sleeping in those days.

For the first few weeks of February, my father dated a chatty frizzy-haired woman named Leanne who worked at the mayor's office scheduling press conferences and talking to reporters. They ordered in Chinese food, and they'd leave the half-empty containers lying out on the counter. They watched movies in his room, and then at some point his door would close. I pretended a few times that it was my mother in there, that she'd slipped in without my knowing, but usually I put my earbuds in to keep from hearing anything.

One night toward the end of that month, he brought home a woman from Los Angeles named Chloe who owned a string of boutiques and wore sparkly eyeliner, low-waisted jeans, and a belly button ring, in winter. She flirted with me when he left the room, quizzing me about my personal life and once touching my knee. She gave me her business card, which listed the address of her New York store. "Come by sometime," she said, with a predatory softness in her eyes. When my father walked back in, there was music I knew he hated booming from the study.

"This okay?" he asked.

"Oh, *Steve*," Chloe said, "we can do better than that." She went and turned the tuner to some kind of lame diva dance music. She started grooving on her way back.

She was about forty, I'd say, but she tossed her hair and gyrated like an extra on a music video.

My father glanced at me and raised his eyebrows. I wrote ABSURD on a piece of notepaper and flashed it quickly so she wouldn't see.

"Both of you come here and *dance*," she said from the dining room.

She looked misplaced vamping next to the long oak dining table and under my grandmother's crystal chandelier. My father moved his shoulders tentatively to the beat. Chloe yelled, "Show your father how to dance, Andy."

"He does just fine for himself," I told her.

I went and hid in my room. When I ventured out an hour later, his door was closed, and I saw her satin jacket and a shiny red purse draped over the reading chair in the living room.

Later that same week, I watched my father pick up the widow of one of his business partners during the intermission of *Into the Woods*. They were sharing notes about the New York Ballet, and she said she had no one to go with, did he know anyone with extra tickets? She came back with us for drinks after the show, and my father put on an old Billie Holiday record my mother had loved.

The widow's name was Patricia Hobson. She was an interior decorator and good looking in a preppy, older-woman way, with attentive eyes, a long thin nose, and a long wiry neck. I kept staring at the cords on her neck as she spoke.

"New York is a fabulous place to be a boy just out of college," she said.

"How so?"

"Well, the ratio is entirely in your favor. There are so many gorgeous, stylish women in the city. I see them absolutely *everywhere*, and they're all single. My lord, Andrew, they'll eat you *up*. What's your type?"

I shrugged.

"He likes tall ones," my father said, because my last girlfriend had been my height.

"Well, my daughter is five-five, but she can wear heels."

"I'm pretty sure I'd be a disappointment," I told her, and she glanced over at my dad and smiled kindly. "I doubt that very much," she said.

She started to size up our apartment then, commenting on the arrangement of the chairs and sofas and the artwork on our walls. "This apartment has so much *potential*," she said. "Give me a few hours some Saturday afternoon, and I'll show you what we can do."

"Let me show you something," my father said. He poured her a Scotch, and they stepped out on the terrace to look out at the lights across Central Park.

"Oh, *boy*," she said, which is what everyone said when they saw our view.

"This is my favorite spot in the world. If you look through the binoculars you can see people jogging around the reservoir."

"I run around that reservoir four days a week," Mrs. Hobson said.

"Let us know next time so we can watch for you," my father said. I thought he was joking until I saw his face.

"I will," she said. "We can wave to each other."

* * *

I slipped out later to get drunk with my high school friend Jonas, but the whole time I was picturing my father and Mrs. Hobson ransacking our underachieving apartment, taking our keepsakes down to the storage lockers in the basement of our building. There were legitimate grounds for my fear: In the last week two framed photographs and four drawers of clothes had vanished. I think my father wanted to disperse my mother's ghost discreetly and respectfully. But every couple of days something else was missing, most recently a picture of my mother and godmother as teenagers, resting on a hammock like lazy goddesses. In its place now was a blank spot on the wall.

It's got to stop, I thought.

Jonas tilted his head, puzzled. I guess I'd said it aloud.

"He's not cheating on her," he said.

"Because she's dead, you mean. I suppose that's technically right." We chugged our beers, then Jonas went to the bar to refill our empty pitcher.

"I have a friend who wants to meet you," he said when he returned. "Actually, she's a little obsessed about it."

"What did you tell her?"

"This and that. You just come up in conversation, and then it's all she wants to talk about."

"She must have an exciting life."

"She does, actually. She's really smart."

"Good looking?"

Jonas paused, as though I'd asked a trick question.

"Sort of. She kind of hides it. She doesn't do much for *me*, but maybe she would if I didn't know her so well."

"You told her about my mother dying?"

He nodded. "When I told her she cried."

"That's just too fucking *weird*," I said. I reached for my father's jacket, which was on the floor next to me, and rested it on my lap.

"It wasn't." He put his cigarette out and lit another. "Anyhow, get comfortable, brother. You're not getting anywhere near that apartment for another couple hours, you got me?"

When we finally made it back we saw her coat on a hanger in the vestibule. Jonas ran his hand across Mrs. Hobson's scarf and then bent over to smell it.

"Your dad is outstanding," he said.

I took a tin of sour candies from her coat pocket, just to do it, really, not because I wanted anything of hers.

Both my father and I were in therapy then. He went two mornings a week to an animated man named Bergman who had a book-lined office on the Upper East Side, and on Wednesday nights I saw a woman named Dr. Helendoerf down in the Village. Bergman and my father started meeting shortly after my mother was diagnosed—at my mother's urging. When my father left therapy he seemed uplifted, which was far from the case with me. He and his therapist talked about my mother, probably, but they also talked about art and politics, even sports. Bergman was constantly finding his way into our breakfast or dinnertime conversations. "Bergman thinks the Mets should trade Piazza," he'd say. Or, "Bergman gave me a list of Polish films for us to rent." They were friends. I once saw them walking down our street together, which seemed like a violation of the patient-therapist relationship. I asked Dr. Helendoerf about it. I asked her if she would ever take a walk with a patient.

She tilted her head slightly to the right. She wore a neutral pashmina that resembled the ones my mother wore.

"Is that something you think you would like to do, take a walk with me?"

"No," I said, too emphatically. "I mean, not especially."

She allowed a long awkward silence.

"Why do you think you asked then?"

I didn't have an answer. I began to hear a buzzing sound like a halogen light turned too high or low.

"Do you think perhaps you're disappointed sometimes when the world doesn't respond to you the way it responds to your father?"

"That's probably true," I said.

I saw her write something down.

"But I don't want that kind of attention."

"Then why do you think it is that you're so angry?"

"I'm not angry," I said.

She didn't respond. She might have raised her eyebrows.

"I just don't get why he's so happy all the time."

She continued to study me. I was fairly used to these standoffs. In the silence the buzzing started up again.

"Do you hear that sound?" I asked.

She paused for a moment. "What sort of sound?"

It was faint now, and probably from somewhere on the street.

"I guess I don't either," I said.

When my mother was sick I was out of the house a lot. I'd go out to work—an entry-level job I'd talked my way into at a public radio station—and then I'd stay out until everyone was asleep. Once I stayed away for nearly two weeks without telling anyone where I went. I missed her birthday party. When I reached my father on the phone he was madder than he'd ever been. And then he forgave me, which was even worse. He said I was distraught, which was true, but for the longest time I just felt numb. He said people cope in different ways. He said he thought of leaving all the time, which I believed and didn't care to hear. I couldn't really say why I needed to be away, and really I was able to put my mother out of my mind most of the time.

Dr. Helendoerf said I was repressing my reactions to my mother's illness and "obfuscating" my emotional responses. And she said that was a big reason why I stayed in the house all the time now; I was trying to keep my family intact by staying at home. I told her that was bullshit, if not in those words.

I called my father to see if I should pick up dinner, and a woman answered the phone. "*Aw, fuck,*" I said and hung up.

On my way into the building, I was spotted again by Mrs. Wiederman, a gaunt red-haired woman who, like four or five others whose names I forgot, invited me to dinner every time she saw me.

"I made a pot of stew you can keep in the freezer and heat up for your suppers," she said, whispering to protect my pride.

"We're eating out mostly," I said.

"Well, I'll just leave it outside your door, then," she said. Dishes in sealed Tupperware, aluminum pans, and plastic Baggies had been dropped off on our doorstep ever since my mother died.

"You know your mother would be so proud of you," she said as we rode the cramped and ancient elevator together.

I thought about the arguments my mother and I'd been having over my lack of direction.

"Why?" I asked.

She seemed confused by the question.

"Because you're a *lovely* young man," she said. She stepped toward me then, held my face in her cold damp hands. I smelled mouthwash and old-lady perfume. Then I felt the walls of the elevator shiver. She was actually going to kiss my face.

"Get *away*," I said, pulling back. "Did you even know my mother?"

She gasped, and then stared at me with her mouth open, as if I was dissolving before her eyes. "Oh . . . " she said. "Oh, dear." When we got to her floor she stumbled out of the elevator.

"And we don't need any more of your shitty dinners," I yelled.

I felt pretty bad about this later.

As we made our way across the park on a Saturday to the Metropolitan Museum of Art, my father told me I hadn't been myself lately. We were walking through the Seventy-ninth Street fields, by Belvedere Castle, and in the cold our voices came out in vapor. "I'm fine," I said. "And you?"

"I know you're not sleeping," he said. A man in a gray Columbia sweatshirt jogged by, with a black Labrador keeping pace.

"It's getting better," I said, though it wasn't. Whenever I dropped off I kept having a dream in which my mother was alive and the two of us had to go around convincing everyone we knew that she hadn't died. "Prove it's you," they'd say. She'd tell them their middle name or their birthday, and they'd tell her she had gotten them wrong. "It's a strange time for everyone," my father said.

We stopped on the path, facing each other. I smoothed a patch of dirt and stones with my foot. The buzzing in my ears was constant now, like the static on a radio station that only partially comes in, or a wiring defect on a speaker you might eventually get used to.

"It isn't my business," I said, "but it might be easier if there weren't so many of them."

"You're right," he said, and sighed. "I need to slow down."

"What the hell, you're living," I said.

He considered this for a moment. Then he put his arm around me like I was twelve again.

In the track-lit lunchroom of the museum, my father was his old self again. He told me how he chased my mother to Europe. He talked while a waiter with a white shirt and black bow tie poured us Heinekens, tipping the glass to keep down the foam. He met her on a Memorial Day weekend when she was a waitress on Martha's Vineyard, then met her again when she was checking coats at a party in New York.

I'd heard this story so often I used to groan when he started, but not this time.

I wanted him to slow down and tell every detail.

"She'd rented a house with your godmother in Nice, a two-story cottage with a yard and a view of two churches and a bakery. I couldn't stand being apart from her," he said. "I took my three weeks of vacation and flew to France. She didn't know what to make of me. We barely knew each other, and there I was, on her doorstep in my shorts and T-shirt with the Michelin guide to Italy and Greece under my arm, like a college kid."

He took a sip of beer and cleared his throat.

"Two weeks later, in Venice, I proposed. She was probably the most beautiful woman I'd ever met," he said. "And far and away the most perceptive. It's like she'd lived a thousand lives because of all the books she read. It sometimes made me uneasy."

"How come?"

"Because I couldn't hide the way I could with other women." I could hear him breathing, heavy and slow.

He held my glance, then put on his glasses and studied the check.

"You remind me of her sometimes," he said without looking up.

That night, for a few hours, my father appeared genuinely haunted, and I was heartened. He sat in his study looking out the window for a while, and then he took out some files from the cabinets in there. He was flipping through my mother's notes and preliminary pages for her book on Paul and Jane Bowles.

For all my father's achievements, my mother was always a step or two ahead of him. She was the one who'd finish the Sunday crossword puzzle, who knew word derivations, who could speak three languages, who had more persuasive things to say about the films and plays we went to. She feared alternately that I would pursue success single-mindedly like my father or that I'd inherit her impractical intelligence, the kind that ensured the vibrancy of their social life but that only recently had earned her—in the form of the Bowles advance—even a modest income. On her deathbed, I was still deciding who to be like, and who to rebel against, though I still had time to fail them both.

I watched him from the doorway. I felt a bit guilty for forcing him into my mood, but it was a mission I'd undertaken.

"Someone should follow up on this," he said. "All this good work shouldn't just go to waste."

"Maybe I will," I said.

His eyes lit up. "Oh, I'd love that. I really would."

Then he gathered up the pages, put them away, and got dressed to go out.

The radio station was on the fifth floor of an old warehouse building on the Lower West Side. I had to call from a pay phone to get someone to open the padlocks on the back door and bring me up a rusted elevator. I assistant-produced for a phone-in issues show (the insurgency in Iraq, corruption in the Justice Department), screening callers for whoever was hosting and gauging people's on-air skills. Their politics didn't matter to me, so long as they had something to say. The most intense conversation I had was with a man whose wife had Alzheimer's who'd called to talk about stem cell research. After forty-five years of marriage his wife barely recognized him, and once, after a meal, she tried to tip him.

I listened to his stories, and then I told him about my mother. Nothing planned.

He spoke and then I did, back and forth, a game of catch. I told him about lying to everyone, making excuses for her thinness. That was her rule. She thought her publisher would cancel her contract if it got out that she was sick. I told him about Thanksgiving, how I kept pushing her to eat. She said politely she didn't want any more, but I insisted. She couldn't hold it down.

She covered her face and ran to the kitchen, my father and me hovering as she leaned over the sink. *My God, I can't do this, I just can't do anything.* She was so terribly sorry, she said, that she'd ruined our Thanksgiving. "It was the last time we ate a meal together, and I screwed it up," I said.

"You're lucky." The caller had an even baritone and a slight Brooklyn accent.

"You're more than lucky she's dead and buried. Dead and alive is what's killing me. It's breaking my heart."

Jonas met me at the Dublin House on Seventy-ninth and Broadway later that night. It was packed, and everyone was drinking as though the end of the world were coming; at least it felt that way to me. We settled down at a dark wood table in the back and made our way through two sizable pitchers. I described how my father appeared to have a steady girlfriend now, a school administrator named Linda.

"Women do great on their own," he said. "But the men from our fathers' generation are kind of clueless. For all their yelling at each other, my dad couldn't go three days without my mother. Remember when my Aunt Beth died? My Uncle Ned remarried within five months."

The buzzing in my head started in again, and then the music got incredibly loud.

Jonas was saying something about the way we're wired, which I couldn't really hear. Then it felt like someone had shoved cotton in my ears.

"I've gone deaf," I said.

He helped me to my feet and pushed me through a maze of beery faces out the door. In the freezing air, my hearing returned.

"Is it possible you're working backward through the healing process," he said.

"Fuck off."

"I'm not knocking it. I think it's admirable."

I threw up on his shoes and felt somewhat better.

Over that weekend Jonas brought me to a Rites of Spring party on Spring Street, endearingly enough. We rode the subway down, then walked there through a late March blizzard. The cars moved soundlessly down the street. From somewhere in the heavens a snowball scraped the top of Jonas's head.

"Took you fucking long enough," a woman's voice yelled. She was leaning out the window of a fourth-floor apartment.

"Took us forever to shovel out the driveway," Jonas yelled back.

The party was packed with downtown hipsters, most about five years older than us, with something already to show for their lives. In what passed as a dining room the snowball hurler, Sylvie, was arranging the hors d'oeuvre platters and mixing margaritas.

"You're Andrew," she said, when I walked by the food table.

The crier, I thought.

She handed me a margarita, then tucked a strand of hair behind her ear. She was nearly my height, pale and possibly sleep deprived, with an oval face, soft features, and dark brown librarian glasses. When we shook hands hers was damp from the snow, or from squeezing limes.

After a minute or two of introductory conversation, she said, "I'm really sorry about your mother."

"Thanks," I said.

Someone called her name, and she excused herself and went to hug a woman in a short skirt and knee-high boots, who introduced her to a white guy with thick dreadlocks.

When she returned she said, "I don't know if Jonas told you, but I went through something similar when I was in high school."

I was starting to understand that having someone close to you die meant hearing everyone else's saddest story.

"You lost your mother?" I said.

"Father. Listen, you probably don't want to talk about this at a party."

"Maybe not," I said, and so we talked about where she went to school and my job at the radio station. She was studying art history at Columbia. She told me all about her roommate, Dana, whom Jonas slept with once ("zero chemistry"), and then she asked me how my father was coping.

Sort of as an experiment, or because I had a buzz on, I decided to tell her the abridged saga of my winter, about the perfumed notes and late-night calls, how I felt sometimes like a dormitory R.A., how

I'd bump into T-shirted women in the kitchen half asleep, how one of them made elaborate snacks in the middle of the night, and how another, the boutique owner, accidentally walked naked into my room, thinking it was my father's.

"Oh, please. You think she went in there by *accident*?" Sylvie said.

"I guess I did."

"*Sweetheart*. When my father died my mother kept me away from the men she was dating." We were side by side and our arms brushed. My body tensed. "I was sixteen, and I think she thought I'd try to seduce them. And I probably would have in my own insecure way. Not literally, but enough to ruin things for her. In any event she stayed over at their apartments. At first it was only on the weekends, but then it was like four nights a week. She'd phone to tell me to order a pizza for me and my brother, or Chinese food, whatever we wanted and to charge it to her American Express card."

She poured me another margarita, then poured herself one. "I could have stayed out in clubs all night, or had huge-ass parties, and she would have never known. I tried it once, throwing a party, but I ended up getting too nervous about all the people there getting drunk and throwing up, so I kicked them all out."

"Did she remarry?"

"Yes, to my stepfather."

"Do you like him?"

"Better than her."

"Seriously?"

"Let's just say he's a lot less complicated."

"I find everything about my father's dating depressing."

"Depressing is when he dates a twenty-year-old."

"He hasn't done that."

"Then count your blessings."

I watched her after that. She was unabashed in a way that usually put me off, but in her there was something heartfelt that I latched onto. She disappeared for a half hour or so and then reappeared at my side.

"Feel like getting out of here?" she said.

"You mean the two of us?"

"You think you could do better?" she said.

I tilted my head in mock judgment. She was kind of gawky, I thought, with narrow hips and long skinny arms and an illegible word written on the back of her wrist. Her hair held the shape of a wool cap she must have worn to the party, but she didn't seem to care.

"All right. Let's go," I said.

It was Sylvie's idea to stop by our house. She wanted to meet my father "in the flesh" and see if he was as dashing as she imagined. When we reached home, Linda was camped in the kitchen, making a pot of coffee.

"Your dad went down to tell the doorman to turn up the heat," she said. She wore a cashmere V-neck sweater of my father's over a white camisole and looked like a late-career Jane Fonda. "It's freezing in here, don't you think?"

"I'm Sylvie," Sylvie said. She took off her ski cap and shook out her hair, sprinkling melting snow into the room and onto her glasses, which she removed and placed in her coat pocket.

"And I'm Linda, Andrew's dad's girlfriend," Linda said. She pulled out three mugs, one that I hadn't seen before, with the Statue of Liberty drinking coffee. She poured us cups and told us about her evening, coaching a room of Bensonhurst kids about writing résumés.

My father buzzed the intercom from downstairs and said he'd be up in ten minutes.

"When he wants things done, he goes out and gets them done," Linda said, smiling. I could have told her that was inaccurate, that when my father wanted things done he convinced others to do them for him, but I figured she'd learn that soon enough.

"It's supposed to get down to single digits by the morning," Linda said. "Are you two in for the night?"

I pretended not to grasp what she was suggesting, but Sylvie said, "No. We just came by to warm up."

When my father came in and saw that I was with a young woman he grinned widely. "Welcome to spring," he said. He asked Sylvie a series of questions about herself, listened with interest to her answers, and then showed her the view. There was something both wistful and very tender in the way he treated us.

* * *

We walked uptown along the park. I didn't know where we were headed, only that Sylvie appeared to have a plan.

We sat on a bench on the path at Eighty-first Street and sipped from a pint bottle of Knob Creek we bought at the corner liquor store, assessing the few passersby who braved the weather. A young guy, two or three years older than me, hobbled across on crutches.

"He's faking," Sylvie said. "Grab one of his crutches."

"What would I do with just one?"

"You could sell it back to him," she said. "Or you could beat him with it."

We traveled then to the benches near the band shell, where Sylvie said she used to roller-skate. I used to ride my skateboard over to watch people like her, I said.

"I was the one in the hot pants."

"Really. I think I kissed you once."

We were at the center of Central Park in the middle of the night. I thought: this is what unbalanced people do. Snow dropped down on us. My feet felt cold and wet, and I took another slug of whiskey. I was getting drunk. She rested her legs over mine, and I warmed them with my hands. It all felt forced, and then it didn't.

As though she'd been working up to the question, she asked me, "What's the weirdest thing you can do with your body?"

"I don't understand."

"I mean, can you do this?"

She touched her elbows together behind her head. "Or this?" She bent her hand back so that her fingertips touched the back of her forearm.

"No," I said. "Nor would I want to."

She looked so distraught that I went ahead and wiggled my left ear, something I hadn't done since grade school.

"I *knew* there was greatness in you," she said.

At some point, because it was on my mind, I told her about walking in the park with my mother, a week after we found out she was sick. I'd been away for the summer and I'd flown back to the city the day before. My mother was critiquing my wardrobe, the holes in my t-shirts and jeans.

"I'm buying you some pants," she said. "Don't be embarrassed."

"I won't," I said.

We went to some stores on Columbus Avenue, and I felt like I was eleven.

She bought me four pairs of pants, two pairs of dress socks, three shirts, and a navy peacoat. It was as though she were outfitting me for a trip. It was the first time I understood there was a finite number of afternoons we'd have together. A hundred. Ninety-nine. The next day it would be ninety-eight.

We never talked about the fact that she was dying, or what she was heading into. I think we both believed there'd be time. But it all went so quickly. The night I came to her with all the questions and thoughts I'd been saving up, her painkillers had made her so dopey she thought I was taking her to the opera. I actually played *Carmen* for her, and she said, head pressed into her pillow, that it was unbearably beautiful. She knew that she was sick, and in bed, but she thought she was young and in bed with the flu. And she asked me on one of her last days if I could make sure her tennis racket was strung, because she'd broken a string the summer before. I took it into a shop, and when they'd finished I brought it back to show her.

When I reached her the nurse had upped her morphine, and from then on she was gone.

When my story ended, Sylvie closed her eyes. "You know, I said everything I wanted to say to my father, and he made his peace with me. But I never played opera for him while he was in bed," she said. "That is such a fucking cool thing to do."

Outside her building Sylvie declared, "It's been a while since I slept with anyone."

I just smiled stupidly.

"You're quite adorable," she said.

Her roommate was away for the weekend. It was a pretty standard grad school apartment, two tiny bedrooms, a kitchenette, a narrow hallway, and a sunken living room decorated with a nice plush armchair and couch that must have come from someone's family. We passed out in our clothes for an hour or two. Then we slept together with them off. Undressed she was far sexier than her boyish clothes and awkward eagerness had forecast, and when she pulled me inside her I felt irrationally as though I might have fallen in love. At around 4:00 A.M. I woke up sweating and startled from a nightmare. My mother wasn't in this one. My father had died and I was sorting through his papers and clothes, and I was showing our apartment to a series of realtors. I asked them each, *Have you seen the view over Central Park?* It took some effort to determine that my father was snoring in his bed a dozen blocks away, and my relief at this understanding was so overwhelming I wept uncontrollably. In the morning I was curious to find myself in a strange apartment and not in my childhood room. I heard car horns and voices outside, a doorman's whistle. I felt tired still, but in a different way, as though I'd been drugged.

I noticed then what wasn't there. The buzzing. I stumbled over to the clock on her desk. 9:34.

"You can go if you want," she said from the bed.

"What do you mean?"

"I mean, I sort of trapped you here last night."

There was something fragile in her eyes I hadn't yet seen.

"I'd much rather stay," I said.

She smiled and curled into her pillow. Her feet dangled from beneath the covers.

I slipped back into bed and drew her to me so that her warm back rested against my chest. I closed my eyes, and in seconds I was out. I slept as I hadn't in years, through that whole snowy day, and when I awoke again it was night. I threw on my pants and padded down the hallway, where I came across her reading a book on the living room sofa, legs curled beneath her. She glanced up at me. "It stopped snowing," she said. "Shall we go get a bite?"

"Yes," I said.

I grabbed the rest of my clothes from the bedroom. We bundled up and headed into the freezing night. On Broadway I felt the wind rip through my pea coat, all the way to my skin, and I was aware then that I had left the first stage of my life and was out in the world in a way I was never before.

CLARE BEAMS

∎

We Show What We Have Learned

FROM *Hayden's Ferry Review*

BEFORE HER DISINTEGRATION, we had long held an absolute and unwavering contempt for Ms. Swenson. She had won that with her uncertainty, which we had sensed in the very first moments of the very first day of fifth grade, the way dogs can smell fear. Waves of it rolled off her, along with the odor of cats and Kleenex and chalk that hung in her sad, pilly sweaters. Ms. Swenson was pitiful, but this did not mean we pitied her. We felt nothing for the faded blue of her eyes, which were like a soft sea creature's underbelly, or for the way she kept them open so wide and blinked so rapidly that she seemed to be seeing us through a mist. Her movements, too, were misty, whereas we were sharp and quick and feral. We did not wonder much about her life. She seemed ageless to us in the way that most adults seemed ageless—we could not have said whether she was twenty-five or forty—but we did know that she was younger than most of the other teachers. This was less because her face was unlined than because she seemed so much more unfinished. Everything Ms. Swenson ever said to us had a question in it, even when she explained to us long division or poetry, things it was clear she understood, and even when she told Mark Peters to stop it when he pulled down Sally Winters's pants and underpants to show us the hair-flecked space between her legs. The question in her voice then was simply more panicked than usual.

The day the disintegration began, we were learning about Indian civilization. We were always learning about Indian civilization—we began each year with it, and then we might, as on that day (when we were supposed to be talking about the southern agricultural system), make several unexpected detours back to revel in the quietude of that life so close to nature. The teachers all loved these lost things, and Ms. Swenson loved them even more than most. We watched while she drew wigwams on the board. Ms. Swenson was very bad at drawing, worse even than the worst of us, because she was crippled by second guessing. She darted in to draw a line, darted back to look at it, darted back in to erase it and start over. "Is that straight?" she asked us, but wasn't it supposed to be rounded, wasn't that the whole point? Finally she sighed in a way that meant she was giving up and settling for the misshapen thing she had produced. "You see, children, the *hole* was put there," she said, pointing, "so that the cooking smells could escape. It's *ingenious.*" Her hands began to wave like vestigial gills that she was trying and failing to breathe with. There was something beautiful about her excitement in these moments, irresistible target though it was. "The early colonists were *never* so ingenious. In many ways, the civilization they would *brutally* overpower was *vastly* superior to their own."

Abner Harris raised his hand. Ms. Swenson never did learn not to call on him. Perhaps she was distracted by the glimmering vision of wigwams in her mind, a whole village of them where she might have lived gently and happily in the absence of us. "Yes, Abner?" Ms. Swenson said.

"Is that what holes are always there for?"

"Is *what* what they're always there for, Abner?"

"So smells can escape? Is that what, like, Sarah's hole is there for?"

"Sarah's hole?" Ms. Swenson said, musingly, failing for so long to understand, though Sarah was already blushing. When Ms. Swenson got there, two high red spots appeared on her cheeks. "Abner, that is inappropriate," she said and yet managed to sound as if she were asking his permission to reprimand him.

"What is?" Mock innocence was mortally wounding to her; she couldn't help taking it at face value. We waited, snuffling into our hands and tasting the salt of our palms, chewing on the skin around our fingernails with the glee of what was coming: her floundering speared-fish flopping.

"To *speak* about the . . . " flop, flip, "private parts of others."

"But Ms. Swenson," said Billy Nichols, drawn to the blood in the water, "which parts *are* private? I forget."

We squeaked our sweaty hands against our desks in joy. Now she would have to *say* them, *say* those words. What could be more wonderful? We would hear them from adult lips.

And that was when it happened. We would wonder, ever after, what caused it: the force of the bottled-up, forbidden words that we were calling forth or the hammering blows of the humiliation we were delivering. Whether the force came from within or without. Ms. Swenson, in her agitation, flicked her webby hair behind her ear, chalk still in hand, and in the process flicked something off of herself. It flew forth with so much force that the act would have seemed intentional but for the puzzlement on her face. An earring, we assumed at first, but the earrings Ms. Swenson wore were not that large.

Hannah Perkins, in the first row, began to scream. She was peering over the edge of her desk at the thing on the floor, and she curled her feet up under her as if to keep them away from a mouse. Without consciously deciding to move, we left our seats and clustered around the space in front of Hannah's desk.

The thing on the ground was an earlobe.

It looked very fleshy, detached, though Ms. Swenson had never before seemed to have especially fleshy ears. It sat on the ground like a fat, self-satisfied earthworm, one that had perhaps eaten its brethren. Ms. Swenson's small gold hoop earring was still in place, puckering the roundest part of the lobe's belly. There was no blood; there was simply one ragged edge. Naturally, we looked from there to the edge of Ms. Swenson's still-attached ear, the matching puzzle piece, the yin to the lobe's yang. No blood there either. Then we looked at her face.

"Hmm," Ms. Swenson said. She turned away. We thought she might begin to scream. Instead she went calmly to her desk, swished a tissue from its box, and returned to the lobe on the carpet. She covered it with the tissue, and for a second it seemed she might leave it there, a small sheet over a small corpse. Then, with an expression of distaste, she reached out and lifted it just as she might have lifted a dog turd. She walked back to her desk, opened the drawer, and placed the lobe inside. She shut the drawer softly. Only then did she look at us. She seemed to have just remembered where she was.

"I can trust you, I think," she said, "not to mention this to anyone." We were surprised by the lack of a question in her voice. We nodded, twenty-six heads in unison, the first grown-up promise we had ever made, one of the few some of us would ever keep. "Now, I believe we were discussing the wigwam."

Here are the parts that Ms. Swenson lost in the days that followed: the tip of a shoulder, three molars, the end of her nose, her lower lip, and assorted fingers and toes, including all of the fingers of her right hand except the thumb. She still managed to hold the chalk by pinning it between thumb and palm. Her penmanship didn't look too different than usual. We applauded this triumph, literally applauded it with our shamelessly whole hands, and she acknowledged the tribute with a nod before continuing with the lesson. There was something different about these lessons now. We were attending to them anew, horrified, rapt. Ms. Swenson was not a dramatically better teacher than she had been before—she still apologized and bobbled, though the missing lower lip gave her an irritated expression—but we were dramatically better students. We wondered which of her words would move her enough to move a part off of her, and the wondering made us really listen to those words, which made us learn from them, in most of our cases for the first time. We learned to multiply and divide gracefully, to conjugate French verbs, to spell "ambiguity"; we learned the order of Civil War battles and the types of rocks, igneous, metamorphic, sedimentary. This progress was so painless it was scarcely noticeable to us. Ms. Swenson had become a mystery, and so she gained our devotion. Our love and our fear of her grew in direct proportion to the little sheeted lumps in her desk drawers. Once, at recess, Tom Milk brought out a tissue bundle he said he had stolen from the desk; he claimed it was the left index finger we had seen her shed two days earlier. His reluctance to let us see it was the tip-off, though, and when Shawn Greggors seized it from him and shook it out, nothing but more tissues emerged, and they danced merrily away across the pavement. You could not have paid us, any of us, enough to touch the genuine relics.

It was two weeks from the first earlobe to the culmination. We had all known for days that some end must be nearing, but still we were unprepared.

Ms. Swenson was explaining the mating rituals of frogs. "The male gives a little call like this: *whoo whoooo*," she said. She sounded more like an owl. She crouched down to approximate a frog with her carriage. "He tries to call as loud as he can. The female hears the call and thinks, *Oh my, what's that?* And then she gives a little hop."

This was where Ms. Swenson forgot her limitations and gave a little hop of her own to demonstrate. It was a small hop, but it was enough. In addition to the thump of her weight as her feet hit the ground, there was a sound like a large wet sock tearing. Both of her legs detached somewhere near the hips and fell away beneath her skirt. Her torso plummeted. "Oof," she said with the impact, and her shoulders separated from her chest, and her head separated from her neck and landed facedown on the carpet.

There was a silence.

"Okay," Ms. Swenson said. Her voice was a little carpet muffled, bright with effort. "That wasn't so bad. Not as bad as I thought it would be. Melanie?" Melanie was the girl at whose socks Ms. Swenson was now staring. "Melanie, would you please put me on that chair?"

Melanie did not want to touch the head, we could all see this, but how do you refuse a request like that? She picked Ms. Swenson up, holding her far away from her own body, and carried her toward a chair at the front of the room. "At least that's over," Ms. Swenson said en route.

When Melanie put her down, though, we could tell that it wasn't over yet. A great hunk of Ms. Swenson's hair came away in Melanie's hand; Melanie shrieked softly and brushed it off against her pants. Ms. Swenson didn't seem to notice. As we watched, one of her eyebrows lifted from her face like peeling paint and fell in a curl to the seat of the chair. Her upper lip was starting to look crooked. "Children, we must be quick, now," Ms. Swenson said. "It is time for you to show what you have learned."

We misunderstood her at first. We rummaged frantically for pencils and paper. Some of us set to work multiplying and dividing; others began to spell out previously elusive words. Still others began lists of facts. We could have filled pages and pages with those facts. We could have wallpapered the classroom with them.

"Not *that!*" Ms. Swenson said. We looked up at her. An eyelid slipped its moorings. "Is that all you know? Is that all I have taught you?" Her panic had set the eyeball beneath the crazily hung eyelid rolling; we wondered if she could still see out of it.

We waited for her to regain her composure and tell us again what we were to do. We wanted to please her as much as we had ever wanted anything.

"Why must you persist in aggravating me? You know what I want," she said. "I want to see you come apart. Haven't I been demonstrating for weeks now? Haven't you been paying attention? All of you ought to know how it is done."

We watched her. Those of us who had understood were hoping we hadn't. Ms. Swenson's patience had run out. "Show me, children!" she screamed. "Perform!"

But the force of that P was too much; it blew her upper lip clear off. She saw it sail away from her, hit the edge of Melanie's desk, and stick, and she seemed to surrender. We had thought the finale would be spectacular. We had been waiting for days for her eyes to pop cartoonishly, for her to fling a moist slab of tongue toward us. These things did not happen. She just gave a sigh, and the head sank to one side a little, and that was all.

All except for the feeling that we felt next.

It began differently for each of us, Ms. Swenson's final lesson. Some of us felt it gathering in the tiny bird-bones of our fingers, some in our hard, pink, healthy gums. For some, it came first to the pristine joints of our vertebrae. For still others, it settled in the unobstructed tunnels, gleaming and smooth, that led into and out of our childish and unscarred hearts. But though it took so many different forms, the beginning itself was universal. Not even the most whole among us was exempt. You would not have seen a difference to look at us, but we had changed, were changing, as our seams learned how to loosen. We were becoming divisible. In this way, Ms. Swenson prepared us. For the future is gated, and there are tolls to be paid.

JOSHUAH BEARMAN

■

Art of the Steal

FROM *Wired*

THE PLANE SLOWED AND LEVELED out about a mile above-
ground. Up ahead, the Viennese castle glowed like a fairy tale pal-
ace. When the pilot gave the thumbs-up, Gerald Blanchard looked
down, checked his parachute straps, and jumped into the darkness.
He plummeted for a second, then pulled his cord, slowing to a nice
descent toward the tiled roof. It was early June 1998, and the evening
wind was warm. If it kept cooperating, Blanchard would touch down
directly above the room that held the Koechert Diamond Pearl. He
steered his parachute toward his target.

A couple of days earlier, Blanchard had appeared to be just another twentysomething on vacation with his wife and her wealthy
father. The three of them were taking a six-month grand European
tour: London, Rome, Barcelona, the French Riviera, Vienna. When
they stopped at the Schloss Schönbrunn, the Austrian equivalent of
Versailles, his father-in-law's VIP status granted them a special preview peek at a highly prized piece from a private collection. And
there it was: In a cavernous room, in an alarmed case, behind bulletproof glass, on a weight-sensitive pedestal—a delicate but dazzling
10-pointed star of diamonds fanned around one monstrous pearl.
Five seconds after laying eyes on it, Blanchard knew he would try to
take it.

The docent began to describe the history of the Koechert Diamond Pearl, better known as the Sisi Star—it was one of many similar pieces specially crafted for Empress Elisabeth to be worn in her

magnificently long and lovely braids. Sisi, as she was affectionately known, was assassinated 100 years ago. Only two stars remain, and it has been 75 years since the public had a glimpse of . . .

Blanchard wasn't listening. He was noting the motion sensors in the corner, the type of screws on the case, the large windows nearby. To hear Blanchard tell it, he has a savant-like ability to assess security flaws, like a criminal Rain Man who involuntarily sees risk probabilities at every turn. And the numbers came up good for the star. Blanchard knew he couldn't fence the piece, which he did hear the guide say was worth $2 million. Still, he found the thing mesmerizing and the challenge irresistible.

He began to work immediately, videotaping every detail of the star's chamber. (He even coyly shot the NO CAMERAS sign near the jewel case.) He surreptitiously used a key to loosen the screws when the staff moved on to the next room, unlocked the windows, and determined that the motion sensors would allow him to move—albeit very slowly—inside the castle. He stopped at the souvenir shop and bought a replica of the Sisi Star to get a feel for its size. He also noted the armed guards stationed at every entrance and patrolling the halls.

But the roof was unguarded, and it so happened that one of the skills Blanchard had picked up in his already long criminal career was skydiving. He had also recently befriended a German pilot who was game for a mercenary sortie and would help Blanchard procure a parachute. Just one night after his visit to the star, Blanchard was making his descent to the roof.

Aerial approaches are a tricky business, though, and Blanchard almost overshot the castle, slowing himself just enough by skidding along a pitched gable. Sliding down the tiles, arms and legs flailing for a grip, Blanchard managed to save himself from falling four stories by grabbing a railing at the roof's edge. For a moment, he lay motionless. Then he took a deep breath, unhooked the chute, retrieved a rope from his pack, wrapped it around a marble column, and lowered himself down the side of the building.

Carefully, Blanchard entered through the window he had unlocked the previous day. He knew there was a chance of encountering guards. But the Schloss Schönbrunn was a big place, with more than

1,000 rooms. He liked the odds. If he heard guards, he figured, he would disappear behind the massive curtains.

The nearby rooms were silent as Blanchard slowly approached the display and removed the already loosened screws, carefully using a butter knife to hold in place the two long rods that would trigger the alarm system. The real trick was ensuring that the spring-loaded mechanism the star was sitting on didn't register that the weight above it had changed. Of course, he had that covered, too: He reached into his pocket and deftly replaced Elisabeth's bejeweled hairpin with the gift-store fake.

Within minutes, the Sisi Star was in Blanchard's pocket and he was rappelling down a back wall to the garden, taking the rope with him as he slipped from the grounds. When the star was dramatically unveiled to the public the next day, Blanchard returned to watch visitors gasp at the sheer beauty of a cheap replica. And when his parachute was later found in a trash bin, no one connected it to the star, because no one yet knew it was missing. It was two weeks before anyone realized that the jewelry had disappeared.

Later, the Sisi Star rode inside the respirator of some scuba gear back to his home base in Canada, where Blanchard would assemble what prosecutors later called, for lack of a better term, the Blanchard Criminal Organization. Drawing on his encyclopedic knowledge of surveillance and electronics, Blanchard became a criminal mastermind. The star was the heist that transformed him from a successful and experienced thief into a criminal virtuoso.

"Cunning, clever, conniving, and creative," as one prosecutor would call him, Blanchard eluded the police for years. But eventually he made a mistake. And that mistake would take two officers from the modest police force of Winnipeg, Canada, on a wild ride of high tech capers across Africa, Canada, and Europe. Says Mitch McCormick, one of those Winnipeg investigators, "We had never seen anything like it."

Blanchard pulled off his first heist when he was a six-year-old living with his single mother in Winnipeg. The family couldn't afford milk, and one day, after a long stretch of dry cereal, the boy spotted some recently delivered bottles on a neighbor's porch. "I snuck over there between cars like I was on some kind of mission," he says. "And no one saw me take it." His heart was pounding, and the milk was somehow sweeter than usual. "After that," he says, "I was hooked."

Blanchard moved to Nebraska, started going by his middle name, Daniel, and became an accomplished thief. He didn't look the part—slim, short, and bespectacled, he resembled a young Bill Gates—but he certainly played it, getting into enough trouble to land in reform school. "The way I met Daniel was that he stole my classroom VCR," recalls Randy Flanagan, one of Blanchard's teachers. Flanagan thought he might be able to straighten out the soft-spoken and polite kid, so he took Blanchard under his wing in his home-mechanics class.

"He was a real natural in there," Flanagan says. Blanchard's mother remembers that even as a toddler he could take anything apart. Despite severe dyslexia and a speech impediment, Blanchard "was an absolute genius with his hands," the teacher recalls. In Flanagan's class, Blanchard learned construction, woodworking, model building, and automotive mechanics. The two bonded, and Flanagan became a father figure to Blanchard, driving him to and from school and looking out for him. "He could see that I had talent," Blanchard says. "And he wanted me to put it to good use."

Flanagan had seen many hopeless kids straighten out—"You never know when something's going to change forever for someone," he says—and he still hoped that would happen to Blanchard. "But Daniel was the type of kid who would spend more time trying to cheat on a test than it would have taken to study for it," Flanagan says with a laugh.

In fact, by early in his high school years, Blanchard had already abandoned his afterschool job stocking groceries to pursue more lucrative opportunities, like fencing tens of thousands of dollars in goods stolen by department store employees he had managed to befriend. "I could just tell who would work with me," he says. "It's a gift, I guess."

Blanchard began mastering the workings of myriad mechanical devices and electronics. He became obsessed with cameras and surveillance: documenting targets, his own exploits, and his huge piles of money. Befitting a young tech enthusiast, he emptied an entire RadioShack one Easter Sunday. At age 16, he bought a house with more than $100,000 in cash. (He hired a lawyer to handle the money and sign the deal on his behalf.) When he moved in, Blanchard told his mother that the home belonged to a friend. "She looked the other way," Blanchard says. "And I tried to keep it all from her."

Around this time, Blanchard was arrested for theft. He did several months behind bars and was released into Flanagan's custody after the older man vouched for him at a hearing. "He was great with our own kids," Flanagan says. "And I still thought he might come around." But Blanchard's burgeoning criminal career was hard to ignore, as he often flaunted his ill-gotten gains. "I wasn't surprised when the FBI came knocking one day," Flanagan says. "He'd pull out a fistful of hundreds and peel one off to pay for pizza."

In April 1993, Blanchard was nabbed by the cops in Council Bluffs, Iowa, for a suspected car arson and brought back to police headquarters. "They kept me in the interrogation room past midnight," Blanchard says. "And at a certain point, I managed to sneak into the next room and slip through the tiles into the ceiling." Undetected, he heard the cops run down the hall, thinking he'd gone out the fire escape. After waiting a couple of hours, Blanchard lowered himself down into the mostly empty station, stole a police coat, badge, radio, and revolver. After leaving a single bullet on the desk of his interrogator, he took the elevator to the main floor and strolled right past the front desk on his way out of the station. He hitchhiked at dawn back to Omaha on the back of a motorcycle, holding his purloined police cap down in the wind. "Why are you wearing a uniform?" the driver asked. "Costume party," Blanchard said as the sun came up. "Really fun time."

The next day, Blanchard was re-apprehended by a SWAT team, which had to use flash grenades to extricate him from his mother's attic. But he surprised the cops by escaping yet again, this time from the back of a police cruiser. "They got out of the car and left the keys," Blanchard says. "There was no barrier, so I fiddled with the cuffs until I got my hands in front of me, locked the doors, slipped up front, and put it in gear." The authorities gave chase until Blanchard swerved into a steak-house parking lot, fled on foot, and was finally recaptured.

This time, Blanchard served four years and his sentence came with a deportation order attached. In March 1997, he was released to his Canadian homeland and barred from returning to the United States for five years.

"After that," Flanagan says, "I heard from Daniel once or twice a year, thanking me for what I had done for him." Blanchard sent pictures of himself vacationing around the world, on exclusive beaches, posing in front of Viennese castles. He said he had his own security business. "I wanted that to be true," Flanagan says. "But I had a hunch he was more likely in the anti-security business."

In 2001, Blanchard was driving around Edmonton when he saw a new branch of the Alberta Treasury Bank going up. His internal algorithm calculated low risk, and he began to case the target meticulously. It had been three years since the Sisi Star theft, and it was time to try something big and new.

As the bank was being built, Blanchard frequently sneaked inside — sometimes at night, sometimes in broad daylight, disguised as a delivery person or construction worker. There's less security before the money shows up, and that allowed Blanchard to plant various surveillance devices in the ATM room. He knew when the cash machines were installed and what kind of locks they had. He ordered the same locks online and reverse engineered them at home. Later he returned to the Alberta Treasury to disassemble, disable, and remount the locks.

The take at this bank was a modest 60 grand, but the thrill mattered more than the money anyway. Blanchard's ambition flowered, as did his technique. As Flanagan had observed, Blanchard always wanted to beat the system, and he was getting better at it. Blanchard targeted a half-dozen banks over the next few years. He'd get in through the air-conditioning ductwork, at times contorting his body to fit inside really tight spaces. Other times, he would pick the locks. If there were infrared sensors, he'd use IR goggles to see the beams. Or he'd simply fool the sensor by blocking the beam with a lead film bag. He assembled an arsenal of tools: night-vision cameras, long-range lenses, high-gain antennas that could pick up the feeds from the audio and video recorders he hid inside a bank, scanners programmed with the encryption keys for police frequencies. He always had a burglary kit on hand containing ropes, uniforms, cameras, and microphones. In the Edmonton branch of the Bank of Nova Scotia, which he hit in 2002, he installed a metal panel near the AC ducts to create a secret crawl space that he could disappear into if surprised by police.

Such evasive action was never required, however, in part because Blanchard had also memorized the mechanics of the Mas-Hamilton and La Gard locks that many banks used for their ATMs. (These are big, complicated contraptions, and when police later interrogated Blanchard, they presented him with a Mas-Hamilton lock in dozens of pieces. He stunned them by reassembling it in 40 seconds.)

Blanchard also learned how to turn himself into someone else. Sometimes it was just a matter of donning a yellow hard hat from Home Depot. But it could also be more involved. Eventually, Blanchard used legitimate baptism and marriage certificates—filled out with his assumed names—to obtain real driver's licenses. He would even take driving tests, apply for passports, or enroll in college classes under one of his many aliases: James Gehman, Daniel Wall, or Ron Aikins. With the help of makeup, glasses, or dyed hair, Blanchard gave James, Daniel, Ron, and the others each a different look.

Over the years, Blanchard procured and stockpiled IDs and uniforms from various security companies and even law enforcement agencies. Sometimes, just for fun and to see whether it would work, he pretended to be a reporter so he could hang out with celebrities. He created VIP passes and applied for press cards so he could go to NHL playoff games or take a spin around the Indianapolis Motor Speedway with racing legend Mario Andretti. He met the prince of Monaco at a yacht race in Monte Carlo and interviewed Christina Aguilera at one of her concerts.

That's where, in July 2000, Blanchard met Angela James. She had flowing black hair and claimed to work for Ford Models. They got along right away, and Blanchard was elated when she gave him her number. He sensed that the teenager was "down with crime"—someone he could count on for help.

Blanchard liked having a sidekick. James was a fun, outgoing party animal who had plenty of free time. She eventually began helping Blanchard on bank jobs. They'd tag team on daylight reconnaissance, where her striking looks provided a distraction while Blanchard gathered information. At night, she'd be the lookout.

Though they were never involved romantically, James and Blanchard traveled together around the world, stopping in the Caribbean to stash his loot in offshore accounts. They camped out at resorts in Jamaica and the Turks and Caicos islands, depositing money in $10,000 increments into some of Blanchard's 13 pseudonymously held accounts. The money in the offshore accounts was to pay for his jet-setting lifestyle. The money back in Canada would bankroll his real estate transactions. The funds sitting in Europe were there, well, in case anything happened to him.

After midnight on Saturday, May 15, 2004, as the northern prairie winter was finally giving way to spring, Blanchard walked up to the front door of the Canadian Imperial Bank of Commerce in the Mega Centre, a suburban development in Winnipeg. He quickly jimmied the lock, slipped inside, and locked the door behind him. It was a brand-new branch that was set to open for business on Monday, and Blanchard knew that the cash machines had been loaded on Friday.

Thorough as ever, Blanchard had spent many previous nights infiltrating the bank to do recon or to tamper with the locks while James acted as lookout, scanning the vicinity with binoculars and providing updates via a scrambled-band walkie-talkie. He had put a transmitter behind an electrical outlet, a pinhole video camera in a thermostat, and a cheap baby monitor behind the wall. He had even mounted handles on the drywall panels so he could remove them to enter and exit the ATM room. Blanchard had also taken detailed measurements of the room and set up a dummy version in a friend's nearby machine shop. With practice, he had gotten his ATM-cracking routine down to where he needed only 90 seconds after the alarm tripped to finish and escape with his score.

As Blanchard approached, he saw that the door to the ATM room was unlocked and wide open. Sometimes you get lucky. All he had to do was walk inside. From here he knew the drill by heart. There were seven machines, each with four drawers. He set to work quickly, using just the right technique to spring the machines open without causing any telltale damage. Well rehearsed, Blanchard wheeled out boxes full of cash and several money counters, locked the door behind him, and headed to a van he had parked nearby.

Eight minutes after Blanchard broke into the first ATM, the Winnipeg Police Service arrived in response to the alarm. However, the officers found the doors locked and assumed the alarm had been an error. As the police pronounced the bank secure, Blanchard was zipping away with more than half a million dollars. The following morning was a puzzler for authorities. There were no indications of damage to the door, no fingerprints, and no surveillance recordings—Blanchard had stolen the hard drives that stored footage from the bank's cameras. Moreover, Blanchard's own surveillance equipment was still transmitting from inside the ATM room, so before he skipped town, he could listen in on investigators. He knew their names; he knew their leads. He would call both the bank manager's cell phone and the police, posing as an anonymous informant who had been involved in the heist and was swindled out of his share. It was the contractors, he'd say. Or the Brinks guy. Or the maintenance people. His tips were especially convincing because he had a piece of inside information: One of the bank's ATMs was left untouched. Blanchard had done that on purpose to make it easier to sow confusion.

With the cops outmatched and chasing red herrings, the Winnipeg bank job looked like a perfect crime. Then officials got a call from a vigilant employee at a nearby Walmart, which shared a large parking lot with the bank. He had been annoyed at people leaving cars there, so he took it upon himself to scan the lot. On the night of the break in, he spotted a blue Dodge Caravan next to the bank. Seeing a dolly and other odd equipment inside, he took down the license plate number. Police ran it. The vehicle had been rented from Avis by one Gerald Daniel Blanchard.

Blanchard's use of his real name was as careless as the fingerprints police found inside the getaway van recovered by the rental company. Soon the cops were on his tail.

Because of the heist's sophistication, the investigation fell to Winnipeg's Major Crimes unit. But Blanchard—now divorced and living with his girlfriend, Lynette Tien—learned that he had become a suspect, so he stayed out of their sights. Two years passed, and many of the investigators who had dealt with the initial leads retired or were transferred.

The case went cold until early 2006, when Mitch McCormick, a veteran officer in his fifties, started working on major crimes and decided to take a look at the unsolved robbery. Intrigued, he called his longtime colleague Larry Levasseur, a wiretap ace who had just been transferred to the Commercial Crimes division.

One night in early February, McCormick and Levasseur sat down at the King's Head bar, a favorite local police haunt. Levasseur went through several pints of amber ale, and McCormick had his usual double rye and a Coke tall. McCormick filled him in on the Blanchard leads and gave him the case file to take home.

The two were interested, but McCormick's boss was skeptical. Why spend money chasing a criminal who was committing most of his crimes outside their jurisdiction? Eventually, though, the two stubborn cops made such a fuss that the department brass relented. "But we got no resources and had to put together a task force out of thin air," McCormick says. "It was like the set of *Barney Miller*. We knew it was bad when we had to buy our own Post-its."

They quickly started filling up those Post-its and arranging them on a corkboard, mapping Blanchard's sprawling network. The case was overwhelming, but they eventually unraveled his tangle of 32 false names. Their preliminary checks also showed that Blanchard was a person of interest in many crimes, including the unsolved theft of the Sisi Star nearly 10 years earlier. They assembled roughly 275 pages of documentation, enough to persuade a judge to let them tap Blanchard's 18 phones. Now they were in business. They were taking a professional flier on this case. They dubbed their investigation Project Kite.

Usually wiretaps are a waiting game; cops will listen to secretive organized crime syndicates for years, hoping for one little slip. But Blanchard was surprisingly loose-lipped. The second weekend the wires went live, McCormick and Levasseur heard him directing a team of underlings in a product-return fraud at a Best Buy. More scams followed. They heard him wheeling and dealing in real estate.

They listened in as he planned his next bank job. They learned about a vast network of sophisticated crime. For a smart criminal, McCormick and Levasseur thought, this guy sure did talk a lot.

Then, on November 16, 2006, Blanchard got a particularly intriguing call. "Hello, Danny," a man with a thick British accent said. "Are you ready? I have a job for you. How soon can you get to Cairo?"

McCormick and Levasseur listened with astonishment as Blanchard immediately set about recruiting his own small team to meet up with another group in Egypt. Blanchard referred to his contact as the Boss—he couldn't pronounce his real name—and explained to his cohorts that there was money to be made with this guy.

James was in. But her parents were in town visiting, and her mother didn't want her to go. James put her mom on the phone so Blanchard could talk the woman into giving her daughter permission to join him in a criminal escapade across the globe. "We're going to make a lot of money," he said. "But don't worry. Everything will be fine."

Several of his regular guys couldn't make it, so Blanchard called his neighbor, a Congolese immigrant named Balume Kashongwe. When Blanchard explained the job, Kashongwe volunteered right away. With his team assembled, Blanchard thought, "This is going to be easy. What could go wrong?" Just a few hours after the Boss' call, Blanchard, Kashongwe, and James were in the air, en route to Cairo.

Blanchard had first met the Boss a few months earlier in London at an electronics store. He could tell they were kindred spirits by a glance at the Boss' purchases: eight DVR recorders. Blanchard knew you didn't buy a load like that for anything but surveillance. The two struck up a conversation.

Later that day, a car arrived to take Blanchard to a London café, where the Boss and a dozen Kurdish henchmen, most from northern Iraq, were waiting in the basement, smoking hookahs. The Boss filled Blanchard in on his operation, which spanned Europe and the Middle East and included various criminal activities, including counterfeiting and fraud. The latest endeavor was called skimming: gleaning active debit and credit card numbers by patching into the ISDN lines that companies use to process payments. The group manufactured counterfeit cards magnetized and embossed with the stolen numbers and then used them to withdraw the maximum daily limits before the fraud was reported. It was a lucrative venture for the Boss' network, which funneled a portion of its take to Kurdish separatists in Iraq.

Living up to his new nickname, the Boss gave Blanchard a trial job: taking 25 cards to Canada to retrieve cash. Blanchard returned to London with $60,000, and the Boss was pleased. He found the younger man charming and steady as well. "We have something big coming," he told Blanchard over dinner at a Kurdish restaurant. "I'll keep you posted."

With that job now at hand, Blanchard's crew arrived in Egypt and checked into the Cairo Marriott Hotel & Omar Khayyam Casino, settling into a couple of suites with sweeping views of the Nile. The next day, three men Blanchard remembered from the London café showed up. They brought roughly one thousand pirated cards, which the group immediately started using in teams of two. Kashongwe and the Kurds from London blended in easily. Blanchard and James bought burkas in the souk as disguises. The Boss directed operations from London.

They went from ATM to ATM for twelve hours a day, withdrawing Egyptian pounds and stuffing the bills into backpacks and suitcases. Blanchard and James folded their cash into pouches hidden beneath the burkas. And as usual, Blanchard filmed the entire adventure: the wandering through Cairo's Byzantine streets, the downtime in the city, the money pouring in.

Back in their bare-bones Winnipeg office, McCormick and Levasseur were monitoring their target's e-mail accounts and calls back to Tien, who was managing travel arrangements and other administrative details from Blanchard's condo in Vancouver. The Canadian cops were stunned. They never imagined they'd come across anything this big. They learned about the loot piling up four feet high in the suites at the Marriott. And then they learned that everything had gone to hell.

In the course of a week, the team collected the equivalent of more than two million dollars. But the individual ATM payouts were small, so after a couple of days Blanchard sent Kashongwe south to Nairobi, Kenya, with fifty cards to find more-generous machines. Kashongwe had no cell phone, though, and he went suspiciously incommunicado. Soon it became clear that Kashongwe was AWOL. Blanchard wasn't happy. And neither was the Boss.

Blanchard was in over his head. In his many years of crime, guns had never been involved. The Boss, however, seemed inclined to change that. Blanchard promised to track down Kashongwe. "Good," the Boss said. "Otherwise, we'll find him. And he won't be happy when we do."

McCormick and Levasseur listened to the calls in and out of Cairo as temperatures rose. They could hear Blanchard calling Tien back in Vancouver, trying desperately to reach Kashongwe. He called Kashongwe's sister in Brussels and his brother in Ottawa. He sounded frantic at times. But Blanchard had no luck; Kashongwe had vanished.

Things took another turn for the worse when the Boss told Blanchard he couldn't leave Cairo until the missing cards were accounted for. Two more men arrived to "keep an eye on things." The Marriott suites had turned into a hostage scene.

But Blanchard's natural charm worked on the Boss, too. He took full responsibility, promised to personally pay back Kashongwe's share, and calmly argued that James didn't have anything to do with the double cross. The Boss eventually told his men to let James go. Then he agreed to let Blanchard travel to London to smooth things out in person. "I'm pretty honest about that kind of thing," Blanchard says. "And the Boss could see that I was taking responsibility for my guy."

The two decided to set aside the Kashongwe problem in the interest of business. The Boss' men would meet Blanchard back in Canada with a new batch of cards. "After all," Blanchard says, "why fight when there was more money to be made?"

On December 3, 2006, Blanchard landed in Vancouver, where he immediately rented a car and drove straight to a branch of the Bank of Nova Scotia, sixty-five miles east in Chilliwack. He'd started prepping to burglarize the bank before his trip. The Kashongwe fiasco ended up nearly costing Blanchard money, and now he was after a sizable payday. Chilliwack was good for $800,000, he figured, and he would work through the holidays to get it done.

McCormick and Levasseur had both been on duty during the holidays before, but never had a case so consumed them. They were spending 18-hour days in their makeshift headquarters or at the King's Head, poring over transcripts and evidence. They got no overtime pay. The strain grew, as did the pressure from higher-ups.

Lucky for them, Blanchard's disarray was compounding his mistakes. As soon as he touched down, McCormick and Levasseur picked up Blanchard live, discussing Cairo, his next bank, and the potential whereabouts of Kashongwe. While Blanchard was en route to Chilliwack, they listened to him and the Boss discuss details about the arrival of a team in Montreal the next day.

McCormick and Levasseur called officials at the Montreal airport with names and flight information. As the targets strode through the airport, the cops swarmed in. The team was detained, and police seized dozens of blank credit cards, a card writer, and computers overflowing with evidence that filled in the blanks on the Cairo operation. To top it off, the hard drives also contained some of Blanchard's comprehensive amateur crime video of that job. Now the police could not only hear him talking about crimes, they could see him committing them.

The Boss phoned the very next day, panicked. But the call caught Blanchard at an inopportune moment. "I can't talk right now," Blanchard whispered. "I'm doing my thing inside the bank right now." It was 12:30 A.M., and Blanchard was crawling through the bank's ductwork.

"Listen, my guys got arrested in the airport, and I need to find out why," the Boss said. Blanchard was making his way painstakingly through the air vents, en route to the ATM room. His earpiece was taped in and the phone was on auto-answer, in case he got a call that the police were nearby. "What's going on with my guys in Montreal?" the Boss demanded. "They got pulled in!"

"I have no idea," Blanchard said softly. "But it's too much of a coincidence that customs knew. The phones must be tapped."

The Boss pressed on, asking for news about Kashongwe, but

Blanchard interrupted. "I'm looking down. There's a security guard down there right now," he breathed. He was deep into the building, making it hard to shimmy his way out in case he needed an emergency escape. "I have too much invested in this job," he said. "I have to go."

"We need to fix this, Danny," the Boss said.

As Blanchard whispered back, McCormick and Levasseur were triangulating the call's location. Now they knew Blanchard was targeting Chilliwack's Bank of Nova Scotia. In late January, investigators from Toronto, Edmonton, and Vancouver as well as provincial police and the Mounties had joined McCormick and Levasseur's small operation. "Project Kite was ready to be reeled in," McCormick says.

At four A.M. on January 23, 2007, more than a dozen SWAT team members swarmed Blanchard's Vancouver condo, where they found Blanchard and Tien. Several other search warrants were executed simultaneously across Canada, turning up half a dozen accomplices, including Angela James and Blanchard's cousin Dale Fedoruk.

Blanchard was busted. At his various residences and storage facilities, police confiscated 10 pallets of material: 60,000 documents, cash in various currencies, smoke bombs, firearms, and 300 electronic devices, including commercial card printers, card readers, and all manner of surveillance equipment. In his condo, police discovered a hidden room stocked with burglary kits and well-organized, itemized documentation of all Blanchard's fake identities. He was initially charged with 41 crimes, ranging from fraud to possession of instruments for forging credit cards.

The Boss called Blanchard in jail on the prison phone. "Why you, Danny?" he asked. "Why would little Winnipeg go to all that trouble? You must have upset the establishment. It's like we say in England: You fuck with the Queen, and they fuck with you."

As McCormick and Levasseur listened in, Blanchard said it wasn't the establishment, or the Queen. "It was these Keystone Kops out here in Winnipeg."

Blanchard says that he could have escaped from jail again, but there was no point. The police had all the evidence, including 120 video-

and audiotapes detailing everything. They'd just find him again, and he was tired of running anyhow.

Blanchard refused to make statements about any of his associates, but he eventually decided to cooperate with authorities about his own case. "He's a flamboyant guy," McCormick says. "And an extrovert, recording everything. Some part of him just wanted to tell his story." He had another incentive, too: Revealing his methods, which would help the banking industry improve its security practices, could earn him a lighter prison sentence.

The first day that Levasseur sat down with Blanchard in Vancouver, the investigator felt like he "was talking to a wall." But in later interviews, Blanchard became more courteous and helpful. Finally, after some negotiations through his lawyer, Blanchard offered to take them to the Sisi Star. "It's right here in my grandmother's basement in Winnipeg," he said. Blanchard had tried to steer clear of his family since his arrest; he didn't want to embarrass them further. But now he had to call. "I need to come to the house," he said. "And I'm bringing the police."

Blanchard, in handcuffs and leg shackles, hugged his grandmother at the door and took McCormick and Levasseur directly into the basement. He disappeared into a crawl space with Levasseur. It was quiet except for the sound of them grappling with the insulation. Eventually, Levasseur removed a square of Styrofoam and pulled out the star.

They brought it out into the light, where the detectives marveled at the beauty of the piece. They'd never seen anything like it. That kicked off nearly a month of debriefing. The cops had gotten some stuff right, but Blanchard set them straight on the rest. "Never in policing does the bad guy tell you, 'Here's how I did it, down to the last detail,' " McCormick says. "And that's what he did."

After spending so much time chasing Blanchard—and then talking to him— McCormick and Levasseur developed a grudging regard for his abilities. And Blanchard grew to admire their relentless investigation. Like a cornered hacker who trades his black hat for white, Blanchard took on a new challenge: working the system from the inside. He provided such good information that McCormick and Levasseur were able to put together an eight-hour presentation for law enforcement and banking professionals. "When those guys hear what Blanchard told us," McCormick says, "you can hear their assholes pucker shut."

Blanchard's full participation came under consideration when he pled guilty to sixteen charges on November 7, 2007. He agreed to sell his four condos and pay restitution to the Canadian government. And he was willing to take a longer sentence for himself in exchange for leniency toward his coaccused, whom he refused to testify against. None of his partners served jail time.

Blanchard also surprised the court by having his lawyer issue an unusual statement: an expression of gratitude for being arrested. "My client wishes to recognize that this huge lie that he had been living could now finally fall apart." It added that Blanchard was looking forward to moving on. "He recognizes that the men and women of the Winnipeg Police Service made that all possible."

Instead of the maximum of 164 years, Blanchard got eight. And then last summer, after serving less than two, he was released into carefully guarded probation. He now lives in a Vancouver halfway house, where he is prohibited from going anywhere near certain types of surveillance equipment and talking to any of his former associates. One of the people he can call is Randy Flanagan, his old mentor from high school.

"He filled me in about the past ten years," Flanagan says. "I was surprised, but not that surprised, about what our little former son had been up to." Blanchard told Flanagan he wanted to turn his life around. Working with McCormick and Levasseur had convinced him that he could become a consultant to the banks. "Who knows?" Flanagan says. "Maybe he will get that security business he talked about off the ground after all."

The judge had a similar thought during Blanchard's plea hearing. The banks "should hire him and pay him a million dollars a year," he said. And right before sentencing, the judge turned directly to Blanchard. "I think that you have a great future ahead of you if you wish to pursue an honest style of life," he said. "Although I'm not prepared to sign a letter of reference."

SLOANE CROSLEY

■

Le Paris!

FROM *How Did You Get This Number*

IT'S INCREDIBLY DIFFICULT to get yourself banished from a city. A country is not so tough. There are words for that on both sides of the border. *Emigrate. Defect. Deport.* But when New Yorkers use those words to explain their residency here, what they really mean is that they packed their bags and got on a plane and it meant more to them than it did to anyone else. No one stopped them. No one checked their papers in Hoboken. No one kept them in quarantine in Queens. No one earns a living being stationed at the Lincoln Tunnel and scowling. At least not technically, they don't. Because as it is with most cities, this one is porous. We absorb the new and sweat out the old and put about as much conscious effort into it as we do into actually sweating. Once you're in, you really have to get creative to be pushed back out.

It's not so tough to get yourself banished from a person's apartment. Smoke in the freshly painted bathroom. Feed the dog chocolate. Ask the hosts if they think it's weird that their two-year-old hasn't started talking yet. The door shuts, the bolt locks, the whispers commence, and your passport to game night gets revoked faster than you can say "baby fish mouth." But in order to get bounced from a city, that place in between, you have to break the public transit system. Or execute some very specific offense on par with killing your young lover's cousin in a vicious street fight in Verona. Or run for office.

I didn't do any of those things to Paris. I loved Paris. Which is why it's especially painful knowing that, like a boarding school reject, I will not be "asked back" anytime soon. Though I was not formally banished, Paris has made it clear that it would prefer to continue on in its Frenchness *sans moi*. To sweat me out. Imagine what it is to be rejected by the most sophisticated and casually stunning place in the world. A place filled with the highest percentage of women on the planet able to pull off chinchilla wraps with jeans. To not be welcome in the City of Love is tantamount to being rejected by love itself. Why couldn't I have gotten thrown out of Akron, Ohio, City of Rubber?

My friend Louise had sublet an apartment in Paris for a month, so I found the cheapest red-eye possible and booked my flight. Because this is what you do when your friend calls from Paris to tell you how wonderful the very worst of everything is over there. You go out and buy an international adapter plug kit, lay the plug heads on your bed, and stare at the beveled prongs. You feel the sudden urge to travel sixteen hours to Fiji just to plug something in. A toaster, maybe. But Fiji, she will have to wait. Paris is calling! The entire city is spinning with sophistication, like a child's top. The Eiffel Tower is the handle.

Having just successfully deplaned, I was already trying on the Parisian version of myself. This version of my personhood was distinctly laid-back. Sometimes forcefully, if the situation required it. *What? No, honestly, take this taxi. You were here first in spirit.* Laid-back Me was sewn to my heels, a shadow with its own motivations and interests. A silhouette with a joint in one hand, a package of Ding Dongs in the other, and bunny slippers on its feet. Not that the shadow wasn't adaptable. That was part of the deal. If I had gone to Montana, I would have been laid-back and prone to liking horses. If I had gone to Tokyo, I would have been laid-back and unfazed by pornographic comic books and confounding soft-drink packaging. If I had gone to Rome, I would have done as they do. Now I had returned to Paris to be laid-back and—who knew what? *The shadow knows.* Consume unseemly quantities of macaroons, maybe.

This laid-back version of me decided to surprise Louise by navigating public transport from the airport to her apartment. Having been to Paris once before, I had a vague sense of its layout. In New York, I couldn't find my way out of a paper bag. Or, more accurately, a used paper bag. I forgot the paths to the same locations no sooner than I had found them. But the Parisian streets were generous with me, rewarding my instinct to veer left or turn right with the correct street names drilled to the walls of each corner. When I located Louise's address, I realized she was right: the worst of the worst here looks a lot like the best of our best. Everything about the building was perfect, right down to the doors—sturdy but worn wooden twins that earned their distress. Like a great pair of jeans. I exchanged grins with a woman who entered the building ahead of me. This would be a double surprise. Any closer and Louise would wake up with me sitting creepily at the end of her bed, watching her sleep.

"*Bonjour*, Louise," I'd say, all *Hello, Clarice*.

Maybe just inside the door was far enough.

The woman held the door. I was still mute with embarrassment, my tongue like the neck of a turtle retracted in the shell of my face. I speak "get by" French. Also known as "*bicyclette rouge* French" to anyone who's ever cracked open a blue, white, and red textbook. *Est-ce que vous avez une bicyclette rouge? Oui, ici est ma bicyclette rouge.* If McGraw-Hill is to be believed, red bicycles are government-issued in France. Also, everyone in France is *très fatigué* all the time, likely from their late nights buttering bread and sending telegrams.

The woman allowed me to follow her, rolling my suitcase clumsily over the cobblestone of the courtyard. When she slid a key into a door on the first floor, she glanced back over her shoulder and smiled again, this time more furtively, which I translated to mean "You gonna be okay out here?" but which probably meant something along the lines of "Please don't kill my family with whatever's in that bag." I sat on my suitcase and called Louise, somewhat horrified by the expensive trip the signal took, ricocheting between hemispheres.

"Well, hello there," I said, anxious to surprise her with my presence not at the *métro* stop, as planned, but delivered right to her front door. *Quel service!*

"Guess where I am."

"At the metro stop?"

"*Non!* In your courtyard."

"What?"

"In your courtyard?"

I didn't understand why she couldn't get on board with my enthusiasm. I had saved her much clunking up metro steps with an obvious fellow tourist, and this allowed her another day of native make-believe. One's own touristicity is easily submerged—watch what you put on your feet, lose the raincoat, try not to look up so much—but *two* tourists are a different story. It's the same principle that allows one to dart like a pixilated frog across oncoming traffic when alone but forces one to wait for a blinking light when with a group, watching old ladies with walkers and mothers with strollers dart past. It's why spies don't have friends and serial killers don't start book clubs. There is no safety in numbers.

"That's impossible," said Louise, waking up.

"Well"—I gave my haughtiest chuckle—"the laws of time and space would beg to differ."

"I don't have a courtyard."

In a moment of temporary dyslexia, Louise had e-mailed me the wrong address. Worse, she couldn't recall her own address. *This is not a problem!* said my laid-back-ness, as it waited for Louise to go downstairs and consult her front door. But when I went to leave I discovered that the giant doors to the street had locked behind me. The metal knobs refused to turn, despite my repeated attempts to convince them. I shook them, imagining how futile a couple of vibrating doors on a bustling Parisian avenue appeared from the other side. I went back into the courtyard, but there were no signs of life, just a few curtains blowing in the open windows above and some very annoying birds. It was nine A.M. I glanced at the door on the first floor. *This is not a problem!* said my laid-back self. Louise got back on the phone, at which point I explained that I was being held hostage by this strange building.

"Okay," she said. "I'm coming to find you."

I didn't know how French blocks worked. I knew only that I was somewhere on a street as long as Broadway and the address had been botched using four digits. I had some time. The first pangs of jet lag washed over me. Sometimes the worst of the worst is actually the worst. Tired of fiddling with the lock, I stepped back and roundhouse kicked it for my own amusement. I did this at the exact right angle to set off the security alarm. Like its cousin, the ambulance siren, this alarm blared in a French accent—singsongy and oddly un-urgent. But it echoed like a bitch.

This is not a problem! said my laid-back-ness. I needed to unstitch this slacker shadow before I punched it.

"For who are you *cherch*ing?" said an elderly Frenchman who appeared from absolutely nowhere. He was angry and quasi-bilingual. He spoke while charging at me and tightening his bathrobe. The rough hair springing from his ears was just long enough to allow for mobility, and it waved with his marching. I looked over his shoulder, searching for a hallway or a stairwell or a dumbwaiter. Right now I was *cherch*ing for any possible Crazy French Dude point of origin.

"You *Frenchfrenchfrench* idiot. I get the *Frenchfrenchfrench* police!"

"*Zut,*" I said, hands in the air. Are you even allowed to threaten to call the police in your bathrobe anymore?

"*Je suis très desolé.*"

That's another thing about *bicyclette rouge* French. No one in France ever finds himself moderately hungry or reasonably happy. They are always very everything.

"*Mais,*" I continued, as he eyed my suitcase stuffed with hypothetically stolen goods, "*je pense que j'ai le mal building.*"

Because I could not think of the word for "wrong," I used the word for "bad." Ah, influency, recipe for extremes. I had broken into this gentlemen's building to insult it. Which, come to think of it, seemed like something a French robber would do.

Perhaps I had inadvertently stumbled on the word "cocksucker" as well, because then came a torrent of French followed by a mercifully dry spitting gesture. The veins of French vocabulary may run thin with a low word count, but they know how to bleed. I have reason to believe I was called a squirrel at one point. But he may also have been calling me a school. I cocked my head at him. Had the use of "school" as a verb crossed continents? And would this man, with his astonishingly wiry nose hair, be familiar with it? One thing was certain: I was being schooled, run over like a half-dead squirrel. Bump, bump.

"*S'il vous plaît,*" I reasoned with him through the sound of the siren, "*pas de polizia. Je suis normale!*"

"*Normale?*" "Ish."

"*D'accord.* Go, go, go," he said in English, shoving me aside to perform a series of doorknob twists befitting a Rubik's Cube.

I peeked outside, hesitant as a cat to leave her cage at the vet's office. Louise was not there yet. When she finally did arrive, I was sitting on my suitcase, ignoring the coolly revolted glares of people passing by and playing with a zipper. My arms extended, I buried my head in my elbows.

"I feel like I should give you money." Louise bent down and hugged me.

"That's so weird." I looked up. "I also feel like you should give me money."

Not being the most reliable navigator, I would get Louise lost many times in the coming days. After a while, it was as much her fault as it was mine for deciding to follow me. But I couldn't blame her. Looking at a map requires an activation of concentration even if you don't have spatial relations issues, the same way cooking raw chicken requires an activation of "let's just get through this part" even if you're not a vegetarian. Because we were staying in the Marais, a neighborhood defined by narrow sidewalks and independent shops and very small cups of coffee, neither of us minded the winding routes home. Nothing seemed to take that long, and when it did, we didn't care: we were in Paris. If we swung especially far off course, we'd pass the old man's building.

"Look"—Louise would point, with a shopping bag-weighted arm—"your fake apartment building."

We took pictures of it. It became our anti-landmark, how we knew we were headed in the wrong direction. And I'd look at the door and think of how thoroughly unappealing it seemed from the other side. I'd think of the last thing the old man said to me as he escorted me off his property. He gestured at the courtyard, then at me, then at the negative space of the open door.

"*Frenchfrenchfrench*," he said. "I do not *Frenchfrench* think you should come to this place again."

He probably meant just the apartment building. But I took it to mean all of Paris.

After that first day, I awoke to the vague but identifiable smell of cheese. The kind of cheese where if you didn't know it was cheese, you'd think someone took a crap on the metro and set it on fire. And then put it out with milk. I meandered into the kitchen to see a composition of French consumption on the table: bottles of red wine, baguettes, leeks, an entire wheel of Brie, and a jar of something that may or may not have been mayonnaise. It also may have been marshmallow fluff. I wouldn't know. The nutritional information orbited along the outermost rings of my French vocabulary.

"I think that's mayonnaise," Louise said, sneaking up behind me and cracking a chocolate croissant in half. "What's French for mayonnaise?"

"*Mayonnaise.*"

"Then what's marshmallow?"

"Presumably *marshmalleaux.*"

Any word over ten letters in English is the same word in French. Fact.

"What is all this, anyway?" I said, gesturing with the jar. It was the same way I would gesture with it in a drunken stupor two nights hence, causing it to slip from my hand, fall straight out the window and onto the street, smashing into a carnage of goop and glass. Which, to our credit, the French pigeons were also at a loss to identify.

"This is the *le beauty* of *le sublet*," she cried. "Cooking!"

Louise, a key-carrying subletter, had gone on a *supermarché* sweep. She opened a plastic container of creamed fish and spread it over her second cliché-stuffed pastry. "Are you pregnant?"

"What?"

"*Le* knocked up. Are you?"

"No." She laughed and explained her subletting enchantment. "I just like bringing groceries back to a house. With a house, even when you've powered down for the day, you're still in a kind of cultural-immersion program."

Who was I to argue? Without even trying to take in Paris, I had already slept in someone else's low bed. I had touched their funny toilet paper, opened their medicine cabinet, banged on their faucets like a monkey, and then maneuvered their low-hanging showerhead, mumbling, *What is this, Thailand?* until I resigned myself to defeat and squatted to bathe, also like a monkey.

The one thing I was most determined to see in Paris I wasn't sure I'd be able to find again. It wasn't mobile like a boat on the Seine or perishable like a macaroon but a public fountain rooted to the ground. The problem was that I had embellished this particular fountain in my head, applied such importance to it that the contextual scenery had all but faded away. I had held the image of it like a pearl ring, loosely pronged and unscratched. It was a peaceful place—overgrown, quaint, and stone, with cigarette butts crushed into the dirt around it. But that didn't exactly narrow it down.

But then Louise began talking about the Luxembourg Gardens. A place, I pointedly explained, where I wanted my ashes scattered one day.

"You should know this," I said, as we walked through the front gates, "so in case I die tomorrow, it's on you to pipe up."

I felt destined for it the way teenagers feel destined for inanimate objects and public spaces. *The walls of this museum know I'm special. No one understands me but this coffee mug.* I also had a fantasy about my descendants—grown, sophisticated, lovely descendants—easing their jetpacks onto the garden grounds on their way to colonize Uranus, commenting on the striking difference between this decrepit fountain crafted from earth matter and their all-white space cars made of microelectric essence. Upon seeing my final resting place, they would be reminded of their humanity and the connective thread between my ashes and the freeze-dried meat pies they ate for breakfast.

This, as it turns out, was a bust. The fountain is not quaint. Nor is its existence much of a mystery, given the fact that it is *the* fountain in the Luxembourg Gardens, measuring 8.9 million meters tall by 9.8 million meters wide and ladled with statues of historical figures and saints and curls of concrete. It had started to rain. We snapped open our shared umbrella and stood at the base. Tourists took photographs and consulted their guidebooks to confirm what they were seeing. "Wow," Louise offered. "Think much of yourself?"

"I don't remember it being this . . . grand."

"I see gargoyles."

"It was more modest the last time."

The fountain was, as most fountains are, symbolic of something else. This one was symbolic of a larger problem I seemed to be having with Paris. My brain had misfiled the entire city, and instead of remembering it from small to big, like a stuffed animal that seems huge when you're a child and stuffed animal–sized when it's being sold at a tag sale, I remembered it from big to small. Paris ran backward. If I thought a monument or a creperie was two streets away, it was two miles away. If I thought a street looked familiar, I was wrong.

Louise read the history-explaining plaque.

"Are you even allowed to have your ashes scattered in a public fountain?"

"It's a body of water."

"It's practically stagnant," she said, pointing to the low-pressure streams meekly pouring from the Bastille-era plumbing.

"Shouldn't you just get buried, anyway? I thought Jews didn't believe in cremation."

I scoffed.

"What does this mean, 'believe in'? Makes it sound like we're living in caves and don't think it exists. Like we're all, 'Oh, fire, what's that? Is something burning? Man, this knish looks like a wheel, except I don't have that reference because I don't know what a wheel is.'"

"So you know what I mean, then." I stared at the watery muck. "I want to get down and dirty with the pennies and the algae."

The truth was, I knew it didn't matter how my corporeal being was disposed of. Bury me, freeze me, deep-fry me like a Mars bar, send me to a giant corporate building with a giant corporate sign that reads SCIENCE. Nothing I did in this life would have any bearing on the path I took in the next one. I had sealed my fate ten years prior, during my first Parisian excursion. Sealed it and spat on it and locked it in, as if trapped behind a Parisian apartment door. I never did have much of a sense of direction, but I knew that when I died, I would not be going north.

My friend Emily and I were backpacking around Europe together in a lopsided horseshoe path that began in Spain and would end in Turkey. More than any other destination, both of us were eager to reach Paris. How could we not be? A.) Paris is awesome, and we could sense its awesomeness in advance; B.) Emily wanted to see Notre Dame before she died; C.) *Somebody* had misread the train schedule leaving Barcelona, thus resulting in an Alps-obscuring overnight train trip in which we woke up in Geneva, Switzerland, and proceeded to get into a massive fight at a train station café, which culminated in my saying something about overrated chocolate, looping my arms into my backpack, and storming out of said station to wander the streets of Geneva, thinking it would be less trouble to spend the rest of my life in a Swiss bus shelter than to sort out the next southbound train.

When I eventually returned, Emily was gone. I thought perhaps she had gone back to Spain. I wouldn't have blamed her. The weather was more pleasant in Barcelona, as was our friendship. But when I reached the appropriate platform, there she was, chin in hand, sitting on her own overstuffed backpack as if it were a giant mushroom. I plopped down next to her.

"I'm sorry," I said, which in retrospect was the right thing to say when you abandon someone in a foreign country with no sign of returning. But which I probably didn't mean at the time. Fatigue had rendered me impervious to Switzerland's neutrality vibes. Emily unstuck her hand, hung her head, and spoke to the platform.

"I tried to buy a bagel, but they won't accept French francs. I offered them fifty francs for a bagel."

"That's just sad."

"Isn't it?" she said, looking up and smiling at me. "How can we have this much difficulty getting to Paris? What would happen to us in Bogotá?"

"We'd sell our bodies to the night in exchange for cocaine and corn on sticks."

"That sounds nice."

Since we arrived a day late, the beds in our hostel of choice had been filled by a pair of German lesbian equestrians. They were in town for a convention, though we couldn't say if it was for Germans or lesbians or equestrians. Either way, we didn't put up a fight. Instead, we wandered the streets, checking into the cheapest one-fifth-of-a-star hotel we could find. Located kind of near Les Halles, it was a hotel only in the sense that a lot of people who didn't live there slept there at night. Or, rather, during the day. Like raccoons.

Hygienic hostels and grimy hotels are a little like employees in a large corporation. When graduating from entry-level, there's a gap of time in which you are no longer an assistant and thus stop receiving overtime. Your salary actually decreases. Your quality of life was better before the upgrade. Sitting in this "hotel" on a partially up-holstered bench with wool protruding from the edges was like a de-motion, with Emily and me doing twice the grunt work for half the perks.

"Do you think they have the Internet?" She straightened up.

"No, I don't think they have the Internet."

Meanwhile, the manager sat in a bulletproof booth and dug through a drawer of keys. I think if he had escorted us anywhere but a lit hallway, we would have run.

"Look at that." I tapped Emily on the arm and gestured toward a completely naked man down the hall. His puckered slabs of fat folded on top of one another as he bent down to feed two less judg-mental cats.

I am a firm believer in not letting disgusting things be witnessed alone. Once, as I watched an old cockroach crawl across the back of my living room sofa, I called my squeamish roommate to tell her the precise measurements and trajectory of the roach. If I had to con-tinue living in our apartment knowing where it had been, I was tak-ing her down with me.

When we got to our room, I shut the sliding lock behind us, and Emily propped a desk chair beneath the doorknob, a move I was pretty sure both of us had seen only in fictional form. There was a dried bar of used soap and a child's dirty sock on the windowsill. We took photos of each other in chalk-outline formation, pretending to be dead on the floor. We slept with our passports in our underwear—a double score for any would-be rapist! In a fit of hygiene control, I turned my shirt inside out and used it as a pillowcase, sleeping on what looked like a dismembered pregnant lady. And the next morn-ing, in a spasm of realism regarding weeks of dirty laundry, I put the shirt right back on. We couldn't let the room win. It didn't matter how many heroin addicts we found slumped in the communal bath-room or prostitutes running drunk through the halls. It didn't matter how many Gauloises we had to smoke to mask the scent of armpits unwashed and dreams deferred. We were going to love Paris. This trip was our cultural vaccination. We'd see and do everything touristy we could so that one day we might come back as real adults and not have to go to a single museum or dead person's mansion. It was like tapas vacation. On day one, Emily planned our first course: a whole day around cathedrals, culminating in her beloved Notre Dame. In pencil, she drew crosses on her map, most of which looked like X's. Which made the map as a whole look like that serial-killer-trailing one on police bulletin boards. I had moved past the Geneva train debacle and was happy to cede control in the matter of churches. Best, I thought, to get God out of the way as quickly as possible.

It's a strange concept, visiting a cathedral. A park is built expressly for visitors. So is a museum. Even the most avant-garde museums don't hang the art on the walls as it's being painted. But a cathedral has a whole other utilitarian life running parallel to the shrinelike patina of history. It's like visiting a work in progress. And the more elaborate the work, the more one feels as if one is intruding. Emily's reaction to this was different from mine. Her experience seemed to be bolstered by the presence of real Parisians praying in pews. In one day, we had been to the Basilique du Sacré-Coeur, Saint Pierre de Montmartre, and the stained-glass light show that was Sainte Chapelle. By the time we hit Notre Dame, Emily had completely detached from the secular world in which she was raised. Maybe it was the buttresses. Maybe it was the tiers of votive candles or the embalmed saints. But my companion, a Protestant by birth, decided she wanted to confess.

"Noooo." I shook my head.

"Yessss." She nodded hers.

This seemed like too sudden a leap, just as all of Catholicism always seemed like too sudden a leap, regardless of the board from which one dove. Because we had a Christmas tree, I was never one of those Jewish kids who felt cheated out of the pageantry of an awesome winter holiday. There is a very specific frustration that accompanies an irreparably tangled string of lights, and I am familiar with it. But the downside to this candy-cane familiarity was a heightened curiosity about Christianity in general and Catholicism in specific. So one winter I asked my mother to explain to me the difference between most Christian denominations and Catholics. Which she obliged over cherry frosted Pop-Tarts.

"Protestants, for example," she said, cracking off a piece of Pop-

Tart against a piece of Bounty, "believe that when they take the Eucharist, it's the symbol of the body of Christ."

I nodded. Symbolism was something I could get behind. The seder plate was an orgy of murderous analogies on a tray.

"Catholics, on the other hand, believe that they are literally taking in the blood and body of Christ."

"So, the cracker turns into Christ when they eat it?"

I imagined the safari-themed sponge capsules we used to get from the toy store. It's all neon-colored horse pills until you put them in the bathroom sink and boom: a hippo.

"Something like that," she agreed, putting the bloody toaster pastry between her lips.

Thus began my awe and fascination with the Catholics. The Catholics had magical powers. And damn it if they didn't know how to decorate. Christmas? Christmas was nothing. The first time I went to Easter services with a family friend, gilded eggs hung from the rafters. Women wore generously brimmed hats. They had the instincts to duck and weave the way civilians should but didn't with umbrellas. At the end of the sermon, an old man to my right said, "Peace be with you," and spontaneously hugged me.

"Oh," I whispered, and froze.

Eventually I gave in to this man's embrace, leaning into his musk. I had watched him brace against his walker and receive Communion, and now I was encircled by the arms of a person who had eaten Jesus. There was something admirable about this way of thinking, something attractive about the sure leap into the invisible. An unadulterated bag of crazy? Yes. But admirable. No matter what your own beliefs may be, the mental fortitude required to think that *your* saliva has Rumpelstiltskinesque powers is something to be respected. Which is why I didn't want Emily fucking with it.

"I don't know if that's a good idea," I said, pointing at the palm of my hand and nodding toward a statue of the Virgin Mary.

Have you ever covered a flashlight with your fingers just to watch your blood light up? That's how Emily looked at me—right through my skin and into my soul. Her eyes filled with hope.

In all likelihood, they were just irritated from the hotel sheets and watering because we misread the label on contact solution and bought mouthwash instead. But standing there in a cool stone corridor in Notre Dame, I knew we wouldn't be leaving unless she confessed. The power of Christ compelled her. Of course, confessing in Notre Dame is not quite the same thing as confessing in your standard red velvet phone booth to the Almighty. This sin-purging line was fifteen people deep and at least half an hour long. And what it led to was not a curtain but a *très* large and *très* see-through glass office between two of the ancient pillars. From the outside, you could make out the backs of sinners' heads, bowing through a checklist of bad habits. It reminded me of the open cubicles of street-level bank branches in Manhattan, financial pet store windows. I am consistently impressed by their inhabitants' ability to keep their attention focused on their clients and their staplers so neatly aligned with their tape dispensers. Perhaps priests were able to do the same with God, lay him out on the desk and staple him into each wayward soul. Also like a bank branch, we lined up between slack velvet ropes. Up front was a paper sign slid into a metal frame. It read FRENCH/ENGLISH.

"Where do I start?" Emily was giddy with intimidation.

I hadn't thought of this—if you are nineteen and have never confessed, do you begin with the cigarette inhaled before noon this morning or the time you stole a package of sparkly pipe cleaners from your second-grade art class and kept them in the bottom of your closet for two years, eventually throwing them out because you felt so guilty? Do you mention the lying, the drinking, the cheating, the gambling, the masturbation, the *schadenfreude*, the disrespecting of your parents, the disrespecting of other people's parents, the doing of the drugs, the shoplifting of the gum, the coveting of worldly goods, the advantage-taking, the responsibility-foisting, the tone you use with food delivery people when you're alone and they're foreign, that time you had a hangnail on your toe so you stuck your foot in your mouth and you bit it off like a monkey? Or is that all kind of a given by now?

As we moved up the line, Emily kicking her giant backpack ahead of her, visitors solemnly but efficiently wove their way between the pews. They seemed disproportionately thrilled to be in a place that allowed flash photography. I feared for my friend's soul. If the End of Days came and it turns out the Catholics were right, would her soul come out like a deformed baby because she confessed only once? Was that not like getting half a piercing? We inched forward, ineffectively attempting to speed time by closing the space between us and the buxom Brit in front of us. She glared back at me, judge-y and annoyed. I took a step back and looked away. There was tourism and there was religion. Since when was it a good idea to cross the streams?

"Hey." Emily took me gently by the shoulder. "This is what churches are here for. To take people in and redeem them. It's on the Statue of Liberty."

"That doesn't make any sense."

"Yes, it does. The Statue of Liberty was a gift . . . from *France*."

It was Emily's turn. She stepped up, leaving me to fidget on the smooth stone floor. I looked around at the frozen pageantry of it all. My feet ached from traipsing from God's house to God's house all day. This man slept around more than George Washington. Similarly, one got the sense that God didn't actually *live* in all of these places. Sainte Chapelle was breathtaking, but Sainte Chapelle was a *pied-à-terre*. Notre Dame was home base.

"Are you waiting for your friend?" a man behind me asked in a heavy Italian accent. I was wearing very American shoes.

He was hoping I'd go sit in one of the pews. It wouldn't speed up his wait time, but at least it would provide the physical illusion. Which, it dawned on me, is all any of this was about, anyway. *Give me your tired, your poor, your Godless masses.* It was then that I made a decision that I'm sure had my grandmother rolling into the fetal position in her grave. I peeked through the glass to see Emily gesticulating wildly across from the priest.

"No, I'm actually waiting."

Ten minutes later, Emily opened the door. And the priest followed. *Oh, lord*, I thought. *What does one have to say to warrant being escorted out of confession? I told her not to mention the toe biting.* But while Emily met me in line, boasting the gratified look of the blessed, the priest put a new sign into the metal frame behind her. This one read FRENCH/JAPANESE.

Even God's servants need to change shifts.

A new priest appeared. Avoiding eye contact like a bartender on a

Saturday night, he shut the glass door behind him and commenced readjusting the swivel chair behind the desk. I felt that internal conflict, that eternal struggle: Do I stay in this line now that I've waited this long or cut my losses and leave the building/movie theater/subway platform? I find it's better to stay and be frustrated than to leave and wonder. I brushed past Emily and sat across from Priest 2.0. Deducing that I was not Japanese, he rattled off something priestly in French. I smiled at him. *Don't wink don't wink don't wink don't wink.*

"*Je suis une Juden!*" I blurted out.

This is what comes from seeing too many Holocaust films.

"But," I explained—my two favorite words in any foreign language are "but" and "because," the universal time-buyers—"but I think that it is true that we have the same God."

The priest put his elbows on the table and leaned forward, studying my face. Was this a prank? Why else would I willingly enter into a situation in which I couldn't function unless it was to mock God? I wanted to explain to him that I willingly enter into situations in which I can't function all the time, and it rarely has anything to do with God.

"English?"

"American!" I said, far too proudly. This was during a time when it was common to glue a Canadian flag patch on your backpack so that the natives would be thrown off your Yankee scent. Never mind the fact that anyone with a flag patch glued to their bag should probably have the crap beat out of them. I had been in utero the last time this priest had uttered a coherent string of English, which he explained to me in words that were not only broken but utterly shattered. Like Helen-Keller-and-Jodie-Foster-in-*Nell*-had-a-love-childshattered. What a rare combination of languages lived in his godly head. What if it turns out that it's not an issue of beliefs but linguistics, and Saint Peter speaks only French and Japanese? Bummer.

The priest cleared his throat. We then proceeded to have the most awkward conversation of my life, potentially of his as well. Through the stilted silences, the rough combination of languages, and the pesky little fact that I did not believe in Jesus or wallpaper in kitchens came the following conclusions.

A.) Paris was so beautiful because it made you look up at the sky/

God; B.) If God had meant the French people to make sushi, he wouldn't have given them cows; C.) Little things in life can produce a smile on your face, like the pen he mindlessly clicked in his right hand, which he also let me click.

I could sense that our time was running out. I could also sense his feeling self-conscious about chucking me out, afraid I'd think it was because I was Jewish. He encouraged me to come back the next week when he was sure there would be an English-speaking priest manning God's fort.

"Ah, *oui*" — I looked at the clock — "but the week that is after this week I will not be here. I will be home."

At which point he got up from the desk and came over to my chair. I stood, and he took my hand.

"God is always home," he said, grinning.

I felt good, relieved, which is pretty much the equivalent of feeling good in organized religion. Relief. You're alive. God doesn't hate you. Your livestock is healthy. No one gave you boils today. Plus, the priest complimented my French.

"For how long have you it learned?"

The truth was, my French was atrocious for how long I it had learned. After a lifetime of flash cards and poetry recitation, I should have graduated from my *bicyclette rouge* French. I should have been speaking sound-barrier-breaking Concord Rouge French. Out of my mouth came:

"*Deux ans.*" Two years.

The priest looked at me long and hard.

"*Vraiment? Deux ans?*"

I gulped and pried my hand away from his. Yup. Uh-huh. Two years.

"*Merveilleux.*"

"Oh . . . Mercy."

"You're welcome."

I flew out of the glass chamber and found Emily, who was standing beneath a large bloody cross. I pulled Emily's arm as if I were her toddler child and she wanted to go lingerie shopping. I had to get out of there immediately. I was a Jew, and I'd just lied to a priest in confession. In Notre Dame. I was going to get the shit smote out of me.

I had incurred God's permanent wrath and purchased myself a one-way ticket to hell. They only sell round-trips to zombies. At the very least, I was going wherever they send Jews who confess to priests and then lie to them. Oklahoma, maybe. But Emily was reluctant to leave. Apparently, her priest was multitalented. Not only was he a fluent English speaker but in her brief meeting with him, he had caused Emily to question her entire religious purpose on this earth, giving her a whole lot more to chew on than a wafer. She wanted to light candles and read pamphlets.

"Are you kidding me?" I said, eyeing the vaulted ceilings for signs of imminent collapse.

A security guard came over and tapped me on the shoulder. He asked me to keep it down.

"I'm sorry," I said, walking back toward the arches of sunlight coming from the main entrance. But when I turned around, I saw that Emily was still standing at the end of a pew. I whistled, the sound echoing in her direction.

Roused from her religious reverie, she picked up her giant backpack and made her way toward me. But not before one of her straps brushed against the table of prayer candles, knocking a corner one to the ground. Emily froze. The mess did not look dissimilar from, say, a jar of French mystery spread dropped out a window. I shut my eyes and exhaled. Surely, I thought, this happens all the time. Who puts a candle so close to the edge of a table? Who is so careless with other people's prayers?

The security guard glared at me. Between the two of us, I had been the first to get in trouble and was thus responsible for all subsequent offenses, even Emily's.

"I do not think you should come to this place again," he said, ushering us out with his eyes.

When we got outside, Emily unfolded her map, running her finger along the fold to find the next X. But I couldn't bring myself to go to another cathedral. We had seen the crown jewel. And I had gotten us escorted away from it.

Wasn't the whole idea of a tapas vacation to partake of a little of everything, anyway? I don't think God would want me to overdo it. I think he would want me to have a crêpe. So Emily and I compromised. No more cathedrals with low-lying fire, but we had to check *something* off the list. We went to the Luxembourg Gardens, where I stumbled upon my fountain. I stood in front of it while Emily checked out the sculpture garden, growing frustrated not with her map but with the actual sculptures if they weren't where they were meant to be. And because fountains are inanimate, and thus polylingual, I took the opportunity to use this particular fountain as my church. I apologized to God for everything I had ever done. Except for the stuff that was kind of a given.

The rain had stopped, so Louise snapped the umbrella shut. The fountain water was calm once more. Louise peered into it, her reflection blotched by the texture of the water. One woman's stagnant is another woman's still.

The remainder of our trip was spent in a less morbid fashion, imbibing the holy trinity of vacation beverages: coffee, wine, and liquor. For all its faults, tapas vacation had worked, and during round two, I felt no pressure to catalog every single Impressionist painter in one day. Instead, I discovered what I had slept through the first time: French nightlife. We accidentally found ourselves in a French strip club, where a Thai stripper named Cali kept touching Louise's hair. We went to bars, where I did the same thing in French as I do in English when people are shouting at me at close range but I still can't understand what they're saying. I shout back in extremely animated gibberish, which invariably results in much nodding and moving along of the conversation. Except I did this in an exaggerated French accent. It's better than the alternative—bellowing "*What?*" at thirty-second intervals, in which case everybody loses.

The last day of my visit, we went to a giant French flea market. I was determined to take a real piece of Paris back with me. For a long time, if people asked if they could bring me anything from their travels, I used to request a rock or a pebble. You shouldn't spend your time obligation shopping when you're on vacation. Plus, picking up a rock from the street was more legitimate than bringing back a snow globe not even manufactured in the corresponding country. I stopped making this request when a friend came back from South America and handed me a cloth sack with a rock—and a stowaway in the form of a dead insect serious enough to have an inch-thick exoskeleton.

At the flea market, I attempted to purchase a giant ostrich egg. I was bolstered by my ability to say *l'ouef* but ultimately thwarted by the *über mal* prospect of packing a forty-euro egg that was sure to break in my suitcase. In sixth grade, we conducted a science experiment in which all the students in the class had to drop an egg from the top of the school's building, protecting it from breaking using homemade devices. What brand of "science" this fell under, I couldn't say. Some kids cradled their egg in cotton-ball nests, some suspended it with rubber bands between sticks like a canopy bed. I squeezed an industrial-sized bottle of Palmolive into a large plastic bag, adding the egg halfway. Palmolive, as it turns out, is not as viscous as you'd think. Not only did the egg break but the bag exploded. It looked like someone had aborted a green chicken in the parking lot.

Louise and I were on our way out of the flea market, me resigned to allowing my *bicyclette rouge* French to deflate in the decade ahead, when I spotted a large antique wall thermometer. The dials were many and crafted; the glass was unbroken. How much could one, in good conscience, charge for a questionably functional wall thermometer? Five ostrich eggs' worth, apparently. It was a very nice-looking thermometer.

"Two hundred euro," the antiques dealer repeated as if it were a fact, a number measured using the object in question.

I bristled at the price, again employing "*mal*," but this time it was exactly what I meant. After enough time in Paris my French had actually improved. But I was done talking. The first rule of any negotiation is be prepared to walk away. Or maybe that's the first rule of eating blowfish. Either way, it was a rule and it was out there and it was time to employ it. And then something happened. For the first time since Paris and I had gotten to know each other, one of its citizens asked me to return.

"One hundred seventy-five euro," said the antiques dealer.

Actually, he didn't say this, he wrote it down, employing the long French 1. My French had gotten better but not that better. Large numbers were on the same ring of vocabulary as nutritional information. Once he gave in a little, it was all the bolstering I needed to negotiate down, until it was only two ostrich eggs' worth. There is a bittersweet capitalist tingle when one gets too good a bargain. The glee of separating yourself from the idiot who pays full price is quickly replaced by the fact that someone was trying to rip you off in the first place. Everyone's the idiot eventually.

On the crowded metro back to the center of town, I attempted to protect the thermometer. It was wrapped in layers of newspaper and bubble wrap, but I was dubious about its prospects for staying in one piece. I didn't even have any dish soap.

"*S'il vous plaît*," I'd say when jostled, melodramatically cradling the thermometer. "*C'est un violon.*"

Louise whipped around to look at me. "*Ceci n'est pas un violon*," she whisper-shouted.

"Shut it, Magritte. It is now."

Though "thermometer" surely falls under the ten-letter translation rule, I have no idea how to say "valuable antique wall *thermomèteuuur*" in French. Even if I did, I assume the average person's ability to conjure an image of such a thing is on par with my ability to produce the words to describe it. Plus, there are benefits to lying about such things. If you are over the age of ten and in possession of a classical musical instrument, people think you are a genius. They think you have an innate gift that you have harnessed into a tangible life skill. They look admiringly at your hands.

Back in the sublet, the thermometer leaned a good foot beyond my suitcase despite my generous angling of it. *This is not a problem!* said my laid-back self, recalling the time it had run through the Miami airport with two carry-ons and an oversized lamp made out of a lawn flamingo and still made the flight.

Shut up and eat your Ding Dongs, I thought, and left the room.

My flight was the first one out of Paris. Louise and I stayed up all night, eating cheese and drinking the last of the wine. I left for the airport while it was still dark outside, making sure to leave time to call a taxi and then for the taxi not to come. I hailed a cab on the street and loaded my suitcase in the trunk but held the thermometer close to my chest. The streets of Paris were utterly abandoned as the taxi darted through them. I lowered my window to take in my last moments of Parisian air. Then I put it back up as we drove past a garbage dump and a gas station.

I tore open the bubble wrap on the thermometer. I just wanted to touch it. Finally, something pertaining to Paris had worked out in my favor. Back when his ostrich-egg count was still at four, the antiques dealer said he purchased the thermometer at an estate sale. I imagined the original owners and hoped that they would not be too upset to see it go home with an American. I felt a seam of some sort on the back of it. Curious, I tore a little further to feel a sliding brass hook. I looked up at the cabdriver through the rearview mirror. I put the thermometer on my lap and pushed the hook, opening the back panel like a grandfather clock. I thought I might find a treasure map. *The Goonies* was a movie, sure, but a very realistic one. Or perhaps I'd discover a copy of the French Declaration of Independence. Certainly not *our* Declaration of Independence. Copies of *that* thing turn up only behind maps of West Virginia and velvet Elvis paintings. We are the least classy treasure hunters on the planet.

Treasure Hunter's Assistant: *Do you think the scroll is beneath the seventeenth-century farmhouse? Or maybe in this dusty urn I just found? Looks like it's from Greece.*

Treasure Hunter in Charge: *Nahh. Crack open that keepsake ornament with the glitter bonnet. I'm pretty sure it's in there.*

My thermometer was scroll-free. However, if there was ever any doubt about the thermometer being from the 1800s, I had my answer: in lieu of pendulums and chimes, it was filled with vials of mercury. Not just a bead or two, as in twentieth-century thermometers, but a post-apocalyptic supply dangling from chain after chain. For a moment I entertained the idea that the silver was on the outside of the glass, painted on there for some olden-timey reason I couldn't fathom but which would make perfect sense if explained to me on a guided tour of Versailles. *As you can see here, folks, the toilets were sealed shut with beeswax each night. Can anyone tell me why? That's right, to ward off pig ghosts . . .*

Maybe the vials themselves were empty. But when I turned them upside down, the mercury did what mercury does — holds on for a heartbeat, fighting gravity like ice at the end of a glass before it comes crashing down on your teeth.

"Fuck."

"*Pardon?*" My cabdriver looked at me through the mirror.

"*Rien.*" I sighed, reattaching the tape. *Okay, this is a bit of a problem!*

Having just checked the airline's website for the most current regulations regarding hair conditioner, I knew that mercury was not among the substances welcomed by the TSA. I think it's generally important—nay, American—to know why you're being told a rule exists. Which is why I went online to begin with. But if it's four A.M. and you're full of French wine, there's really nothing funnier than the TSA website. There is no personality type untouched, no scenario unexplored, no rare-weapons collector unaddressed. The more obscure the warning, the better. I like to think I would be seated next to the guy who pitched a fit because he didn't realize he had to check his throwing stars and "realistic replicas of explosives." He'd probably gnaw his plastic water cup into a shiv out of resentment. It was in the midst of all this that I learned that, in addition to causing lockjawed flipper babies, mercury will eat through aluminum. Which is what planes are made of.

So it's not actually the explosiveness of mercury that's a problem, no more than the handle of the knife or the center of the throwing star is a problem. You have to be a pretty genius terrorist to know how to make a bomb out of mercury. But you have to be only an average idiot to poke a hole in the plane.

My plan was, for once, to stay very still and do nothing. In stressful situations, people often talk about a fight-or-flight response. Which, in my opinion, doesn't give enough credit to the more common reaction of curling up into a little ball. My history of explaining myself in Paris was peppered with failure. For once, I made the decision to play it cool. Or stupid. Whichever came first.

The good news is that I arrived at the airport with plenty of time to be detained by security. Apparently, grinning like a moron as you slide sketchily wrapped prohibited substances through an X-ray machine will not make it okay that you have them on your person. I attempted to buddy up to the security personnel by getting them on my team, being overly cooperative as they escorted me into a small glass-paneled room noticeably reminiscent of the confession booth in Notre Dame. This was not the first time I had been taken to the special "threat to society" security room at the airport. The first time was when I had booked a sudden and nonsensical jaunt to Portugal and back. But at least in that instance, I possessed the confidence of innocence.

Three guards, two women and a man with boobs, put on latex gloves, and one of them handed me a pair of scissors so that I might autopsy the mysterious package myself. For no particular reason beyond being given a knifelike object, I imagined stabbing one of them with the closed scissors. An excessive means of teaching them the hypocrisies of airport security? Sure, but in the visual, I also knew karate. So I hoped it wouldn't come to that.

Two of the guards stood behind me as I sliced open the top of the bubble wrap. I thought this would be satisfactory. You could see the wooden top of something decorative. No wires or egg timers here. Still, they encouraged me to keep cutting. As I roughly sliced through layers of tape and plastic, I thought, *If I was going to blow up a plane, why would I do it so conspicuously?* Terrorism isn't customarily the terrain of reverse psychology. *Ceci n'est pas un ticking suitcase!* The whole Trojan horse bit doesn't have a place in the era of metal detectors.

No matter, I still retained a skeptical appreciation for the law. Sometimes the best way to see your tax dollars at work and protectors in action is to get caught yourself. It's when they gestured for me to take off my shirt that I lost that.

"Pardon?"

"Your shirt," said one of the female guards, pointing to make herself clear. In my carelessness with the scissors, I had actually managed to cut my shirt along with the bubble wrap. *Surely*, I thought, *this will get me off the hook. I can't even cut bubble wrap successfully. Who's going to blow up a plane? Not I.*

She picked up the thermometer and held it the way one might hold a rabbit one has just shot. She quickly felt along the body for any irregularities but found none. She set it down and they all ran cotton swabs over the thermometer and consulted their military-style computer. They took turns frowning at one another, then at the thermometer, and then at the hole in my shirt. Something was showing up on the screen, but they couldn't categorize it. Whatever traditional bombs are made out of, this was not it. There must be some rarely registered airport security category that also includes gunpowder. If you are guilty of possession of these rudimentary explosives, men in wigs and brass-buttoned coats take you into yet another room and slap you senseless with their gloves. Only then may you board the plane.

Man Boobs called in a supervisor, a diminutive but determined gentleman with bags under his eyes that looked like mine but permanent. He asked me to have a seat. He wanted to know where I got the thermometer, and I told him. He wanted to know when I had purchased it, and I told him. He wanted to know if I had purchased it or if someone had purchased it for me, and I told him, adding an "I wish." He wanted to know how much I had paid for it, and I beamed when I told him. But I wasn't about to tell them about the mercury. I had made it this far. The thermometer was the one piece of Paris that was mine. I was a terrible godless lying American idiot, but the fucking thermometer was mine.

Bracing for the possibility of a lie-detector test, I tried to wind my mind back like a speedometer. Only a few hours earlier I was still ignorant of the thermometer's innards. I looked at the digital clock on the desk. I could feel myself about to confess. All I wanted was to crack open a fleece blanket as the flight attendants encouraged me to peruse my options for duty-free grilling equipment and Clinique.

"Okay." The supervisor clicked his pen and slid it into his shirt pocket. "Just make sure you declare it at customs when you land."

You mean if I land, I thought. If I really did have designs on blowing up the plane between here and New York, notifying customs was a bit of a moot point. It made me wonder what else they were willing to let go. I yanked my shirt down so that the hole was more of a slit and less of a belly-button peep show. I put the thermometer underneath my arm like the musical instrument it wasn't. A woman's voice came through the PA system, first in French and then in English. My plane was starting to board. I got up and thanked them for detaining me.

TIM CROTHERS

■

Game of Her Life

FROM *ESPN The Magazine*

SHE FLIES TO SIBERIA *in late September with nine teammates, all in their twenties, much older than she is. When she won the match that put her on this plane, she had no idea what it meant. Nobody had told her what was at stake, so she just played, like always. She had no idea that she'd qualified for the Olympiad; no idea what the Olympiad was. She had no idea that her win would send her to the city of Khanty-Mansiysk, in remote Russia; no idea where Russia was. When she learned all this, she asked just one question: "Is it cold there?"*

But here she is, journeying with her countrymen twenty-seven hours across the globe. And though she has known many of them for a few years, they have no idea where she is from or where she aspires to go, because Phiona Mutesi is from a place where girls like her don't talk about that.

Agape Church could collapse at any moment. It is a ramshackle structure that lists alarmingly to one side, held together by scrap wood, rope, a few nails, and faith. It is rickety, like everything else around it. At the church on this Saturday morning in September are thirty-seven children whose lives are equally fragile. They wander in to play a game none had heard of before they met Coach Robert, a game so foreign that there's no word for it in Luganda, their native language.

Chess.

When they walk through the door, grins crease their faces. This is home as much as any place, a refuge, the only community they know. These are their friends, their brothers and sisters of chess, and there is relative safety and comfort here. Inside Agape church it is almost possible to forget the chaos outside, in Katwe, the largest of eight slums in Kampala, Uganda, and one of the worst places on earth.

There are only seven chessboards at the church, and chess pieces are so scarce that sometimes an orphan pawn must stand in for a king. A child sits on each end of a wobbly pew, both straddling the board between their knobby knees, with captured pieces guarded in their laps. A five-year-old kid in a threadbare Denver Broncos number seven jersey competes against an eleven-year-old in a frayed t-shirt that reads *J'Adore Paris*. Most of the kids are barefoot. Some wear flip-flops. One has on black wingtips with no laces.

It is rapid-fire street chess. When more than a few seconds elapse without a move, there is a palpable restlessness. It is remarkably quiet except for the thud of one piece slaying another and the occasional dispute over the location of a piece on a chessboard so faded that the dark spaces are barely distinguishable from the light ones. Surrender is signaled by a clattering of captured pieces on the board. A new match begins immediately without the slightest celebration.

Coach Robert Katende is here. So are Benjamin and Ivan and Brian. And up near the pulpit sits Phiona. One of two girls in the room, Phiona is juggling three matches at once and dominating them with her aggressive style, checkmating her young opponents while drawing a flower in the dirt on the floor with her toe. Phiona is fourteen, and her stone face gives no sign that the next day she will travel to Siberia to compete against the very best chess players in the world.

Ice? The opening ceremonies at the 2010 Chess Olympiad take place in an ice arena. Phiona has never seen ice. There are also lasers and dancers inside bubbles and people costumed as chess pieces marching around on a giant chessboard. Phiona watches it all with her hands cupping her cheeks, as if in a wonderland. She asks if this happens every night in this place, and she is told by her coach no, the arena normally serves as a home for hockey, concerts, and the circus. Phiona has never heard of those things.

She returns to the hotel, which at fifteen floors is the tallest building Phiona has ever entered. She rides the elevator with trepidation. She stares out of her window amazed by how people on the ground look so tiny from the sixth floor. She takes a long shower, washing away the slum.

* * *

Phiona Mutesi is the ultimate underdog. To be African is to be an underdog in the world. To be Ugandan is to be an underdog in Africa. To be from Katwe is to be an underdog in Uganda. And finally, to be female is to be an underdog in Katwe.

She wakes at five each morning to begin a two-hour trek through Katwe to fill a jug with drinkable water, walking through low land that is often so severely flooded by Uganda's torrential rains that many residents sleep in hammocks near their ceilings to avoid drowning. There are no sewers, and the human waste from downtown Kampala is dumped directly into the slum. There is no sanitation. Flies are everywhere. The stench is appalling.

Phiona walks past dogs, rats, and long-horned cattle, all competing with her to survive in a cramped space that grows more crowded every minute. She navigates carefully through this place where women are valued for little more than sex and childcare, where fifty percent of teen girls are mothers. It is a place where everybody is on the move but nobody ever leaves; it is said that if you are born in Katwe you die in Katwe, from disease or violence or neglect. Whenever Phiona gets scared on these journeys, she thinks of another test of survival. "Chess is a lot like my life," she says through an interpreter. "If you make smart moves you can stay away from danger, but you know any bad decision could be your last."

Phiona and her family have relocated inside Katwe six times in four years, once because all of their possessions were stolen, another time because their hut was crumbling. Their current home is a room ten feet by ten feet, its only window covered by sheet metal. The walls are brick, the roof corrugated tin held up by spindly wood beams. A curtain is drawn across the doorway when the door is open, as it always is during the sweltering daytime in this country bisected by the equator. Laundry hangs on wash lines crisscrossing the room. The walls are bare, except for etched phone numbers. There is no phone.

The contents of Phiona's home are: two water jugs, wash bin, small charcoal stove, teapot, a few plates and cups, toothbrush, tiny mirror, Bible, and two musty mattresses. The latter suffice for the five people who regularly sleep in the shack: Phiona, mother Harriet, teenage brothers Brian and Richard, and her six-year-old niece, Winnie. Pouches of curry powder, salt, and tea leaves are the only hints of food.

Phiona enters the competition venue, an indoor tennis arena packed with hundreds of chessboards, and quickly notices that she is among the youngest of more than 1,000 players from 149 countries. She is told that this is the most accomplished collection of chess talent ever assembled, which makes her nervous. She is the second-seeded player for the Ugandan team, but she isn't playing against kids anymore; her competitors are women. She keeps thinking to herself, Do I really belong here?

Her first opponent is Dina Kagramanov, the Canadian national champion. Kagramanov, born in Baku, Azerbaijan, the hometown of former men's world champion Garry Kasparov, learned the game at age six. She is competing in her third Olympiad and, at twenty-four, has been playing elite chess longer than Phiona has been alive.

Kagramanov preys on Phiona's inexperience, setting a trap early and gaining a pawn advantage that Phiona stubbornly tries and fails to reverse. After her win, Kagramanov is shocked to learn that this is Phiona's first international match against an adult. "She's a sponge," Kagramanov says. "She picks up on whatever information you give her, and she uses it against you. Anybody can be taught moves and how to react to those moves, but to reason like she does at her age is a gift that gives her the potential for greatness."

When asked about early memories, Phiona can recall only loss. "I remember I went to my dad's village when I was about three years old to see him when he was very sick, and a week later he died of AIDS," she says. "After the funeral my family stayed in the village for a few weeks, and one morning when I woke up, my older sister, Juliet, told me she was feeling a headache. We got some herbs and gave them to her, and then she went to sleep. The following morning we found her dead in the bed. That's what I remember."

She tells also of being gravely ill when she was eight. Harriet begged her sister for money to take Phiona to the hospital, and though they were never given a diagnosis, Harriet believes her daughter had malaria. Phiona lost consciousness, doctors removed fluid from her spine, and Harriet was sure she'd have to bury another daughter. She later told Phiona, "You died for two days."

Harriet, who is often sick, is sometimes gone from the shack for days trying to make money for her family's daily meal of rice and tea. She wakes at 2 A.M. to walk five kilometers and buy the avocados and eggplants that she resells at a street market. Phiona, who never knows when her mother will return, is left to care for her siblings.

Phiona does not know her birthday. Nobody bothers to record such things in Katwe. There are few calendars. Fewer clocks. Most people don't know the date or the day of the week. Every day is just like the last.

For her entire life, Phiona's main challenge has been to find food. One afternoon in 2005, when she was just nine but had already dropped out of school because her family couldn't afford it, she secretly followed Brian out of their shack in hopes he might lead to the first meal of the day. Brian had recently taken part in a project run by Sports Outreach Institute, a Christian mission that works to provide relief and religion through sports to the world's poorest people. Phiona watched Brian enter a dusty hallway, sit on a bench, and begin playing with some black and white objects. Phiona had never seen anything like these pieces, and she thought they were beautiful. She peeked around a corner again and again, fascinated by the game and also wondering if there might be some food there. Suddenly, she was spotted. "Young girl," said Coach Robert. "Come in. Don't be afraid."

She is lucky to be here. Uganda's women's team has never participated in an Olympiad before because it is expensive. But this year, according to members of the Ugandan Chess Federation, the president of FIDE (chess's governing body) is funding their trip. Phiona needs breaks like that.

On the second day of matches, she arrives early to explore. She sees Afghan women dressed in burkas, Indian women in saris and Bolivian women in ponchos and black bowler hats. She spots a blind player and wonders how that is possible. She sees an Iraqi kneel and begin to pray toward Mecca. As she approaches her table, Phiona is asked to produce her credential to prove she is actually a competitor, perhaps because she looks so young, or perhaps because with her short hair, baggy sweater, and sweatpants, she is mistaken for a boy.

Before her match begins against Elaine Lin Yu-Tong of Taiwan, Phiona slips off her sneakers. She isn't comfortable playing chess in shoes. Midway through the game, Phiona makes a tactical error, costing her two pawns.

Her opponent makes a similar blunder later, but Phiona doesn't realize it until it's too late. From then on, she stares crestfallen at the board as the rest of the moves play out predictably, and she loses a match she thinks she should have won. Phiona leaves the table and bolts to the parking lot. Katende warned her never to go off on her own, but she boards a shuttle bus alone and returns to the hotel, then runs to her room and bawls into her pillow. Later that evening, Katende tries his best to comfort her, but Phiona is inconsolable. It is the only time chess has ever brought her to tears. In fact, she cannot remember the last time she cried.

Robert Katende was a bastard child who lived his early years with his grandmother in the village of Kiboga, outside Kampala. It wasn't until he was reunited with his mother in Kampala's Nakulabye slum, when he was four, that he learned his first name. Until then he'd been known only as Katende.

Robert's mother died in 1990, when he was eight. He then began a decade-long odyssey from aunt to aunt and from school to school. He'd started playing soccer as a small boy in Kiboga, kicking a ball made of banana leaves. He grew into a center forward of such speed and skill that whenever his guardian of the moment could not afford to send him to school, a headmaster would hear of his soccer prowess and usher him in through a back door.

When Robert was fifteen, he suffered a severe head injury crashing into a goalkeeper. He lapsed into a coma, and everyone at school assumed he was dead. Robert emerged from the coma the next morning but spent three months in the hospital, where doctors told him he would never play soccer again. They were wrong.

Nine months after his injury, despite excruciating headaches, Robert returned to the soccer field. The game provided the only money he could earn. After a club soccer match in 2003, his coach told him about a job at Sports Outreach, and Robert, a born-again Christian, found his calling. He started playing for the ministry's team and was also assigned to Katwe, where he began drawing kids from the slum with the promise of soccer and postgame porridge. After several months, he noticed some children just watching from the sidelines, and he searched for a way to engage them. He found a solution in a nearly forgotten relic, a chess set given to him by a friend back in secondary school. "I had my doubts about chess in Katwe," Katende admits. "With their education and their environment, I wondered, *Can these kids really play this game?*"

Katende started offering chess after soccer games, beginning with a group of six boys who came to be known as The Pioneers. Two years later, the program had twenty-five children. That's when a barefoot nine-year-old girl in a torn and muddied skirt peeked into the entryway, and Coach Robert beckoned her inside.

Chess. Chess. Chess. After a long day at the Olympiad, the players return to the hotel to talk about—what else?—chess. If they are not talking chess, they are playing it.

Dina Kagramanov approaches Phiona in the hotel lobby and hands her two books on advanced chess. Then, with Katende interpreting, the two players break down their first-round match, Kagramanov explaining the strategy behind her own moves and asking about the decisions Phiona made instinctively.

Like each day she will spend in Siberia, Phiona is engulfed by chess, pausing only to visit the hotel restaurant where she dines three times a day at an all-you-can-eat buffet. At the first few meals, Phiona makes herself sick by overeating. Even during dinner, chess moves are replayed with salt and pepper shakers.

"When I first saw chess, I thought, *What could make all these kids so silent?*" Phiona recalls. "Then I watched them play the game and get happy and excited, and I wanted a chance to be that happy."

Katende showed Phiona the pieces and explained how each was restricted by rules about how it could move. The pawns. The rooks. The bishops. The knights. The king. And finally the queen, the most powerful piece on the board. How could Phiona have imagined at the time where those thirty-two pieces and sixty-four squares would deliver her?

Phiona started walking six kilometers every day to play chess. During her early development, she played too recklessly. She often sacrificed crucial pieces in risky attempts to defeat her opponents as quickly as possible, even when playing black—which means going second and taking a defensive posture to open the match. Says

Phiona, "I must have lost my first fifty matches before Coach Robert persuaded me to act more like a girl and play with calm and patience."

The first match Phiona ever won was against Joseph Asaba, a young boy who had beaten her before by utilizing a tactic called the Fool's Mate, a humiliating scheme that can produce victory in as few as four moves. One day Joseph wasn't aware that Katende had prepared Phiona with a defense against the Fool's Mate that would capture Joseph's queen. When Phiona finally checkmated Joseph, she didn't even know it until Joseph began sobbing because he had lost to a girl. While other girls in the project were afraid to play against boys, Phiona relished it. Katende eventually introduced Phiona to Ivan Mutesasira and Benjamin Mukumbya, two of the project's strongest players, who agreed to tutor her. "When I first met Phiona, I took it for granted that girls are always weak, that girls can do nothing, but I came to realize that she could play as well as a boy," Ivan says. "She plays very aggressively, like a boy. She likes to attack, and when you play against her, it feels like she's always pushing you backward until you have nowhere to move."

News eventually spread around Katwe that Katende was part of an organization run by white people, known in Uganda as *mzungu*, and Harriet began hearing disturbing rumors. "My neighbors told me that chess was a white man's game, and that if I let Phiona keep going there to play, that *mzungu* would take her away," she says. "But I could not afford to feed her. What choice did I have?"

Within a year, Phiona could beat her coach, and Katende knew it was time for her and the others to face better competition outside the project. He visited local boarding schools, where children from more privileged backgrounds refused to play the slum kids because they smelled bad and seemed like they might steal from them. But Katende kept asking until ten-year-old Phiona was playing against teens in fancy blazers and knickers, beating them soundly. Then she played university players, defeating them, as well.

She has learned the game strictly through trial and error, trained by a coach who has played chess recreationally off and on for years, admitting he didn't even know all of the rules until he was given *Chess for Beginners* shortly after starting the project. Phiona plays on instinct instead of relying on opening and end-game theory like more refined players. She succeeds because she possesses that precious chess gene that allows her to envision the board many moves ahead, and because she focuses on the game as if her life depended on it, which in her case might be true.

Phiona first won the Uganda Women's Junior Championship in 2007, when she was eleven. She won that title three years in a row, and it would have been four, but the Uganda Chess Federation didn't have the funds to stage it in 2010. She is still so early in her learning curve that chess experts believe her potential is staggering. "To love the game as much as she does and already be a champion at her age means her future is much bigger than any girl I've ever known," says George Zirembuzi, Uganda's national team coach, who has trained with grandmasters in Russia. "When Phiona loses, she really feels hurt, and I like that, because that characteristic will help her keep thirsting to get better."

Although Phiona is already implausibly good at something she has no business even doing, she is, like most girls and women in Uganda, uncomfortable sharing what she's thinking. Normally, nobody cares. She tries to answer any questions about herself with a shrug. When Phiona is compelled to speak, she is barely audible and usually staring at her feet. She realizes that chess makes her stand out, which makes her a target in Katwe, among the most dangerous neighborhoods in Uganda. So she is conditioned to say as little as possible. "Her personality with the outside world is still quite reserved, because she feels inferior due to her background," Katende says. "But in chess I am always reminding her that anyone can lift a piece, because it is so light. What separates you is where you choose to put it down. Chess is the one thing in Phiona's life she can control. Chess is her one chance to feel superior."

Chess is not a spectator sport. During matches at the Olympiad, it is not uncommon for twenty minutes to elapse without a single move. Players often leave the table for a bathroom break or to get a cup of tea or to psyche out an opponent by pretending that it isn't even necessary to sit at the board to conquer it. Phiona never leaves the table. She doesn't know what it means to psyche out an opponent or, fortunately for her, what it means to be psyched out.

But she is restless. These games progress too slowly for her, nothing like chess back in Uganda. She has spent two matches fidgeting and slouching in her seat, desperate for her opponents to get on with it.

Wary after Phiona's breakdown following the second match, Katende is ruing the Uganda Chess Federation's decision to place Phiona as her team's number two seed, where she must face the top players from other teams rather than lower-seeded players with less experience, whom he suspects she could be defeating.

Phiona's third match is against a grandmaster from Egypt, Khaled Mona. Pleased by Mona's quick pace of play, Phiona gets lured into her opponent's rhythm and plays too fast, leading to fatal errors. Mona plays flawlessly and needs just twenty-four moves to win. When Phiona concedes after less than an hour, Katende looks worried, but Phiona recognizes that on this day she's been beaten by a better player. Instead of being discouraged, she is inspired. Phiona walks straight over to Katende and says, "Coach, I will be a grandmaster someday."

She looks relieved, and a bit astonished, to have spoken those words.

Chess had transported Phiona out of Katwe once before. In August 2009, she traveled with Benjamin and Ivan to Juba, Sudan, where the three represented Uganda in Africa's International Children's Chess Tournament. Several other players who had qualified to join them on the national team refused to go with the slum kids.

It was Phiona's first trip out of Uganda, her first visit to an airport. "It felt like taking someone from the nineteenth century and plunging them into the present world," says Godfrey Gali, the Uganda Chess Federation's general secretary. "Everything at the airport was so strange to her; security cameras, luggage conveyors, so many white people. Then when the plane flew above the clouds, Phiona asked me, 'Mr. Gali, are we about to reach heaven?' She was totally sincere."

At their hotel in Sudan, Phiona had her own bed for the first time in her life. She had never before used a toilet that flushed. At the hotel restaurant she was handed a huge menu, a strange notion for someone who had never had a choice of what to eat at a meal before. "I could never have imagined this world I was visiting," Phiona says. "I felt like a queen."

In the tournament, the Ugandan trio, by far the youngest team in the competition, played against teams from sixteen other African nations. In her opening match, Phiona faced a Kenyan who had a reputation as the best young female player in Africa. Despite her hands trembling with each early move, Phiona built a position advantage, isolated the enemy king, then checkmated her surprised opponent. Phiona won all four matches she played. Benjamin and Ivan were undefeated as well, and the three kids from Katwe won the team championship and a trophy too big to fit into any of their tiny backpacks.

A stunned Russian chess administrator, Igor Bolotinsky, approached Phiona after the tournament and told her, "I have a son who is an international chess master, and he was not as good at your age as you are."

When the Ugandan delegation returned to Kampala, Katende met them at the airport. He tried to congratulate Phiona, but she was too busy laughing and teasing her teammates, something he had never seen her do before. For once, he realized, Phiona was just being the kid that she is.

But as Phiona, Benjamin, and Ivan were driven back into Katwe for a victory celebration, a psychological shift took place. Windows in their van were reflexively shut and backpacks pushed out of sight. Smiling faces turned solemn, the mask of the slum. The three children discussed who would keep the trophy, and it was decided that none of them could because it would surely be stolen. They were greeted with cheers and chants of "Uganda! Uganda! Uganda!" But they were also met with some strange questions: *Did you fly on the silver bird? Did you stay indoors, or in the bush? Why did you come back here?*

"It struck me how difficult it must have been for them to go to another world and return," says Rodney Suddith, the director of Sports Outreach. "Sudan might as well be the moon to people in the slum. The three kids couldn't share their experience with the others because they just couldn't connect. It puzzled me at first, and then it made me sad, and then I wondered, *Is what they have done really a good thing?*"

As Phiona left the celebration headed for her home that night, someone excitedly asked her, "What is the first thing you're going to say to your mother?"

"I need to ask her," Phiona said, "'Do we have enough food for breakfast?'"

* * *

Who is she? Is Phiona trying to prove that she's no better than anyone else or that she's better than everyone else? Imagine that psychological tug-of-war inside the mind of the least secure creature on earth, a teenage girl, as she sits at a chessboard nearly five thousand miles from home.

Phiona's opponent in her fourth match, an Angolan, Sonia Rosalina, keeps staring at Phiona's eyes, which Rosalina will later say are the most competitive she has faced in chess. Phiona is behind for most of the match, but refuses to surrender. She battles back and has a chance to force a draw in the end game, but at the critical moment, she plays too passively, too defensively, not like herself. After more than three hours and 144 moves, Phiona grudgingly submits, admitting that she didn't have her "courage" when she needed it most. She promises herself that she will never let that happen again.

No matter how far chess has taken Phiona Mutesi, a ten-foot by ten-foot home in Katwe remains her destination—the life of the ultimate underdog is still her routine. Although Phiona is back in school through a grant from Sports Outreach, she is just learning to read and write. Also, Phiona faces a potential hazard that could make her life even more challenging: Her father died of AIDS, and her mother worries her constant illnesses are because she is HIV-positive, but she is too afraid to be tested. Phiona has never been tested either.

Phiona says that her dream for the future is to build a house outside Katwe for her mother so that she would never have to move again. When Harriet is asked if her daughter can escape the slum, she says, "I have never thought about that." Ugandan universities are not handing out scholarships for chess, and, without benefactors stepping in again, a trip to the 2012 Olympiad in Istanbul, Turkey, is unlikely.

Katende, when pressed to describe Phiona's realistic blueprint out of Katwe, can come up only with a vision he's had about starting an academy where the children of the chess project earn money teaching the game to kids of wealthy families. He says he hopes through her chess that Phiona can begin to blaze a trail out of the slum for all of his chess kids to follow. To do that, though, Phiona must produce on a world stage like no other Ugandan, man or woman, has ever achieved.

September 30, 2010. In Khanty-Mansiysk it is cold and dreary, like every other day at the Olympiad. Phiona hates Russian weather but loves the hotel room, the clean water, the three meals a day. She is dreading her return home in four days, when she must begin scrapping for food again.

She sits at the chessboard for her fifth match wearing a white knit hat, a black overcoat and woolly beige boots that are several sizes too large, all gifts from various mzungu. *Her opponent is an Ethiopian, Haregeweyn Abera, who, like Phiona, is an African teenager. For the first time in the tournament, Phiona sees someone across the table she can relate to. She sees herself. For the first time in the tournament, she is not intimidated at all.*

Phiona plays black but remains patient and gradually shifts the momentum during the first twenty moves of the match until she creates an opening to attack. Suddenly she feels like she is back at Agape church, pushing and pushing and pushing Abera's pieces into retreat until there is nowhere left for Abera to move.

Abera extends her hand in defeat. Phiona tries and fails to suppress her gap-toothed grin, then rises and skips out of the hall into the frigid Siberian air. This dismissed girl from a dismissed world cocks her head back and unleashes a blissful shriek into the slate gray sky, loud enough to startle players still inside the arena.

WILLIAM DERESIEWICZ

■

Solitude and Leadership

FROM *The American Scholar*, originally delivered to a recent plebe
class at the United States Military Academy at West Point

MY TITLE MUST SEEM LIKE A CONTRADICTION. What can solitude
have to do with leadership? Solitude means being alone, and leadership necessitates the presence of others—the people you're leading.
When we think about leadership in American history we are likely to
think of Washington, at the head of an army, or Lincoln, at the head
of a nation, or King, at the head of a movement—people with multitudes behind them, looking to them for direction. And when we
think of solitude, we are apt to think of Thoreau, a man alone in the
woods, keeping a journal and communing with nature in silence.

Leadership is what you are here to learn—the qualities of character
and mind that will make you fit to command a platoon, and beyond
that, perhaps, a company, a battalion, or, if you leave the military, a
corporation, a foundation, a department of government. *Solitude* is
what you have the least of here, especially as plebes. You don't even
have privacy, the opportunity simply to be physically alone, never
mind solitude, the ability to be alone with your thoughts. And yet I
submit to you that solitude is one of the most important necessities
of true leadership. This lecture will be an attempt to explain why.

We need to begin by talking about what leadership really means. I just
spent ten years teaching at another institution that, like West Point,
liked to talk a lot about leadership, Yale University. A school that
some of you might have gone to had you not come here, that some of
your friends might be going to. And if not Yale, then Harvard, Stan-

ford, MIT, and so forth. These institutions, like West Point, also see their role as the training of leaders, constantly encourage their students, like West Point, to regard themselves as leaders among their peers and future leaders of society. Indeed, when we look around at the American elite, the people in charge of government, business, academia, and all our other major institutions—senators, judges, CEOs, college presidents, and so forth—we find that they come overwhelmingly either from the Ivy League and its peer institutions or from the service academies, especially West Point.

So I began to wonder, as I taught at Yale, what leadership really consists of. My students, like you, were energetic, accomplished, smart, and often ferociously ambitious, but was that enough to make them leaders? Most of them, as much as I liked and even admired them, certainly didn't seem to me like leaders. Does being a leader, I wondered, just mean being accomplished, being successful? Does getting straight As make you a leader? I didn't think so. Great heart surgeons or great novelists or great shortstops may be terrific at what they do, but that doesn't mean they're leaders. Leadership and aptitude, leadership and achievement, leadership and even excellence have to be different things, otherwise the concept of leadership has no meaning. And it seemed to me that that had to be especially true of the kind of excellence I saw in the students around me.

See, things have changed since I went to college in the eighties. Everything has gotten much more intense. You have to do much more now to get into a top school like Yale or West Point, and you have to start a lot earlier. We didn't begin thinking about college until we were juniors, and maybe we each did a couple of extracurriculars. But I know what it's like for you guys now. It's an endless series of hoops that you have to jump through, starting from way back, maybe as early as junior high school. Classes, standardized tests, extracurriculars in school, extracurriculars outside of school. Test prep courses, admissions coaches, private tutors. I sat on the Yale College admissions committee a couple of years ago. The first thing the admissions officer would do when presenting a case to the rest of the committee was read what they call the "brag" in admissions lingo, the list of the student's extracurriculars. Well, it turned out that a student who had six or seven extracurriculars was already in trouble. Because the students who got in—in addition to perfect grades and top scores—usually had ten or twelve.

So what I saw around me were great kids who had been trained to be world-class hoop jumpers. Any goal you set them, they could achieve. Any test you gave them, they could pass with flying colors. They were, as one of them put it herself, "excellent sheep." I had no doubt that they would continue to jump through hoops and ace tests and go on to Harvard Business School, or Michigan Law School, or Johns Hopkins Medical School, or Goldman Sachs, or McKinsey Consulting, or whatever. And this approach would indeed take them far in life. They would come back for their twenty-fifth reunion as a partner at White & Case, or an attending physician at Mass General, or an assistant secretary in the Department of State.

That is exactly what places like Yale mean when they talk about training leaders. Educating people who make a big name for themselves in the world, people with impressive titles, people the university can brag about. People who make it to the top. People who can climb the greasy pole of whatever hierarchy they decide to attach themselves to.

But I think there's something desperately wrong, and even dangerous, about that idea. To explain why, I want to spend a few minutes talking about a novel that many of you may have read, *Heart of Darkness.* If you haven't read it, you've probably seen *Apocalypse Now,* which is based on it. Marlow in the novel becomes Captain Willard, played by Martin Sheen. Kurtz in the novel becomes Colonel Kurtz, played by Marlon Brando. But the novel isn't about Vietnam; it's about colonialism in the Belgian Congo three generations before Vietnam. Marlow, not a military officer but a merchant marine, a civilian ship's captain, is sent by the company that's running the country under charter from the Belgian crown to sail deep upriver, up the Congo River, to retrieve a manager who's ensconced himself in the jungle and gone rogue, just like Colonel Kurtz does in the movie.

Now everyone knows that the novel is about imperialism and colonialism and race relations and the darkness that lies in the human heart, but it became clear to me at a certain point, as I taught the novel, that it is also about bureaucracy—what I called, a minute ago, hierarchy. The Company, after all, is just that: a company, with rules and procedures and ranks and people in power and people scrambling for power, just like any other bureaucracy. Just like a big law firm or a governmental department or, for that matter, a university. Just like—and here's why I'm telling you all this—just like the bureaucracy you are about to join. The word *bureaucracy* tends to have negative connotations, but I say this in no way as a criticism, merely a description, that the U.S. Army is a bureaucracy and one of the largest and most famously bureaucratic bureaucracies in the world. After all, it was the Army that gave us, among other things, the indispensable bureaucratic acronym "snafu": "situation normal: all fucked up"—or "all fouled up" in the cleaned-up version. That comes from the U.S. Army in World War II.

You need to know that when you get your commission, you'll be joining a bureaucracy, and however long you stay in the Army, you'll be operating within a bureaucracy. As different as the armed forces are in so many ways from every other institution in society, in that respect they are the same. And so you need to know how bureaucracies operate, what kind of behavior—what kind of character—they reward, and what kind they punish.

So, back to the novel. Marlow proceeds upriver by stages, just like Captain Willard does in the movie. First he gets to the Outer Station. Kurtz is at the Inner Station. In between is the Central Station, where Marlow spends the most time, and where we get our best look at bureaucracy in action and the kind of people who succeed in it. This is Marlow's description of the manager of the Central Station, the big boss:

> He was commonplace in complexion, in features, in manners, and in voice. He was of middle size and of ordinary build. His eyes, of the usual blue, were perhaps remarkably cold .... Otherwise there was only an indefinable, faint expression of his lips, something stealthy—a smile—not a smile—I remember it, but I can't explain .... He was a common trader, from his youth up employed in these parts—nothing more. He was obeyed, yet he inspired neither love nor fear, nor even respect. He inspired uneasiness. That was it! Uneasiness. Not a definite mistrust—just uneasiness—nothing more. You have no

idea how effective such a . . . faculty can be. He had no genius for organizing, for initiative, or for order even . . . . He had no learning, and no intelligence. His position had come to him—why? . . . He originated nothing, he could keep the routine going—that's all. But he was great. He was great by this little thing that it was impossible to tell what could control such a man. He never gave that secret away. Perhaps there was nothing within him. Such a suspicion made one pause.

Note the adjectives: *commonplace, ordinary, usual, common.* There is nothing distinguished about this person. About the tenth time I read that passage, I realized it was a perfect description of the kind of person who tends to prosper in the bureaucratic environment. And the only reason I did is because it suddenly struck me that it was a perfect description of the head of the bureaucracy that I was part of, the chairman of my academic department—who had that exact same smile, like a shark, and that exact same ability to make you uneasy, like you were doing something wrong, only she wasn't ever going to tell you what. Like the manager—and I'm sorry to say this, but like so many people you will meet as you negotiate the bureaucracy of the Army or for that matter of whatever institution you end up giving your talents to after the Army, whether it's Microsoft or the World Bank or whatever—the head of my department had no genius for organizing or initiative or even order, no particular learning or intelligence, no distinguishing characteristics at all. Just the ability to keep the routine going, and beyond that, as Marlow says, her position had come to her—why?

That's really the great mystery about bureaucracies. Why is it so often that the best people are stuck in the middle and the people who are running things—the leaders—are the mediocrities? Because excellence isn't usually what gets you up the greasy pole. What gets you up is a talent for maneuvering. Kissing up to the people above you, kicking down to the people below you. Pleasing your teachers, pleasing your superiors, picking a powerful mentor and riding his coattails until it's time to stab him in the back. Jumping through hoops. Getting along by going along. Being whatever other people want you to be, so that it finally comes to seem that, like the manager of the Central Station, you have nothing inside you at all. Not taking stupid risks like trying to change how things are done or question why they're done. Just keeping the routine going.

I tell you this to forewarn you, because I promise you that you will meet these people and you will find yourself in environments where what is rewarded above all is conformity. I tell you so you can decide to be a different kind of leader. And I tell you for one other reason. As I thought about these things and put all these pieces together—the kind of students I had, the kind of leadership they were being trained for, the kind of leaders I saw in my own institution—I realized that this is a national problem. We have a crisis of leadership in this country, in every institution. Not just in government. Look at what happened to American corporations in recent decades, as all the old dinosaurs like General Motors or TWA or U.S. Steel fell apart. Look at what happened to Wall Street in just the last couple of years.

Finally—and I know I'm on sensitive ground here—look at what happened during the first four years of the Iraq War. We were stuck. It wasn't the fault of the enlisted ranks or the noncoms or the junior officers. It was the fault of the senior leadership, whether military or civilian or both. We weren't just not winning, we weren't even changing direction.

We have a crisis of leadership in America because our overwhelming power and wealth, earned under earlier generations of leaders, made us complacent, and for too long we have been training leaders who only know how to keep the routine going. Who can answer questions, but don't know how to ask them. Who can fulfill goals, but don't know how to set them. Who think about *how* to get things done, but not whether they're worth doing in the first place. What we have now are the greatest technocrats the world has ever seen, people who have been trained to be incredibly good at one specific thing, but who have no interest in anything beyond their area of expertise. What we *don't* have are leaders.

What we don't have, in other words, are *thinkers*. People who can think for themselves. People who can formulate a new direction: for the country, for a corporation or a college, for the Army—a new way of doing things, a new way of looking at things. People, in other words, with *vision*.

Now some people would say, *Great. Tell this to the kids at Yale, but why bother telling it to the ones at West Point?* Most people, when they think of this institution, assume that it's the last place anyone would want to talk about thinking creatively or cultivating independence of mind. It's the Army, after all. It's no accident that the word *regiment* is the root of the word *regimentation.* Surely you who have come here must be the ultimate conformists. Must be people who have bought in to the way things are and have no interest in changing it. Are not the kind of young people who think about the world, who ponder the big issues, who question authority. If you were, you would have gone to Amherst or Pomona. You're at West Point to be told what to do and how to think.

But you know that's not true. I know it, too; otherwise I would never have been invited to talk to you, and I'm even more convinced of it now that I've spent a few days on campus. To quote Colonel Scott Krawczyk, your course director, in a lecture he gave last year to English 102:

> From the very earliest days of this country, the model for our offi-cers, which was built on the model of the citizenry and reflective of democratic ideals, was to be different. They were to be possessed of a democratic spirit marked by independent judgment, the freedom to measure action and to express disagreement, and the crucial respon-sibility never to tolerate tyranny.

All the more so now. Anyone who's been paying attention for the last few years understands that the changing nature of warfare means that officers, including junior officers, are required more than ever to be able to think independently, creatively, flexibly. To deploy a whole range of skills in a fluid and complex situation. Lieutenant colonels who are essentially functioning as provincial governors in Iraq, or captains who find themselves in charge of a remote town somewhere in Afghanistan. People who know how to do more than follow orders and execute routines.

Look at the most successful, most acclaimed, and perhaps the fin-est soldier of his generation, General David Petraeus. He's one of those rare people who rises through a bureaucracy for the right rea-sons. He is a thinker. He is an intellectual. In fact, *Prospect* magazine named him Public Intellectual of the Year in 2008—that's *in the world*. He has a Ph.D. from Princeton, but what makes him a thinker is not that he has a Ph.D. or that he went to Princeton or even that he taught at West Point. I can assure you from personal experience that there are a lot of highly educated people who don't know how to think at all.

No, what makes him a thinker—and a leader—is precisely that he is able to think things through for himself. And because he can, he has the confidence, the *courage*, to argue for his ideas even when they aren't popular. Even when they don't please his superiors. Courage: There is physical courage, which you all possess in abundance, and then there is another kind of courage, moral courage, the courage to stand up for what you believe.

It wasn't always easy for him. His path to where he is now was not a straight one. When he was running Mosul in 2003 as commander of the 101st Airborne and developing the strategy he would later formulate in the *Counterinsurgency Field Manual* and then ultimately apply throughout Iraq, he pissed a lot of people off. He was way ahead of the leadership in Baghdad and Washington, and bureaucracies don't like that sort of thing. Here he was, just another two-star, and he was saying, implicitly but loudly, that the leadership was wrong about the way it was running the war. Indeed, he was not rewarded at first. He was put in charge of training the Iraqi army, which was considered a blow to his career, a dead-end job. But he stuck to his guns, and ultimately he was vindicated. Ironically, one of the central elements of his counterinsurgency strategy is precisely the idea that officers need to think flexibly, creatively, and independently.

That's the first half of the lecture: the idea that true leadership means being able to think for yourself and act on your convictions. But how do you learn to do that? How do you learn to think? Let's start with how you *don't* learn to think. A study by a team of researchers at Stanford came out a couple of months ago. The investigators wanted to figure out how today's college students were able to multitask so much more effectively than adults. How do they manage to do it, the researchers asked? The answer, they discovered—and this is by no means what they expected—is that they don't. The enhanced cognitive abilities the investigators expected to find, the mental faculties that enable people to multitask effectively, were simply not there. In other words, people do not multitask effectively. And here's the really surprising finding: the more people multitask, the worse they are, not just at other mental abilities, but at multitasking itself.

One thing that made the study different from others is that the researchers didn't test people's cognitive functions while they were multitasking. They separated the subject group into high multitaskers and low multitaskers and used a different set of tests to measure the kinds of cognitive abilities involved in multitasking. They found that in every case the high multitaskers scored worse. They were worse at distinguishing between relevant and irrelevant information and ignoring the latter. In other words, they were more distractible. They were worse at what you might call "mental filing": keeping information in the right conceptual boxes and being able to retrieve it quickly. In other words, their minds were more disorganized. And they were even worse at the very thing that defines multitasking itself: switching between tasks.

Multitasking, in short, is not only not thinking, it impairs your ability to think. *Thinking means concentrating on one thing long enough to develop an idea about it.* Not learning other people's ideas, or memorizing a body of information, however much those may sometimes be useful. Developing your own ideas. In short, thinking for yourself. You simply cannot do that in bursts of 20 seconds at a time, constantly interrupted by Facebook messages or Twitter tweets, or fiddling with your iPod, or watching something on YouTube.

I find for myself that my first thought is never my best thought. My first thought is always someone else's; it's always what I've already heard about the subject, always the conventional wisdom. It's only by concentrating, sticking to the question, being patient, letting all the parts of my mind come into play, that I arrive at an original idea. By giving my brain a chance to make associations, draw connections, take me by surprise. And often even that idea doesn't turn out to be very good. I need time to think about it, too, to make mistakes and recognize them, to make false starts and correct them, to outlast my impulses, to defeat my desire to declare the job done and move on to the next thing.

I used to have students who bragged to me about how fast they wrote their papers. I would tell them that the great German novelist Thomas Mann said that a writer is someone for whom writing is more difficult than it is for other people. The best writers write much more slowly than everyone else, and the better they are, the slower they write. James Joyce wrote *Ulysses*, the greatest novel of the twentieth century, at the rate of about a hundred words a day—half the length of the selection I read you earlier from *Heart of Darkness*—for seven years. T. S. Eliot, one of the greatest poets our country has ever produced, wrote about 150 pages of poetry over the course of his entire twenty-five-year career. That's half a page a month. So it is with any other form of thought. You do your best thinking by slowing down and concentrating.

Now that's the third time I've used that word, *concentrating*. Concentrating, focusing. You can just as easily consider this lecture to be about concentration as about solitude. Think about what the word means. It means gathering yourself together into a single point rather than letting yourself be dispersed everywhere into a cloud of electronic and social input. It seems to me that Facebook and Twitter and YouTube—and just so you don't think this is a generational thing, TV and radio and magazines and even newspapers, too—are all ultimately just an elaborate excuse to run away from yourself. To avoid the difficult and troubling questions that being human throws in your way. Am I doing the right thing with my life? Do I believe the things I was taught as a child? What do the words I live by—words like *duty*, *honor*, and *country*—really mean? Am I happy?

You and the members of the other service academies are in a unique position among college students, especially today. Not only do you know that you're going to have a job when you graduate, you even know who your employer is going to be. But what happens after you fulfill your commitment to the Army? Unless you know who you are, how will you figure out what you want to do with the rest of your life? Unless you're able to listen to yourself, to that quiet voice inside that tells you what you really care about, what you really believe in—indeed, how those things might be evolving under the pressure of your experiences. Students everywhere else agonize over these questions, and while you may not be doing so now, you are only post-poning them for a few years.

Maybe some of you *are* agonizing over them now. Not everyone who starts here decides to finish here. It's no wonder and no cause for shame. You are being put through the most demanding training anyone can ask of people your age, and you are committing your-self to work of awesome responsibility and mortal danger. The very rigor and regimentation to which you are quite properly subject here naturally has a tendency to make you lose touch with the passion that brought you here in the first place. I saw exactly the same kind of thing at Yale. It's not that my students were robots. Quite the re-verse. They were intensely idealistic, but the overwhelming weight of their practical responsibilities, all of those hoops they had to jump through, often made them lose sight of what those ideals were. Why they were doing it all in the first place.

So it's perfectly natural to have doubts, or questions, or even just difficulties. The question is, what do you do with them? Do you sup-press them, do you distract yourself from them, do you pretend they don't exist? Or do you confront them directly, honestly, courageously? If you decide to do so, you will find that the answers to these dilem-mas are not to be found on Twitter or Comedy Central or even in *New York Times*. They can only be found within—without distractions, without peer pressure, in solitude.

But let me be clear that solitude doesn't always have to mean intro-spection. Let's go back to *Heart of Darkness*. It's the solitude of con-centration that saves Marlow amidst the madness of the Central Station. When he gets there he finds out that the steamboat he's sup-posed to sail upriver has a giant hole in it, and no one is going to help him fix it. "I let him run on," he says, "this *papier-mâché* Mephistoph-eles"—he's talking not about the manager but his assistant, who's even worse, since he's still trying to kiss his way up the hierarchy, and who's been raving away at him. You can think of him as the In-ternet, the ever-present social buzz, chattering away at you 24/7:

> I let him run on, this papier-mâché Mephistopheles and it seemed to
> me that if I tried I could poke my forefinger through him, and would

find nothing inside but a little loose dirt . . . . It was a great comfort to turn from that chap to . . . the battered, twisted, ruined, tin-pot steamboat . . . . I had expended enough hard work on her to make me love her. No influential friend would have served me better. She had given me a chance to come out a bit—to find out what I could do. No, I don't like work. I had rather laze about and think of all the fine things that can be done. I don't like work—no man does—but I like what is in the work,—the chance to find yourself. Your own reality—for yourself, not for others—what no other man can ever know.

"The chance to find yourself." Now that phrase, "finding yourself," has acquired a bad reputation. It suggests an aimless liberal-arts college graduate—an English major, no doubt, someone who went to a place like Amherst or Pomona—who's too spoiled to get a job and spends his time staring off into space. But here's Marlow, a mariner, a ship's captain. A more practical, hardheaded person you could not find. And I should say that Marlow's creator, Conrad, spent nineteen years as a merchant marine, eight of them as a ship's captain, before he became a writer, so this wasn't just some artist's idea of a sailor. Marlow believes in the need to find yourself just as much as anyone does, and the way to do it, he says, is work, solitary work. Concentration. Climbing on that steamboat and spending a few uninterrupted hours hammering it into shape. Or building a house, or cooking a meal, or even writing a college paper, if you really put yourself into it.

"Your own reality—for yourself, not for others." Thinking for yourself means finding yourself, finding your own reality. Here's the other problem with Facebook and Twitter and even *New York Times*. When you expose yourself to those things, especially in the constant way that people do now—older people as well as younger people—you are continuously bombarding yourself with a stream of other people's thoughts. You are marinating yourself in the conventional wisdom. In other people's reality: for others, not for yourself. You are creating a cacophony in which it is impossible to hear your own voice, whether it's yourself you're thinking about or anything else. That's what Emerson meant when he said that "he who should inspire and lead his race must be defended from travelling with the souls of other men, from living, breathing, reading, and writing in the daily, time-worn yoke of their opinions." Notice that he uses the word *lead*. Leadership means finding a new direction, not simply putting yourself at the front of the herd that's heading toward the cliff.

So why is reading books any better than reading tweets or wall posts? Well, sometimes it isn't. Sometimes, you need to put down your book, if only to think about what you're reading, what *you* think about what you're reading. But a book has two advantages over a tweet. First, the person who wrote it thought about it a lot more carefully. The book is the result of *his* solitude, *his* attempt to think for himself.

Second, most books are old. This is not a disadvantage: this is precisely what makes them valuable. They stand against the conventional wisdom of today simply because they're not *from* today. Even if they merely reflect the conventional wisdom of their own day, they say something different from what you hear all the time. But the great books, the ones you find on a syllabus, the ones people have continued to read, don't reflect the conventional wisdom of their day. They say things that have the permanent power to disrupt our habits of thought. They were revolutionary in their own time, and they are still revolutionary today. And when I say "revolutionary," I am deliberately evoking the American Revolution, because it was a result of precisely this kind of independent thinking. Without solitude—the solitude of Adams and Jefferson and Hamilton and Madison and Thomas Paine—there would be no America.

So solitude can mean introspection, it can mean the concentration of focused work, and it can mean sustained reading. All of these help you to know yourself better. But there's one more thing I'm going to include as a form of solitude, and it will seem counterintuitive: friendship. Of course friendship is the opposite of solitude; it means being with other people. But I'm talking about one kind of friendship in particular, the deep friendship of intimate conversation. Long, uninterrupted talk with one other person. Not Skyping with three people and texting with two others at the same time while you hang out in a friend's room listening to music and studying. That's what Emerson meant when he said that "the soul environs itself with friends, that it may enter into a grander self-acquaintance or solitude."

Introspection means talking to yourself, and one of the best ways of talking to yourself is by talking to another person. One other person you can trust, one other person to whom you can unfold your soul. One other person you feel safe enough with to allow you to acknowledge things — to acknowledge things to yourself — that you otherwise can't. Doubts you aren't supposed to have, questions you aren't supposed to ask. Feelings or opinions that would get you laughed at by the group or reprimanded by the authorities.

This is what we call thinking out loud, discovering what you believe in the course of articulating it. But it takes just as much time and just as much patience as solitude in the strict sense. And our new electronic world has disrupted it just as violently. Instead of having one or two true friends that we can sit and talk to for three hours at a time, we have 968 "friends" that we never actually talk to; instead we just bounce one-line messages off them a hundred times a day. This is not friendship, this is distraction.

I know that none of this is easy for you. Even if you threw away your cell phones and unplugged your computers, the rigors of your training here keep you too busy to make solitude, in any of these forms, anything less than very difficult to find. But the highest reason you need to try is precisely because of what the job you are training *for* will demand of you.

You've probably heard about the hazing scandal at the U.S. naval base in Bahrain that was all over the news recently. Terrible, abusive stuff that involved an entire unit and was orchestrated, allegedly, by the head of the unit, a senior noncommissioned officer. What are you going to do if you're confronted with a situation like that going on in *your* unit? Will you have the courage to do what's right? Will you even know what the right thing is? It's easy to read a code of conduct, not so easy to put it into practice, especially if you risk losing the loyalty of the people serving under you, or the trust of your peer officers, or the approval of your superiors. What if you're not the commanding officer, but you see your superiors condoning something you think is wrong?

How will you find the strength and wisdom to challenge an unwise order or question a wrongheaded policy? What will you do the first time you have to write a letter to the mother of a slain soldier? How will you find words of comfort that are more than just empty formulas?

These are truly formidable dilemmas, more so than most other people will ever have to face in their lives, let alone when they're twenty-three. The time to start preparing yourself for them is now. And the way to do it is by thinking through these issues for yourself—morality, mortality, honor—so you will have the strength to deal with them when they arise. Waiting until you have to confront them in practice would be like waiting for your first firefight to learn how to shoot your weapon. Once the situation is upon you, it's too late. You have to be prepared in advance. You need to know, already, who you are and what you believe: not what the Army believes, not what your peers believe (that may be exactly the problem), but what *you* believe.

How can you know that unless you've taken counsel with yourself in solitude? I started by noting that solitude and leadership would seem to be contradictory things. But it seems to me that solitude is the very essence of leadership. The position of the leader is ultimately an intensely solitary, even intensely lonely one. However many people you may consult, you are the one who has to make the hard decisions. And at such moments, all you really have is yourself.

ANTHONY DOERR

■

The Deep

FROM *Zoetrope: All-Story*

TOM IS BORN IN 1914 IN DETROIT, a quarter mile from International Salt. His father is offstage, unaccounted for. His mother operates a six-room, under-insulated boarding house populated with locked doors, behind which drowse the grim possessions of itinerant salt workers: coats the colors of mice, tattered mucking boots, aquatints of undressed women, their breasts faded orange. Every six months a miner is laid off, gets drafted, or dies, and is replaced by another, so that very early in his life Tom comes to see how the world continually drains itself of young men, leaving behind only objects—empty tobacco pouches, bladeless jackknives, salt-caked trousers—mute, incapable of memory.

Tom is four when he starts fainting. He'll be rounding a corner, breathing hard, and the lights will go out. Mother will carry him indoors, set him on the armchair, and send someone for the doctor.

Atrial septal defect. Hole in the heart. The doctor says blood sloshes from the left side to the right side. His heart will have to do three times the work. Lifespan of sixteen. Eighteen if he's lucky. Best if he doesn't get excited.

Mother trains her voice into a whisper. *Here you go, there you are, sweet little Tomcat.* She moves Tom's cot into an upstairs closet—no bright lights, no loud noises. Mornings she serves him a glass of buttermilk, then points him to the brooms or steel wool. *Go slow,* she'll murmur. He scrubs the coal stove, sweeps the marble stoop. Every so often he peers up from his work and watches the face of the oldest boarder, Mr. Weems, as he troops downstairs, a fifty-year-old man hooded against the cold, off to descend in an elevator a thousand feet underground. Tom imagines his descent, sporadic and dim lights passing and receding, cables rattling, a half-dozen other miners squeezed into the cage beside him, each thinking their own thoughts, men's thoughts, sinking down into that city beneath the city where mules stand waiting and oil lamps burn in the walls and glittering rooms of salt recede into vast arcades beyond the farthest reaches of the light.

Sixteen, thinks Tom. *Eighteen if I'm lucky.*

School is a three-room shed aswarm with the offspring of salt workers, coal workers, ironworkers. Irish kids, Polish kids, Armenian kids. To Mother the schoolyard seems a thousand acres of sizzling pandemonium. *Don't run, don't fight*, she whispers. No games. His first day, she pulls him out of class after an hour. *Shhh*, she says, and wraps her arms around his like ropes.

Tom seesaws in and out of the early grades. Sometimes she keeps him out of school for whole weeks at a time. By the time he's ten, he's in remedial everything. *I'm trying*, he stammers, but letters spin off pages and dash against the windows like snow. *Dunce*, the other boys declare, and to Tom that seems about right.

Tom sweeps, scrubs, scours the stoop with pumice one square-inch at a time. *Slow as molasses in January*, says Mr. Weems, but he winks at Tom when he says it.

Every day, all day, the salt finds its way in. It encrusts washbasins, settles on the rims of baseboards. It spills out of the boarders, too: from ears, boots, handkerchiefs. Furrows of glitter gather in the bed-sheets: a daily lesson in insidiousness.

Start at the edges, then scrub out the center. Linens on Thursdays. Toilets on Fridays.

He's twelve when Ms. Fredericks asks the children to give reports. Ruby Hornaday goes sixth. Ruby has flames for hair, Christmas for a birthday, and a drunk for a daddy. She's one of two girls to make it to fourth grade.

She reads from notes in controlled terror. *If you think the lake is big you should see the sea. It's three quarters of Earth. And that's just the surface.* Someone throws a pencil. The creases on Ruby's forehead deepen. *Land animals live on ground or in trees rats and worms and gulls and such. But sea animals they live everywhere they live in the waves and they live in mid water and they live in canyons six and a half miles down.*

She passes around a red book. Inside are blocks of text and full-color photographic plates that make Tom's heart boom in his ears. A blizzard of toothy minnows. A kingdom of purple corals. Five orange starfish cemented to a rock.

Ruby says, *Detroit used to have palm trees and corals and seashells. Detroit used to be a sea three miles deep.*

Ms. Fredericks asks, *Ruby, where did you get that book?* but by then Tom is hardly breathing. See-through flowers with poison tentacles and fields of clams and pink spheres with a thousand needles on their backs. He tries to ask, *Are these real?* but quicksilver bubbles rise from his mouth and float up to the ceiling. When he goes over, the desk goes over with him.

The doctor says it's best if Tom stays out of school and Mother agrees. *Keep indoors,* the doctor says. *If you get excited, think of something blue.* Mother lets him come downstairs for meals and chores only. Otherwise he's to stay in his closet. *We have to be more careful, Tomcat,* she whispers, and sets her palm on his forehead.

Tom spends long hours on the floor beside his cot, assembling and reassembling the same jigsaw puzzle: a Swiss village. Five hundred pieces, nine of them missing. Sometimes Mr. Weems reads to Tom from adventure novels. They're blasting a new vein down in the mines and in the lulls between Mr. Weems's words, Tom can feel explosions reverberate up through a thousand feet of rock and shake the fragile pump in his chest.

He misses school. He misses the sky. He misses everything. When Mr. Weems is in the mine and Mother is downstairs, Tom often slips to the end of the hall and lifts aside the curtains and presses his forehead to the glass. Children run the snowy lanes and lights glow in the foundry windows and train cars trundle beneath elevated conduits. First-shift miners emerge from the mouth of the hauling elevator in groups of six and bring out cigarette cases from their overalls and strike matches and spill like little, salt-dusted insects out into the night, while the darker figures of the second-shift miners stamp their feet in the cold, waiting outside the cages for their turn in the pit.

In dreams he sees waving sea fans and milling schools of grouper and underwater shafts of light. He sees Ruby Hornaday push open the door of his closet. She's wearing a copper diving helmet; she leans over his cot and puts the window of her helmet an inch from his face.

He wakes with a shock. Heat pools in his groin. He thinks, *Blue, blue, blue.*

One drizzly Saturday, the bell rings. When Tom opens the door, Ruby Hornaday is standing on the stoop in the rain.

Hello. Tom blinks a dozen times. Raindrops set a thousand intersecting circles upon the puddles in the road. Ruby holds up a jar: six black tadpoles squirm in an inch of water.

Seemed like you might be interested in water creatures.

Tom tries to answer, but the whole sky is rushing through the open door into his mouth.

You're not going to faint again, are you?

Mr. Weems stumps into the foyer. *Jesus, boy, she's damp as a church, you got to invite a lady in.*

Ruby stands on the tiles and drips. Mr. Weems grins. Tom mumbles, *My heart.*

Ruby holds up the jar. *Keep 'em if you want. They'll be frogs before long.* Drops shine in her eyelashes. Rain glues her shirt to her clavicles. *Well, that's something,* says Mr. Weems. He nudges Tom in the back. *Isn't it, Tom?*

Tom is opening his mouth. He's saying, *Maybe I could*—when Mother comes down the stairs in her big, black shoes. *Trouble,* hisses Mr. Weems.

Mother dumps the tadpoles in a ditch. Her face says she's composing herself but her eyes say she's going to wipe all this away. Mr. Weems leans over the dominoes and whispers, *Mother's as hard as a cobblestone but we'll crack her, Tom, you wait.*

Tom whispers, *Ruby Hornaday,* into the space above his cot. *Ruby Hornaday. Ruby Hornaday.* A strange and uncontainable joy inflates dangerously in his chest.

Mr. Weems initiates long conversations with Mother in the kitchen. Tom overhears scraps: *Boy needs to move his legs. Boy should get some air.*

Mother's voice is a whip. *He's sick.*

He's alive! What're you saving him for?

Mother consents to let Tom retrieve coal from the depot and tinned goods from the commissary. Tuesdays he'll be allowed to walk to the butcher's in Dearborn. *Careful, Tomcat, don't hurry.*

Tom moves through the colony that first Tuesday with something close to rapture in his veins. Down the long gravel lanes, past pit cottages and surface mountains of blue and white salt, the warehouses like dark cathedrals, the hauling machines like demonic armatures. All around him the monumental industry of Detroit pounds and clangs. The boy tells himself he is a treasure hunter, a hero from one of Mr. Weems's adventure stories, a knight on important errands, a spy behind enemy lines. He keeps his hands in his pockets and his head down and his gait slow, but his soul charges ahead, weightless, jubilant, sparking through the gloom.

In May of that year, 1929, fourteen-year-old Tom is walking along the lane thinking spring happens whether you're paying attention or not; it happens beneath the snow, beyond the walls — spring happens in the dark while you dream — when Ruby Hornaday steps out of the weeds. She has a shriveled rubber hose coiled over her shoulder and a swim mask in one hand and a tire pump in the other. *Need your help.* Tom's pulse soars.

I got to go to the butcher's.

Your choice. Ruby turns to go. But really there is no choice at all.

She leads him west, away from the mine, through mounds of rusting machines. They hop a fence, cross a field gone to seed, and walk a quarter mile through pitch pines to a marsh where cattle egrets stand in the cattails like white flowers.

In my mouth, she says, and starts picking up rocks. *Out my nose. You pump, Tom. Understand?* In the green water two feet down Tom can make out the dim shapes of a few fish gliding through weedy enclaves.

Ruby pitches the far end of the hose into the water. With waxed cord she binds the other end to the pump. Then she fills her pockets with rocks. She wades out, looks back, says, *You pump,* and puts the hose into her mouth. The swim mask goes over her eyes; her face goes into the water.

The marsh closes over Ruby's back, and the hose trends away from the bank. Tom begins to pump. The sky slides along overhead. Loops of garden hose float under the light out there, shifting now and then. Occasional bubbles rise, moving gradually farther out.

One minute, two minutes. Tom pumps. His heart does its fragile work. He should not be here. He should not be here while this skinny, spellbinding girl drowns herself in a marsh. If that's what she's doing. One of Mr. Weems's similes comes to him: *You're trembling like a needle to the pole.*

After four or five minutes underwater, Ruby comes up. A neon mat of algae clings to her hair, and her bare feet are great boots of mud. She pushes through the cattails. Strings of saliva hang off her chin. Her lips are blue. Tom feels dizzy. The sky turns to liquid.

Incredible, pants Ruby. *Fucking incredible.* She holds up her wet, rock-filled trousers with both hands, and looks at Tom through the wavy lens of her swim mask. His blood storms through its lightless tunnels.

He has to trot to make the butcher's and get back home by noon. It is the first time Tom can remember permitting himself to run, and his legs feel like glass. At the end of the lane, a hundred yards from home, he stops and pants with the basket of meat in his arms and spits a pat of blood into the dandelions. Sweat soaks his shirt. Dragonflies dart and hover. Swallows inscribe letters across the sky. The street seems to ripple and fold and straighten itself out again.

Just a hundred yards more. He forces his heart to settle. *Everything*, Tom thinks, *follows a path worn by those who have gone before: egrets, clouds, tadpoles. Everything everything everything.*

The following Tuesday Ruby meets him at the end of the lane. And the Tuesday after that. They hop the fence, cross the field; she leads him places he's never dreamed existed. Places where the structures of the saltworks become white mirages on the horizon, places where sunlight washes through groves of maples and makes the ground quiver with leaf-shadow. They peer into a foundry where shirtless men in masks pour molten iron from one vat into another; they climb a tailings pile where a lone sapling grows like a single hand thrust up from the underworld. Tom knows he's risking everything—his freedom,

Mother's trust, even his life—but how can he stop? How can he say no? To say no to Ruby Hornaday would be to say no to the world.

Some Tuesdays Ruby brings along her red book with its images of corals and jellies and underwater volcanoes. She tells him that when she grows up she'll go to parties where hostesses row guests offshore and everyone puts on special helmets to go for strolls along the sea bottom. She tells him she'll be a diver who sinks herself a half mile into the sea in a steel ball with one window. In the basement of the ocean, she says, she'll find a separate universe, a place made of lights: schools of fish glowing green, living galaxies wheeling through the black.

In the ocean, says Ruby, *half the rocks are alive. Half the plants are animals.*

They hold hands; they chew Indian gum. She stuffs his mind full of kelp forests and seascapes and dolphins. *When I grow up*, says Ruby. *When I grow up . . .*

Four more times Ruby walks around beneath the surface of a River Rouge marsh while Tom stands on the bank working the pump. Four more times he watches her rise back out like a fever. *Amphibian*, she laughs. *It means two lives.*

Then Tom runs to the butcher's and runs home, and his heart races, and spots spread like ink blots in front of his eyes. Sometimes in the afternoons, when he stands up from his chores, his vision slides away in violet streaks. He sees the glowing white of the salt tunnels, the red of Ruby's book, the orange of her hair—he imagines her all grown up, standing on the bow of a ship, and feels a core of lemon yellow light flaring brighter and brighter within him. It spills from the slats between his ribs, from between his teeth, from the pupils of his eyes. He thinks: *It is so much! So much!*

So now you're fifteen. And the doctor says sixteen?

Eighteen if I'm lucky.

Ruby turns her book over in her hands. *What's it like? To know you won't get all the years you should?*

I don't feel so shortchanged when I'm with you, he wants to say but his voice breaks at *short* and the sentence fractures.

They kiss only that one time. It is clumsy. He shuts his eyes and leans in, but something shifts and Ruby is not where he expects her to be. Their teeth clash. When he opens his eyes, she is looking off to her left, smiling slightly, smelling of mud, and the thousand tiny blonde hairs on her upper lip catch the light.

The second-to-last time Tom and Ruby are together, on the last Tuesday of October, 1929, everything is strange. The hose leaks, Ruby is upset, a curtain has fallen somehow between them.

Go back, Ruby says. *It's probably noon already. You'll be late.* But she sounds as if she's speaking to him through a tunnel. Freckles flow and bloom across her face. The light goes out of the marsh.

On the long path through the pitch pines it begins to rain. Tom makes it to the butcher's and back home with the basket and the ground veal, but when he opens the door to Mother's parlor the curtains blow inward. The chairs leave their places and come scraping toward him. The daylight thins to a pair of beams, waving back and forth and Mr. Weems passes in front of his eyes, but Tom hears no footsteps, no voices: only an internal rushing and the wet metronome of his exhalations. Suddenly he's a diver staring through a thick, foggy window into a world of immense pressure. He's walking around on the bottom of the sea. Mother's lips say, *Haven't I given enough? Lord God, haven't I tried?* Then she's gone.

In something deeper than a dream Tom walks the salt roads a thousand feet beneath the house. At first it's all darkness, but after what might be a minute or a day or a year, he sees little flashes of green light out there in distant galleries, hundreds of feet away. Each flash initiates a chain reaction of further flashes beyond it, so that when he turns in a slow circle he can perceive great flowing signals of light in all directions, tunnels of green arcing out into the blackness—each flash glowing for only a moment before fading, but in that moment repeating everything that came before, everything that will come next.

He wakes to a deflated world. The newspapers are full of suicides; the price of gas has tripled. The miners whisper that the saltworks are in trouble.

Quart milk bottles sell for a dollar apiece. There's no butter, hardly any meat. Fruit becomes a memory. Most nights Mother serves only cabbage and soda bread. And salt.

No more trips to the butcher; the butcher is closed anyway. By November, Mother's boarders are vanishing. Mr. Beeson goes first, then Mr. Fackler. Tom waits for Ruby to come to the door but she doesn't show. Images of her climb the undersides of his eyelids, and he rubs them away. Each morning he clambers out of his closet and carries his traitorous heart down to the kitchen like an egg.

The world is swallowing people like candy, boy, says Mr. Weems. *No one is leaving addresses.*

Mr. Hanson goes next, then Mr. Heathcock. By April the saltworks is operating only two days a week, and Mr. Weems, Mother, and Tom are alone at supper.

Sixteen. Eighteen if he's lucky. Tom moves his few things into one of the empty boarders' rooms on the first floor, and Mother doesn't say a word. He thinks of Ruby Hornaday: her pale blue eyes, her loose flames of hair. *Is she out there in the city, somewhere, right now? Or is she three thousand miles away?* Then he sets his questions aside.

Mother catches a fever in 1932. It eats her from the inside. She still puts on her high-waisted dresses, ties on her apron. She still cooks every meal and presses Mr. Weems's suit every Sunday. But within a month she has become somebody else, an empty demon in Mother's clothes — perfectly upright at the table, eyes smoldering, nothing on her plate.

She has a way of putting her hand on Tom's forehead while he works. Tom will be hauling coal or mending a pipe or sweeping the parlor, the sun cold and white behind the curtains, and Mother will appear from nowhere and put her icy palm over his eyebrows, and he'll close his eyes and feel his heart tear just a little more.

Amphibian. It means two lives.

Mr. Weems is let go. He puts on his suit, packs up his dominoes, and leaves an address downtown.

I thought no one was leaving addresses.

You're true as a map, Tom. True as the magnet to the iron. And tears spill from the old miner's eyes.

One blue morning not long after that, for the first time in Tom's memory, Mother is not at the stove when he enters the kitchen. He finds her upstairs sitting on her bed, fully dressed in her coat and shoes and with her rosary clutched to her chest. The room is spotless, the house wadded with silence.

Payments are due on the fifteenth. Her voice is ash. *The flashing on the roof needs replacing. There's ninety-one dollars in the dresser.*

Mother, Tom says.

Shhh, Tomcat, she hisses. *Don't get yourself worked up.*

Tom manages two more payments. Then the bank comes for the house. He walks in a daze through blowing sleet to the end of the lane and turns right and staggers through the dry weeds till he finds the old path and walks beneath the creaking pitch pines to Ruby's marsh. Ice has interlocked in the shallows, but the water in the center is as dark as molten pewter.

He stands there a long time. Into the gathering darkness he says, *I'm still here, but where are you?* His blood sloshes to and fro, and snow gathers in his eyelashes, and three ducks come spiraling out of the night and land silently on the water.

The next morning he walks past the padlocked gate of International Salt with fourteen dollars in his pocket. He rides the trackless trolley downtown for a nickel and gets off on Washington Boulevard. Between the buildings the sun comes up the color of steel, and Tom raises his face to it but feels no warmth at all. He passes catatonic drunks squatting on upturned crates, motionless as statues, and storefront after storefront of empty windows. In a diner a goitrous waitress brings him a cup of coffee with little shining disks of fat floating on top.

The streets are filled with faces, dull and wan, lean and hungry; none belong to Ruby. He drinks a second cup of coffee and eats a plate of eggs and toast. A woman emerges from a doorway and flings a pan out onto the sidewalk, and the wash water flashes in the light a moment before falling. In an alley a mule lies on its side, asleep or dead. Eventually the waitress says, *You moving in?* and Tom goes out. He walks slowly toward the address he's copied and recopied onto a sheet of Mother's writing paper. Frozen furrows of plowed snow are shored up against the buildings, and the little golden windows high above seem miles away.

It's a boarding house. Mr. Weems is at a lopsided table playing dominoes by himself. He looks up, says, *Holy shit sure as gravity*, and spills his tea.

By a miracle Mr. Weems has a grandniece who manages the owl shift in the maternity ward at City General. Maternity is on the fourth floor. In the elevator Tom cannot tell if he is ascending or descending. The niece looks him up and down and checks his eyes and tongue for fever and hires him on the spot. *World goes to Hades but babies still get born*, she says, and issues him white coveralls.

Rainy nights are the busiest. Full moons and holidays are tied for second. God forbid a rainy holiday with a full moon. Ten hours a night, six nights a week, Tom roves the halls with carts of laundry, taking soiled blankets and diapers down to the cellar, bringing clean blankets and diapers up. He brings up meals, brings down trays.

Doctors walk the rows of beds injecting expecting mothers with morphine and something called scopolamine that makes them forget. Sometimes there are screams. Sometimes Tom's heart pounds for no reason he can identify. In the delivery rooms there's always new blood on the tiles to replace the old blood Tom has just mopped away.

The halls are bright at every hour, but out the windows the darkness presses very close, and in the leanest hours of those nights Tom gets a sensation like the hospital is deep underwater, the floor rocking gently, the lights of neighboring buildings like glimmering schools of fish, the pressure of the sea all around.

He turns eighteen. Then nineteen. All the listless figures he sees: children humped around the hospital entrance, their eyes vacant with hunger; farmers pouring into the parks; families sleeping without cover—people for whom nothing left on earth could be surprising. There are so many of them, as if somewhere out in the countryside great farms pump out thousands of ruined men every minute, as if the ones shuffling down the sidewalks are but fractions of the immense multitudes behind them.

And yet is there not goodness, too? Are people not helping one another in these ruined places? Tom splits his wages with Mr. Weems. He brings home discarded newspapers and wrestles his way through the words on the funny pages. He turns twenty, and Mr. Weems bakes a mushy pound cake full of eggshells and sets twenty matchsticks in it, and Tom blows them all out.

He faints at work: once in the elevator, twice in the big, pulsing laundry room in the basement. Mostly he's able to hide it. But one night he faints in the hall outside the waiting room. A nurse named Fran hauls him into a closet. *Can't let them see you like that,* she says, and wipes his face and he washes back into himself.

The closet is more than a closet. The air is warm, steamy; it smells like soap. On one wall is a two-basin sink; heat lamps are bolted to the undersides of the cabinets. Set in the opposite wall are two little doors.

Tom returns to the same chair in the corner of Fran's room whenever he starts to feel dizzy. Three, four, occasionally ten times a night, he watches a nurse carry an utterly newborn baby through the little door on the left and deposit it on the counter in front of Fran.

She plucks off little knit caps and unwraps blankets. Their bodies are scarlet or imperial purple; they have tiny, bright red fingers, no eyebrows, no kneecaps, no expression except a constant, bewildered wince. Her voice is a whisper: *Why here she is, there he goes, OK now, baby, just lift you here.* Their wrists are the circumference of Tom's pinkie.

Fran takes a new washcloth from a stack, dips it in warm water, and wipes every inch of the creature—ears, armpits, eyelids—washing away bits of placenta, dried blood, all the milky fluids that accompanied it into this world. Meanwhile the child stares up at her with blank, memorizing eyes, peering into the newness of all things. Knowing what? Only light and dark, only mother, only fluid.

Fran dries the baby and splays her fingers beneath its head and diapers it and tugs its hat back on. She whispers, *Here you are, see what a good girl you are, down you go,* and with one free hand lays out two new, crisp blankets, and binds the baby—wrap, wrap, turn—and sets her in a rolling bassinet for Tom to wheel into the nursery, where she'll wait with the others beneath the lights like loaves of bread.

* * *

In a magazine Tom finds a color photograph of a three-hundred-year-old skeleton of a bowhead whale, stranded on a coastal plain in a place called Finland. He tears it out, studies it in the lamplight. *See,* he murmurs to Mr. Weems, *how the flowers closest to it are brightest? See how the closest leaves are the darkest green?*

Tom is twenty-one and fainting three times a week when, one Wednesday in January, he sees, among the drugged, dazed mothers in their rows of beds, the unmistakable face of Ruby Hornaday. Flaming orange hair, freckles sprayed across her cheeks, hands folded in her lap, and a thin gold wedding ring on her finger. The material of the ward ripples. Tom leans on the handle of his cart to keep from falling.

Blue, he whispers. *Blue, blue, blue.*

He retreats to his chair in the corner of Fran's washing room and tries to suppress his heart. *Any minute,* he thinks, *her baby will come through the door.*

Two hours later, he pushes his cart into the post-delivery room, and Ruby is gone. Tom's shift ends; he rides the elevator down. Outside, rain settles lightly on the city. The streetlights glow yellow. The early morning avenues are empty except for the occasional automobile, passing with a damp sigh. Tom steadies himself with a hand against the bricks and closes his eyes.

A police officer helps him home. All that day Tom lies on his stomach in his rented bed and recopies the letter until little suns burst behind his eyes. *Deer Ruby, I saw you in the hospital and I saw your baby to. His eyes are viry prety. Fran sez later they will probly get blue. Mother is gone and I am lonely as the arctic see.*

That night at the hospital Fran finds the address. Tom includes the photo of the whale skeleton from the magazine and sticks on an extra stamp for luck. He thinks: *See how the flowers closest to it are brightest. See how the closest leaves are the darkest green.*

He sleeps, pays his rent, walks the thirty-one blocks to work. He checks the mail every day. And winter pales and spring strengthens and Tom loses a little bit of hope.

One morning over breakfast, Mr. Weems looks at him and says,

You ain't even here, Tom. You got one foot across the river. You got to pull back to our side.

But that very day, it comes. *Dear Tom, I liked hearing from you. It hasn't been ten years but it feels like a thousand. I'm married, you probably guessed that. The baby is Arthur. Maybe his eyes will turn blue. They just might.*

A bald president is on the stamp. The paper smells like paper, nothing more. Tom runs a finger beneath every word, sounding them out. Making sure he hasn't missed anything.

I know your married and I dont want anything but happyness for you but maybe I can see you one time? We could meet at the acquareyem. If you dont rite back thats okay I no why.

Two more weeks. *Dear Tom, I don't want anything but happiness for you, too. How about next Tuesday? I'll bring the baby, okay?*

The next Tuesday, the first one in May, Tom leaves the hospital after his shift. His vision flickers at the edges, and he hears Mother's voice: *Be careful, Tomcat. It's not worth the risk.* He walks slowly to the end of the block and catches the first trolley to Belle Isle, where he steps off into a golden dawn.

There are few cars about, all parked, one a Ford with a huge present wrapped in yellow ribbon on the backseat. An old man with a crumpled face rakes the gravel paths. The sunlight hits the dew and sets the lawns aflame.

The face of the aquarium is Gothic and wrapped in vines. Tom finds a bench outside and waits for his pulse to steady. The reticulated glass roofs of the flower conservatory reflect a passing cloud. Eventually a man in overalls opens the gate, and Tom buys two tickets, then thinks about the baby and buys a third. He returns to the bench with the three tickets in his trembling fingers.

By eleven the sky is filled with a platinum haze and the island is busy. Men on bicycles crackle along the paths. A girl flies a yellow kite.

Tom?

Ruby Hornaday materializes before him—shoulders erect, hair newly short, pushing a chrome-and-canvas baby buggy. He stands quickly, and the park bleeds away and then restores itself.

Sorry I'm late, she says.

She's dignified, slim. Two quick strokes for eyebrows, the same narrow nose. No makeup. No jewelry. Those pale blue eyes and that hair.

She cocks her head slightly. *Look at you. All grown up.*

I have tickets, he says.

How's Mr. Weems?

Oh, he's made of salt, he'll live forever.

They start down the path between the rows of benches and the shining trees. Occasionally she takes his arm to steady him, though her touch only disorients him more.

I thought maybe you were far away, he says. *I thought maybe you went to sea.*

Ruby parks the buggy and lifts the baby to her chest—he's wrapped in a blue afghan—and then they're through the turnstile.

The aquarium is dim and damp and lined on both sides with glass-fronted tanks. Ferns hang from the ceiling, and little boys lean across the brass railings and press their noses to the glass. *I think he likes it,* Ruby says. *Don't you, baby?* The boy's eyes are wide open. Fish swim slow ellipses through the water.

They see translucent squid with corkscrew tails, sparkling pink octopi like floating lanterns, cowfish in blue and violet and gold. Iridescent green tiles gleam on the domed ceiling and throw wavering patterns of light across the floor.

In a circular pool at the very center of the building, dark shapes race back and forth in coordination. *Jacks,* Ruby murmurs. *Aren't they?*

Tom blinks.

You're pale, she says.

Tom shakes his head.

She helps him back out into the daylight, beneath the sky and the trees. The baby lies in the buggy sucking his fist, examining the sky with great intensity, and Ruby guides Tom to a bench.

Cars and trucks and even a limousine pass slowly along the white bridge, high over the river. The city glitters in the distance.

Thank you, says Tom.

For what?

For this.

How old are you now, Tom?

Twenty-one. Same as you. A breeze stirs the trees, and the leaves vibrate with light. Everything is radiant.

World goes to Hades but babies still get born, whispers Tom.

Ruby peers into the buggy and adjusts something, and for a moment the back of her neck shows between her hair and collar. The sight of those two knobs of vertebrae, sheathed in her pale skin, fills Tom with a longing that cracks the lawns open. For a moment it seems Ruby is being slowly dragged away from him, as if he is a swimmer caught in a rip, and with every stroke the back of her neck recedes farther into the distance. Then she sits back, and the park heals over, and he can feel the bench become solid beneath him once more.

I used to think, Tom says, *that I had to be careful with how much I lived. As if life was a pocketful of coins. You only got so much and you didn't want to spend it all in one place.*

Ruby looks at him. Her eyelashes whisk up and down.

But now I know life is the one thing in the world that never runs out. I might run out of mine, and you might run out of yours but the world will never run out of life. And we're all very lucky to be part of something like that.

She holds his gaze. *Some deserve more luck than they've gotten.*

Tom shakes his head. He closes his eyes. *I've been lucky, too. I've been absolutely lucky.*

The baby begins to fuss, a whine building to a cry. Ruby says, *Hungry.*

A trapdoor opens in the gravel between Tom's feet, black as a keyhole, and he glances down.

You'll be OK?

I'll be OK.

Good-bye, Tom. She touches his forearm once, and then goes, pushing the buggy through the crowds. He watches her disappear in pieces: first her legs, then her hips, then her shoulders, and finally the back of her bright head.

And then Tom sits, hands in his lap, alive for one more day.

NEIL GAIMAN

■

Orange

FROM *Southwest Airlines Spirit Magazine*

CONFIDENTIAL POLICE FILE

(Third subject's responses to investigator's written questionnaire)

1.

Jemma Glorfindel Petula Ramsey.

2.

17 on June the 9th.

3.

The last 5 years. Before that we lived in Leesburg (Florida). Before that, Kalamazoo (Michigan).

4.

I don't know. I think he's in magazine publishing now. He doesn't talk to us anymore. The divorce was pretty bad and Mom wound up paying him a lot of money. Which seems sort of wrong to me. But maybe it was worth it just to get free of him.

5.

An inventor and entrepreneur. She invented the Stuffed Muffin™, and started the Stuffed Muffin chain. I used to like them when I was a kid, but you can get kind of sick of stuffed muffins for every meal, especially because Mom used us as guinea pigs. The Complete Tur-key Dinner Christmas Stuffed Muffin was the worst. But she sold out her interest in the Stuffed Muffin chain about five years ago, to start work on My Mom's Colored Bubbles (not actually ™ yet).

6.

Two. My sister Lilias, who was just 15, and my brother Marshall, 12.

7.

Several times a day.

8.

No.

9.

Through the Internet. Probably on eBay.

10.

She's been buying colors and dyes from all over the world ever since she decided that the world was crying out for brightly colored Day-Glo bubbles. The kind you can blow, with the bubble mixture.

11.

It's not really a laboratory. I mean, she calls it that, but really it's just the garage. Only she took some of the Stuffed Muffins™ money and converted it, so it has sinks and bathtubs and Bunsen burners and things, and tiles on the walls and the floor to make it easier to clean.

12.

I don't know. Lilias used to be pretty normal. When she turned 13 she started reading these magazines and putting pictures of these strange bimbo women up on her wall like Britney Spears and so on. Sorry if anyone reading this is a Britney fan ;) but I just don't get it. The whole orange thing didn't start until last year.

13.

Artificial tanning creams. You couldn't go near her for hours after she put it on. And she'd never give it time to dry after she smeared it on her skin, so it would come off on her sheets and on the fridge door and in the shower leaving smears of orange everywhere. Her friends would wear it too, but they never put it on like she did. I mean, she'd slather on the cream, with no attempt to look even human-colored, and she thought she looked great. She did the tanning salon thing once, but I don't think she liked it, because she never went back.

14.

Tangerine Girl. The Oompaloompa. Carrot-top. Go-Mango. Orangina.

15.

Not very well. But she didn't seem to care, really. I mean, this is a girl who said that she couldn't see the point of science or math because she was going to be a pole dancer as soon as she left school. I said, nobody's going to pay to see you in the altogether, and she said how do you know? She's a sort of squarish shape, for a start.

16.

German measles, mumps, and I think Marshall had chicken pox when he was staying in Orlando with the Grandparents.

17.

In a small pot. It looked a bit like a jam jar, I suppose.

18.

I don't think so. Nothing that looked like a warning label anyway. But there was a return address. It came from abroad, and the return address was in some kind of foreign lettering.

19.

You have to understand that Mom had been buying colors and dyes from all over the world for five years. The thing with the Day-Glo bubbles is not that someone can blow glowing colored bubbles, it's that they don't pop and leave splashes of dye all over everything. Mom says that would be a lawsuit waiting to happen. So, no.

20.

There was some kind of shouting match between Lilias and Mom to begin with, because Mom had come back from the shops and not bought anything from Lilias's shopping list except the shampoo. Mom said she couldn't find the tanning cream at the supermarket but I think she just forgot. So Lilias stormed off and slammed the door and went into her bedroom and played something that was probably Britney Spears really loudly. I was out the back, feeding the three cats, the chinchilla, and a guinea pig named Roland who looks like a hairy cushion, and I missed it all.

21.

On the kitchen table.

22.

When I found the empty jam jar in the back garden the next morning. It was underneath Lilias's window. It didn't take Sherlock Holmes to figure it out.

23.

Honestly, I couldn't be bothered. I figured it would just be more yelling, you know? And Mom would work it out soon enough.

24.

Yes, it was stupid. But it wasn't uniquely stupid, if you see what I mean. Which is to say, it was par-for-the-course-for-Lilias stupid.

25.

That she was glowing.

26.

A sort of pulsating orange.

27.

When she started telling us that she was going to be worshipped like a god, as she was in the dawn times.

28.

Marshall said she was floating about an inch above the ground. But I didn't actually see this. I thought he was just playing along with her newfound weirdness.

29.

She didn't answer to "Lilias" anymore. She described herself mostly as either My Immanence or The Vehicle. ("It is time to feed The Vehicle.")

30.

Dark chocolate. Which was weird because in the old days I was the only one in the house who even sort-of like it. But Marshall had to go out and buy her bars and bars of it.

31.

No. Mom and me just though it was more Lilias. Just a bit more imaginatively weirdo Lilias than usual.

32.

That night, when it started to get dark. You could see the orange pulsing under the door. Like a glowworm or something. Or a light show. The weirdest thing was that I could still see it with my eyes closed.

33.

The next morning. All of us.

34.

It was pretty obvious by this point. She didn't really even look like Lilias any longer. She looked sort of smudged. Like an after-image. I thought about it, and it's . . . okay. Suppose you were staring at something really bright, that was a blue color. Then you closed your eyes, and you'd see this glowing yellowy-orange after-image in your eyes? That was what she looked like.

35.

They didn't work either.

36.

She let Marshall leave to get her more chocolate. Mom and I weren't allowed to leave the house anymore.

37.

Mostly I just sat in the back garden and read a book. There wasn't very much else I really could do. I started wearing dark glasses, so did Mom, because the orange light hurt our eyes. Other than that, nothing.

38.

Only when we tried to leave or call anybody. There was food in the house, though. And Stuffed Muffins™ in the freezer.

39.

"If you'd just stopped her wearing that stupid tanning cream a year ago we wouldn't be in this mess!" But it was unfair, and I apologized afterward.

40.

When Marshall came back with the dark chocolate bars. He said he'd gone up to a traffic cop and told him that his sister had turned into a giant orange glow and was controlling our minds. He said the man was extremely rude to him.

41.

I don't have a boyfriend. I did, but we broke up after he went to a Rolling Stones concert with the evil bottle-blond former friend whose name I do not mention. Also, I mean, the Rolling Stones? These little old goat-men hopping around the stage pretending to be all rock and roll? Please. So, no.

42.

I'd quite like to be a vet. But then I think about having to put animals down, and I don't know. I want to travel for a bit before I make any decisions.

43.

The garden hose. We turned it on full, while she was eating her chocolate bars, and distracted, and we sprayed it at her.

44.

Just orange steam, really. Mom said that she had solvents and things in the garage, if we could get in there, but by now Her Immanence was hissing mad (literally), and she sort of fixed us to the floor. I can't explain it. I mean, I wasn't stuck, but I couldn't leave or move my legs. I was just where she left me.

45.

About two feet above the carpet. She'd sink down a bit to go through the door, so she didn't bump her head. And after the hose incident she didn't go back to her room, just stayed in the main room and floated about frumpily, the color of a luminous carrot.

46.

Complete world domination.

47.

I wrote it down on a piece of paper and gave it to Marshall.

48.

He had to carry it back. I don't think Her Immanence really understood money.

49.

I don't know. It was Mom's idea more than mine. I think she hoped that the solvent might remove the orange. And at that point, it couldn't hurt. Nothing could have made things worse.

50.

It didn't even upset her, like the hose-water did. I'm pretty sure she liked it. I think I saw her dipping her chocolate bars into it, before she ate them, although I had to sort of squint up my eyes to see anything where she was. It was all a sort of great orange glow.

51.

That we were all going to die. Mom told Marshall that if the Great Oompaloompa let him out to buy chocolate again, he just shouldn't bother coming back. And I was getting really upset about the animals—I hadn't fed the chinchilla or Roland the guinea pig for two days, because I couldn't go into the back garden. I couldn't go anywhere. Except the bathroom, and then I had to ask.

52.

I suppose because they thought the house was on fire. All the orange light. I mean, it was a natural mistake.

53.

We were glad she hadn't done that to us. Mom said it proved that Lilias was still in there somewhere, because if she had the power to turn us into goo, like she did the firefighters, she would have done so. I said that maybe she just wasn't powerful enough to turn us into goo at the beginning and now she couldn't be bothered.

54.

You couldn't even see a person in there anymore. It was a bright orange pulsating light, and sometimes it talked straight into your head.

55.

When the spaceship landed.

56.

I don't know. I mean, it was bigger than the whole block, but it didn't crush anything. It sort of materialized around us, so that our whole house was inside it. And the whole street was inside it too.

57.

No. But what else could it have been?

58.

A sort of pale blue. They didn't pulse, either. They twinkled.

59.

More than six, less than twenty. It's not that easy to tell if this is the same intelligent blue light you were just speaking to five minutes ago.

60.

Three things. First of all, a promise that Lilias wouldn't be hurt or harmed. Second, that if they were ever able to return her to the way she was, they'd let us know, and bring her back. Thirdly, a recipe for fluorescent bubble mixture. (I can only assume they were reading Mom's mind, because she didn't say anything. It's possible that Her Immanence told them, though. She definitely had access to some of the Vehicle's memories.) Also, they gave Marshall a thing like a glass skateboard.

61.

A sort of a liquid sound. Then everything became transparent. I was crying, and so was Mom. And Marshall said "Cool beans," and I started to giggle while crying, and then it was just our house again.

62.

We went out in the back garden and looked up. There was something blinking blue and orange, very high, getting smaller and smaller, and we watched it until it was out of sight.

63.

Because I didn't want to.

64.

I fed the remaining animals. Roland was in a state. The cats just seemed happy that someone was feeding them again. I don't know how the chinchilla got out.

65.

Sometimes. I mean, you have to bear in mind that she was the single most irritating person on the planet, even before the whole Her Immanence thing. But yes, I guess so. If I'm honest.

66.

Sitting outside at night, staring up at the sky, wondering what she's doing now.

67.

He wants his glass skateboard back. He says that it's his, and the government has no right to keep it. (You are the government, aren't you?) Mom seems happy to share the patent for the Colored Bubble recipe with the government though. The man said that it might be the basis of a whole new branch of molecular something or other. Nobody gave me anything, so I don't have to worry.

68.

Once, in the back garden, looking up at the night sky. I think it was only an orangeyish star, actually. It could have been Mars, I know they call it the red planet. Although once in a while I think that maybe she's back to herself again, and dancing, up there, wherever she is, and all the aliens love her pole dancing because they just don't know any better, and they think it's a whole new art-form, and they don't even mind that she's sort of square.

69.

I don't know. Sitting in the back garden talking to the cats, maybe. Or blowing silly-colored bubbles.

70.

Until the day I die.

I attest that this is a true statement of events.

Signed:

Date:

MOHAMMED HANIF

■

Butt and Bhatti

FROM *Granta*

TEDDY HAS BROUGHT A MAUSER to his declaration of love. He has brought a story about the moon as well but he is not sure where to start. The story is romantic in an old-fashioned kind of way; the Mauser has three bullets in it. He is hoping that the Mauser and the story about the moon will somehow come together to produce the kind of love song that makes old acquaintances run away together.

Before resorting to gunpoint poetry, Teddy Butt tries the traditional route to romancing a medical professional; he pretends to be sick and then, like a truly hopeless lover, starts believing that he is sick, recognizes all the little symptoms—sudden fevers, heart palpitations, lingering migraine, even mild depression. He cries while watching a documentary about a snow leopard stranded on a melting glacier.

He lurks around the Outpatients Department on a Sunday afternoon, when Sister Alice Bhatti is alone. She pretends to be busy counting syringes, boiling needles, polishing grimy surfaces, and only turns round when he coughs politely, like you are supposed to do when entering a respectable household so that women have the time to cover themselves. Sister Alice Bhatti doesn't understand this polite-cough protocol and stares at him as if telling him, *See? This is what smoking does to your lungs.*

Teddy Butt is too vain to bring up anything like stomach troubles or a skin rash, both conditions he frequently suffers from. Boldabolics play havoc with his digestion. His bodybuilder's weekly regime of waxing his body hair has left certain parts of his body looking like abstract kilim designs. For his first consultation with Sister Alice he has thought up something more romantic.

"I can't sleep."

He says this sitting on a rickety little stool as Sister Alice takes notes in a khaki-coloured register. "For how long have you not been able to sleep?" With any other patient Alice would have reached for the wrist to take the pulse, would have listened to their chest with a stethoscope, but she knows that Teddy is not that kind of patient.

"Since I have seen you," is what Teddy wants to say but he hasn't rehearsed it, he is not ready yet.

"I do go to sleep. But then I have dreams and I wake up," he says and feels relieved at having delivered a full sentence without falling off the stool.

Alice Bhatti wants to tell him to go to the OPD in Charya Ward, that is where they deal in dreams. The whole place is a bad dream. But she knows that he wants to be her patient and Senior Sister Hina Alvi has taught her that when a patient walks in with intent you listen to them, even if you know they are making up their symptoms.

She can also see the outline of a muzzle in the crotch of his yellow Adidas trousers. He looks like a freak with two cocks.

"What kind of dreams?"

Teddy has only ever had one dream, the one with a river and a kaftan-wearing God in it. The dream always ends badly as a drowning Teddy discovers that he can't walk on water even in his dream. God stands at the edge of a silvery, completely walkable river and shakes His head in disappointment as if saying, it's your dream, what do you expect me to do? But somehow bringing up God and His kaftan and His disapproval right now seems inappropriate. "I see a river in my dream." He conveniently leaves God out.

"A river?" Alice Bhatti taps the pen on the register without writing anything.

Teddy feels he is being told that his dream is not sick enough.

"It's a river of blood. Red."

Sister Alice looks at him with interest. This Teddy boy might be a police tout but he has a poetic side to him, she thinks.

"Any boats in that river of yours?" she asks with an encouraging smile, as if urging him to go on sharing more of his dream with her, to go ahead and dream for her. Teddy accepts the challenge. "It has bodies floating in it and severed heads, bobbing up and down." He realizes that his dream doesn't sound very romantic. "And some flowers also."

"Do you recognize any of these people in the river? In your dream, I mean." Teddy shuts his eyes as if trying hard to recognize a face from the river. Teddy was hoping that somehow his midnight yearning for Alice and his insomnia would walk hand in hand and form a rhyming, soaring declaration of love that would reverberate through the corridors of the hospital. Instead he is stuck with embellishing details for a bad dream.

"I can't really stop your dreams but I can give you something that will ensure that you sleep well. And if you sleep well then you might start having better dreams." She scribbles a prescription for Lexotanil then puts it aside. "Actually I might have one here. An hour before you sleep. Never on an empty stomach. And no warm milk at night. Sometimes indigestion can give you bad dreams."

Sister Alice gives him a curt smile, turns round and goes back to counting her syringes. She does it with such studied concentration that it seems the health of the nation depends on getting this count right.

Teddy Butt stumbles into the OPD the following morning, bleary-eyed, moving slowly. Even his voice seems to be coming from underwater. There is a sleepy calm about him. Even the muzzle of the gun in his trousers seems flaccid. "I didn't have any dreams. What did you give me? What did you mix in that pill?" Teddy's words are accusatory but his tone is grateful.

"I didn't mix anything. It was a Glaxo original, supposed to help you sleep. Do you want more?" She reaches into her drawer and stops. She notices that he is wearing a little cross on a gold chain around his neck. She shows the slight, spontaneous irritation that natives feel when tourists try and dress up like them. "What's that thing you are wearing?"

"A chain," Teddy Butt says. "A friend from Dubai got it for me." The man whose neck Teddy snatched it from was indeed visiting from Dubai. One ear and the side of his face were blown off in an unfortunate accident during an interrogation. The man from Dubai had almost strangled Teddy with his handcuffs before Inspector Malangi put his Repeater near his left ear, shouted at Teddy, "Knee on the left, *bhai*. Your left, not mine,"—and shot him. The chain with the cross was the reward Inspector Malangi gave him for keeping the man pinned down at that difficult moment. Teddy hadn't killed the man; he was only holding him down. It was his job. If he hadn't done it someone else would have. If he hadn't done this job he would definitely have to do some other job. And who knows what he might be required to do in that new job? He runs his forefinger along his chain and presses the cross into his chest with the satisfaction of someone who is lucky enough not to get the worst job in the city. He had felt the man's breath on his knee when he tried to bite him before getting shot.

For a moment Teddy wonders whether he can source a matching necklace for her.

"It's a cross, not jewellery. Why would a man want to wear jewellery anyway?" She scribbles a prescription for Lexotanil on her pad and turns away.

Teddy Butt is flummoxed and walks away without answering, without asking anything. He goes to his room in Al Aman apartments and sleeps the whole day. He doesn't have any dreams but after he wakes up and starts doing weights he watches a fascinating documentary about Komodo dragons who hypnotize their prey before going for the underside of their throat.

Teddy decides that he is going to tell Alice Bhatti everything but he will need her full attention. From what Teddy can tell, women are always distracted, trying to do too many things at the same time, always happy to go off on tangents; that's why they make good nurses and politicians but not good chefs and truck drivers. He realizes that he can't do it without his Mauser. He also realizes that he'll have to wait for the coming Sunday when there is only skeleton staff on duty.

Teddy is one of those people who are only articulate when they talk about cricket. The rest of the time they rely on a combination of grunts, hand gestures and repeat the snippets of what other people have just said to them. He also has very little experience of sharing his feelings.

He has been a customer of women and occasionally their tormentor but never a lover. He believes that being a lover is something that falls somewhere between paying them and slapping them around. Twice he has come close to conceding love. Once he gave a fifty-rupee tip to a prostitute who looked fourteen but claimed to be twenty-two. Encouraged by his generosity she also demanded a poster of Imran Khan and that put him off. Teddy promised to get it but never went back because he thought Imran Khan was a failed batsman pretending to be a bowler. On another occasion he only pretended to take his turn with a thirty-two-year-old Bangladeshi prisoner after a small police contingent had shuffled out of the room. He only sat there and played with her hair while she sobbed and cursed in Bengali. The only word he could understand was Allah. He had walked out adjusting his fly, pretending to be exhausted and satisfied, even joking with the policemen: *It was like fucking an oil spill.*

But Teddy Butt can be very articulate, even poetic, with a Mauser in his hand, and after much thought this is what he decides to do. He tries practising in front of the full-length mirror in his room. "You live in my heart." With every word he jabs the Mauser in the air like an underprepared lawyer trying to impress a judge. The gun might send the wrong signal but Teddy is convinced that he will be able to explain himself. People always listen and try their best to understand when their life depends on listening properly.

"You can't go around in the Ortho Ward with that," Alice Bhatti has emerged carrying a bedpan in one hand and a discarded, blood-smeared bandage in the other and starts admonishing him while walking away from him. "Don't waste your bullets, this hospital will kill them all anyway." Teddy feels the love of his life slipping from his hands, his plan falling apart at the very first hurdle. He grips the Mauser, stretches his arm and blocks her way.

Alice Bhatti looks confused for a moment and then irritated. "What do you want to rob me of? This piss tray?"

With the Mauser extended, Teddy finds his tongue. "I can't live like this. This life is too much."

"Nobody can live like this." Alice Bhatti is attentive now and sympathetic. "If these cheap guns don't kill you, those Boldabolic pills will. Get a job as a PT master. Or come to think of it, you could get a nurse's diploma and work here. There is always work for a man nurse. There are parts of this place where even women doctors don't go. Charya Ward for example hasn't had a . . . "

Teddy doesn't listen to the whole thing, the word PT master triggers off a childhood memory that he had completely forgotten—a very tall, very fat PT teacher holds him by his ears, swings him round and then hurls him on the ground and walks away laughing. The other children run around him in a circle and decide to change his nickname from "Nappy" to "Yo-yo." Teddy takes the gun to Alice Bhatti's temple and snarls in his high-pitched, sing-song voice.

"Give me one good reason why somebody wouldn't shoot in this hospital? Why shouldn't I shoot you right here and end all my troubles?"

"Mine too," she wants to say but Teddy's hand holding the Mauser is trembling and one thing Sister Alice doesn't want in her life is a shoot-out in her workplace.

He orders Alice Bhatti to put her tray and bandages down, which she does. She has realized that Teddy is serious. Suicidal serious maybe, but he is the kind of suicidal serious who in the process of taking their own life would cause some grievous bodily harm to those around them.

Ortho Ward is unusually quiet at this time of day. Number fourteen, who is always shouting about an impending plague caused by computer screens is calm and only murmurs about the itch in his plastered leg. A ward boy enters the corridor carrying a water cooler on a wheelbarrow, and when he sees Alice and Teddy, he stops in his tracks. Embarrassed as if he has stumbled on to someone's private property and found the owners in a compromising position, he backtracks, taking the wheelbarrow with him. Sister Alice doesn't expect him to inform anyone.

"What do you want, Mr. Butt?" Alice Bhatti tries to hide her fear behind a formal form of address. She has learned all the wrong things from Senior Sister Hina Alvi.

"You live in my heart," Teddy Butt wants to say but only jabs the air with his Mauser, five times. In her limited experience with guns and madmen, Sister Alice Bhatti knows that when men are unable to talk you are in real trouble. She looks at him expectantly as if she has understood what his Mauser has just said, likes it and now wants to hear more.

Mixed-up couplets about her lips and hair, half-remembered speeches about a life together, names of their children, pledges of undying love, a story about the first time he saw her, what she wore, what she said, a half-sincere eulogy about her professionalism which he was sure she would appreciate, her shoulder blades, all these things rush through Teddy Butt's head and then he realizes that he has already delivered his opening line by pulling out a gun.

Now, he can start anywhere.

Alice Bhatti thinks that she should not do Sunday shifts any more and instead should help her dad with his woodwork. If she lives to see another Sunday, that is.

She looks beyond Teddy, outside the corridor; on the top of the stairs a man sits facing the sun like an ancient king waiting to receive his subjects. His legs amputated just above the knees, he sits on the floor, wearing full-length trousers that sometimes balloon up in the wind. He has a stack of large X-rays next to him. He picks them up one by one, holds them against the sun and looks at them for a long time as if contemplating old family pictures.

Teddy Butt decides to start with her garbage bin. "I go through your garbage bin. I know everything about you. I see all the prayers you scribble on prescriptions. You never write your own name. But I can tell from the handwriting." He sobs violently and holds the Mauser with both hands to steady himself. The muzzle of his gun slides down a degree like an erection flashbacking to a sad memory. Sister Alice sees it as a sign from God. Bless Our Lord who descended from the heavens. God accepts her gratitude with godlike indifference. And Teddy straightens his gun. He seems to have found his groove and starts to speak in paragraphs as if delivering the manifesto of a new political party which wants to eradicate poverty and pollution during its first term in power.

"The love that I feel for you is not the love I feel for any other human being. The world might think it's the love of your flesh. I can understand this world and their thinking. I have wondered about this and thought long and hard and realized that this is a world full of sinners so I do understand what they think but I don't think like that. When I think about you, do I think about these milk pots?" He waves his Mauser across her chest. Alice looks at his gun and feels nauseous and wonders if the peace and quiet of this corridor is worth preserving. "I think of your eyes. I think of your eyes only."

The octopus of fear that had clutched Sister Alice's head begins to relax its tentacles.

In her heart of hearts, Alice, who has seen people die choking on their own food, and survive after falling from a sixth floor on to a paved road, knows that Teddy means every word of what he has said. And he isn't finished yet.

"I was standing outside the hospital hoping to catch a glimpse of you. It was a full Rajab moon. Then I looked up at the balcony of Ortho Ward and saw you empty a garbage bin. I saw your face for a moment and then you disappeared. Then I looked up again and saw that the moon had disappeared too. I rubbed my eyes, I shut them, I opened them again. I stood and kept looking up for forty-five minutes. People gathered around me, I held them from their collars, made them look towards the sky and kept asking them where the moon had gone. And they said what moon? We have seen no moon. Did you just escape from the Charya Ward? And then I knew that I couldn't live without you."

A thick March cloud has cloaked the sun outside. The perfect spring afternoon turns into its own wintry ghost. The man with the X-rays is trying to shoo away a kite, which, confused by the sudden change in light, thinks it's dusk, and swoops down in a last desperate attempt to take something home.

The final bell rings in the neighbouring St Xavier's Primary School and eighteen hundred children suddenly start talking to each other in urgent voices like house sparrows at dusk.

Alice Bhatti bends down, picks the piss tray from the floor, holds it in front of her chest and speaks in measured tones. "I know your type," she says. "That little gun doesn't scare me. Your tears don't fool me. You think that a woman, any woman, who wears a uniform, is just waiting for you to show up and she'll take it off. I wish you had just walked in and told me you want me to take this off. We could have had a conversation about that. At the end of which I would have told you what I am telling you now: Fuck off and never show me your face again."

Teddy Butt runs before she is finished. He runs past the legless man, now taking a nap with his face covered with an X-ray, past the ambulance drivers dissecting the evening newspapers, past the hopeful junkies waiting for the hospital accidentally to dispense its bounty.

As he emerges out of the hospital he raises his arm in the air, without thinking, without targeting anything, and shoots his Mauser.

The city stops moving for three days.

The bullet pierces the right shoulder of a truck driver who has just entered the city after a forty-eight-hour journey; his shoulder is almost leaning out of his driver's window, his right hand drumming the door, his fingers holding a finely rolled joint, licked on the side with his tongue for extra smoothness, a ritual treat that he has prepared for the end of the journey. He is annoyed with his own shoulder, he looks at it with suspicion. His shoulder feels as if it has been stung by a bee that travelled with him all the way from his village. His left hand grips the shoulder where it hurts and finds his shirt soaked in red gooey stuff. He jams the brake to the floor. A rickshaw trying to dodge the swerving truck gets entangled in its double-mounted Goodyear tyres and is dragged along for a few yards. Five children, all between seven and nine, in their pristine blue-and-white St Xavier's uniform become a writhing mess of fractured skulls, blood, crayons and Buffy the Vampire Slayer lunch boxes. The truck comes to a halt after gently nudging a cart and overturning a pyramid of the season's last guavas. A size-four shoe is stuck between two Goodyears.

School notebooks are looked at, pockets are searched for clues to the victims' identities, the mob slowly gathers around the truck, petrol is extracted from the tank and sprinkled over its cargo of three tonnes of raw peanuts. Teddy with his broken heart and the truck driver with his bleeding shoulder both realize what is coming even before the mob has made up its mind; they first mingle in the crowd and then start walking in opposite directions.

A lonely fire engine will turn up an hour later but will be pelted at and sent away. The truck and its cargo will smoulder for two days.

In a house twenty miles away a phone rings. A grandmother rushes on to the street beating her chest and wailing. Two motorcycles kick-start simultaneously. Half a dozen jerrycans full of kerosene are hauled into a rickety Suzuki pickup. A nineteen-year-old rummages under his pillow, cocks his TT pistol and runs on to the street screaming, promising to rape every Pathan mother in the land. A second-hand tyre shop owner tries to padlock his store but the boys are already there with their iron rods and bicycle chains. A police-mobile switches on its emergency horn and rushes towards the police commissioner's house. A helicopter hovers over the beach as if defending the Arabian Sea against the burning rubber smell that is spreading through the city. An old colonel walking his dog in the Colonels' Colony asks his dog to hurry up and do its business. A bank teller is shot dead for smiling. Finding the streets deserted, groups of kites and crows descend from their perches and chase wild dogs that lift their faces to the sky and bark joyously. Five size-four coffins wait for three days as ambulance drivers are shot at and sent back to where they came from. Carcasses of burned buses, rickshaws, paan shops and at least one KFC joint seem to have a calming effect on the population. Newspapers start predicting "Normalcy limping back to the city," as if normalcy had gone for a picnic and sprained an ankle.

During the three-day shutdown eleven more are killed; two of them turn up shot and tied together in one gunny bag dumped on a rubbish heap. Three billion rupees-worth of Suzukis, Toyotas and Hinopaks are burned down. During these days Alice Bhatti is actually not that busy. When people are killed while fixing their satellite dishes on their roofs, or their motorbikes are torched while going to buy a litre of milk, they tend to forget about their ailments, they learn to live without dialysis for their kidneys, home cures are found for minor injuries, prayers replace prescription drugs. Sister Alice has time to sit down between her chores, she has time to take a proper lunch and prayer breaks. Between cleaning gun wounds and mopping the A&E floor, Sister Alice has moments of calm and she finds herself thinking about that scared little man with the Mauser, his mad story about the disappearing moon. She wonders if he is caught up in these riots, if he is still having those dreams. She wonders if she has been in one of his dreams.

CHRIS JONES

■

Roger Ebert: The Essential Man

FROM *Esquire*

FOR THE 281ST TIME in the last ten months, Roger Ebert is sitting down to watch a movie in the Lake Street Screening Room, on the sixteenth floor of what used to pass for a skyscraper in the Loop. Ebert's been coming to it for nearly thirty years, along with the rest of Chicago's increasingly venerable collection of movie critics. More than a dozen of them are here this afternoon, sitting together in the dark. Some of them look as though they plan on camping out, with their coats, blankets, lunches, and laptops spread out on the seats around them.

The critics might watch three or four movies in a single day, and they have rules and rituals along with their lunches to make it through. The small, fabric-walled room has forty-nine purple seats in it; Ebert always occupies the aisle seat in the last row, closest to the door. His wife, Chaz, in her capacity as vice-president of the Ebert Company, sits two seats over, closer to the middle, next to a little table. She's sitting there now, drinking from a tall paper cup. Michael Phillips, Ebert's bearded, bespectacled replacement on *At the Movies*, is on the other side of the room, one row down. Steve Prokopy, the guy who writes under the name Capone for *Ain't It Cool News*, leans against the far wall. Jonathan Rosenbaum and Peter Sobczynski, dressed in black, are down front.

"Too close for me," Ebert writes in his small spiral notebook.

Today, Ebert's decided he has the time and energy to watch only one film, Pedro Almodóvar's new Spanish-language movie, *Broken Embraces*. It stars Penélope Cruz. Steve Kraus, the house projectionist, is busy pulling seven reels out of a cardboard box and threading them through twin Simplex projectors.

Unlike the others, Ebert, sixty-seven, hasn't brought much survival gear with him: a small bottle of Evian moisturizing spray with a pink cap; some Kleenex; his spiral notebook and a blue fine-tip pen. He's wearing jeans that are falling off him at the waist, a pair of New Balance sneakers, and a blue cardigan zipped up over the bandages around his neck. His seat is worn soft and reclines a little, which he likes. He likes, too, for the seat in front of him to remain empty, so that he can prop his left foot onto its armrest; otherwise his back and shoulders can't take the strain of a feature-length sitting anymore.

The lights go down. Kraus starts the movie. Subtitles run along the bottom of the screen. The movie is about a film director, Harry Caine, who has lost his sight. Caine reads and makes love by touch, and he writes and edits his films by sound. "Films have to be finished, even if you do it blindly," someone in the movie says. It's a quirky, complex, beautiful little film, and Ebert loves it. He radiates kid joy. Throughout the screening, he takes excited notes—references to other movies, snatches of dialogue, meditations on Almodóvar's symbolism and his use of the color red. Ebert scribbles constantly, his pen digging into page after page, and then he tears the pages out of his notebook and drops them to the floor around him. Maybe twenty or thirty times, the sound of paper being torn from a spiral rises from the aisle seat in the last row.

The lights come back on. Ebert stays in his chair, savoring, surrounded by his notes. It looks as though he's sitting on top of a cloud of paper. He watches the credits, lifts himself up, and kicks his notes into a small pile with his feet. He slowly bends down to pick them up and walks with Chaz back out to the elevators. They hold hands, but they don't say anything to each other. They spend a lot of time like that.

Roger Ebert can't remember the last thing he ate. He can't remember the last thing he drank, either, or the last thing he said. Of course, those things existed; those lasts happened. They just didn't happen with enough warning for him to have bothered committing them to memory—it wasn't as though he sat down, knowingly, to his last supper or last cup of coffee or to whisper a last word into Chaz's ear. The doctors told him they were going to give him back his ability to eat, drink, and talk. But the doctors were wrong, weren't they? On some morning or afternoon or evening, sometime in 2006, Ebert took his last bite and sip, and he spoke his last word.

Ebert's lasts almost certainly took place in a hospital. That much he can guess. His last food was probably nothing special, except that it was: hot soup in a brown plastic bowl; maybe some oatmeal; perhaps a saltine or some canned peaches. His last drink? Water, most likely, but maybe juice, again slurped out of plastic with the tinfoil lid peeled back. The last thing he said? Ebert thinks about it for a few moments, and then his eyes go wide behind his glasses, and he looks out into space in case the answer is floating in the air somewhere. It isn't. He looks surprised that he can't remember. He knows the last words Studs Terkel's wife, Ida, muttered when she was wheeled into the operating room ("Louis, what have you gotten me into now?"), but Ebert doesn't know what his own last words were. He thinks he probably said goodbye to Chaz before one of his own trips into the operating room, perhaps when he had parts of his salivary glands taken out—but that can't be right. He was back on TV after that operation. Whenever it was, the moment wasn't cinematic. His last words weren't recorded. There was just his voice, and then there wasn't.

Now his hands do the talking. They are delicate, long-fingered, wrapped in skin as thin and translucent as silk. He wears his wedding ring on the middle finger of his left hand; he's lost so much weight since he and Chaz were married in 1992 that it won't stay where it belongs, especially now that his hands are so busy. There is almost always a pen in one and a spiral notebook or a pad of Post-it notes in the other—unless he's at home, in which case his fingers are feverishly banging the keys of his MacBook Pro.

He's also developed a kind of rudimentary sign language. If he passes a written note to someone and then opens and closes his fingers like a bird's beak, that means he would like them to read the note aloud for the other people in the room. If he touches his hand to his blue cardigan over his heart, that means he's either talking about something of great importance to him or he wants to make it clear that he's telling the truth. If he needs to get someone's attention and they're looking away from him or sitting with him in the dark, he'll clack on a hard surface with his nails, like he's tapping out Morse code. Sometimes—when he's outside wearing gloves, for instance—he'll be forced to draw letters with his finger on his palm. That's his last resort.

C-O-M-C-A-S-T, he writes on his palm to Chaz after they've stopped on the way back from the movie to go for a walk.

"Comcast?" she says, before she realizes—he's just reminded her that people from Comcast are coming over to their Lincoln Park brownstone not long from now, because their Internet has been down for three days, and for Ebert, that's the equivalent of being buried alive: C-O-M-C-A-S-T. But Chaz still wants to go for a walk, and, more important, she wants her husband to go for a walk, so she calls their assistant, Carol, and tells her they will be late for their appointment. There isn't any debate in her voice. Chaz Ebert is a former lawyer, and she doesn't leave openings. She takes hold of her husband's hand, and they set off in silence across the park toward the water.

They pass together through an iron gate with a sign that reads AL-FRED CALDWELL LILY POOL. Ebert has walked hundreds of miles around this little duck pond, on the uneven stone path under the trees, most of them after one operation or another. The Eberts have lost track of the surgeries he has undergone since the first one, for thyroid cancer, in 2002, followed by the one on his salivary glands in 2003. After that, they disagree about the numbers and dates. "The truth is, we don't let our minds dwell on these things," Chaz says. She kept a journal of their shared stays in hospitals in Chicago and Seattle and Houston, but neither of them has had the desire to look at it. On those rare occasions when they agree to try to remember the story, they both lose the plot for the scenes. When Chaz remembers what she calls "the surgery that changed everything," she remembers its soundtrack best of all. Ebert always had music playing in his hospital room, an esoteric digital collection that drew doctors and nurses to his bedside more than they might have been otherwise inclined to visit. There was one song in particular he played over and over: "I'm Your Man," by Leonard Cohen. That song saved his life.

Seven years ago, he recovered quickly from the surgery to cut out his cancerous thyroid and was soon back writing reviews for the *Chicago Sun-Times* and appearing with Richard Roeper on *At the Movies*. A year later, in 2003, he returned to work after his salivary glands were partially removed, too, although that and a series of aggressive radiation treatments opened the first cracks in his voice. In 2006, the cancer surfaced yet again, this time in his jaw. A section of his lower jaw was removed; Ebert listened to Leonard Cohen. Two weeks later, he was in his hospital room packing his bags, the doctors and nurses paying one last visit, listening to a few last songs. That's when his carotid artery, invisibly damaged by the earlier radiation and the most recent jaw surgery, burst. Blood began pouring out of Ebert's mouth and formed a great pool on the polished floor. The doctors and nurses leapt up to stop the bleeding and barely saved his life. Had he made it out of his hospital room and been on his way home—had his artery waited just a few more songs to burst—Ebert would have bled to death on Lake Shore Drive. Instead, following more surgery to stop a relentless bloodletting, he was left without much of his mandible, his chin hanging loosely like a drawn curtain, and behind his chin there was a hole the size of a plum. He also underwent a tracheostomy, because there was still a risk that he could drown in his own blood. When Ebert woke up and looked in the mirror in his hospital room, he could see through his open mouth and the hole clear to the bandages that had been wrapped around his neck to protect his exposed windpipe and his new breathing tube. He could no longer eat or drink, and he had lost his voice entirely. That was more than three years ago.

Ebert spent more than half of a thirty-month stretch in hospitals. His breathing tube has been removed, but the hole in his throat remains open. He eats through a G-tube—he's fed with a liquid paste, suspended in a bag from an IV pole, through a tube in his stomach. He usually eats in what used to be the library, on the brownstone's second floor. (It has five stories, including a gym on the top floor and a theater—with a neon marquee—in the basement.) A single bed with white sheets has been set up among the books, down a hallway filled with Ebert's collection of Edward Lear watercolors. He shuffles across the wooden floor between the library and his living room, where he spends most of his time in a big black leather recliner, tipped back with his feet up and his laptop on a wooden tray. There is a record player within reach. The walls are white, to show off the art, which includes massive abstracts, movie posters (*Casablanca, The*

Stranger), and aboriginal burial poles. Directly in front of his chair is a black-and-white photograph of the Steak 'n Shake in Champaign-Urbana, Illinois, one of his hometown hangouts.

He believes he's had three more surgeries since the removal of his lower jaw; Chaz remembers four. Each time, however many times, surgeons carved bone and tissue and skin from his back, arm, and legs and transplanted them in an attempt to reconstruct his jaw and throat. Each time, he had one or two weeks of hope and relief when he could eat a little and drink a little and talk a little. Once, the surgery looked nearly perfect. ("Like a movie star," Chaz remembers.) But each time, the reconstructive work fell apart and had to be stripped out, the hole opened up again. It was as though the cancer were continuing to eat away at him, even those parts of him that had been spared. His right shoulder is visibly smaller than his left shoulder; his legs have been weakened and riddled with scars. After each attempt at reconstruction, he went to rehabilitation and physical therapy to fix the increasing damage done. (During one of those rehabilitation sessions, he fell and broke his hip.) He still can't sit upright for long or climb stairs. He's still figuring out how to use his legs.

At the start of their walk around the pond, Ebert worries about falling on a small gravel incline. Chaz lets go of his hand. "You can do it," she says, and she claps when Ebert makes it to the top on his own. Later, she climbs on top of a big circular stone. "I'm going to give my prayer to the universe," she says, and then she gives a sun salutation north, south, east, and west. Ebert raises his arms into the sky behind her.

They head home and meet with the people from Comcast, who talk mostly to Chaz. Their Internet will be back soon, but probably not until tomorrow. Disaster. Ebert then takes the elevator upstairs and drops into his chair. As he reclines it slowly, the entire chair jumps somehow, one of its back legs thumping against the floor. It had been sitting on the charger for his iPhone, and now the charger is crushed. Ebert grabs his tray and laptop and taps out a few words before he presses a button and speakers come to life.

"What else can go wrong?" the voice says.

The voice is called Alex, a voice with a generic American accent and a generic tone and no emotion. At first Ebert spoke with a voice called Lawrence, which had an English accent. Ebert liked sounding

English, because he is an Anglophile, and his English voice reminded him of those beautiful early summers when he would stop in London with Chaz on their way home after the annual chaos of Cannes. But the voice can be hard to decipher even without an English accent layered on top of it — it is given to eccentric pronunciations, especially of names and places — and so for the time being, Ebert has settled for generic instead.

Ebert is waiting for a Scottish company called CereProc to give him some of his former voice back. He found it on the Internet, where he spends a lot of his time. CereProc tailors text-to-speech software for voiceless customers so that they don't all have to sound like Stephen Hawking. They have catalog voices — Heather, Katherine, Sarah, and Sue — with regional Scottish accents, but they will also custom-build software for clients who had the foresight to record their voices at length before they lost them. Ebert spent all those years on TV, and he also recorded four or five DVD commentaries in crystal-clear digital audio. The average English-speaking person will use about two thousand different words over the course of a given day. CereProc is mining Ebert's TV tapes and DVD commentaries for those words, and the words it cannot find, it will piece together syllable by syllable. When CereProc finishes its work, Roger Ebert won't sound exactly like Roger Ebert again, but he will sound more like him than Alex does. There might be moments, when he calls for Chaz from another room or tells her that he loves her and says goodnight — he's a night owl; she prefers mornings — when they both might be able to close their eyes and pretend that everything is as it was.

There are places where Ebert exists as the Ebert he remembers. In 2008, when he was in the middle of his worst battles and wouldn't be able to make the trip to Champaign-Urbana for Ebertfest — really, his annual spring festival of films he just plain likes — he began writing an online journal. Reading it from its beginning is like watching an Aztec pyramid being built. At first, it's just a vessel for him to apologize to his fans for not being downstate. The original entries are short updates about his life and health and a few of his heart's wishes. Postcards and pebbles. They're followed by a smattering of Welcomes to Cyberspace. But slowly the journal picks up steam, as

Ebert's strength and confidence and audience grow. *You are the readers I have dreamed of*, he writes. He is emboldened. He begins to write about more than movies; in fact, it sometimes seems as though he'd rather write about anything other than movies. The existence of an afterlife, the beauty of a full bookshelf, his liberalism and atheism and alcoholism, the health-care debate, Darwin, memories of departed friends and fights won and lost—more than five hundred thousand words of inner monologue have poured out of him, five hundred thousand words that probably wouldn't exist had he kept his other voice. Now some of his entries have thousands of comments, each of which he vets personally and to which he will often respond. It has become his life's work, building and maintaining this massive monument to written debate—argument is encouraged, so long as it's civil—and he spends several hours each night reclined in his chair, tending to his online oasis by lamplight. Out there, his voice is still his voice—not a reasonable facsimile of it, but *his*.

"It is saving me," he says through his speakers.

He calls up a journal entry to elaborate, because it's more efficient and time is precious:

When I am writing my problems become invisible and I am the same person I always was. All is well. I am as I should be.

He is a wonderful writer, and today he is producing the best work of his life. In 1975 he became the first film critic to win the Pulitzer Prize, but his TV fame saw most of his fans, at least those outside Chicago, forget that he was a writer if they ever did know. (His Pulitzer still hangs in a frame in his book-lined office down the hall, behind a glass door that has THE EBERT COMPANY, LTD.: FINE FILM CRITICISM SINCE 1967 written on it in gold leaf.) Even for Ebert, a prolific author—he wrote long features on Paul Newman, Groucho Marx, and Hugh Hefner's daughter, among others, for this magazine in the late 1960s and early '70s and published dozens of books in addition to his reviews for the *Sun-Times*—the written word was eclipsed by the spoken word. He spent an entire day each week arguing with Gene Siskel and then Richard Roeper, and he became a regular on talk shows, and he shouted to crowds from red carpets. He lived his life through microphones.

But now everything he says must be written, either first on his laptop and funneled through speakers or, as he usually prefers, on some kind of paper. His new life is lived through Times New Roman and chicken scratch. So many words, so much writing—it's like a kind of explosion is taking place on the second floor of his brownstone. It's not the food or the drink he worries about anymore—*I went thru a period when I obsessed about root beer + Steak + Shake malts*, he writes on a blue Post-it note—but how many more words he can get out in the time he has left. In this living room, lined with thousands more books, words are the single most valuable thing in the world. They are gold bricks. Here idle chatter doesn't exist; that would be like lighting cigars with hundred-dollar bills. Here there are only sentences and paragraphs divided by section breaks. Every word has meaning.

Even the simplest expressions take on higher power here. Now his thumbs have become more than a trademark; they're an essential means for Ebert to communicate. He falls into a coughing fit, but he gives his thumbs-up, meaning he's okay. Thumbs-down would have meant he needed someone to call his full-time nurse, Millie, a spectral presence in the house.

Millie has premonitions. She sees ghosts. Sometimes she wakes in the night screaming—so vivid are her dreams.

Ebert's dreams are happier. *Never yet a dream where I can't talk*, he writes on another Post-it note, peeling it off the top of the blue stack. *Sometimes I discover—oh, I see! I CAN talk! I just forget to do it.*

In his dreams, his voice has never left. In his dreams, he can get out everything he didn't get out during his waking hours: the thoughts that get trapped in paperless corners, the jokes he wanted to tell, the nuanced stories he can't quite relate. In his dreams, he yells and chatters and whispers and exclaims. In his dreams, he's never had cancer. In his dreams, he is whole.

These things come to us, they don't come from us, he writes about his cancer, about sickness, on another Post-it note. *Dreams come from us.*

We have a habit of turning sentimental about celebrities who are struck down—Muhammad Ali, Christopher Reeve—transforming them into mystics; still, it's almost impossible to sit beside Roger Ebert, lifting blue Post-it notes from his silk fingertips, and not feel as though he's become something more than he was. He has those hands. And his wide and expressive eyes, despite everything, are almost always smiling.

There is no need to pity me, he writes on a scrap of paper one afternoon after someone parting looks at him a little sadly. *Look how happy I am.*

In fact, because he's missing sections of his jaw, and because he's lost some of the engineering behind his face, Ebert can't really do anything but smile. It really does take more muscles to frown, and he doesn't have those muscles anymore. His eyes will water and his face will go red — but if he opens his mouth, his bottom lip will sink most deeply in the middle, pulled down by the weight of his empty chin, and the corners of his upper lip will stay raised, frozen in place. Even when he's really angry, his open smile mutes it: The top half of his face won't match the bottom half, but his smile is what most people will see first, and by instinct they will smile back. The only way Ebert can show someone he's mad is by writing in all caps on a Post-it note or turning up the volume on his speakers. Anger isn't as easy for him as it used to be. Now his anger rarely lasts long enough for him to write it down.

There's a reception to celebrate the arrival of a new ownership group at the *Chicago Sun-Times*, which Ebert feared was doomed to close otherwise. Ebert doesn't have an office in the new newsroom (the old one was torn down to make way for one of Donald Trump's glass towers), but so long as the newspaper exists, it's another one of those outlets through which he can pretend nothing has changed. His column mug is an old one, taken after his first couple of surgeries but before he lost his jaw, and his work still dominates the arts section. (A single copy of the paper might contain six of his reviews.) He's excited about seeing everybody. Millie helps him get dressed, in a blue blazer with a red pocket square and black slippers. Most of his old clothes don't fit him anymore: "For meaningful weight loss," the voice says, "I recommend surgery and a liquid diet." He buys his new clothes by mail order from L.L.Bean.

He and Chaz head south into the city; she drives, and he provides direction by pointing and knocking on the window. The reception is at a place that was called Riccardo's, around the corner from the Billy Goat. Reporters and editors used to stagger into the rival joints after filing rival stories from rival newsrooms. Riccardo's holds good memories for Ebert. But now it's something else — something called

Phil Stefani's 437 Rush, and after he and Chaz ease up to the curb and he shuffles inside, his shoulders slump a little with the loss of another vestige of old Chicago.

He won't last long at the reception, maybe thirty or forty minutes. The only chairs are wooden and straight-backed, and he tires quickly in a crowd. When he walks into the room of journalistic luminaries—Roeper, Lynn Sweet, Rick Telander—they turn toward him and burst into spontaneous applause. They know he's earned it, and they don't know even half of what it's taken him just to get into the room, just to be here tonight, but there's something sad about the wet-eyed recognition, too. He's confronted by elegies everywhere he goes. People take longer to say goodbye to him than they used to. They fuss over him, and they linger around him, and they talk slowly to him. One woman at the party even writes him a note in his notepad, and Ebert has to point to his ears and roll his eyes. He would love nothing more than to be holding court in a corner of the room, telling stories about Lee Marvin and Robert Mitchum and Russ Meyer (who came to the Eberts' wedding accompanied by Melissa Mounds). Instead he's propped on a chair in the middle of the room like a swami, smiling and nodding and trying not to flinch when people pat him on the shoulder.

He took his hardest hit not long ago. After Roeper announced his departure from *At the Movies* in 2008—Disney wanted to revamp the show in a way that Roeper felt would damage it—Ebert disassociated himself from it, too, and he took his trademarked thumbs with him. The end was not pretty, and the break was not clean. But because Disney was going to change the original balcony set as part of its makeover, it was agreed, Ebert thought, that the upholstered chairs and rails and undersized screen would be given to the Smithsonian and put on display. Ebert was excited by the idea. Then he went up to visit the old set one last time and found it broken up and stacked in a dumpster in an alley.

After saying their goodbyes to his colleagues (and to Riccardo's), Ebert and Chaz go out for dinner, to one of their favorite places, the University Club of Chicago. Hidden inside another skyscraper, there's a great Gothic room, all stone arches and stained glass. The room is filled mostly with people with white hair—there has been a big push to find younger members to fill in the growing spaces in the membership ranks—and they nod and wave at him and Chaz. They're given a table in the middle of the room.

Ebert silently declines all entreaties from the fussy waiters. Food arrives only for Chaz and a friend who joins them. Ebert writes them notes, tearing pages from his spiral notepad, tapping his fingers together for his words to be read aloud. Everyone smiles and laughs about old stories. More and more, that's how Ebert lives these days, through memories of what things used to feel like and sound like and taste like. When his friend suddenly apologizes for eating in front of him, for talking about the buttered scallops and how the cream and the fish and the wine combine to make a kind of delicate smoke, Ebert shakes his head. He begins to write and tears a note from the spiral.

No, no, it reads. *You're eating for me.*

Gene Siskel died eleven years ago, in February 1999, from a brain tumor. He was fifty-three years old. He had suffered terrible headaches in those last several months, but he was private about his pain. He didn't talk about being sick or how he felt or what he expected or hoped for. He was stoic and solitary and quiet in his death. Siskel and Ebert were both defined, for most of their adult lives, by comparative measures: the fat one, the bald one, the loud one, the skinny one. Siskel was also the careful one. He joked that Ebert's middle name was "Full Disclosure." Ebert's world has never had many secrets in it. Even at the end, when Siskel knew what was coming, he kept his secrets. He and Ebert never once spoke about his looming death.

There are pictures of Siskel all over the brownstone—on the grand piano, in the kitchen, on bookshelves. The biggest one is in the living room; Ebert can see it from his recliner. In almost all the pictures, Siskel and Ebert—never Ebert and Siskel—are standing together, shoulder to shoulder, smiling, two big thumbs-up. In the picture in the living room, they're also wearing tuxedos.

"Oh, Gene," Chaz says, and that's all she says.

All these years later, the top half of Ebert's face still registers sadness when Siskel's name comes up. His eyes well up behind his glasses, and for the first time, they overwhelm his smile. He begins to type into his computer, slowly, deliberately. He presses the button and the speakers light up. "I've never said this before," the voice says, "but we were born to be Siskel and Ebert." He thinks for a moment before he begins typing again. There's a long pause before he hits the button. "I just miss the guy so much," the voice says. Ebert presses the button again. "I just miss the guy so much."

Last February, to mark the tenth anniversary of Siskel's death, Ebert wrote an entry in his online journal called "Remembering Gene." He calls it up on his screen. It is beautifully written, filled with stories about arguments, even pitched battles, but nearly every memory is tinged with love and humor. Ebert scrolls through each paragraph, his eyes brimming, the smile winning again. The first lousy balcony set had painted pop bottles for rail supports. Siskel had courtside tickets for the Bulls and thought Phil Jackson was a sage. His beautiful daughters, Cate and Callie, were the flower girls for the Eberts' wedding.

And then comes the turn. Gene's first headache struck in the back of a limo on their way to be on *Leno*, which was broadcasting from Chicago. In front of the audience, Siskel could manage only to agree with everything Ebert said; they made it a gag. That night Siskel went to the Bulls game because they were in the playoffs, but the next day he underwent some tests. Not long after that, he had surgery, but he never told anyone where he was going to have it. He came back and for a time he continued taping the show with Ebert. Siskel's nephew would help him to his seat on the set, but only after the set was cleared.

Our eyes would meet, the voice reads from Ebert's journal, *unspoken words were between us, but we never spoke openly about his problems or his prognosis. That's how he wanted it, and that was his right.*

Gene Siskel taped his last show, and within a week or two he was dead. Ebert had lost half his identity.

He scrolls down to the entry's final paragraph.

We once spoke with Disney and CBS about a sitcom to be titled Best Enemies. *It would be about two movie critics joined in a love/hate relationship. It never went anywhere, but we both believed it was a good idea. Maybe the problem was that no one else could possibly understand how meaningless was the hate, how deep was the love.*

Ebert keeps scrolling down. Below his journal he had embedded video of his first show alone, the balcony seat empty across the aisle. It was a tribute, in three parts. He wants to watch them now, because he wants to remember, but at the bottom of the page there are only three big black squares. In the middle of the squares, white type reads: "Content deleted. This video is no longer available because it has been deleted." Ebert leans into the screen, trying to figure out what's happened. He looks across at Chaz. The top half of his face turns red, and his eyes well up again, but this time, it's not sadness surfacing. He's shaking. It's anger.

Chaz looks over his shoulder at the screen. "Those fu—," she says, catching herself.

They think it's Disney again—that they've taken down the videos. Terms-of-use violation.

This time, the anger lasts long enough for Ebert to write it down. He opens a new page in his text-to-speech program, a blank white sheet. He types in capital letters, stabbing at the keys with his delicate, trembling hands: MY TRIBUTE appears behind the cursor in the top left corner. ON THE FIRST SHOW AFTER HIS DEATH. But Ebert doesn't press the button that fires up the speakers. He presses a different button, a button that makes the words bigger. He presses the button again and again and again, the words growing bigger and bigger and bigger until they become too big to fit the screen, now they're just letters, but he keeps hitting the button, bigger and bigger still, now just shapes and angles, just geometry filling the white screen with black like the three squares. Roger Ebert is shaking, his entire body is shaking, and he's still hitting the button, bang, bang, bang, and he's shouting now. He's standing outside on the street corner and he's arching his back and he's shouting at the top of his lungs.

His doctors would like to try one more operation, would like one more chance to reclaim what cancer took from him, to restore his voice. Chaz would like him to try once more, too. But Ebert has refused. Even if the cancer comes back, he will probably decline significant intervention. The last surgery was his worst, and it did him more harm than good. Asked about the possibility of more surgery, he shakes his head and types before pressing the button.

"Over and out," the voice says.

Ebert is dying in increments, and he is aware of it.

I know it is coming, and I do not fear it, because I believe there is nothing on the other side of death to fear, he writes in a journal entry titled "Go Gently into That Good Night." *I hope to be spared as much pain as possible on the approach path. I was perfectly content before I was born, and I think of death as the same state. What I am grateful for is the gift of intelligence, and for life, love, wonder, and laughter. You can't say it wasn't interesting. My lifetime's memories are what I have brought home from the trip. I will require them for eternity no more than that little souvenir of the Eiffel Tower I brought home from Paris.*

There has been no death-row conversion. He has not found God. He has been beaten in some ways. But his other senses have picked up since he lost his sense of taste. He has tuned better into life. Some things aren't as important as they once were; some things are more important than ever. He has built for himself a new kind of universe. Roger Ebert is no mystic, but he knows things we don't know.

I believe that if, at the end of it all, according to our abilities, we have done something to make others a little happier, and something to make ourselves a little happier, that is about the best we can do. To make others less happy is a crime. To make ourselves unhappy is where all crime starts. We must try to contribute joy to the world. That is true no matter what our problems, our health, our circumstances. We must try. I didn't always know this, and am happy I lived long enough to find it out.

Ebert takes joy from the world in nearly all the ways he once did. He has had to find a new way to laugh—by closing his eyes and slapping both hands on his knees—but he still laughs. He and Chaz continue to travel. (They spent Thanksgiving in Barbados.) And he still finds joy in books, and in art, and in movies—a greater joy than he ever has. He gives more movies more stars.

But now it's getting late, which means he has his own work to do. Chaz heads off to bed. Millie, for the moment, hasn't been seized by night terrors, and the brownstone is quiet and nearly dark. Just the lamp is lit beside his chair. He leans back. He streams Radio Caroline—the formerly pirate radio station—and he begins to write. Everything fades out but the words. They appear quickly. Perfect sentences, artful sentences, illuminating sentences come out of him at a ridiculous, enviable pace, his fingers sometimes struggling to keep up.

Earlier today, his publisher sent him two copies of his newest book, the silver-jacketed *Great Movies III*, wrapped in plastic. Ebert turned them over in his hands, smiling with satisfaction—he wrote most of it in hospital beds—before he put them on a shelf in his office, by the desk he can no longer sit behind. They filled the last hole on the third shelf of his own published work; later this year, another book—*The Pot and How to Use It*, a collection of Ebert's rice-cooker recipes—will occupy the first space on a fourth shelf. Ebert's readers have asked him to write his autobiography next, but he looks up from his laptop and shrugs at the thought. He's already written a lot about himself on his journal, about his little childhood home in Champaign-Urbana and the days he spent on TV and in hospitals, and he would rather not say the same thing twice.

Besides, he has a review to finish. He returns his attention to his laptop, its glow making white squares in his glasses. Music plays. Words come.

Pedro Almodóvar loves the movies with lust and abandon and the skill of an experienced lover. Broken Embraces *is a voluptuary of a film, drunk on primary colors, caressing Penélope Cruz, using the devices of a Hitchcock to distract us with surfaces while the sinister uncoils beneath. As it ravished me, I longed for a freeze-frame to allow me to savor a shot.*

Ebert gives it four stars.

CHARLIE LEDUFF

■

What Killed Aiyana Stanley-Jones?

FROM *Mother Jones*

IT WAS JUST AFTER MIDNIGHT on the morning of May 16 and the neighbors say the streetlights were out on Lillibridge Street. It is like that all over Detroit, where whole blocks regularly go dark with no warning or any apparent pattern. Inside the lower unit of a duplex halfway down the gloomy street, Charles Jones, twenty-five, was pacing, unable to sleep.

His seven-year-old daughter, Aiyana Mo'nay Stanley-Jones, slept on the couch as her grandmother watched television. Outside, Television was watching them. A half-dozen masked officers of the Special Response Team—Detroit's version of SWAT—were at the door, guns drawn. In tow was an A&E crew filming an episode of *The First 48*, its true-crime program. The conceit of the show is that homicide detectives have forty-eight hours to crack a murder case before the trail goes cold. Thirty-four hours earlier, Je'Rean Blake Nobles, seventeen, had been shot outside a liquor store on nearby Mack Avenue; an informant had ID'd a man named Chauncey Owens as the shooter and provided this address.

The SWAT team tried the steel door to the building. It was unlocked. They threw a flash-bang grenade through the window of the lower unit and kicked open its wooden door, which was also unlocked. The grenade landed so close to Aiyana that it burned her blanket. Officer Joseph Weekley, the lead commando—who'd been featured before on another A&E show, *Detroit SWAT*—burst into the house. His weapon fired a single shot, the bullet striking Aiyana in the head and exiting her neck. It all happened in a matter of seconds.

"They had time," a Detroit police detective told me. "You don't go into a home around midnight. People are drinking. People are awake. Me? I would have waited until the morning when the guy went to the liquor store to buy a quart of milk. That's how it's supposed to be done."

But the SWAT team didn't wait. Maybe because the cameras were rolling, maybe because a Detroit police officer had been murdered two weeks earlier while trying to apprehend a suspect. This was the first raid on a house since his death.

Police first floated the story that Aiyana's grandmother had grabbed Weekley's gun. Then, realizing that sounded implausible, they said she'd brushed the gun as she ran past the door. But the grandmother says she was lying on the far side of the couch, away from the door.

Compounding the tragedy is the fact that the police threw the grenade into the wrong apartment. The suspect fingered for Blake's murder, Chauncey Owens, lived in the *upstairs* flat, with Charles Jones's sister.

Plus, grenades are rarely used when rounding up suspects, even murder suspects. But it was dark. And TV may have needed some pyrotechnics.

"I'm worried they went Hollywood," said a high-ranking Detroit police official, who spoke on the condition of anonymity due to the sensitivity of the investigation and simmering resentment in the streets. "It is not protocol. And I've got to say in all my years in the department, I've never used a flash-bang in a case like this."

The official went on to say that the SWAT team was not briefed about the presence of children in the house, although the neighborhood informant who led homicide detectives to the Lillibridge address told them that children lived there. There were even toys on the lawn.

"It was a total fuck-up," the official said. "A total, unfortunate fuck-up."

Owens, a habitual criminal, was arrested upstairs minutes after Aiyana's shooting and charged for the slaying of Je'Rean. His motive, authorities say, was that the teen failed to pay him the proper respect. Jones, too, later became a person of interest in Je'Rean's murder—he allegedly went along for the ride—but Jones denies it, and he's lawyered up and moved to the suburbs.

As Officer Weekley wept on the sidewalk, Aiyana was rushed to the trauma table, where she was pronounced dead. Her body was transferred to the Wayne County morgue.

Dr. Carl Schmidt is the chief medical examiner there. There are at least fifty corpses on hold in his morgue cooler, some unidentified, others whose next of kin are too poor to bury them. So Dr. Schmidt keeps them on layaway, zipped up in body bags as family members wait for a ship to come in that never seems to arrive.

The day I visited, a Hollywood starlet was tailing the doctor, studying for her role as the medical examiner in ABC's new Detroit-based murder drama *Detroit 1-8-7*. The title is derived from the California penal code for murder: 187. In Michigan, the designation for homicide is actually 750.316, but that's just a mouthful of detail.

"You might say that the homicide of Aiyana is the natural conclusion to the disease from which she suffered," Schmidt told me.

"What disease was that?" I asked.

"The psychopathology of growing up in Detroit," he said. "Some people are doomed from birth because their environment is so toxic."

Was it so simple? Was it inevitable, as the doctor said, that abject poverty would lead to Aiyana's death and so many others? Was it death by TV? By police incompetence? By parental neglect? By civic malfeasance? About 350 people are murdered each year in Detroit. There are some 10,000 unsolved homicides dating back to 1960. Many are as fucked up and sad as Aiyana's. But I felt unraveling this one death could help diagnose what has gone wrong in this city, so I decided to retrace the events leading up to that pitiable moment on the porch on Lillibridge Street.

People my mother's age like to tell me about Detroit's good old days of soda fountains and shopping markets and lazy Saturday night drives. But the fact is Detroit and its suburbs were dying forty years ago. The whole country knew it, and the whole country laughed. *A bunch of lazy, uneducated blue-collar incompetents. The Rust Belt. Forget about it.*

When I was a teenager, my mother owned a struggling little flower shop on the East Side, not far from where Aiyana was killed. On a hot afternoon around one Mother's Day, I was working in the back greenhouse. It was a sweatbox, and I went across the street to the liquor store for a soda pop. A small crowd of agitated black people was gathered on the sidewalk. The store bell jingled its little requiem as I pulled the door open.

Inside, splayed on the floor underneath the rack of snack cakes near the register, was a black man in a pool of blood. The blood was congealing into a pancake on the dirty linoleum. His eyes and mouth were open and held that milky expression of a drunk who has fallen asleep with his eyes open. The red halo around his skull gave the scene a feeling of serenity.

An Arab family owned the store, and one of the men—the one with the pocked face and loud voice—was talking on the telephone, but I remember no sounds. His brother stood over the dead man, a pistol in his hand, keeping an eye on the door in case someone walked in wanting to settle things.

"You should go," he said to me, shattering the silence with a wave of his hand. "Forget what you saw, little man. Go." He wore a gold bracelet as thick as a gymnasium rope. I lingered a moment, backing out while taking it in: the bracelet, the liquor, the blood, the gun, the Ho-Hos, the cheapness of it all.

The flower shop is just a pile of bricks now, but despite what the Arab told me, I did not forget what I saw. Whenever I see a person who died of violence or misadventure, I think about the dead man with the open eyes on the dirty floor of the liquor store. I've seen him in the faces of soldiers when I was covering the Iraq War. I saw him in the face of my sister, who died a violent death in a filthy section of Detroit a decade ago. I saw him in the face of my sister's daughter, who died from a heroin overdose in a suburban basement near the interstate, weeks after I moved back to Michigan with my wife to raise our daughter and take a job with the *Detroit News*.

No one cared much about Detroit or its industrial suburbs until the Dow collapsed, the chief executives of the Big Three went to Washington to grovel, and General Motors declared bankruptcy—one hundred years after its founding. Suddenly, Detroit was historic, symbolic—hip, even. I began to get calls from reporters around the world wondering what Detroit was like, what was happening here. They were wondering if the Rust Belt cancer had metastasized and was creeping to Los Angeles and London and Barcelona. Was Detroit an outlier or an epicenter?

Je'Rean Nobles was one of the rare black males in Detroit who made it through high school. A good kid with average grades, Je'Rean went to Southeastern High, which is situated in an industrial belt of moldering Chrysler assembly plants. Completed in 1917, the school, attended by white students at the time, was considered so far out in the wilds that its athletic teams took the nickname "Jungaleers."

With large swaths of the city rewilding—empty lots are returning to prairie and woodland as the city depopulates—Southeastern was slated to absorb students from nearby Kettering High this year as part of a massive school-consolidation effort. That is, until someone realized that the schools are controlled by rival gangs. So bad is the rivalry that when the schools face off to play football or basketball, spectators from the visiting team are banned.

Southeastern's motto is *Age Quod Agis*: "Attend to Your Business." And Je'Rean did. By wit and will, he managed to make it through. A member of JROTC, he was on his way to the military recruitment office after senior prom and commencement. But Je'Rean never went to prom, much less the Afghanistan theater, because he couldn't clear the killing fields of Detroit. He became a horrifying statistic—one of 103 kids and teens murdered between January 2009 and July 2010.

Je'Rean's crime? He looked at Chauncey Owens the wrong way, detectives say.

It was 2:40 in the afternoon on May 14 when Je'Rean went to the Motor City liquor store and ice-cream stand to get himself an orange juice to wash down his McDonald's. About forty kids were milling around in front of the soft-serve window. That's when Owens, thirty-four, pulled up on a moped.

Je'Rean might have thought it was funny to see a grown man driving a moped. He might have smirked. But according to a witness, he said nothing.

"Why you looking at me?" said Owens, getting off the moped. "Do you got a problem or something? What the fuck you looking at?"

A slender, pimply faced kid, Je'Rean was not an intimidating fig-ure. One witness had him pegged for thirteen years old.

Je'Rean balled up his tiny fist. "What?" he croaked.

"Oh, stay your ass right here," Owens growled. "I got something for you."

Owens sped two blocks back to Lillibridge and gathered up a posse, according to his statement to the police. The posse allegedly included Aiyana's father, Charles "C.J." Jones.

"It's some lil' niggas at the store talking shit—let's go whip they ass," Detective Theopolis Williams later testified that Owens told him during his interrogation.

Owens switched his moped for a Chevy Blazer. Jones and two other men known as "Lil' James" and "Dirt" rode along for Je'Rean's ass-whipping. Lil' James brought along a .357 Magnum—at the be-hest of Jones, Detective Williams testified, because Jones was afraid someone would try to steal his "diamond Cartier glasses."

Je'Rean knew badness was on its way and called his mother to come pick him up. She arrived too late. Owens got there first and shot Je'Rean clear through the chest with Lil' James' gun. Clutching his juice in one hand and two dollars in the other, Je'Rean staggered across Mack Avenue and collapsed in the street. A minute later, a friend took the two dollars as a keepsake. A few minutes after that, Je'Rean's mother, Lyvonne Cargill, arrived and got behind the wheel of the car that friends had dragged him into.

Why would anyone move a gunshot victim, much less toss him in a car? It is a matter of conditioning, Cargill later told me. In Detroit, the official response time of an ambulance to a 911 call is twelve min-utes. Paramedics say it is routinely much longer. Sometimes they come in a Crown Victoria with only a defibrillator and a blanket, be-cause there are no other units available. The hospital was six miles away. Je'Rean's mother drove as he gurgled in the backseat.

"My baby, my baby, my baby. God, don't take my baby."

They made it to the trauma ward, where Je'Rean was pronounced dead. His body was transferred to Dr. Schmidt and the Wayne County morgue.

The raid on the Lillibridge house that took little Aiyana's life came two weeks and at least a dozen homicides after the last time police stormed into a Detroit home. That house, too, is on the city's East Side, a nondescript brick duplex with a crumbling garage whose driveway funnels into busy Schoenherr Road.

Responding to a breaking-and-entering and shots-fired call at 3:30 A.M., Officer Brian Huff, a 12-year veteran, walked into that dark house. Behind him stood two rookies. His partner took the rear entrance. Huff and his partner were not actually called to the scene; they'd taken it upon themselves to assist the younger cops, according to the police version of events. Another cruiser with two officers responded as well.

Huff entered with his gun still holstered. Behind the door was Jason Gibson, twenty-five, a violent man with a history of gun crimes, assaults on police, and repeated failures to honor probationary sentences.

Gibson is a tall, thick-necked man who, like the character Omar from *The Wire*, made his living robbing dope houses. Which is what he was doing at this house, authorities contend, when he put three bullets in Officer Huff's face.

What happened after that is a matter of conjecture, as Detroit officials have had problems getting their stories straight. Neighbor Paul Jameson, a former soldier whose wife had called in the break-in to 911, said the rookies ran toward the house and opened fire after Huff was shot.

Someone radioed in, and more police arrived — but the official story of what happened that night has changed repeatedly. First, it was six cops who responded to the 911 call. Then eight, then eleven. Officials said Gibson ran out the front of the house. Then they said he ran out the back of the house, even though there is no back door. Then they said he jumped out a back window. It was Jameson who finally dragged Huff out of the house and gave him CPR in the driveway, across the street from the Boys & Girls Club. In the end, Gibson was charged with Huff's murder and the attempted murders of four more officers. But police officials have refused to discuss how one got shot in the foot.

"We believe some of them were struck by friendly fire," the high-ranking cop told me. "But our ammo's so bad, we can't do ballistics testing. We've got nothing but bullet fragments."

A neighbor who tends the lawn in front of the dope house out of respect to Huff wonders why so many cops came in the first place, given that "the police hardly come around at all, much less that many cops that fast on a home break-in."

But the real mystery behind Officer Huff's murder is why Gibson was out on the street in the first place. In 2007, he attacked a cop and tried to take his gun. For that he was given simple probation. He failed to report. Police caught him again in November 2009 in possession of a handgun stolen from an Ohio cop. Gibson bonded out last January and actually showed up for his trial in circuit court on February 17.

The judge, Cynthia Gray Hathaway, set his bond at $20,000 — only ten percent of which was due upfront — and adjourned the trial without explanation, according to the docket. Known as "Half-Day" Hathaway, the judge was removed from the bench for six months by the Michigan Supreme Court a decade ago for, among other things, adjourning trials to sneak away on vacation.

Predictably, Gibson did not show for his new court date. The day after Huff was killed, and under fire from the police for her leniency toward Gibson, Judge Hathaway went into the case file and made changes, according to notations made in the court's computerized docket system. She refused to let me see the original paper file, despite the fact that it is a public record, and has said that she can't comment on the case because she might preside in the trial against Gibson.

More than 4,000 people attended Officer Huff's funeral at the Greater Grace Temple on the city's Northwest Side. Police officers came from Canada and across Michigan. They were restless and agitated and pulled at the collars of dress blues that didn't seem to fit. Bagpipes played and the rain fell.

Mayor Dave Bing spoke. "The madness has to stop," he said.

But the madness was only beginning.

It might be a stretch to see anything more than Detroit's problems in Detroit's problems. Still, as the American middle class collapses, it's worth perhaps remembering that the East Side of Detroit — the place where Aiyana, Je'Rean, and Officer Huff all died — was once its industrial cradle.

Henry Ford built his first automobile assembly-line plant in Highland Park in 1908 on the east side of Woodward Avenue, the thoroughfare that divides the east of Detroit from the west. Over the next fifty years, Detroit's East Side would become the world's machine shop, its factory floor. The city grew to 1.3 million people from 300,000 after Ford opened his Model T factory. Other auto plants sprang up on the East Side: Packard, Studebaker, Chrysler's Dodge Main. Soon, the Motor City's population surpassed that of Boston and Baltimore, old East Coast port cities founded on maritime shipping when the world moved by boat.

European intellectuals wondered at the whirl of building and spending in the new America. At the center of this economic dynamo was Detroit. "It is the home of mass-production, of very high wages and colossal profits, of lavish spending and reckless instalment-buying, of intense work and a large and shifting labour-surplus," British historian and MP Ramsay Muir wrote in 1927. "It regards itself as the temple of a new gospel of progress, to which I shall venture to give the name of 'Detroitism.'"

Skyscrapers sprang up virtually overnight. The city filled with people from all over the world: Arabs, Appalachians, Poles, African Americans, all in their separate neighborhoods surrounding the factories. Forbidden by restrictive real estate covenants and racist custom, the blacks were mostly restricted to Paradise Valley, which ran the length of Woodward Avenue. As the black population grew, so did black frustration over poor housing and rock-fisted police.

Soon, the air was the color of a filthy dishrag. The water in the Detroit River was so bad, it was said you could bottle it and sell it as poison. The beavers disappeared from the river around 1930.

But pollution didn't kill Detroit. What did?

No one can answer that fully. You can blame it on the John Deere mechanical cotton-picker of 1950, which uprooted the sharecropper and sent him north looking for a living—where he found he was locked out of the factories by the unions. You might blame it on the urban renewal and interstate highway projects that rammed a freeway down the middle of Paradise Valley, displacing thousands of blacks and packing the Negro tenements tighter still. (Thomas Sugrue, in his seminal book *The Origins of the Urban Crisis*, writes that residents in Detroit's predominantly black lower East Side reported 206 rat bites in 1951 and 1952.)

You might blame postwar industrial policies that sent the factories to the suburbs, the rural South, and the western deserts. You might blame the 1967 race riot and the white flight that followed. You might blame Coleman Young—the city's first black mayor—and his culture of cronyism. You could blame it on the gas shocks of the '70s that opened the door to foreign car competition. You might point to the trade agreements of the Clinton years, which allowed American manufacturers to leave the country by the back door. You might blame the UAW, which demanded things like full pay for idle workers, or myopic Big Three management who, instead of saying no, simply tacked the cost onto the price of a car.

Then there is the thought that Detroit is simply a boomtown that went bust the minute Henry Ford began to build it. The car made Detroit, and the car unmade Detroit. The auto industry allowed for sprawl. It also allowed a man to escape the smoldering city.

In any case, Detroit began its long precipitous decline during the 1950s, precisely when the city—and the United States—was at its peak. As Detroit led the nation in median income and homeownership, automation and foreign competition were forcing companies like Packard to shutter their doors. That factory closed in 1956 and was left to rot, pulling down the East Side, which pulled down the city. Inexplicably, its carcass still stands and burns incessantly.

By 1958, 20 percent of the Detroit workforce was jobless. Not to worry: The city had its own welfare system, decades before Lyndon Johnson's Great Society. The city provided clothing, fuel, rent, and $10 every week to adults for food; children got $5. Word of the free milk and honey made its way down South, and the poor "Negroes" and "hillbillies" flooded in.

But if it wasn't for them, the city population would have sunk further than it did. Nor is corruption a black or liberal thing. Louis Miriani, the last Republican mayor of Detroit, who served from 1957 to 1962, was sent to federal prison for tax evasion when he couldn't explain how he made nearly a quarter of a million dollars on a reported salary of only $25,000.

Today—seventy-five years after the beavers disappeared from the Detroit River—"Detroitism" means something completely different. It means uncertainty and abandonment and psychopathology. The city reached a peak population of 1.9 million people in the 1950s, and it was 83 percent white. Now Detroit has fewer than 800,000 people, is 83 percent black, and is the only American city that has surpassed a million people and dipped back below that threshold.

"There are plenty of good people in Detroit," boosters like to say. And there are. Tens of thousands of them, hundreds of thousands. There are lawyers and doctors and auto executives with nice homes and good jobs, community elders trying to make things better, teachers who spend their own money on classroom supplies, people who mow lawns out of respect for the dead, parents who raise their children, ministers who help with funeral expenses.

For years it was the all-but-official policy of the newspapers to ignore the black city, since the majority of readers lived in the predominantly white suburbs. And now that the papers do cover Detroit, boosters complain about a lack of balance. To me, that's like writing about the surf conditions in the Gaza Strip. As for the struggles of a generation of living people, the murder of a hundred children, they ask me: "What's new in that?"

Detroit's East Side is now the poorest, most violent quarter of America's poorest, most violent big city. The illiteracy, child poverty, and unemployment rates hover around fifty percent.

Stand at the corner of Lillibridge Street and Mack Avenue and walk a mile in each direction from Alter Road to Gratiot Avenue (pronounced Gra-*shit*). You will count thirty-four churches, a dozen liquor stores, six beauty salons and barber shops, a funeral parlor, a sprawling Chrysler engine and assembly complex working at less than half-capacity, and three dollar stores—but no grocery stores. In fact, there are no chain grocery stores in all of Detroit.

There are two elementary schools in the area, both in desperate need of a lawnmower and a can of paint. But there is no money; the struggling school system has a $363 million deficit. Robert Bobb was hired in 2009 as the emergency financial manager and given sweeping powers to balance the books. But even he couldn't stanch the tsunami of red ink; the deficit ballooned more than $140 million under his guidance.

Bobb did uncover graft and fraud and waste, however. He caught a lunch lady stealing the children's milk money. A former risk manager for the district was indicted for siphoning off $3 million for personal use. The president of the school board, Otis Mathis, recently admitted that he had only rudimentary writing skills shortly before being forced to resign for fondling himself during a meeting with the school superintendent.

The graduation rate for Detroit schoolkids hovers around 35 percent. Moreover, the Detroit public school system is the worst performer in the National Assessment of Educational Progress tests, with nearly 80 percent of eighth-graders unable to do basic math. So bad is it for Detroit's children that Education Secretary Arne Duncan said last year, "I lose sleep over that one."

Duncan may lie awake, but many civic leaders appear to walk around with their eyes sealed shut. As a reporter, I've worked from New York to St. Louis to Los Angeles, and Detroit is the only big city I know of that doesn't put out a crime blotter tracking the day's mayhem. While other American metropolises have gotten control of their murder rate, Detroit's remains where it was during the crack epidemic. Add in the fact that half the police precincts were closed in 2005 for budgetary reasons, and the crime lab was closed two years ago due to ineptitude, and it might explain why five of the nine members of the city council carry a firearm.

To avoid the embarrassment of being the nation's perpetual murder capital, the police department took to cooking the homicide statistics, reclassifying murders as other crimes or incidents. For instance, in 2008 a man was shot in the head. ME Schmidt ruled it a homicide; the police decided it was a suicide. That year, the police said there were 306 homicides—until I began digging. The number was actually 375. I also found that the police and judicial systems were so broken that in more than 70 percent of murders, the killer got away with it. In Los Angeles, by comparison, the unsolved-murder rate is 22 percent.

The fire department is little better. When I moved back to Detroit two years ago, I profiled a firehouse on the East Side. Much of the firefighters' equipment was substandard: Their boots had holes; they were alerted to fires by fax from the central office. (They'd jerry-rigged a contraption where the fax pushes a door hinge, which falls on a screw wired to an actual alarm.) I called the fire department to ask for its statistics. They'd not been tabulated for four years.

Detroit has been synonymous with arson since the '80s, when the city burst into flames in a pre-Halloween orgy of fire and destruction known as Devil's Night. At its peak popularity, 810 fires were set in a three-day span. Devil's Night is no longer the big deal it used to be, topping out last year at around 65 arsons. That's good news until you realize that in Detroit, some 500 fires are set every single month. That's five times as many as New York, in a city one-tenth the size.

As a reporter at the *Detroit News*, I get plenty of phone calls from people in the neighborhoods. A man called me once to say he had witnessed a murder, but the police refused to take his statement. When I called the head of the homicide bureau and explained the situation, he told me, "Oh yeah? Have him call me," and then hung up the phone. One man, who wanted to turn himself in for a murder, gave up trying to call the Detroit police; he drove to Ohio and turned himself in there.

The police have been working under a federal consent decree since a 2003 investigation found that detectives were locking up murder witnesses for days on end, without access to a lawyer, until they coughed up a name. The department was also cited for excessive force after people died in lockup and at the hands of rogue cops.

Detroit has since made little progress on the federal consent decree. Newspapers made little of it—until the U.S. Attorney revealed that the federal monitor of the decree was having an affair with the priapic mayor Kwame Kilpatrick, who was forced to resign, and now sits in prison convicted of perjury and obstruction of justice.

The Kilpatrick scandal, combined with the murder rate, spurred the newly elected mayor, Dave Bing—an NBA Hall of Famer—to fire Police Chief James Barrens last year and replace him with Warren Evans, the Wayne County sheriff. The day Barrens cleaned out his desk, a burglar cleaned out Barrens' house.

Evans brought a refreshing honesty to a department plagued by ineptitude and secrecy. He computerized daily crime statistics, created a mobile strike force commanded by young and educated go-getters, and dispatched cops to crime hot spots. He assigned the SWAT team the job of rounding up murder suspects, a task that had previously been done by detectives.

Evans told me then that major crimes were routinely underreported by 20 percent. He also told me that perhaps 50 percent of Detroit's drivers were operating without a license or insurance. "It's going to stop," he promised. "We're going to pull people over for traffic violations and we're going to take their cars if they're not legal. That's one less knucklehead driving around looking to do a drive-by."

His approach was successful, with murder dropping more than 20 percent in his first year. If that isn't a record for any major metropolis, it is certainly a record for Detroit. (And that statistic is true; I checked.)

So there should have been a parade with confetti and tanks of lemonade, but instead, the complaints about overaggressive cops began to roll in. Then Evans' own driver shot a man last October. The official version was that two men were walking in the middle of a street on the East Side when Evans and his driver told them to walk on the sidewalk. One ran off. Evans' driver—a cop—gave chase. The man stopped, turned, and pulled a gun. Evans' driver dropped him with a single shot. An investigation was promised. The story rated three paragraphs in the daily papers, and the media never followed up. Then Huff got killed. Then Je'Rean was murdered. Then came the homicide-by-cop of little Aiyana.

Chief Evans might have survived it all, had he, too, not been drawn to the lights of Hollywood. As it turns out, he was filming a pilot for his own reality show, entitled *The Chief.*

The program's six-minute sizzle reel begins with Evans dressed in full battle gear in front of the shattered Michigan Central Rail Depot, cradling a semiautomatic rifle and declaring that he would "do whatever it takes" to take back the streets of Detroit. I saw the tape and wrote about its existence after the killing of Aiyana, but the story went nowhere until two months later, when someone in City Hall leaked a copy to the local ABC affiliate. Evans was fired.

But in Evans' defense, he seemed to understand one thing: After the collapse of the car industry and the implosion of the real estate bubble, there is little else Detroit has to export except its misery.

And America is buying. There are no fewer than two TV dramas, two documentaries, and three reality programs being filmed here. Even *Time* bought a house on the East Side last year for $99,000. The gimmick was to have its reporters live there and chronicle the decline of the Motor City for one year.

Somebody should have told company executives back in New York that they had wildly overpaid. In Detroit, a new car costs more than the average house.

Aiyana's family retained Geoffrey Fieger, the flamboyant, brass-knuckled lawyer who represented Dr. Jack Kevorkian—a.k.a. Dr. Death. With Chief Evans vacationing overseas with a subordinate, Fieger ran wild, holding a press conference where he claimed he had seen videotape of Officer Weekley firing into the house from the porch. Fieger alleged a police cover-up. Detroit grew restless.

I went to see Fieger to ask him to show me the tape. Fieger's suburban office is a shrine to Geoffrey Fieger. The walls are covered with photographs of Geoffrey Fieger. On his desk is a bronze bust of Geoffrey Fieger. And during our conversation, he referred to himself in the third person—Geoffrey Fieger.

"What killed Aiyana is what killed the people in New Orleans and the rider on the transit in Oakland, and that's police bullets and police arrogance and police cover-up," Geoffrey Fieger said. "People call it police brutality. But Geoffrey Fieger calls it police arrogance. Even in Detroit, a predominantly black city. They killed a child and then they lied about it."

I asked Fieger if Charles Jones should accept some culpability in his daughter's death, considering his alleged role in Je'Rean's murder, the stolen cars found in his backyard, and the fact that his daughter slept on the couch next to an unlocked door.

"So what?" Fieger barked. "I'm not representing the father; I'm speaking for the daughter." He also pointed out that while Jones remains a person of interest in Je'Rean's murder, he has not been arrested. "It's police disinformation."

As for the videotape of the killing, Geoffrey Fieger said he did not have it.

I was allowed to meet with Charles Jones the following morning at Fieger's office, but with the caveat that I could only ask him questions about the evening his daughter was killed.

Jones, twenty-five, a slight man with frizzy braids, wore a dingy t-shirt. An eleventh-grade dropout and convicted robber, he said he supported his seven children with "a little this, a little that—I got a few tricks and trades."

He has three boys with Aiyana's mother, Dominika Stanley, and three boys with another woman, whom he had left long ago.

Jones' new family had been on the drift for the past few years as he tried to pull it together. His mother's house on Lillibridge, he said, was just supposed to be a way station to better things.

They had even kept Aiyana in her old school, Trix Elementary, because it was something consistent in her life, a clean and safe school in a city with too few. They drove her there every morning, five miles.

"I can accept the shooting was a mistake," Jones said about his daughter's death as a bleary-eyed Stanley sat motionless next to him. "But I can't accept it because they lied about it. I can't heal properly because of it. It was all for the cameras. I don't want no apology from no police. It's too late."

I asked him if the way he was raising his daughter, the people he exposed her to, or the neighborhood where they lived—with its decaying houses and liquor stores—may have played a role.

Stanley suddenly emerged from her stupor: "What's that got to do with it?" she hissed.

"My daughter got love, honor, and respect. The environment didn't affect us none," Jones said. "The environment got nothing to do with kids."

Aiyana was laid to rest six days after her killing. The service was held at Second Ebenezer Church in Detroit, a drab cake-shaped megachurch near the Chrysler Freeway. A thousand people attended, as did the predictable plump of media.

The Rev. Al Sharpton delivered the eulogy, though his heart did not seem to be in it. It was a white cop who killed the girl, but Detroit is America's largest black city with a black mayor and a black chief of police. The sad and confusing circumstances of the murders of Je'Rean Blake and Officer Huff, both black, robbed Sharpton of some of his customary indignation.

"We're here today not to find blame, but to find out how we never have to come here again," said Sharpton, standing in the grand pulpit. "It's easy in our anger, our rage, to just vent and scream. But I would be doing Aiyana a disservice if we just vented instead of dealing with the real problems."

He went on: "This child is the breaking point."

Aiyana's pink-robed body was carried away by a horse-drawn carriage to the Trinity Cemetery, the same carriage that five years earlier had taken the body of Rosa Parks to Woodlawn Cemetery on the city's West Side. Once at Aiyana's graveside, Charles Jones released a dove.

Sharpton left and the Rev. Horace Sheffield, a local version of Sharpton, got stiffed for $4,000 in funeral costs, claiming Aiyana's father made off with the donations people gave to cover it.

"I'm trying to find him," Sheffield complained. "But he doesn't return my calls. It's always like that. People taking advantage of my benevolence. They went hog wild. I mean, hiring the Rosa Parks carriage?"

"I don't owe Sheffield shit," says Jones. "He got paid exactly what he was supposed to be paid."

While a thousand people mourned the tragic death of Aiyana, the body of Je'Rean Blake Nobles sat in a refrigerator at a local funeral parlor; his mother was too poor to bury him herself and too respectful to bury him until after the little girl's funeral, anyhow. The mortician charged $700 for the most basic viewing casket, even though the body was to be cremated.

Sharpton's people called Je'Rean's mother, Lyvonne Cargill, promising to come over to her house after Aiyana's funeral. She waited, but Sharpton never came.

"Sharpton's full of shit," said Cargill, a brassy 39-year-old who works as a stock clerk at Target. "He came here for publicity. He's from New York. What the hell you doing up here for? The kids are dropping like flies—especially young black males—and he's got nothing but useless words."

The Rev. Sheffield came to see Cargill. He gave her $800 for funeral costs.

As summer dragged on, the story of Aiyana faded from even the regional press. As for the tape that Geoffrey Fieger claimed would show the cops firing on Aiyana's house from outside, A&E turned it over to the police. The mayor's office is said to have a copy, as well as the Michigan State Police, who are now handling the investigation. Even on Lillibridge Street, the outrage has died down. But the people of

Lillibridge Street still look like they've been picked up by their hair and dropped from the rooftop. The crumbling houses still crumble. The streetlights still go on and off. The landlord of the duplex, Edward Taylor, let me into the Jones apartment. A woman was in his car, the motor running.

"They still owe me rent," he said with a face about the Joneses. "Don't bother locking it. It's now just another abandoned house in Detroit."

And with that, he was off.

Inside, toys, Hannah Montana shoes, and a pyramid of KFC cartons were left to rot. The smell was beastly. Outside, three men were loading the boiler, tubs, and sinks into a trailer to take to the scrapyard.

"Would you take a job at that Chrysler plant if there were any jobs there?" I asked one of the men, who was sweating under the weight of the cast iron.

"What the fuck do you think?" he said. "Of course I would. Except there ain't no job. We're taking what's left."

I went to visit Cargill, who lived just around the way. She told me that Je'Rean's best friend Chaise Sherrors, seventeen, had been murdered the night before—an innocent bystander who took a bullet in the head as he was on a porch clipping someone's hair.

"It just goes on," she said. "The silent suffering."

Chaise lived on the other side of the Chrysler complex. He, too, was about to graduate from Southeastern High. A good kid who showed neighborhood children how to work electric clippers, his dream was to open a barbershop. The morning after he was shot, Chaise's clippers were mysteriously deposited on his front porch, wiped clean and free of hair. There was no note.

If such a thing could be true, Chaise's neighborhood is worse than Je'Rean's. The house next door to his is rubble smelling of burnt pine, pissed on by the spray cans of the East Warren Crips. The house on the other side is in much the same state. So is the house across the street. In this shit, a one-year-old played next door, barefoot.

Chaise's mother, Britta McNeal, thirty-nine, sat on the porch staring blankly into the distance, smoking no-brand cigarettes. She thanked me for coming and showed me her home, which was clean and well kept. Then she introduced me to her fourteen-year-old son De'Erion, whose remains sat in an urn on the mantel. He was shot in the head and killed last year.

She had already cleared a space on the other end of the mantel for Chaise's urn.

"That's a hell of a pair of bookends," I offered.

"You know? I was thinking that," she said with tears.

The daughter of an autoworker and a home nurse, McNeal grew up in the promise of the black middle class that Detroit once offered. But McNeal messed up—she admits as much. She got pregnant at 15. She later went to nursing school but got sidetracked by her own health problems. School wasn't a priority. Besides, there was always a job in America when you needed one.

Until there wasn't. Like so many across the country, she's being evicted with no job and no place to go.

"I want to get out of here, but I can't," she said. "I got no money. I'm stuck. Not all of us are blessed."

She looked at her barefoot grandson playing in the wreckage of the dwelling next door and wondered if he would make it to manhood.

"I keep calling about these falling-down houses, but the city never comes," she said.

McNeal wondered how she was going to pay the $3,000 for her son's funeral. Desperation, she said, feels like someone's reaching down your throat and ripping out your guts.

It would be easy to lay the blame on McNeal for the circumstances in which she raised her sons. But is she responsible for police officers with broken computers in their squad cars, firefighters with holes in their boots, ambulances that arrive late, a city that can't keep its lights on and leaves its vacant buildings to the arsonist's match, a state government that allows corpses to stack up in the morgue, multinational corporations that move away and leave poisoned fields behind, judges who let violent criminals walk the streets, school stewards who steal the children's milk money, elected officials who loot the city, automobile executives who couldn't manage a grocery store, or Wall Street grifters who destroyed the economy and left the nation's children with a burden of debt? Can she be blamed for that?

"I know society looks at a person like me and wants me to go away," she said. "'Go ahead, walk in the Detroit River and disappear.' But I can't. I'm alive. I need help. But when you call for help, it seems like no one's there.

"It feels like there ain't no love no more."

I left McNeal's porch and started my car. The radio was tuned to NPR and *A Prairie Home Companion* came warbling out of my speakers. I stared through the windshield at the little boy in the diaper playing amid the ruins, reached over, and switched it off.

J. ROBERT LENNON

■

Weber's Head

FROM *Salamander*

JOHN WEBER, THE FIRST PERSON to answer my ad, appeared pleasant enough, tall and round-faced with a receding cap of curls, sloped shoulders, and an easy, calm manner. He nodded constantly as I showed him around the place, as if willing to accept and agree with every single thing in the world for the rest of his life. At the time, these seemed like good portents. I didn't like searching for roommates and I didn't like dealing with people, so I told him he was welcome to the room and accepted his check.

He moved in the next day with the help of a wan, stringy-haired woman in hiking shorts, though it was late October and forty degrees outside. The woman did not smile, and hauled his boxes in the door with practiced efficiency while Weber began unpacking in his room. I asked her if she wanted any help.

"No," she said.

"Are you sure?" I wasn't doing anything, just waiting for noon to come along so that I could catch my bus.

She shook her head vigorously, her hair falling over her face. I returned to my coffee and magazine and left her alone.

When I came home from work that night, John Weber was standing alone in the kitchen with an apron around his waist. Various things were hissing and bubbling in pots and pans, and he beckoned me over with his spatula. The kitchen table was set with two place-mats—they must have belonged to him because I had never owned any in my life—and there were separate glasses for water and wine. I didn't recognize the silverware, either. It was heavy and bright and lay upon folded cloth napkins.

"Expecting a guest?" I was thinking of the woman from that morning.

"Nope. Just a roommate!"

He was grinning, waiting for a reaction.

"You mean me?"

"You're my only roommate!" he laughed. "Take a load off!"

His manner could be described as bustling. He pulled out my chair for me, took the briefcase from my hand, and set it on the floor behind me. "Red or white?"

I looked at the table, and back at him. "What?"

"Red or white?"

"Uh . . . "

He rolled, jocularly, his large, slightly bulging gray eyes, then gestured toward the counter, where two bottles of wine stood, uncorked. One of them, the white, was tucked into a cylindrical stone bottle cooler, the kind you keep in the freezer. I had never seen one before, outside of a cooking supply catalog, and had never considered that somebody might actually own one.

"Uh . . . red," I said.

"You sure not white?"

"Yes."

"Because the white spoils faster once you open it."

"I'm sorry," I said. "White wine gives me a headache."

He rolled his eyes again, not so jocularly this time, and snatched the white wine off the counter. Back in the fridge it went with a clatter, and then the cooler into the freezer. He poured my red wine with unnecessary haste and some of it slopped over onto the tablecloth, which must also have been his.

"How was your day?" he asked a minute later, his back to me, his arms working over the pots and pans.

"Fine." I took a swig of wine. It was not the gamy plonk I usually drank. "How was yours?"

"Exciting! I'm glad to be here."

"Is your room all put together?"

"Sure!" He turned off each burner and began transferring food to a pair of china plates. "I don't have many possessions," he went on. "I don't believe in them."

"Well, what about the napkins and placemats and tablecloth and all that?"

"Oh, someone gave them to me."

With a flourish, he whipped off his apron and hung it on a wall hook which I was certain he had installed there himself for this express purpose. In response to this effort, the landlord would no doubt someday withhold twenty dollars of the security deposit. Then John Weber lifted the two plates high into the air and glided them onto the placemats. With a similar motion, he seated himself, and then grinned at me again, awaiting my reaction.

Before me lay a lovely-looking lamb chop, overlaid with a coarse sauce of what appeared to be diced tomatoes, onions, and rosemary. There was a little pile of roasted new potatoes and some spears of asparagus. It was really very impressive, and I looked at it in dismay as the sounds of rending and smacking reached me from across the table. It was quite a sight, John Weber digging in; he pulled little shreds of lamb from the chop with his incisors and pressed entire spears of asparagus against his face, folding them roughly into his mouth. He wasn't a slob, exactly—he was too tidy for that, constantly dabbing at the corners of his mouth with a napkin—but his ardent champing had its closest analogue in the desperate feast of a hyena hunched over a still-twitching zebra. It was unsettling. I tried not to make any sound.

"Hey," he said, his pupils dilated, his shoulders faintly heaving. "What's the matter?"

"John," I said. "I'm sorry to tell you this. I already ate."

The fork slowly descended to the plate.

"Why didn't you *say*?"

"You'd already cooked it."

"You could have called home."

"John," I said, meeting his hurt and angry gaze. "I don't know you. You moved in this morning. Why would I expect you to cook dinner for me?"

He waved his hand in front of his face, sweeping the question away. "We're roommates," he said. "We have to show one another a little bit of respect."

I should have kicked him out right then and there. But I didn't. How could I? You don't kick a man out of his home for making you dinner. And I had already cashed the check.

"All right," I said. "I'm sorry." And I picked up my knife and fork and went to work.

The apartment building in question stood, or rather lay, at the bottom of a mountain. It was a one-story strip of six units, with four arranged in a row and two more at an angle, to accommodate a rock outcropping in the back. Our apartment was one of the ones on the angle, and our back windows looked out at the outcropping. We didn't get a single ray of sunlight until one in the afternoon.

The mountain was called Mount Peak—a terrible name for a mountain. It didn't even have a peak: it was rounded on top. It was part of the western foothills of the Rockies, and though this all sounds very bracing and natural, the fact is that Mount Peak was, in almost every sense, a thoroughly shitty mountain. The southern third had been completely chopped off to make way for a highway, its western face had been logged and stood bare and weedy, and an abandoned housing project jutted out to the north like a tumor. In addition, about a hundred feet above our apartment, the local high school had spelled out the name of its team, BEAVERS, in white-painted stones, and a few of these would roll down each week and thump against our back wall. Sometimes one of them would ricochet off a tree stump and crash through a window.

Even the wildlife looked scraggly and sick. Mangy elk could often be found mornings, standing around in the parking lot looking confused. You would have to honk at them in order to leave, if you were lucky enough to own a car. We once found a dead bighorn sheep lying on our front stoop, and another time we had to cancel a dinner date because a scrawny, insane-looking mountain lion was standing outside our door, growling.

By "we" I don't mean John Weber and me; I mean Ruperta and me. Ruperta was my girlfriend. She left me because we had sex problems—specifically, the not having of it. It was my fault. I didn't want to do it anymore. All I wanted to do was read and reread from my library of books about trains. It was my interest in trains that caused me to rent this place, with Ruperta, five years before; if you hiked to the south end of the mountain you got a great view of the tracks down below. But a few months after we moved in, the only freight

company that used the tracks went out of business, and they fell
into disrepair.

Honestly, I don't know what was wrong with me. I felt like I was
slowing down. I had moved to this town to go to graduate school in
environmental and land use law. I read a lot of thick, boring books,
and went on a field trip to see how various ranches diverted creek water. Then, one day, while inspecting a barbed-wire fence as part of a
summer internship, I fell into a ravine and broke my arm. When I
got out of the hospital, I had lost all interest in returning to school,
and I started begging off when Ruperta wanted to get it on. She put
up with that for a very long time, and this reasonableness caused me
to lose all respect for her, a respect I regained the moment she left. I
missed her terribly.

Since quitting school, I had worked for eight dollars an hour editing the newsletter of a hunting and conservation outfit. The work
took about three hours each week, so I spent the rest of the time pretending to do it and posting on Internet message boards under a variety of names. I chatted all day long about knitting, veganism, soccer,
scrapbooking, and dog grooming, none of which I knew anything
about, nor cared to learn. I was thoroughly debased, and at thirty-two
felt like I'd been an old man for a long time. I saw no way of escaping the life I'd made for myself, save for the mountain falling down
and crushing me.

Weber was also probably around thirty, but his girlfriend, Sandy,
looked closer to forty. Forty-two, if I had to make a precise guess. She
came twice a week to spend the night in Weber's room, where some
kind of new age harp CD was cued up and left to repeat all night
long. I asked Weber if he could turn the music off after midnight,
and he laughed. "Of course not!" he said.

"Why not? It's hard to sleep."

"Well, Sandy can't sleep without it."

"But Sandy doesn't live here. I live here."

"Sandy is a guest." He shook his head. "I'm disappointed in you.
You don't know how to treat a guest, do you. You should be ashamed
of yourself."

I spent a fair amount of time alone with Sandy, since Weber liked to sleep in on the mornings after her visits—he was still in school, studying I don't know what—and she, like me, was an early riser. We sat across from one another at the table, me with the paper, she with nothing, drinking from a gigantic mug of coffee. She made cryptic little pronouncements in a withered, weary voice.

"John doesn't like coffee."

"There's a nuclear missile near here, I bet you didn't know that."

"John used to race bicycles competitively."

"It's possible to get certain diseases from fish, you know."

One morning in late autumn she said, incredibly, "John is a genius, you know."

I could not resist. "He is?"

Beneath its hay-like skirt of hair, her chin seemed to nod very slightly.

"What's he a genius of?"

"Art," she replied.

"Art?"

"Sculpture. He's a sculpturist."

"I would never have guessed."

It was hard to see what her eyes were up to under there, but I had the feeling they were glaring at me. We drank our coffees.

"Don't be an asshole," Sandy said.

It was another week before I found out exactly what type of sculpturism Weber was getting up to in his room. He had invited me in there more than once, usually to hear one or another horrible song that he was grooving on.

"Hey, come listen to this!"

"I can hear it from out here," I would reply from the living room.

"No, you can't. You need to get the full audio spectrum."

"John, I can hear enough out here to know I don't want to come in there and hear it better."

A moment of silence that suggested deep puzzlement, and then he would emerge wearing a pained expression. "You mean you don't *like* it?"

"No."

"How can you not like this?" Gesturing back toward the room.

"By hearing it, and then considering my feelings about it, and then deciding I don't like it."

"You know," he said on one of these occasions, "it really hurts my feelings when you won't listen to my music."

At which point I set down *Small-Gauge Railways of the American Northeast,* carefully marking the page with a magazine subscription card, and said, "One, it isn't *your* music, John. You didn't compose it or perform it. It's somebody else's music that you happen to like. And two, we don't have to like the same things. Do I keep asking you to look at pictures of trains?"

"No, and maybe you should." He crossed his freckled arms over his scrawny chest. "Trains are cool. I like trains. Why don't you show me your stuff more often?"

"I don't want to."

"Right! There's the problem! Sometimes I think we should see a counselor or something."

"A *roommate* counselor?"

"A relationship counselor."

"We're not in a relationship."

"We're in a *roommate* relationship."

In this manner I had managed to avoid being lured into the dark heart of Weber's personal space, which in my opinion had, in the form of his incessant demand for attention and approval, encroached upon the rest of the apartment enough already. But then, apparently dissatisfied by my resistance to his overtures, he began to borrow my books. I came home from work one night, ate — I had managed to get him to stop serving me meals, though not to stop demanding grocery money for the meals he would continue to offer to make me — showered, put on my pajamas, and got into bed with a good heavy train book. Then John Weber walked in.

"Hey dude."

"What do you want, John."

He came and sat on the edge of my futon, which lay on the floor in the corner as it had ever since Ruperta took our bed. I scootched my legs over and pulled up the covers to my chest.

"I wanted to return your book," he said, and handed me *New Innovations in Rail Travel 1982–1992.*

"Where did you get this?"

"I borrowed it."

"From *where*?" I demanded.

"Right there, man." He pointed to one of the enormous sagging homemade bookshelves that lined the walls of my room.

"You came in here and took my book?"

"Not *took*. *Borrowed*. There's a difference."

I wanted very badly to debate the precise difference between taking and borrowing, and establish definitively which of the two he had done. But the more I argued, the longer John Weber would remain sitting on my futon. I capitulated. "Thank you," I said, and stared daggers at him until he left.

But the next night, when he was at Sandy's place, I couldn't find a particular hobo oral history I was looking for, and I became convinced that Weber had taken it away to his inner sanctum. And so, without hesitation, I threw open his door and plunged in, expertly flipping the oddly placed switch—it was two feet from the doorjamb and about nine inches too high—that I remembered clearly from the days when Ruperta used the room as an office. At which time I saw that Weber was not, in fact, at Sandy's—he was right there in his room. Except he was a uniform medium-gray color and his body was missing below the neck.

Of course I screamed. You, too, would have screamed. I want to scream today, remembering it. Weber's head. It sat on top of—appeared, in fact, to be growing out of—a miniature chest of drawers in the corner of his room. It was made of modeling clay. John Weber, sculpturist. The head was life-size; it rested upon a sturdy neck, which thickened into what should have been shoulders, but in fact was merely a broad smearing of clay that covered the top of the bureau and extended partway down the sides. This head was extraordinarily, horrifyingly realistic. The flared nostrils, the slightly uneven ears, the chinless chin—they were all perfect. The head was so fabulously accomplished that it brought out details I didn't know I'd noticed on the real John Weber—the lines around the eyes, the pockmarks on the forehead, the crookedness of the teeth. He even had the smile down right—that awful half-smirk, simultaneously innocent and calculating, relaxed and desperate, brilliant and moronic.

How was it possible that John Weber could see himself so clearly? He was the most obstinately unobservant person I had ever met. Of course, there was his epic, heroic narcissism; that probably explained it. To one side of the head, attached to the wall, was a foot-square mirror where, no doubt, he studied his face as he worked. This, I surmised, must have been the real reason he invited me into his room. The music was a ruse. He wanted me to see—to admire—the head.

When he came home late the next morning, I watched him more closely than usual, hoping to learn how I had missed this hidden talent. He seemed to appreciate the extra attention and became voluble.

"Have a good night?" he asked me.

It gave me a bit of a shock. Did he know, somehow, that I had gone into his room? I was feeling bad about it, as I had later found the hobo book hidden by a corner of my futon. "Fine," I said, cautiously. "And you?"

"Oh," he said, with a smarmy touch of wistfulness. "I guess so."

"Is something wrong?"

He exhaled loudly, pretended to consider before speaking. "Let me ask you something."

"Okay . . . "

"What do you think of Sandy?"

"Ahh . . . she seems . . . very nice."

"Well, of course she's *nice*. She's very *nice*. What I mean is . . . I'm afraid maybe we're a bad match."

"How so?"

I'd been alone on the couch, and now Weber flopped down next to me, and swung one leg over the other. He wore a thick fleece zippered sweatshirt and, like Sandy, an unseasonable pair of many-pocketed khaki hiking shorts.

"Well, there's the age difference, for one thing."

I shrugged. "She's not *that* much older."

"You mean younger. *I'm* not that much older, you mean. That's it, though, I kind of am. I mean, I think she thinks of me as being like a mentor or something. You know? I'm so much more talented and mature than her, it's like I'm like her father. Or really I'm nothing like her father, I'm like *another* father."

"How old is she, exactly?"

"She's nineteen."

I could only stare blankly.

"I know, I know, robbing the cradle, right?" He stood up now and began to pace. "Her parents totally hate me. They think I'm corrupting her or something. Which is totally crazy since I don't even believe in sex before marriage."

"You don't?" I said.

John Weber laughed. "No, of course not, are you nuts? That's a recipe for disaster. And don't tell her I told you because this is totally private and secret but Sandy is *not* a virgin *at all*, and her parents don't know obviously, and that's what's crazy, I'm keeping her on the straight and narrow, not corrupting her!"

"Wow."

"And I am very cool with that. With her having sex, like, in her past. I mean, I still respect her and all. But I dunno, I mean, she wants to have sex and kiss and all that, because she's used to it I guess, but at this point if I did that stuff it would be like doing it to my daughter or something, on account of this being-like-her-father thing. *Not* like her father," he self-corrected, "like a *second* father."

"You don't kiss?"

"On the cheek." He blushed. "Sort of neck, too."

That was enough for me. I stood up. "I have to go to work," I said.

"No you don't. It's only ten-thirty."

"There are errands I need to do."

"The next bus won't be here for half an hour."

"I am going to walk to town."

His raised his eyebrows. "You are? That's so cool. I am coming with you." He went to the coat rack and shrugged on his jacket. "I have to get some fresh air and straighten all this out in my head."

Did he say "my head" with special, slightly fey, significance? I believed that he did. I did not want to walk the two miles to town, let alone with John Weber, but that's what I ended up doing, and in retrospect it was a good thing because I bumped into Ruperta. In order to get away from Weber as quickly as possible, I pretended to need something at the first retail business we passed, which was a fishing and hunting supply store at the edge of town.

"What do you need *here*?"

"Some very strong filament. Fishing line. For hanging something."

Weber seemed to recoil. "Well, I'm not going in *there* with you."

"Okay," I said, perhaps too readily.

"I don't believe in killing animals," he went on. "That place is basically an animal-murdering supply store."

I couldn't help myself. "But . . . don't you eat meat?"

He snorted. "Well, yeah, but that's different. That's meat animals. This is wildlife."

The discussion might have gone on all day. I said goodbye and left him to his cognitive dissonance. From inside, I watched his hunched back as he slouched toward town. When I turned around, I saw Ruperta behind the counter.

"What are you doing here?" she said.

"What are *you* doing here?"

She shrugged. "Bernice fired me." Bernice was her old boss, the owner of a catering company that Ruperta had been the manager of. "For no reason! She said I was spying on her through her windows at night. Which obviously I wasn't. She's fired half the staff. She'll be out of business by New Year's and in the loony bin by Groundhog Day. Who's the big guy?"

I explained as best I could about Weber and told her about the head. She nodded, smiling wryly. I was in love with her. And here I thought I had made so much progress.

"Still on those train books?"

"No," I said, "I've kind of lost interest."

"Huh," she said. "Well. Goodbye."

I hadn't intended to leave. But I said goodbye and walked the rest of the way into town.

For the next two weeks, I hoped daily that Weber would spend the night at the home of his immoral, withered teen sex addict so that I could go snoop in his bedroom. When he did, I explored every corner, digging through his stuff carefully at first, and later with desperate abandon. The room produced more fascinating artifacts than I would have imagined—love letters from various adolescent girls (boringly, they seem to have been written when Weber, too, was an adolescent);

photographs of Weber and some other people at a party, in which only Weber appeared sober; several books on sculptural technique (which, oddly, didn't appear ever to have been opened); and, inside a special little carved Indian-looking hinged box lined with crushed velvet, a single, foil-wrapped, six-months-expired, spermicidally lubricated condom. I could not help but let out a little bark of laughter when I saw it. But then I remembered that it was Weber who was the object of a woman's desire, not me, and I licked my lips in bitter humiliation.

The head, meanwhile, had improved. It had become even creepier; it had a life force. Weber had turned it, so that now it faced the window and gazed at Mount Peak with admiration, respect, and not a little irony, as if it and the mountain had made a pact. The freckles and blotches that populated the real John Weber's face had been reproduced here, somehow, as slight depressions or perhaps microscopically thin plateaus; their monochrome relief gave them a quality of terrible realness, and I could not refrain from touching them. Then, in the harsh glare from Weber's daylight-corrected lamp, I saw that my fingerprints had marred, subtly, the surface of the head, and mixed with Weber's own. I thought of Ruperta and emitted a small whimper.

Have I described her? I don't think that I have. Ruperta was an arrangement of pleasing roundnesses, all balls stuck to balls, a snowman of flesh. Wide round eyes nestled in wide round glasses, surrounded by black parentheses of hair set atop a full, pink melon head. She was my type — indeed, the perfect expression of it. I walked to town every day now, in order to pass by the animal-murdering supply store, where she allowed me to speak to her briefly each day, to construct the elaborate illusion that I was leading a respectable and appealing life. She told me that she had learned to fire a rifle and to tie trout flies, and that she liked these things a great deal, and what did I think of that? I liked that very much, I said, and as I said it, it became true. I felt the possibility of reinvention, of reconciliation. Some days I wept as I walked the rest of the way to work.

John Weber did not seem himself. I found him one morning sitting at the kitchen table, gazing out the window at the mountain. In the next room, I recalled, the head was doing exactly the same thing.

"John," I said. "What's the matter?"

"Nothing."

I stood there, unsure what I should do. Had John Weber just turned down an opportunity to speak? He looked so glum. So serious.

"No, what?" I persisted.

He turned to me now, slowly, and regarded me as though he were deciding what sort of person I was, whether I could be trusted with what he had to say. After a moment, he came to a decision.

"Well, to be honest, for a while, there, I wasn't sure about you. You're a little self-absorbed, you know. But I guess we're really friends now, aren't we?"

"Sure." I thought of the condom, nestled in its tiny secret bed, and felt guilty.

"I've decided to ask Sandy to get engaged."

I tried, but failed, not to say, "Really?"

"Yes. And if she agrees, I am going to make love with her."

Regret flooded my body—I had passed up the chance to never hear this!

"I have a plan," Weber said, brightening. "I'm going to invite her on a hike. Up Mount Peak. And we're going to go all the way to the Beavers sign. And I'll propose to her, and if she says yes, I'm going to point down at our roof and say, 'See that? That's where I'm going to make passionate love to you as soon as we get down there.'"

"Umm, you want me to make myself scarce?"

He waved his hand. "Ahh, no, doesn't matter, hang around if you want. Anyway, then we're each going to take a white stone from the Beavers sign and we're going to bring them down here and lay them next to the bed while we do it. That's the plan."

"There's a big pile of the stones out back," I pointed out.

"The stones aren't the point, roommate," he said. "*Getting* the stones is the point."

"I see."

"And plus," he said, his dark mood utterly dispelled now, "I have something else for her. A very special thing I've been making."

"Wow."

"Do you want to see it?"

"I think that's just between you two."

"That's a good point. I can't show it to you. What was I thinking? It has to be pure."

"That's romantic," I said.

He was euphoric now. "Really? You think so?" He stood up. "Oh man, this is so awesome. I am so gonna get engaged to her." And before I could stop him, he came to me and hugged me. "Thanks, man. You're the greatest. I was so wrong about you."

"You're welcome," I said uncertainly, and withdrew from our embrace. Weber threw on his coat and marched out the door, presumably to go set up his Big Day.

That day came quickly. The following Saturday the two of them appeared at our door in their excursion getups: fleece jackets, tan shorts lousy with zippered pockets (new ones, with more pockets than ever before), sleek boots of synthetic fabrics in natural colors, and matching backpacks with a single, diagonal padded strap. Weber looked elated. Sandy looked skeptical. The backpack strap was very wide and kept pressing into one or the other of her small breasts, forcing her to adjust it every thirty seconds or so.

"I got us some stuff," Weber said.

"I can see that," I replied.

"It's all for our special day."

Sandy said, "I still don't see what's so special about it."

"*Everything*," Weber said, taking her hands. "Everything about it is very special." I caught a glimpse of Sandy rolling her eyes.

They turned and headed out. But after a moment, Weber came back. He hurried over to me and laid his hands on my shoulders. Even through my oxford shirt I could feel how damp they were.

"I won't be the same when I come back. You need to understand that, roomie."

"Okay . . . "

"Old John Weber will be no more." His face appeared beatific, or perhaps just flushed. "You won't be able to count on my advice—new John Weber might be beyond all that. So I just want to tell you now—you need to change, too."

"Do I?"

"Put it all behind you. The trains and stuff. All your Internet groups. Find purpose for your life. That's all." He lifted his hands and brought them down on my shoulders a second time, perhaps a bit too heartily.

"Did you look on my computer?" I asked him.

But he only shook his head, his real head, the less intelligent of the two. "So long," he said, and marched out the door.

Here's what had happened the night before: I strolled right into the fishing and hunting shop just before it closed and asked Ruperta if she'd let me take her out to dinner. She said yes. We got into her car and drove east around Mount Peak, and then south behind its much more impressive twin, Mount Clark. Eventually we came to the large log structure that housed Pappy's Best Steaks Ever Grill, where, if you had the money and, more importantly, the desire, you could walk around back and pick out, from a meadow, which grass-fed steer you wanted to eat that night. They would slaughter it on the spot, and when you were through eating, they would load the leftover butchered cuts, wrapped in white paper and packed into cardboard boxes, onto the bed of your pickup truck.

We did not choose that option, though. Ruperta had some prime rib and I ordered barbecued chicken.

"You're not going all hippie vegetarian on me, are you?" she asked.

"Chicken's not a vegetable," I argued.

"It's close."

We didn't say much during the meal. Afterward we drove out to the all-night shooting range and I watched Ruperta spray a man-shaped target with hot lead underneath the arc lights. I was impressed—she was very good. When she was through we sat in the car and made out, and she lay her fat little hand on my crotch.

"Is this real?" she quipped.

"Ha ha."

"You should know I slept with my boss a couple of times."

"Oh," I said. I had assumed, of course, that she would go seeking amorous companionship, but it was hard to imagine it really happening. I felt very small.

She frowned and removed her hand. "Hmm. Just like old times."

And so all this was on my mind as I sat and watched through the kitchen window as Weber and Sandy scaled the mountain. Now, I am not big on epiphanies. But as their bunched, indistinguishably hairy calves vanished from the frame, I felt a bottomless hole open up in the floor of my soul, and I knew with sickening certainty that if I did not leave this place immediately, I was going to die here. John Weber would marry his weathered nymph, and they would keep me, like a son or drooling pet, in this hideous little clapboard prison. Or worse, Sandy would decline to wed, and then Weber and I would be alone. One way or another, I would never escape Weber. His avidity was more powerful than my aversion. He had a life-force—he had *joie de vivre*. All I had was a collection of train books and an intimidating ex-girlfriend.

Maybe he was right about me.

I went to Weber's room and pawed, once again, through his possessions. I had my own things, of course, mementos of an unremarkable life, stored away in boxes and crates in the closet, but they didn't interest me. I knew Weber's better than mine. The head still stood on its pedestal, gazing out at the mountain's cheesy face, and was I imagining it, or did it look a little smugger these days, a little more glib? I don't know what made me do what I did next—some uncharacteristic upwelling of personality, maybe—but I dropped the packet of state-themed postcards I was holding, took three steps across the room, and mashed in Weber's nose with my thumb. I gasped, as if having just watched someone else do it. The face was ruined of course; the jolly ape Weber had always secretly resembled was revealed in all its glory, with my whorled print in the center of it.

That was that. I was gone. I would leave it all behind. I ran to the bedroom; snatched up my wallet, an extra pair of eyeglasses, and my only pair of clean socks; and bolted for the door, shouldering on my coat as I went.

I made it to the middle of the gravel lot before I changed my mind. The air was chill, the sun was nowhere to be found, and I had already lost heart. I couldn't just leave. I couldn't just start over. What had I been thinking? I was not that kind of man; rather, I was the kind of man who endured, ignored, and took his lumps. Perhaps I could mound the nose back into shape. I turned and drew a deep breath.

There was a rumbling. Thunder, I surmised—or a big rig passing on the freeway. But I could feel it in my stomach, in my bowels, and I knew that this was something else, a new sound, low and terrible.

A moment later, dozens of animals, their patchy fur standing on end, came pouring around the sides of our building—squirrels, deer and elk, grouse and chukkar, a mountain cat and a lone galloping moose—and streamed past me as if I were a rock or tree. I did not understand what it was I was seeing. The animals fled, the rumble grew in intensity, and I looked up to see an avalanche fast approaching, scouring the mountain clean: a white wave of little boulders, ten years of Sisyphean teenage ambition loosed from the tyranny of the text. The BEAVERS sign, ruined, and on the rampage.

A hundred lifetimes might have passed in those awful moments, as the stones screamed down the rock face—a hundred of my lifetime, anyway, which might as well have been lived in a second, for all the good it had done anyone—and buried our lousy little shack of a home. *Buried* is the wrong word, perhaps. *Annihilated* is more like it. Our apartment unit, all of the apartment units, were crushed. The wave stopped at my feet, half-surrounding me in an implausible arc of evident magnetic repulsion, and I stood there blinking at the dusty ruins.

Of course there would be lawsuits, lots of them. There would be resignations, elections, excuses, exhortations. The landlord would flee. The Open Space Committee would be formed. The high school would change the name of its mascot. And, in time, the crushed bodies of Weber and his girl would be found in the rubble, and upon her broken finger, an engagement ring. This last, of course, is the detail that would be best remembered: a love so strong, it brought down a mountain.

My own life, though, would never be so romantic. I would merely shack back up with Ruperta, regain my potency, and happily apply myself to a life of connubial resignation. When a heart attack claimed her lovesick employer, Ruperta would buy the business for a song and open three more across the state. She would become mildly famous throughout the region for her amusing television ads in which she lured whitetail deer with a come-hither glance. And when I proposed marriage to her, she would respond by driving us to the courthouse to get it over with.

As for Mount Peak, it still stands, renamed Mount Sandy, thanks to the passionate lobbying efforts of Weber's fiancée's mother and father. (Weber's family, for their part, just wanted to put everything behind them.) Nature has been allowed to reclaim it—the logging roads closed, the housing project bulldozed, the forest reseeded. From our taxidermy-festooned house across town, the saplings seem to shroud it in a haze of new green, like a girl in a peek-a-boo teddy. By the time we're old, it will be wearing a heavy coat, like a stout old fellow with a war wound.

This I am looking forward to seeing from the picnic table on the back deck, where I have learned to tie flies for my domineering wife. It is a pastime designed to endure, a tedium of infinite small variations. Weber *was* right about me, that I would be better off with some kind of purpose. I'm not a man, not really, just the gray clammy shadow of one—startlingly realistic at times, sure, but the product of hands not my own. I sit, bent over my vise, under the watchful eye of Mount Sandy, and expect to be here, still doing the same thing, when I drop dead of old age.

MAC McCLELLAND

■

For Us Surrender Is Out of the Question

FROM *Mother Jones*

"DO YOU WANT A CIGARETTE?" I ask Htan Dah, holding up a pack of Thai-issue Marlboros. We are sitting on opposite sides of a rectangular table, talking over the spread: three bottles of vodka, two cartons of orange juice, plates of sugared citrus slices, nearly empty bottles of beer and bowls of fried pork, sweet corn waffles, pad thai, a chocolate cake. We share the benches with two guys each, and half a dozen others hover.

The men are all in their twenties. Most of them are solid and strong and hunky; their faces shine because they're drunk, and it's July. They could be mistaken for former frat boys unwinding after another tedious workday.

Except that they're stateless. They are penniless. They speak three or four languages apiece. Two of them had to bribe their way out of Thai police custody yesterday, again, because they're on the wrong side of the border between this country and the land-mine-studded mountains of their own. Htan Dah's silky chin-length hair slips toward his eyes as he leans forward. My Marlboros are adorned with a legally mandated photographic deterrent, a guy blowing smoke in a baby's face, but it doesn't deter Htan Dah. Nor is he deterred by the fact that he doesn't smoke. Tonight, he is flushed with heat and booze and the virility and extreme hilarity of his comrades. Tonight, as always, he is celebrating the fact that he's still alive. He takes a cigarette. "Never say no," he says, and winks at me.

* * *

I'd arrived at Mae Sot a few weeks before. This city in western central Thailand is a major hub for people, teak, gems, and other goods
that enter the country illegally from Burma. The place is rife with
smugglers, dealers, undocumented immigrants, and slaves. My bus
arrived in the late afternoon. I wasn't connected to any aid or charity
organization—I'd just happened on a website of a group that said it
was promoting democracy in the Texas-size military dictatorship of
Burma, and eventually volunteered, via e-mail, to help its activists living in Thailand learn English. (As I was to discover, the particulars
of their mission were far more dangerous, and illegal, so I'll refer to
them as Burma Action.)

At the station, I was met by The Guy, whose name wasn't The Guy,
but whose actual name I didn't catch when he mumbled it twice and
then just shook his head and laughed when I asked him to repeat it
one more time. After a brief ride in a three-wheeled tuk-tuk, we arrived at a gold-detailed black gate that stood heavy sentry at the road.
Behind it stood Burma Action's local HQ, a big but run-down house,
two stories of worn wood and dirty concrete with a balcony on the
left, cement garage on the right. The Guy gave me a quick tour. The
"kitchen" had a sink and some dishes; cooking took place out in the
dining room/garage. He took a few steps farther. "Bathroom." He
gestured into a cement-walled room through an oversize wooden
door. There was a squat toilet set into the floor, and in lieu of toilet
paper a shallow well with a little plastic bowl floating on top. There
was also, running the length of the left wall, a giant waist-high cement trough filled with water and dead mosquitoes.

"What's that?" I asked.

"A bath."

I looked at it, jet-lagged. "How does it work?" I asked.

He exhaled hard through his nose, a whispery snort. "Like this,"
he said, pantomiming filling a bowl with water and dumping it over
his head. "Are you hungry?"

I asked The Guy what was in the soup he offered me.

"I don't know the word in English," he said. "Leaves?"

Close. Twigs, actually. The Guy pulled a stump of wood up next to me
at the table, and watched me chew through the sautéed woody stems.

"So, where are you from?" I asked.

"Me?"

I nodded.

"I am kuh-REN. Everybody here, we are all kuh-REN."

Oh, man. It was starting to come together now.

When I'd landed in Bangkok, a Burma Action employee had picked me up at the airport to make sure I found the bus station and the right eight-hour bus north. She was tiny and Thai and heavily accented, and repeatedly told me during our cab ride that everyone I was about to be working with was Korean. It seemed sort of weird that a bunch of Koreans would move to Thailand together to work for peace in Burma, but I thought that was nice, I guessed, and even wrote in my journal, relievedly, "Koreans tend to have excellent English skills."

When I'd arrived at the Mae Sot bus station, The Guy had asked if I was his new volunteer.

"Yes," I'd said. "You're not *Korean*."

I'd done my homework before leaving the States. I had read about the Karen. But I'd only seen the word written down, and had assumed that it sounded like the name of my parents' blond divorced friend. I didn't know how it was pronounced any more than most Westerners would've been certain how to say "Darfur" 10 years ago.

When I turned the corner from the kitchen into the large living room, four pairs of dark eyes looked up from a small TV screen. I smiled, but The Guy, leaning against the wall with his arms folded, didn't make any introductions, so I sat on the marble floor among the legs of the white plastic chairs the guys were sitting in, quiet amid the rise and fall of their soft tonal syllables, deep, bubbling, like slow oil over stones. The TV blared Thai. Mosquitoes sauntered in through the screenless windows, possible hosts to malaria, dengue fever, Japanese encephalitis. I'd no natural resistance to the latter two, and I'd opted against taking the sickening drugs for the former. Not wanting to be the white girl who ran upstairs to hide under a mosquito net at dusk, I watched the guys laughing and talking, like a partygoer who didn't know anyone. I pulled my air mattress out of my bag and started blowing it up. I got bit. I scratched. I shifted my sit bones on the shiny tile. Finally, I stood up.

"I'm going to bed," I told The Guy.

He nodded, and looked at me for a second. It was 7:30. "Are you okay?" he asked. I'd just taken twenty-seven hours of planes and automobiles. I'd glanced at the phrases "Forced marriage" and "Human trafficking" on a piece of paper taped to the wall behind the computers in the adjacent room. I said that I was fine and headed upstairs. I dropped my air mattress under the big blue mosquito net and lay down. I had no real idea who these people were, or what they did here, or even what I was supposed to do here. I appeared to have my work, whatever it was, cut out for me, since The Guy (real name: The Blay) seemed to be among the few who spoke English. My digestive system had its work cut out for it, too, since these guys apparently ate sticks. Lying there, listening to my housemates laugh and holler downstairs, I comforted myself with the thought that these Karen seemed nice. I couldn't have guessed then, drifting to sleep to the sound of their amiable chatter, that every last one of them was a terrorist.

Imagine, for a moment, that Texas had managed to secede from the union, and that you live there, in the sovereign Republic of Texas. Imagine that shortly after independence, a cadre of old, paranoid, greedy men who believed in a superior military caste took over your newly autonomous nation in a coup. Your beloved president, who had big dreams of prosperity and Texan unity, whom you believed in, was shot, and now the army runs your country. It has direct or indirect control over all the businesses. It spends 0.3 percent of GDP on health care, and uses your oil and natural gas money to buy weapons that Russia, Pakistan, and North Korea have been happy to provide. It sends your rice and beans to India and China, while your countrymen starve. There is no free press, and gatherings of more than five people are illegal. If you are arrested, a trial, much less legal representation, is not guaranteed. In the event of interrogation, be prepared to crouch like you're riding a motorbike for hours or be hung from the ceiling and spun around and around and around, or burned with cigarettes, or beaten with a rubber rod. They might put you in a ditch with a dead body for six days, lock you in a room with wild, sharp-beaked birds, or make you stand to your neck in a cesspool full of maggots that climb into your nose and ears and mouth. If you do manage to stay out of the prisons, where activists and dissidents have been rotting for decades, you will be broke and starving. Your children have a 10 percent chance of dying before they reach their fifth birthday, and a 32 percent chance they'll be devastatingly malnourished if they're still alive. What's more, you and 50 million countrymen are trapped inside your 268,000-square-mile Orwellian nightmare with some 350,000 soldiers. They can snatch people—maybe your kid—off the street and make them join the army. They can grab you as you're going out to buy eggs and make you work construction on a new government building or road—long, hard hours under the grueling sun for days or weeks without pay—during which you'll have to scavenge for food. You'll do all this at gunpoint, and any break will be rewarded with a pistol-whipping. Your life is roughly equivalent to a modern-day Burmese person's.

Now imagine that you belong to a distinct group, Dallasites, or something, that never wanted to be part of the Republic in the first place, that wanted to either remain part of the United States, which had treated you just fine, or, failing that, become your own free state within the Republic of Texas, since you already had your own infrastructure and culture. Some Dallasites have, wisely or unwisely, taken up arms to battle the Texas military government, and in retaliation whole squads of that huge army have, for decades, been dedicated to terrorizing your city. You and your fellow Dallasites are regularly conscripted into slavery, made to walk in front of the army to set off land mines that they—and your own insurgents—have planted, or carry one hundred pound loads of weaponry while being severely beaten until you're crippled or die. If you're so enslaved, you might accompany the soldiers as they march into your friends' neighborhoods and set them on fire, watch them shoot at fleeing inhabitants as they run, capturing any stragglers. If you're one of those stragglers, and you're a woman, or a girl five or older, prepare to be raped, most likely gang-raped, and there's easily a one-in-four chance you'll then be killed, possibly by being shot, possibly through your vagina, possibly after having your breasts hacked off. If you're a man, maybe you'll be hung by your wrists and burned alive. Maybe a soldier will drown you by filling a plastic bag with water and tying it over your head, or stretch you between two trees and use you as a hammock, or cut off your nose, pull out your eyes, and then stab you in both ears before killing you, or string you up by your shoulders and club you now and again for two weeks, or heat up slivers of bamboo and push them into your urethra, or tie a tight rope between your dick and your neck for a while before setting your genitals on fire, or whatever else hateful, armed men and underage boys might dream up when they have orders to torment, and nothing else to do. And though you've been sure for decades that the United States can't possibly let this continue, it has invested in your country's oil and will not under any circumstances cross China, which is your country's staunch UN defender and economic ally, so you really need to accept that America is decidedly not coming to save you. Nobody is.

Now your life is pretty much equivalent to a modern-day Burmese Karen's.

Shortly after dawn, someone dropped a pile of thinly sliced onions and whole garlic cloves with the skins still on into a wok of hot soybean oil. As the smell wafted up, I climbed out from under my mosquito net and walked softly out of my room.

Htan Dah—whose name was pronounced, to my unceasing delight, the same as the self-satisfied English interjection "tada!"—stood at the gas range, which spat oil at his baggy long-sleeved shirt. He tilted the wok, concentrating harder than he needed to on the swirling oil. Htan Dah was worried about me. As the office manager of Burma Action for the past two years, he'd heard the nighttime weeping of plenty of self-pitying philanthropists, who tended to arrive tired and instantly homesick. The last girl, a Canadian with a lot of luggage, had started sobbing almost as soon as he'd picked her up, and couldn't be calmed even by the hours she spent taking calls from her boyfriend back home. She'd cried for days.

Indeed, I'd had a very sad moment the night before when, after my air mattress deflated and my angles pressed into hard floor, and I realized that the ants patrolling the grounds were trekking right through my hair, I actually hoped that I had contracted malaria or Japanese encephalitis from the mosquito bites raging hot and itchy so I would have a legitimate excuse to bail back to the States. That way I wouldn't have to be mad at myself for being too chickenshit to hack it through loneliness and less-than-ideal bathing arrangements. I'd even considered taking the bus back to Bangkok. If there wasn't an immediate flight out, I could just hang out on Khao San Road and read books. I hated Khao San Road, with its hennaed European back-packers and incessant techno and beer specials, but at least it was familiar. I'd realized then that I might start crying, but I was deter-mined not to. Instead, I saved the tearing up for when Htan Dah put another bowl of stick soup in front of me now and asked, "How long are you staying?"

"Six weeks," I said.

"Six weeks!" he hollered. "Why not four months? Or six months?"

"Six weeks is a long time to go out of the country in America," I said. "Besides, I was in Thailand for a month two years ago."

"How many times have you been here?"

"Twice."

"Wow," he said. Then, more softly, "You have traveled a lot. That's nice." He had no idea, even.

"Have you traveled?"

"No, I cannot."

"Why not?"

"Because! I am Karen!"

"So what?"

"So, I cannot go anywhere." He dumped chunks of raw, pink meat into the oil, which sputtered furiously. "If I go outside, I can be arrested."

"Really?"

"Yes! I am refugee!"

Htan Dah's exclamations suggested that none of this should have been news to me—though I soon realized that this was also just how he talked. But my books hadn't said much about refugees, or men-tioned that most of the Burmese refugees in Thailand were Karen, and Burma Action hadn't told me that my housemates were refugees, and certainly not refugees who'd run away from camp to live and work illegally in that house. I, after all, was the one who'd just figured out that no one here was Korean.

"I'm sorry," I said. "Why would you be arrested because you're a refugee?"

"Because! I don't have Thai ID. I am not Thai citizen, so, I cannot go outside refugee camp."

"Really?"

"Yes! I can be fined, maybe 3,000 baht"—nearly $100 in a country where the average annual income was about $3,000—"I can go to jail, or maybe, be deported ... " We looked at each other, and he nodded in my silence, emphasizing his point with a sharp dip of his chin. "You have a lot of experience. You have been to a lot of places."

"Did you live in a refugee camp before?"

"Yes. Before I came to BA."

"How long have you lived here?"

"In Thailand?" Htan Dah asked. "I was born in Thailand."

To be a Karen refugee in Thailand is to be unwelcome. The Royal Thai Government, already sanctuary to evacuees from other Southeast Asian wars by the time the Karen showed up in the '80s, was hardly in a hurry to recognize and protect them as refugees—and, not having signed the 1951 UN Convention Relating to the Status of Refugees, it didn't have to. This is only the latest misfortune in the Karen's long history of troubles. They were massively oppressed and enslaved before Burma became a British colony in 1886, but their relations with the Burmese were nothing so nasty as after they played colonialists' pet and then joined the Allies in World War II. British officers promised the Karen independence for helping us fight the Burmese and Japan. They lied. The Karen resistance started, and the Karen National Union formed, about as soon as the ink was dry on Burma's postwar independence agreement. Their oath had four parts: *(1) For us surrender is out of the question. (2) Recognition of Karen State must be completed. (3) We shall retain our arms. (4) We shall decide our own political destiny.* The Karen had been well trained and well armed by Westerners. They nearly took the capital in 1949, and when they were pushed back to the eastern hills, they built the largest insurrection (among many) against the Burmese junta. By the '80s, the KNU claimed that its annual income, from taxing smuggled products flowing through the porous Thai border, was in the tens of millions of dollars a year.

The junta responded with Four Cuts. You've never heard of Four

Cuts, but it's a Burmese army strategy that every Karen child knows very well: cutting off the enemy's sources of food, finance, intelligence, and recruits (and, some say, their heads). Unfortunately for villagers, these sources of support include the villagers themselves, in addition to their rice and livestock. It's the same strategy the British used to extinguish uprisings back in their day: "We simply wiped out the village and shot everyone we saw," wrote Sir James George Scott, an intrepid administrator who, in addition to killing Burmese, introduced soccer to them. "Burned all their crops and houses." Htan Dah's parents were among the first wave of Karen to flee the wrath of the Burmese army. Today the Burmese camp population in Thailand is 150,000, and the number one answer people give when asked why they left Burma is "running away from soldiers."

I asked Htan Dah, on my third day, how many people lived in our office/house. I'd been working on lesson plans all day for the soon-to-start English classes. Men had been working alongside me at the other computers, keeping to themselves.

"Maybe ten," he said.

A lot more dudes than that had been milling around. Many of them were dudes in Che Guevara T-shirts. Htan Dah said that in addition to present staff, there were visitors from other offices and NGOs, plus staff currently "inside"—in Burma.

"Doing what?" I asked.

"Doing interviewww, taking videooo, taking picturrre . . . " he said, drawing out the final syllables. "They go to the village, and they tell about what is going on in Burma, and about how to unite for democracy. Also, they ask, 'Have you seen Burma army? Have they raped you, or shot you, or burned your village?'" This explained the "Human Rights Vocabulary" translation cheat sheet I'd noticed on my first night. I'd since gotten a better look at it, studying the fifteen most-used phrases. One side listed words in Karen script, a train of round characters, with loops that extended lines or swirls above and below the baseline. The other side was in English: (1) Killings (2) Disappearances (3) Torture/inhumane treatments (4) Forced labor (5) Use of child soldiers (6) Forced relocation (7) Confiscation/destruction of property (8) Rape (9) Other sexual violence (10) Forced prostitution (11) Forced marriage (12) Arbitrary/illegal arrest/detention (13) Human trafficking (14) Obstruction of freedom of movement (15) Obstruction of freedom/expression/assembly. These were going to be English classes like no other I'd taken or taught.

"Then what?"

"Then they enter information into Martus."

"Into . . . what?"

"Human rights violation database."

"Then what happens to the information?"

"We can share, with other HRD."

"With other . . . "

"Human rights documenter."

"So you guys collect it all . . . "

Htan Dah stared at me.

"And then what? Then it just sits there?"

Htan Dah shrugged.

"How do the guys get to the villages?"

"They walk."

This explained the physique of Htoo Moo, he of the silent h and the constant smiling and the never talking to me and the stupefyingly round and hard-looking ass. "How long are they gone?"

"Depends. Maybe three months."

"Do they just hide around the jungle that whole time?"

"Yes!" Htan Dah said. "If they are caught, they could die."

Here's how it worked: Somebody had to document what was going on in Burma — and stealthily. One activist who gave an interview to a foreign reporter served seven years in prison. Another was sentenced to twenty-five years for giving an interview critical of the regime to the BBC in 1997. Of the 173 nations in the Reporters Without Borders Press Freedom Index 2008, Burma ranked 170th, behind every other country except the "unchanging hells" of Turkmenistan, North Korea, and Eritrea. Burma has the third most journalists in jail. As for coverage of *eastern* Burma, ground zero of the Karen war . . . forget about it.

So a couple of times a year, Htoo Moo, one of Burma Action's human rights documenters, shouldered a bag carrying what he wasn't wearing of nine shirts, three pairs of pants, two pairs of shorts, four pairs of underwear, and two pairs of socks—plus a tape recorder, six tapes, a notebook, three pens, a digital camera, a battery charger, a kilo of sugar, cold, sinus, and stomach medicines, a bottle of water, and 150 bucks' worth of Thai currency—and trekked clandestinely into his homeland.

His most recent trip had started with a six-hour drive, five hours in a long-tail boat watching the banks of the Salween River and a darkening sky, and two days of walking over mountains and jungle trade paths subsisting on just sugar and found water until he reached a village. Even by Karen standards, this settlement was pretty remote; a fish-paste purchase was a day's walk away. At night, he slept outside on the ground, and during the day he stood thigh-deep in a river, trying—though he couldn't get the hang of the procedure, however effortless the villagers made it look—to net fish while chatting up villagers about abuses by the State Peace and Development Council (SPDC), which is what the government of Burma calls itself.

After a month, Htoo Moo walked two days to interview escaped porters. He took pictures of lesions the straps left in their shoulders—raw, pink holes infested with flies and maggots. The porters told of being starved and dehydrated and repeatedly beaten with fists, kicks, and bamboo, of how prisoners who still fail to get up are shot or left to die, of doing double duty as minesweepers. SPDC offenses can be partially charted by the trail of porters' corpses.

Dodging land mines, Htoo Moo walked to the next small village. He entered it to find that some sort of plague had landed on all ten houses, and most of the people were dying. One house contained a dead boy whose father, the only family member left, was too sick to bury him. The villagers encouraged Htoo Moo to look, to bear witness, and he did, but left after a few days, because there was nothing else to be done.

By the time he walked two days to another village, listened to and documented the story of a boy who was shot along with his father and brother by Burmese soldiers while cultivating rice, by the time he'd looked at the fresh bullet holes in the boy's shoulder and ass, and at the bloody track another round had grazed into the side of his head, by the time the boy had explained how he'd sent other villagers back to the field to get his brother and father as soon as he'd staggered home but it was too late, they were already dead, by the time he took pictures of the boy's wounds, which had been treated with only boiled water and cotton dressing, Htoo Moo was ready for a rest.

"The SPDC is coming," the chief told him.

So this is the drill: You flee, carrying everything you can—big heavy loads, as much rice as you can stand on your back in giant baskets, any clothes or anything else you want to own for maybe the rest of your life, your baby. Htoo Moo helped the villagers hide rice, salt, fish paste, and some extra sets of clothing among the surrounding trees before they all took off together in the early evening. He followed the eighty villagers along a path hidden beneath tall grass. Figuring a six-hour walk put them far enough out of harm's way, they stopped at midnight and Htoo Moo slept, finally, on the forest floor.

But the next morning, a scout told them the SPDC was coming; everyone needed to leave. Htoo Moo had slept through breakfast, and there wasn't time to make more. Neighboring villages had evidently joined the flight; there were 200 people in the makeshift camp now. They had with them one KNU soldier. Not wanting to further strain the villagers' rations, Htoo Moo stalked an enormous rat he'd spied lumbering around and killed it with one strike of a piece of bamboo. When he smiled, pleased with his efficiency, an old man next to him laughed. "Before you woke up," he said, "I tried to kill that. I think it was already tired."

The villagers fled until noon. Some of the children with no shoes lost flesh and bled as their feet pounded the ground, and some of them cried silently as they ran. Htoo Moo carried his bag on his back, the dead rat in one hand, his digital camera in the other, occasionally snapping pictures of the exodus. When they stopped, he dug his fingers into the rat's skin and ripped it off. He tore the meat into pieces and went in on lunch with another man, who provided a pot, chilies, and salt. Five minutes later, his belly was full of seared rat meat. He closed his eyes as sleep slowly started to overtake him, and then—gunshots.

Gunshots. He clutched his bag and jumped to his feet. Nobody screamed. The boy with the bullet holes started running, new blood rushing from the wound in his ass. Htoo Moo took off, ahead of even the village chief, reaching a flat-out run, crashing shoulder-first through tall croppings of bamboo in his path, before realizing he had no idea where he should be going. He stopped, turned around a couple of times, and considered ditching his camera. What if the SPDC caught him? What if they saw that he'd been taking pictures of gun-shot farmers, prisoner-porters with skin disease, cigarette burns, knife wounds, raw and infected shoulders that bore the permanent scars of carrying over mountains for days or weeks at a time? Though he felt like a coward, he fell back into the middle of the throng. By the time they stopped at nightfall, news had spread through the crowd that one man in the rear had been shot dead.

Htoo Moo listened to the men next to him talking. Of the 200 people, four had guns, four or five rounds apiece. One admitted that he had only three bullets left. "No problem," another told him. "You will just aim very well."

After three days of squatting and swatting bugs in the jungle, Htoo Moo told the chief that he wanted to leave. Sometimes, villagers hide out for weeks because they don't know if it's safe to go back yet. Sometimes, it never is. Htoo Moo needed to get back to work.

"I will take you myself," the chief said. "I am ready." He was in no hurry now. He'd heard over the radio that the soldiers had killed the pigs and the chickens, and then burned the village to the ground. There was nothing to go back to.

To slow down the SPDC advance, the KNU had set up scores of new land mines, and the way in was no longer a safe way out. Htoo Moo and the chief trudged through the jungle for three days to a KNU headquarters, where they shook hands and parted, and Htoo Moo asked a KNU insurgent to guide him the rest of the way. Shortly after they started off, the parasites that had been multiplying in his liver since entering his body via mosquito burst through the cells that hosted them and flooded Htoo Moo's bloodstream. He trekked slowly, through his fever, stopping when the retching brought him to his knees. "Don't rest there!" his guide screamed when he moved toward a smooth patch of soil just to the side of the path. He'd nearly knelt on a land mine. It took another two days to reach the riverbank, where he bought antimalarial tablets with his last few baht and boarded the boat toward Thailand—which had, by default, become home.

* * *

"Do you have picture?" Htan Dah asked one evening. "Of your friends?"

"Let's go to the computer room," I replied. Thus were several Karen refugee activists of Mae Sot, Thailand, bestowed with one of democracy's greatest gifts: that of wasting exorbitant amounts of time on social networking websites. I logged in to MySpace, and clicked through some of my pals' profiles, talking about who they were, or where they were, or what they were doing in the pictures. Htoo Moo, working diligently at the next computer, glanced over as nonchalantly as possible. Htan Dah said very little. Once, he asked me to clarify the gender of the girl I was pointing to on the screen. "Are you sure?" he asked. "She looks like a boy." I laughed and told him that she was a lesbian, my ex-girlfriend, actually, which seemed to clear it up for him. Other than that, he mostly just stared at the monitor in stunned silence, for so long that it started to weird me out.

"What do you think?" I asked him when I'd finished the tour.

"Wow," he said quietly.

"So, those are my friends," I said. He made no move to get up or take his eyes off the page.

I asked him if he wanted to see how the website worked. I showed him the browse feature, dropping down the long list of countries whose citizens we could gawk at. "How about Myanmar?" he asked, spying the junta's official name for Burma among the options.

I was surprised it was there, and even more surprised that our first search turned up 3,000 profiles. The junta has some awesome restrictions on owning electronics, especially computers. In 1996, Leo Nichols, former honorary consul for Scandinavian countries and friend of Burmese activists, was sentenced to three years for the illegal possession of fax machines and phones. (Taken into custody, he was tortured and died.) There are Internet cafés, but café workers are required to capture customers' screenshots every five minutes and submit their Web histories, along with home addresses and phone numbers, to the state. Humanitarian geeks in other countries, though, work full time to give Burma's citizens Internet access, with proxy servers that they update when the government figures out how to block them. From the look of it, they were doing their job.

On MySpace, ink-haired Burmese teens and twentysomethings stared at us: the chin-down-sexy-eyes-up shot, the haughty chin up/

eyes half-closed look, the profile with eyes askance. Their faces were surrounded by HTML-coded sparkles, animated hearts and stars, slaughtered English colloquialisms. Htan Dah paused long and hard at each picture that came up.

"I don't know them," he said finally.

This conclusion struck me as pretty foregone, since he'd never lived in Burma. "Did you think you would?"

He looked at me, realizing his mistake. "I don't know," he said softly. We made Htan Dah his own profile, and he stayed logged in long after I'd gone to bed.

At dinner the next day, Htan Dah, Htoo Moo, and another refugee, Ta Mla, spent a fair amount of time watching me and muttering to each other in Karen.

"Something on your mind, tiger?" I asked Htan Dah.

"We are talking about your girlfriend," he said.

Yeah, I'd thought that conversation had ended a little too easily. "All right. You can talk about it with me."

"Do you ever have boyfriend?"

"Yes. I've had boyfriends and girlfriends."

This produced a moment of confused silence, which I filled with a lame description of the sexuality continuum, along with an explanation of the somewhat loose sexual mores of modern American gals like myself. Htan Dah responded by telling me that they had heard of gay people, since a visitor to the house had informed them of their existence—last year.

"Last year!" I hollered.

"Yes!" he yelled back. "In Karen culture, we do not have."

"There's never been a gay person in a Karen village in the history of Karen society." All three men shook their heads. "Come on."

"If there was a gay person, they would leave," Htan Dah said. "It is not our culture."

"Let's just say there was a gay person," I said. "Couldn't they stay in the village?"

"No," Htan Dah said. "I would not allow gay people in my village."

"Are you kidding me?!"

Htan Dah held my gaze, though his seemed more uncertain the longer it went on.

"Are you going to make *me* leave?"

"No! For you, in your culture, it is okay," he said. "You are not Karen. But in our culture, it does not belong." Htoo Moo and Ta Mla were nodding, and I scowled at them.

"You're a refugee," I said. "And it sucks. It's ruining your life. But you would force another villager to become a refugee because they were gay?"

Nobody said no. I turned on Htan Dah; I was maddest at him, and he was probably the only one who could follow my fast, heated English. "If there was peace in Burma and you lived in a village and there was a gay Karen person," I asked again, "you would want to make that person another Karen refugee by making them leave?"

That, or my anger, shut him up. "I am interested in your ideas," he said, evenly, after a minute. "I think it is important to keep an open mind."

I shut up, too, and focused on eating rice for a few awkward moments.

"So," I said eventually. "Do you guys have sex?"

Htoo Moo and Ta Mla shook their heads while Htan Dah said, "Sometimes."

"Ever?" I asked Htoo Moo.

"No," he said.

"Why not?"

"Because, I am not married."

"What about you?" I asked Htan Dah.

"Yes," he said, nodding hard once. "I am married."

"You're *married*?"

Htan Dah laughed. "Yes! I am married."

"I didn't know that. Where is your wife?"

"She is in camp. With my kid."

"You have a kid?"

Other things I didn't know: that everyone currently in the house—save The Blay and Htan Dah, who were married, apparently—was a virgin. This extended even to kissing. They hailed from the parts of Burma that had been heavily influenced by Christian missionaries, and premarital sex was taboo. Htoo Moo volunteered that he wasn't actively looking for a girlfriend, and that he wouldn't know what to do with her even if he found one.

Htan Dah told me I had to show them MySpace again. We

crowded around a computer, our cheeks flushed with satiety and humidity and new camaraderie. Htoo Moo interjected burning questions about American life as they came to him.

"Do you eat rice in America?"

"Yes. Usually I eat brown rice."

"Brown rice?"

"It's rice with the hull still on it. Do you know what I'm talking about?"

"No. I don't believe that . . . Have you ever eat tiger?"

"*Eaten* tiger. No."

"Have you ever eat . . . monkey?

"'Have you ever *eaten* monkey,' you mean. No."

"Are there black lady in America?"

"*Ladies.* Yes . . . "

"What language do they speak?" Htan Dah chimed in.

"English."

"Really?"

I gaped at him, disbelieving, but before I could formulate a response, Htoo Moo said, "In America, you have cream to grow hair." He ran his hand over his baby-smooth jawline.

"Yeah. I think that's true. I think it's generally for people who are bald, though."

"Do you have that?"

"Hair-growing cream? Oh, yeah. I use it on my ass."

The sarcasm seemed to translate, since they laughed for minutes.

We made Ta Mla a MySpace profile, and he and Htan Dah started giving the other guys tutorials as they wandered in. My work here was done.

A few days earlier, when I'd asked my students what they did for fun, I'd had to explain the concept of "fun" for about five minutes before anyone could answer me, and then the answers were "Nothing," "Nothing," "Watch TV," and three "Talk"s. By the time I went upstairs, every computer screen was lit, the guys scrolling through the faces of Burma, a window into a world they considered home but where some had never been and probably none would ever live again.

* * *

Htan Dah diligently kept me company during meals. "You are so slow," he said one morning, watching me chew every bit of rice into oblivion. "Why don't you eat fast?"

"Why should I?" I asked. "I'm not in a hurry."

"But what if you are under attack, or have to run away?"

I scoffed at him. "I'm from Ohio."

"Yes, but I am refugee! We are taught to eat fast."

Be that as it may, we were in peacetime Thailand, so this attack seemed like an incredibly hypothetical scenario, and even though Htan Dah had mentioned something about refugee camps getting burned down on the very first day of class, I'd kind of dismissed it.

So boy did I feel like an asshole when he turned in an essay with this intro the next day:

Having been fallen a sleep at midnight, my parents, sister, aunt and I heard the children's screaming and the voice of the shelling mortars simultaneously came about, and suddenly jumped through the ladder from the top to the bottom of the house to get away from the attacking troops' ammunitions without grabbing any facility.

For a while, Htan Dah's family and all those other asylum-seekers in Thailand were safe, relative to the Karen still in Burma. If they ventured out of the squalid camps, they were subject to harassment and arrest from one of the world's most corrupt police forces, but at least Burmese soldiers were less likely to march into a sovereign country to attack them.

What the Burmese army could do, though, was help a rival Karen faction to do so. They called themselves the Democratic Karen Buddhist Army, or DKBA. There had been discontent within the Christian-led KNU for years, complaints of abuses of power, religious discrimination, and grueling jungle-warfare conditions. In 1994, by which point there were 80,000 Karen living in the Thai camps, a government-allied monk persuaded several hundred Buddhist KNU soldiers to defect. The junta was only too happy to support their cause—which included attacking refugee camps filled with Christian Karen.

The huts at Htan Dah's settlement of Huay Kaloke were cloaked in thick, warm Thai darkness as DKBA soldiers moved in on the 7,000 refugees living there in January 1997. Residents generally went to bed early; there was no electricity, and flammable materials cost money nobody had. But Htan Dah's mother sometimes hired herself out as a laborer, plowing fields for about a dollar a day. That was far less than what the legal Thai workers alongside her made, but she needed money to buy nails—her scavenged-bamboo-and-thatch hut wasn't going to hold itself together—and candles, since she wasn't wild about her kids using homemade lamps, essentially tin cans filled with gasoline.

The small encampment had become overpopulated, so that there wasn't even enough space to play soccer, and Htan Dah barely ever left it. But a Christian organization had donated some books, and NGOs were running a full school system now. Htan Dah had exams the next day; he had stayed up past sundown studying and had been asleep for hours by the time the sound of gunshots reached his family's shelter. Some children somewhere screamed as they leapt out of the elevated hut. They ran, backs and knees bent, low to the dirt, for the surrounding woods as DKBA troops set fire to the camp. The huts burned hot and fast. Htan Dah kept his head down, so that he hardly registered the other people running alongside, not even noticing that some were in their underwear. "Please, God," he prayed. "Oh my God. Save me. Save my life," over and over again. It was a few days before his sixteenth birthday. He prayed and ran until he reached the forest, where, like everyone else, he stopped, turned around, and stood silently watching the camp—bedrooms, books, photos, shoes, a shirt woven by a grandmother—burn to the ground.

The next day, the refugees returned to the smoldering plot and made beds in the ash. They began slowly rebuilding, though none could have any illusions that the Thai security posted at the front gate would protect them. They had long ago noted that the function of the guards was not so much keeping danger out as keeping the refugees in, collecting bribes from those who wanted to leave the camp to work or collect firewood or make a trip to the market. Their attackers met no resistance on their way into Huay Kaloke that night. And less than fourteen months later, when vehicles full of DKBA soldiers drove in again, no one stopped them. Again.

"How do you know the Thai soldiers just let them drive right in through the front gate?" I interrupted Htan Dah as he told me this story on the reading bench in my room. That an army would allow raiding foreign troops unfettered access to 7,000 sleeping civilians — twice — seemed frankly a little far-fetched. "Maybe the soldiers were trying to protect the gate, but the DKBA just went around or something."

Htan Dah had told this story before, and to several foreigners, but never to one rude enough to suggest that he was a liar. He cocked his head. "Because," he said, "there is only one road. The only way into the camp is through the front gate!"

For a second time, Htan Dah awoke in the middle of the night to gunfire and shouting; for a second time, he fled with his family and the clothes he was wearing for the safety of the surrounding trees. But this time, the soldiers also shelled the camp. This time, a pregnant woman was shot dead and two girls from Htan Dah's school who hid in a well suffered burns that killed them. This time a seven-year-old died of shrapnel wounds and dozens were injured — and nearly the whole damn camp was burned down again.

"We accept that we were inactive," the secretary general of Thailand's National Security Council conceded later. Thai authorities decided to close the camp. Htan Dah's family set up a temporary shelter made of sticks and a raincoat, under which they lived while they were waiting to be moved elsewhere.

The trucks didn't arrive for almost a year and a half. When they did, Htan Dah and his family were shipped to a camp in the mountains, where the population in exile eventually became 20,000 strong, where Htan Dah eventually grew up and got married and had a baby of his own, where the cold, wet winds cut through the shacks stacked high in the hills of central Thailand, far away enough to be safer from the DKBA.

My days fell into a strange routine. I taught two classes of English a day, beginner and intermediate. After and between classes, and before the evening of drinking began in earnest, I snacked on coconut-fried cashews I bought at the 7-Eleven while helping the guys translate their HRD interviews or fill out applications for asylum. They kept filling out the applications, even though they had little chance of success — certainly no chance of resettling in the United States, which, under the Patriot Act, had effectively declared all Karen from the contested highlands terrorists for providing "material support" to the "terrorist" KNU.

After class one day, one of the guys wanted to show me a word he saw all the time so I could explain its meaning: marginalized. (He grasped the concept pretty quickly.) He also wanted to know what the thing used to bind people's feet together was called. I told him I didn't think we had a word for that in English. (I was wrong. Though archaic in noun form, the word exists: "fetters.") When Htoo Moo asked me later for the word for systematically slicing open the skin on someone's forearm, I told him I didn't think we had a word for that, either.

Another day, I sat outside holding an impromptu pronunciation lesson on some of the words in an HRD's report.

"Repeat after me," I was saying. "*Rape.*"

"Rop."

"Try again. *Rrraaape.*"

Another day, a Burma Action staffer I'll call Lah Lah Htoo asked if I wanted to see a video. He loaded a DVD of some footage taken in eastern Burma by aid workers, mostly Karen, some of whom are also medics, called the Free Burma Rangers.

It starts with war footage, guys shooting guns in tall jungle bush, and loud rocket fire, and a village burning down and screaming women running for their lives, before moving briefly to photo stills: a picture of villagers standing over a group of dead bodies, a picture of a dead woman with her shirt torn open, a picture of murdered children lined up in a row. Then the camera centers on the face of a seventeen-year-old boy with lifeless, unfocused eyes, a *longyi* (sarong) held up below his neck so he can't see his completely exposed lower leg bone, a bloody white stick still hung with a few slick and glistening black-purple sinews, protruding from a bloody knee—a land-mine wound swarmed by flies. Then he's in a thin hammock, with a man in cheap plastic flip-flops at each end of the bamboo pole from which it swings, and another walking alongside holding an IV drip dangling from another piece of wood, being carried through the mountainous terrain. For four days. Which is how long it takes the Ranger team to get him to a clinic on the border, where a proper amputation can be done.

By that point I'd twisted my face into a permanent wince, and it didn't get any easier to watch. A husband and wife sit next to each other while he explains that their two sons and daughter were taken by Burma army troops. Local Karen leaders negotiated the return of the two boys, but they haven't seen the girl since. "We want her back," the woman says, smiling sadly, before dropping her face to her knees, covering it with her pink sweater, and starting to sob. There are people getting ready to run from an attack, little girls running around talking fast directions to each other while they throw shit in baskets and sacks they strap to their foreheads. A man on his back breathing fast and shallow as Free Burma Ranger medics jab their fingers and instruments into the bloody stump below his knee. Skulls and bones on the ground and a Ranger telling how he brought a bunch of children's presents donated by kids overseas only to find that there are no children in this village anymore. Rangers tearing out infected teeth with pliers. Rangers cleaning the gory, festering wound on a little kid's leg as the child stands still, calm, pantsless. Rangers delivering a baby in the darkness by the green glow of the camera's night mode, on the jungle floor. A shot of a Burma army compound, the camera zooming in shakily on the faces of the boys with rifles, the hiding cameramen whispering breathlessly to each other. A man rocking the tiniest sleeping baby; his wife died in childbirth during their flight through the jungle. He worries he has no idea how to take care of this child without her. Tears streaming hard and quiet down the face of a woman mindlessly fingering her jacket zipper with one hand, standing among the ashes of her old village, in which her husband was killed. A toddler barely old enough to stand picking his way through the jungle as his village flees, carefully parting the brush with his chubby little fingers and stepping through with his bare, scratched legs and feet. A Ranger team leaves a group of internally displaced persons and the IDPs call out please don't leave us, please come back. A man keeps hiding his face contorted with sorrow as he sobs convulsively, "I don't understand why they killed my children. They didn't even know their right hand from their left hand," while the woman next to him weeps silently and gnashes her teeth. The video ends with a quote from Galatians on the screen: *Let us not grow weary while doing good. In due season we shall reap if we don't lose heart.*

"What do you think?" Lah Lah Htoo asked me when it ended.

I thought I might like to close myself in the bathroom so I could punch myself in the chest, just a little, to try to release some of the tightness and weight there.

"Good video?" he asked, because I was taking so long to answer.

"Yeah, it's a good video."

He nodded and waited politely for me to continue, but I just sat quietly, awkwardly, before simply nodding back at him. Eventually, I asked him what they did with the videos they made.

"We send them. To human rights organizations, UN, news."

"Do they ever use them?"

Lah Lah Htoo shrugged.

Make no mistake: Though most Americans are woefully uninformed about the shit going down in Burma, your federal lawmakers are *on* it. In 1997, President Bill Clinton barred new U.S. investment in the country. In 2003, Congress introduced the Burmese Freedom and Democracy Act, which banned any Burmese imports, opposed loans to the regime, froze any of its U.S. assets, and denied its leaders entry visas. In 2005, Condoleezza Rice awarded Burma a special designation as an "outpost of tyranny." Bush 43 gave it shout-outs in several State of the Union addresses. ("We will continue to speak out for the cause of freedom in places like Cuba, Belarus, and Burma.") There's a U.S. Senate Women's Caucus on Burma, and Obama just extended sanctions again and said this at his Nobel Peace Prize acceptance: "When there is genocide in Darfur, systematic rape in Congo, repression in Burma — there must be consequences . . . . And the closer we stand together, the less likely we will be faced with the choice between armed intervention and complicity in oppression." Also blacklisting Burma: Australia, which won't sell the regime weapons and has financial sanctions against 463 members of the junta. And the EU has stripped Burma of trading privileges and put an arms embargo in place.

The trouble isn't so much a lack of measures as their total ineffectiveness. Though U.S. investors have had to pull their money out of, say, the garment industry, they can still deal in Burma's oil and gas, which is where the junta's big money comes from. When Congress passed that 1997 law restricting new investment, Unocal got its gas fields grandfathered in. After Chevron absorbed Unocal in 2005, its lobbyists worked tirelessly to ensure that no sanctions would force it to divest. It appeared as though the 2008 Block Burmese JADE (Junta's Anti-Democratic Efforts) Act would finally force Chevron to give up its Burmese holdings, until the Senate Committee on Foreign Relations, chaired by Joe Biden (whose former chief of staff was one Alan Hoffman, once a Unocal lobbyist), stripped out the provision and replaced it with a *suggestion* that the company "consider voluntary divestment over time."

Okay, but if we only fashioned better — and better-targeted — sanctions, advocates say, Burma's economy would collapse and the government might just get packing. But whether or not you believe that sanctions were the straw that broke South Africa's back, you cannot believe that they would have worked in that country if half the world's governments had said, "We're not going to give you money for your stuff anymore" while the other half had said, "Awesome. More for us."

Operation Rescue

"Mordor is the [Burmese government], and guys like us are hobbits," Tha U Wa A Pa says by way of explaining why he built a training base for medics in a land-mine-infested war zone in Burma, where he lives with his wife and three children.

Tha U Wa A Pa and his Free Burma Rangers document the atrocities of the Burmese army and provide medical and tactical help to those fleeing from it. It's a quest requiring almost inconceivable bravery and, in Tha U Wa A Pa's case, a conviction that God has chosen him for this task. Though he uses a Karen nom de guerre (meaning "Father of the White Monkey" — a.k.a. his daughter), he's the son of prominent American missionaries in Thailand, an alum of Texas A&M (BA, poli-sci) and a former U.S. Army Ranger. After graduating from Fuller Seminary in Pasadena, Tha U Wa A Pa became a missionary in Thailand himself. Which is where he was in 1997, when a major SPDC offensive sent a flood of Karen refugees across the border. Tha U Wa A Pa loaded up a backpack full of supplies and, together with a KNU soldier he met along the way, rushed into Burma as if it were a house on fire. The two men treated as many wounded as they could, carrying a guy who'd stepped on a land mine to a hospital to have his leg amputated. Over the next three weeks, they ferried supplies and patients back and forth over the border.

Since then, the Rangers have trained more than 110 roving teams who provide medical assistance to (and document the plight of) the more than half a million internally displaced persons in the eastern Burmese jungle. Rangers have treated some 400,000 people for malaria, AIDS, dysentery, diarrhea, malnutrition, worms, anemia, skin disease, and infections. They pull teeth and deliver babies. Six have lost their lives on the job. As the junta's violence escalates, so do their efforts; the Rangers' budget is up to $1.3 million a year, all donations, mostly from churches and their parishioners. "We're just little guys trying to do some good," Tha U Wa A Pa says. "On the surface it seems like Mordor has all the strength and power and might. But if our fellowship of hobbits stays united, good will defeat evil in the end."

That's the reality in Burma, where China is building an oil pipeline so as to avoid the long trip around the Strait of Malacca. Thailand has the rights to 1.7 trillion cubic feet of natural gas in one concession alone. One Indian firm has signed up for 5 trillion cubic feet. Russia has several firms drilling. A single pipeline operated by France, Thailand, and, yes, Chevron earned the junta more than $1 billion in 2008. The South Korean company Daewoo International plans to earn more than $10 billion over 25 years from its drilling project in Burma's immense Shwe gas reserve; handling Daewoo's exploratory Burma drilling was the American firm Transocean. As a member of the Association of Southeast Asian Nations, Burma is included in a free-trade agreement with India that eliminates tariffs on thousands of products; India plans to invest billions of dollars in two Burmese hydroelectric dams. The EU is discussing a free-trade agreement with ASEAN nations as well, although the UK swears it won't make a deal that would benefit Burma—it's worth noting the UK already has oil and gas dealings there. In 2008 Burma saw a 165 percent increase in the number of Chinese multinational companies involved in Burmese mining, oil and gas, and hydropower development. The regime ran a $2.5 billion trade surplus in 2009, with $5 billion in currency reserves.

The United States can better target its sanctions all it wants, but already they've pushed tens of thousands of Burmese textile workers out of factory jobs—and, as even the State Department has admitted, into sex work. And as Chevron has pointed out, if we pull out our remaining investments, someone else—perhaps someone less conscientious—will gladly fill the gap. The international community can't even agree to stop giving the regime weapons. Even if it could get China to play ball on that front, not so much North Korea. As long as there's money to be made in Burma, a cohesive or constructive policy of international financial disengagement—from an energy-rich country neighbored by the world's two most populous, energy-desperate countries—is never going to happen.

You know a situation is dire when its best chance of a good outcome depends on action by the United Nations Security Council. At the 2005 UN World Summit, member nations resolved that if a government perpetuates or allows any of four "atrocity crimes"—war crimes, ethnic cleansing, crimes against humanity, or genocide—the world body is responsible for taking "timely and decisive" action to protect that nation's people. When in 2007 a draft resolution on Burma was brought before the Security Council, some activists felt that there was a strong case for it to include charges of genocide against the Karen. The UN 1948 Convention on the Prevention and Punishment of the Crime of Genocide defines "genocide" as an attempt "to destroy, in whole or in part, a national, ethnical, racial or religious group" with at least one of five methods. One of them the SPDC isn't guilty of: "Forcibly transferring children of the group to another group." But "killing members of the group"? Check. "Causing serious bodily or mental harm to members of the group"? Check. "Deliberately inflicting on the group conditions of life calculated to bring about its physical destruction in whole or in part"? Clearly. "Imposing measures intended to prevent births within the group"? If you count gang-raping and murdering pregnant women, yes. Since the International Criminal Tribunal for Rwanda, systematic rape has been recognized as a key feature of genocide. In Burma, it's systematic, institutionalized, and indoctrinated into soldiers, who are explicitly ordered, "Your blood must be left in the village."

But not one government has officially leveled the charge at Burma, and some academics and even activists argue that these genocidal actions aren't genocide-like enough to count. We can't just be throwing the word around to describe any old horror. Or as my father put it when I tried to impress upon him the seriousness of my BA housemates' situation, "But how does it compare to Sudan?"

If Sudan is the bar against which we're measuring genocide, okay: Burma was alongside Sudan on the list of the world's worst displacement situations for four years running. Sudan's mortality rate for children under five, a common measure of conflict epidemiology, is 109 per 1,000 live births. In eastern Burma, it's 221. In the Darfur genocide, 400,000 civilians have been killed. A junta chairman once estimated that the body count of Burma's civil war—the Karen are only one of seven major minorities that have been involved in dozens of armed insurgencies—"would reach as high as millions."

It comes down to this: A draft resolution that compellingly charges genocide against a country is a draft resolution that's likely to get passed—because no one wants to be the nation that vetoes that. But the 2007 Security Council draft resolution to declare Burma a threat to international peace and security didn't contain charges of genocide. Nor ethnic cleansing, nor crimes against humanity, nor war crimes. China and Russia vetoed it.

Since I first arrived at Burma Action's Mae Sot offices, four years ago, some 50,000 Burmese refugees have left Thailand for UN-orchestrated resettlement in Western countries. In 2007, the United States waived its material support prohibition for refugees who'd assisted the KNU, and the next year allowed in more than 14,000 refugees, including several BA staff members. In America, they try to make rent with welfare or factory wages, and talk, weirdly, about struggling to survive. I apologized to one, after he was moved to a suburb outside cold, gray Cleveland, for his crushing poverty and loneliness and the weather. "It's okay," he replied. "You can never find a good place to live in the world. Only in heaven."

Though some of the documentary activists have emigrated, their footage and reports gather dust in Thailand, awaiting, the human rights community hopes, the day when they might be used at a trial of the junta or in a truth and reconciliation process. Some Burma Action footage made it out and into the opener for *Rambo IV*, whose producers paid—after some hard haggling—about two grand for it.

Lah Lah Htoo is one of those activists who's stayed behind. At a going-away party my last weekend, he sat with a guitar in his lap. On a previous night he'd played a hard-twanging, pentatonic melody on a stringed Karen instrument while he sang, in flowing minor notes, a traditional song about a river, so haunting that I had nearly drunkenly wept. But now the guitar he held was idle, and he tipped his head back and looked at me through half-closed eyes.

"Do you think that we will see each other again?" he asked, one arm dangling over the body of the guitar.

"Of course we'll see each other again," I said. I looked at Htan Dah. "I'll come back to Thailand soon."

"When?" several voices asked.

"Probably next summer. I have to figure it out with work, and money."

"So," one of the guys said, "we will see each other again maybe next year."

"I hope," I said. "Hopefully next year."

"When we see each other again," Lah Lah Htoo said, "it will be in Burma." The other guys cheered. "When we see each other again, you will come to Burma. And you will not *need* a visa to enter. And *I* will pick you up at the airport." His face was barely wide enough for his smile, and he was hollering a bit, over the approving shouts of the other guys. "In a car. In *my* car!" Lah Lah Htoo had left his village when he was a teenager, when he'd run away with the rest of his family and neighbors, and hadn't been back since. A silence settled over his coworkers in the wake of his fantastic predictions, and they all smiled softly and looked off or at the floor or at the wall as they considered cars and airports, and I thought about doomed POWs in movies who know their fate is sealed but talk anyway about how they're going to eat a big cheeseburger when they get back to America, and I kept quiet as long as the guys were quiet, bowing my head as if in reverence of something that had died.

JOYCE CAROL OATES

■

A Hole in the Head

FROM *The Kenyon Review*

STRANGE! — THOUGH DR. BREDE WORE LATEX gloves when treating patients and never came into direct contact with their skin, when he peeled off the thin rubber gloves to toss them into the sanitary waste disposal in his examination room, his hands were faintly stained with rust-red streaks — *blood?*

He lifted his hands, spread his fingers to examine them. His hands were those of an average man of his height and weight, though his fingers were slightly longer than average and the tips were discernibly tapered. His nails were clipped short and kept scrupulously clean and yet — how was this possible? — inside the latex gloves, they'd become ridged with the dried rust-red substance he had to suppose was blood. He thought *There must be a flaw in the gloves. A tear.*

It wasn't the first time this had happened — this curiosity. In recent months it seemed to be happening with disconcerting frequency. Lucas considered retrieving the used gloves from the trash to inspect them, to see if he could detect minuscule tears in the rubber — but the prospect was distasteful to him.

In the lavatory attached to his office Lucas Brede washed his hands vigorously. A swirl of rust-red water disappeared down the drain. This was a mystery! Few of his patients ever "bled" in his office. Dr. Brede was a cosmetic surgeon, and the procedures he performed on the premises — collagen and Botox injection, microdermabrasion, sclerotherapy, laser (wrinkle removal), chemical peeling, Therma Therapy — involved virtually no blood loss. More complicated surgical procedures — face-lift, rhinoplasty, vein removal, liposuction — were performed at a local hospital with an anesthesiologist and at least one assistant.

On the operating table Dr. Brede's patients bled considerably—the face-lift in particular was bloody, as it involved deep lacerations in both the face and the scalp—but nothing out of the ordinary—nothing that Dr. Brede couldn't stanch with routine medical intervention. But this!—this mysterious evidence of bloodstains, inside the latex gloves!—he couldn't comprehend. There had to be a deficiency in the rubber gloves.

He would ask his nurse-receptionist Chloe to complain to the supplier—to demand that the entire box of defective gloves be replaced. It wouldn't be the first time that medical suppliers had tried to foist defective merchandise on Lucas Brede in recent years; with the worsening of the U.S. economy there'd been a discernible decrease in quality and in business ethics . . . . Lucas hadn't wanted to credit rumors he'd been hearing recently about malpractice settlements certain of his cosmetic surgeon-colleagues had been forced to make, suggesting that medical ethics, too, in some quarters, had become compromised.

In desperate times, desperate measures. Whoever had said that, it had not been Hippocrates.

In the mirror above the sink the familiar face confronted him—a hesitant smile dimpling the left cheek, a narrowing of the eyes as if seeing Lucas Brede at such close quarters he couldn't somehow believe what he was seeing.

Is this me? Or who I've become?

He was Lucas Brede, MD. He was forty-six years old. He was a "plastic" surgeon—his specialty was rhinoplasty. He took pride in his work—in some aspects of his work—and, rare in his profession, he hadn't yet been sued for malpractice. For the past eight years he'd rented an office suite on the first-floor, rear level of Weirlands, a sprawling glass, granite, and stucco medical center set back from a private road on an elegantly landscaped hillside on the outskirts of Hazelton-on-Hudson, Dutchess County, New York. In this late winter season of dark pelting rains—the worsening economic crisis, foreclosures of properties across the nation, "domestic ruin"—and thousands of miles away beyond the U.S. border a spurious and interminable "war to protect freedom" in its sixth year—Lucas Brede and the other physicians-residents at Weirlands were but marginally affected. Most of their patients were affluent, and if the ship of state was sinking, they were of the class destined to float free.

In addition, Dr. Brede's patients were almost exclusively female, and vitally, one might say passionately, devoted to their own well-being: faces, bodies, "lifestyles." They were the wives, ex-wives, or widows of rich men; some were the daughters of rich men; a significant fraction were professional women in high-paying jobs—determined to retain their youthfulness and air of confidence in a ruthlessly competitive marketplace.

Occasionally Lucas happened to see photographs of his patients in the local Hazleton paper, or in New *York Times* society pages—glamorous clothes, dazzling smiles, invariably looking much younger than their ages—and felt a stir of pride. *That face is one of mine.*

He liked them, on the whole. And they liked him—they were devoted to him. For all were attractive women, or had been: their well-being depended upon such attractiveness, maintained *in perpetuity*.

Already in their early forties the blond, fair-skinned women were past the bloom of their beauty and wore dark glasses indoors, expensive moisturizers, and thick creams at night. No cosmetic procedure could quite assuage their anxiety, that they were *looking their age*. Lucas couldn't imagine any husband—any man—embracing one of these women in the night; they must insist upon sleeping alone, as they'd slept alone as girls. (Lucas's wife now slept apart from him. But not because she wanted to preserve her beauty.) His patients were nervous women who laughed eagerly. Or they were edgy women who rarely laughed, fearing laugh lines in their faces. Their eyes watered—they'd had LASIK eye surgery, their tear ducts had been destroyed. Botox injections and face-lifts had left their faces tautly smooth, in some cases flawless as masks. But their necks!—their necks were far more difficult to "lift." And their hands, and the flaccid flesh of their upper arms. In their wish to appear younger than their ages, as beautiful as they'd once been, or more beautiful—*what they were not*—they were childlike, desperate. The more Dr. Brede injected gelatinous liquids into their skin—collagen, Botox, Restylane,

Formula X—the more eager they were for more drastic treatments: chemical peels, dermabrasion, cosmetic surgery. They feared hair-fine wrinkles as one might fear melanomas. They feared soft, crepey flesh beneath their eyes; they feared the slackening of jowls, jawlines as in another part of the world one might fear leprosy.

To assuage their skittishness, for they were hypersensitive to pain, Dr. Brede provided them with small, hard, rubber balls to grip when he injected their faces with his long, transparent needles; he gave them mildly narcotizing creams to rub into their skin before arriving at his office; he gave them tranquilizers, or, occasionally, placebos; it amused him, and sometimes annoyed him, that his patients reacted to pain so disproportionately—sometimes, before he'd actually pushed the needle into their faces. The most delicate procedure was the injection of Botox, Restylane, or Formula X into the patient's forehead where, if Dr. Brede was not exceedingly careful, the needle struck bone, and gave every evidence of being genuinely painful. (Dr. Brede had never injected himself with any of these solutions so had no idea what they felt like, nor did he have any inclination to experiment.) His patients were devoted to him, but they were uneasy and emotional, like children—who could be angry with children?

He wanted to assure them *My touch is magic! I bring you mercy.*

He liked—loved—his work—his practice at Weirlands—but there were times when the prospect of doing what he was doing forever filled him with sick terror.

Leave then. Quit. Do another kind of medicine. Can't you?

His wife hadn't understood. There'd been a willful opacity in her pose of righteousness. He'd tried to explain to her—to a degree—but she hadn't understood. He needed to take on more patients—he needed to convince his patients to upscale their treatment—in the aftermath of this fiscal year that had been so devastating for all. Lucas wanted only to keep his finances—his investments—as they were, without losing more money; he'd had to deceive his wife about certain of these investments, of which she knew virtually nothing. Audrey's signature was easy to come by—trustingly she signed legal and financial documents without reading them closely, or at all; so trustingly, Lucas sometimes skirted the nuisance of involving her and signed her signature—her large, schoolgirl hand—himself.

Certain of his financial problems, he'd confided in no one, for there was no one in whom he could confide. Nor could he share his more exciting, hopeful news — that he'd been experimenting with an original gelatinous substance that resembled Botox chemically but was much cheaper. There was a marginal risk of allergic reactions and chemical "burning" — he knew, and was hypercautious. This magical substance, to which he'd given the name Formula X, Dr. Brede could prepare in his own "lab" in his office suite and be spared the prohibitively high prices the Botox manufacturers demanded.

One day, maybe, Lucas Brede would perfect and patent Formula X and enter into a lucrative deal with a pharmaceutical company — though making money in itself wasn't his intention.

"I'm going *in*."

So matter-of-factly the neurosurgeon spoke, you would not have thought him boastful.

Lucas Brede had entered medical school intending to be a neurosurgeon. Except the training was too arduous, expensive. Except his fellow students — ninety percent of them Jews, from the Metropolitan New York region — were too ambitious, too ruthless, and too smart. Except his instructors showed shockingly little interest in Lucas Brede — as if he were but one of many hundreds of med students, indistinguishable from the rest. As in the Darwinian nightmare struggle for existence, Lucas Brede hadn't quite survived, he'd been devoured by his fierce competitors, he'd been the runt of the litter.

How fascinated he'd been as a medical student, and then an intern, and finally a resident at the Hudson Neurosurgical Institute in Riverdale, New York — how envious — observing with what confidence the most revered neurosurgeons dared to open up the human skull and touch the brain — the *living brain*. He was eager to emulate them — eager to be accepted by this elite tribe of elders — even as in his more realistic moments he knew he couldn't bear it, the very thought of it left him faint, dazed — an incision into the skull, a drilling open of a hole into the skull to expose the *living brain*.

Vividly he remembered certain episodes in his two-year residency at the Institute. Memories he'd never shared with anyone, still less with the woman he married, whose high opinion of Lucas Brede he could not risk sullying.

Ten-, twelve-hour days. Days indistinguishable from nights. He'd assisted at operations—from one to three operations a day, six days a week. He'd interviewed patients, he'd prepped patients. He'd examined CT scans. Once confronted with a CT scan he'd stared and stared at the dense-knotted tangle of wormy arteries and veins amid the sponge-like substance that was the *brain*, and all that he'd learned of the brain seemed to dissolve like vapor. Here was a malevolent life-form—a *thing* of unfathomable strangeness. He'd tasted panic like black bile in his mouth. For more than twenty-four hours he'd gone without sleeping and in his state of exhaustion, laced with caffeine and amphetamines, he'd been both over-excited and lethargic—his thoughts careened like pinballs, or drifted and floated beyond his comprehension. Somehow he was confusing the brain-picture illuminated before him with a picture of his own brain. . . . What he was failing to see was a brainstem glioma, a sinister malignancy like a serpent twined about the patient's brainstem and all but invisible to inexpert eyes. "Ordinarily these tumors are inoperable," the neurosurgeon said, "—but I'm going *in*." Lucas shivered. Never would he have the courage to utter such words. Never would he have such faith in himself. *Going in.*

Not that he dreaded the possibility of irrevocably maiming or killing a patient so much as he dreaded the public nature of such failure, the terrible judgment of others.

He hadn't failed his residency, explicitly. In some ways he'd performed very well. But he'd known, and everyone around him had known, that he would never be a neurosurgeon. A shameful thing had happened when he assisted in his first trepanation, or craniectomy—he'd been the one to drill open the skull—this was the skull of a living person, a middle-aged man being prepped for surgery—handed a heavy power drill and bluntly told, "Go to it." By this time in his residency he'd observed numerous craniectomies—he'd observed numerous brain surgeries. He knew that the human skull is one of the most durable of all natural substances, a bone hard as mineral; to penetrate it you need serious drills, saws, brute force. In the dissection lab in medical school he'd experimented with such drilling, but in this case the head was a living head, the brain encased in the skull was a *living brain* and this fact filled him with horror, as well as the fact that he knew the patient, he'd interviewed the patient, and had gotten along very well with the anxious man. Now, as in a ghoulish comic-book torture, this man had been placed in a sitting position, clamped into position; mercifully, for the resident obliged to drill a hole in his head, he'd been rolled beneath the instrument table and was virtually invisible beneath a sterile covering and towels. All that Lucas was confronted with was the back of the man's head, upon which, in an orange marking pen, the neurosurgeon had drawn the pattern of the opening Lucas was to drill. "Go to it"—the older man repeated. The patient's scalp had been cut, blood had flowed freely and was wiped away, now a flap of the scalp was retracted and the skull—the bone—exposed. Calmly—he was sure he exuded calm—Lucas pressed the power drill against the bone—but couldn't seem to squeeze the trigger until urged impatiently, "Go *on*." Blindly then he squeezed—jerked at—the trigger; there was a high-pitched whining noise; slowly the point of the drill turned, horribly cutting into the skull. Lucas's eyes so flooded with tears, he couldn't see clearly. Blindly he held the drill in place; the instrument was heavy and clumsy in his icy hands and seemed to be pulsing with its own, interior life. How hard the human skull was, and adamant—but the stainless steel drill was more powerful—a mixture of bone-shavings and blood flew from the skull—a flurry of bloodied shavings—the drill ceased abruptly when the point penetrated the skull, to prevent it from piercing the *dura mater* just beyond, a dark-pink, rubbery membrane threaded with blood vessels and nerves. Lucas smelled burned bone and flesh—he'd been breathing bone-dust—he began to gag, lightheaded with nausea. But there was no time to pause for recovery—he had to drill three more holes into the skull, in a trapezoid pattern, first with the large drill and then with a smaller, more precise drill. The smell of burned bone and flesh was overwhelming, hideous—he held his breath not wanting to breathe it in—now with a plier-like instrument pulling and prying at the skull—panting, desperate—turning the holes into a single opening. He thought *This isn't real. None of this is real* yet how ingenious, the "skull" oozed blood, now the single hideous hole in the skull was stuffed with surgical sponges immediately soaked with blood. Then he was speaking to someone—he was speaking calmly and matter-of-factly—the procedure was completed and the next stage of the surgery was now to begin—he was certain that this was so, he'd done all that was required of him and he'd done it without making a single error, yet somehow the tile floor tilted upward, rose to meet him—as all stared the young resident's knees buckled—the nerve-skeleton that bore him aloft and prevented him from dissolving into a puddle of helpless flesh on the floor collapsed, shriveled, and was gone.

It was fatigue. Caffeine, speed. The pressure of his work. The eyes of the others. Dazed and not seeming to know where he was at first—in the corridor outside the OR—not wanting to ask what had happened only if the patient was all right, if he'd completed the craniectomy satisfactorily, and he'd been assured yes, he had.

Nineteen years he'd been a cosmetic surgeon in Hazelton-on-Hudson, New York. Eight years since he'd moved his practice to prestigious Weirlands at the outskirts of town. As a suburban physician Dr. Brede avoided all surgeries involving pathologies and all surgeries except the most familiar and routine, and high-paying—face-lifts were the most lucrative and the most reliable. The procedure was ghastly as a sadist's fantasy and horribly bloody when the facial skin-mask was "lifted" and "stretched"—"stapled" to the scalp—but no one had ever died of a face-lift—at least not one of Dr. Brede's patients. One of these operations was very like another as most human faces, attractive or otherwise, beneath the skin-mask, are very like one another.

Of course he knew—and he resented—that in the pantheon of physicians and surgeons Dr. Lucas Brede's life's work was considered trivial, contemptible. And he himself trivial, contemptible. He knew, and tried not to know. He tried not to be bitter. Thinking *I would feel this way myself, about myself. If my life had gone otherwise.*

In this season of dark-pelting rains. Snow swirling like sticky clumps of mucus out of a sheet-metal sky. His four-fifteen patient Mrs. Druidd, in whose sallow, sagging face he'd been injecting Formula X slowly, carefully—wiping away blood with sterile gauzepads—an itchy film of perspiration on his face—began to be restless, skittish. On her previous visit to Dr. Brede, just before Christmas, Mrs. Druidd had had a chemical peeling; now, follow-up injections to plump out lines and wrinkles in her face, much of this routine except Dr. Brede was substituting his own Formula X for Restylane—a substitution that was entirely ethical, he believed, in the way that substituting generic drugs for pricey brand-name drugs was ethical—but the mild tranquilizer he'd given her didn't seem to be effective, and with each injection she seemed to be feeling more pain. "Squeeze the balls. Both balls"—Dr. Brede advised. His manner was calm, kindly. If he was deeply annoyed, you would never have guessed so from his affable smile.

"Oh! That *hurts*."

Mrs. Druidd had never spoken so petulantly to Dr. Brede—this was a surprise. Lucas saw to his alarm that there were deep bruises in the woman's face, where he'd been injecting Formula X; collagen and Restylane caused bruising too, but nothing like this. And that weltlike mark on one side of the woman's mouth, he knew wouldn't fade readily.

Three to five days was the usual estimate for bruising following injections. Very likely it might be more than a week this time.

Mrs. Druidd asked if this was something new he was injecting into her face—"It feels different. It stings and *burns*."

Lucas hesitated just a moment before assuring her, this was the identical treatment she'd had numerous times in his office.

"I don't remember it stinging so and *burning*. I'm afraid to see what I look like . . . "

The woman was fifty-seven years old, what did she expect? A miracle? Even with the lurid bruising, the effect of Dr. Brede's treatments over the past several years gave Mrs. Druidd the appearance of a woman of thirty-five, perhaps—if you didn't look too closely at the small, damp, fanatic eyes.

Here was a rich man's wife, or ex-wife. Dr. Brede had seen Mrs. Druidd's photograph in the Hazelton paper, he was sure. Chairwoman of the Friends of the Hazelton Public Library. Chairwoman of the Hazelton Medical Clinic's annual Spring Fling. With her dramatic dark hair and flawless-seeming face Mrs. Druidd managed to hold her own with women of her daughter's generation. Her sessions with Dr. Brede, that had more often the air of custom and ritual, usually went more smoothly.

Dr. Brede had no choice but to bring the hand mirror to Mrs. Druidd's face. This was a part of the ritual, he could hardly avoid it. At first Mrs. Druidd drew in her breath sharply, as if she'd been slapped—then she touched her tender, wounded skin—unexpectedly she laughed—"Well! It felt worse than this! I suppose I deserve it—after all." She paused, with a rueful sort of flirtatiousness. "How long will this awful bruising last, Doctor?"

Even now, the woman yearned to trust Dr. Brede, for women yearn to trust men—all women, all men. And Dr. Brede wanted to believe that certainly, yes, he was a man worthy of a woman's trust.

"The usual—three to five days. Unless you become anxious and stressed—stress will exacerbate the bruising, as you know."

"Yes—yes!—'stress.'" Mrs. Druidd spoke as if repentant. Chloe had brought in an ice pack for Mrs. Druidd to take away with her, for a minimum extra charge—standard procedure in Dr. Brede's office and much appreciated by his patients.

Badly he wanted this pathetic woman to depart. He was tugging off his latex gloves impatiently—"Be sure to keep the ice pack on your face as much as possible. If you do—as you know—your face will heal much more quickly." The latex gloves seemed to be sticking to his fingers; he tore them off in haste, as if suffocating. As Mrs. Druidd left his office, pressing the ice bag to her reddened and swollen face, walking as a dazed or drunken woman might walk, the sobering thought came to Dr. Brede *I will never see her again. She will never call.*

His 5:15 P.M. patient, his last of the day, Mrs. Drake, another of his long-term patients, proved even more difficult. There was an edgy querulousness about Mrs. Drake as she climbed up onto the examination table, lay back stiffly, and allowed Chloe to position her; she failed to relax as Dr. Brede indicated on her face in Magic Marker ink, where the injections would be; instead of squeezing the rubber balls Dr. Brede gave her, to deflect pain, as Dr. Brede began the injections she sat up abruptly, touching her face—"That hurts! That *burns!* It doesn't feel like last time."

Calmly Lucas assured her that certainly, it was the same solution—the identical solution—Botox—he'd given her in the
past—"You must be more tense today. Tension heightens sensitivity to even mild discomfort." He was holding the syringe with the two
inch needle in his hand that trembled slightly—though Mrs. Drake
was too distracted to notice.

"Doctor, are you blaming *me*?"

The woman spoke so aggressively, Lucas was taken by surprise.
Long he'd been accustomed to the tractability of his female patients;
it was like them to murmur apologetically for wincing with pain. But
Irena Drake was the wife of a Dutchess County supreme court judge,
a woman with a strident voice and accusing eyes. Her chestnut-col-
ored hair was synthetically lightened and her skin that had once been
luminous and creamy seemed to be now drying out, though she was
only in her late forties. Lucas "lifted" Mrs. Drake's face several years
before and attended to it at three-month intervals; between patient
and doctor there had arisen a quasi-flirtatious rapport, not so much
sexual as social, or so Dr. Brede had imagined. Now Mrs. Drake was
wincing with pain, though he'd hardly touched her.

It was Formula X he was using, having decided to dilute it just
slightly after his experience with Mrs. Druidd. Lucas was certain that
this liquid solution couldn't possibly be causing a "burning" sensation—the hypersensitive woman had to be imagining it. But when
he began to inject her forehead—where fine, white wrinkles had
formed unmistakably since Mrs. Drake's last injection six months
before—Lucas felt the needle slip, and strike bone—the hard bone
just above the eye. Mrs. Drake screamed and shoved him away. "Dr.
Brede! You did that on purpose!"

"I—I certainly did not."

"You did! You did that to hurt me—to punish me!"

"Mrs. Drake—Irena!—why would I want to hurt you?—punish you? Please try to be calm—take a deep breath and release
slowly . . . "

"Have you been drinking, Dr. Brede?"

"Drinking? Of course not."

He'd had only a twenty-minute break between patients, at 2:00.
Eating a late lunch at his desk, on the phone with his accountant
who was preparing his New York State tax documents, he'd had just a

double shot of Johnnie Walker he kept in a cabinet in his office, and he'd rinsed his mouth with Listerine afterward. He was certainly not drunk. Nowhere near drunk. This hysterical woman could not smell alcohol on his breath.

"Then you're—drugged. You're taking something. I've seen TV documentaries—doctors like you. You've hurt me—look at me."

On Mrs. Drake's furrowed forehead was a bright blotch like a birthmark. Where he'd been injecting, with enormous care, minuscule quantities of Formula X to plump out the wrinkles and to "freeze" the nerves, to prevent such unattractive furrowing. All this was routine procedure, or nearly—still it was troubling, the patient's face was hot and swollen to the touch after only a few injections.

"Dr. Brede! I will report you to the county medical board—I will tell my husband. He will know what to do. I am leaving now, and *I am not paying for this treatment.*"

"But, Irena—I haven't completed the injections. I haven't half-completed the treatment. Chloe can put ice on your face and wait a few minutes before proceeding—"

"No. I'm finished. Let me out."

"You can't possibly want to leave without—"

"Yes. I do. I want to leave now."

Like a child in a tantrum, Mrs. Drake tore off the sheet of white paper covering her to the chin and threw it onto the floor. On this paper was a fine lacy pattern of blood-specks like overlapping cobwebs, of a kind Lucas had not noticed before.

"You signed a waiver, Mrs. Drake. Before coming into treatment, you signed a waiver with me."

"'Signed a waiver'! Of course I 'signed a waiver'—doctors like you won't treat patients otherwise. But would such a waiver stand up in court, if I can prove negligence? Malpractice? If I have photos taken of my injured face? I doubt it."

"Your face—is not 'injured.' Swelling and bruising is perfectly normal as you must know . . . "

Dr. Brede was stunned by the woman's unprecedented hostility. In his nineteen years of practice no patient had ever spoken to him like this. Some change had occurred, almost overnight; he couldn't think that it had exclusively to do with him but with the era itself—the plummeting economy, the ongoing wars, the malaise of a protracted winter. He thought *I will have to stop this madwoman. Someone must stop this madwoman*, but the prospect of touching Mrs. Drake, trying to restrain her, was distasteful. If he tried to prevent her leaving—in order to speak to her reasonably—she would react by screaming, and Chloe would hear.

"Goodbye! I'm never coming back! And—*I am not paying.*"

Indignant, Mrs. Drake left the examination room, kicking at the sheet of paper she'd thrown to the floor. Her harridan-face was luridly bruised as if she'd been tattooed by a whimsical and erratic tattooist.

"Dr. Brede?"—there was Chloe gazing at him with concerned eyes.

"It's all right, Chloe. Mrs. Drake had to leave suddenly."

"But—"

"I said it's *all right.*"

"But—shall I send her a bill? Or—"

"No. Don't send her a bill, please. Expunge her."

It was both flattering to Lucas, and discomforting, that his nurse receptionist behaved at times as if she were in love with him; Lucas was too gentlemanly to take advantage of her, though since his separation from his wife, Chloe's tender solicitude toward him was more marked. Now he would have turned away impatiently except Chloe dared to restrain him, as an older sister might—"Dr. Brede? Let me get this"—stooping to swipe at something on his trouser cuff with a tissue—a dark, damp stain? Blood?

Then, as she straightened, Chloe noticed a similar, smaller stain on a cuff of Dr. Brede's white shirt and this, too, she hurriedly swiped at with the tissue.

"A drop of something," she murmured, frowning as if embarrassed, not quite meeting her employer's eye, "—wet."

To his wife he'd pleaded *Have faith in me!*

"'Trepanning'—you know what that is, Doctor?"

"Yes. Of course."

"It's a—controversial medical procedure, I think?"

"Not controversial. Not a 'medical' procedure."

Ms. Steene was a stranger who'd called to make an "emergency appointment" with Dr. Brede for a consultation. He'd assumed that the woman wanted to discuss possible cosmetic treatments to restore a look of youthfulness to her creased face that appeared to be prematurely weathered; she was slender, if not markedly underweight, and wore sweatpants and a sweatshirt embossed with shiny green letters — *Harmony Acres for a Better World*. On the form she'd filled out for Dr. Brede's files she gave her age as fifty-six. Emphatically she'd crossed out the little boxes meant to designate sex and marital state as if in objection to such queries into her personal life.

With an air of correcting the uninformed physician Ms. Steene said reprovingly, "Not a *medical* procedure, Doctor. A *spiritual* procedure."

How unexpected this was, and annoying. One of Dr. Brede's long-term patients had also asked him about trepanning the other day, and Chloe reported calls to the office with similar inquiries. There must have been something about trepanning on television recently, on one of the morning or afternoon interview shows aimed at women viewers. Politely Dr. Brede said, "Trepanning is not a 'spiritual' procedure, any more than it's a medical procedure, Ms. Steene. It's medieval pseudo-science in which holes are drilled into the skull to reduce pressure or to allow 'disease' or evil spirits to escape. It's a thoroughly discredited procedure that's very dangerous—like exorcism."

Stubbornly Ms. Steene said, "It isn't 'medieval,' Doctor. You can say that it predates the history of *Homo sapiens*—there is evidence that Neanderthal man practiced trepanning. Throughout the ancient world—in the East, in Egypt—trepanning has been practiced. In 1999 it was revived, in several parts of the world simultaneously. There are no practitioners in this part of the country, however. I was wondering if—"

"Ms. Steene, no reputable doctor would 'trepan' a patient. That is just not possible. There's no medical purpose to it, and as I said it's very dangerous, as you can surmise. I don't quite see why you came to me . . ."

Ms. Steene wasn't an unattractive woman, but her voice set Lucas's nerves on edge, like sandpaper rubbed against sandpaper. She seemed to be peering at him with an unusual avidity, as if indeed there was a reason that she'd made an appointment to see him, which he wasn't willing to acknowledge. "I came to inquire whether you might administer this treatment to me, Doctor. It's very simple—a single hole to start with. The recommended size is three-quarters inch in diameter in this area of the skull"—with bizarre matter-of-factness the woman indicated a portion of her scalp several inches above her right eye.

Brusquely Dr. Brede said, "I'm sorry. No."

"Just—'no'? But why not? If you do 'face-lifts'—'liposuction'—procedures for mere vanity's sake—why won't you do this, for the sake of the spirit?"

Because there is no such entity as "spirit." Because you are a madwoman.

"I'm afraid not, Ms. Steene. And I don't recommend that you look around for another 'surgeon' to do this ridiculous 'procedure' for you."

On this note the consultation ended abruptly. With a forced courteous smile Dr. Brede showed Ms. Steene to the door. How his face ached, like a mask clamped too tightly in place! Though he was incensed and indignant from the insult to his professional integrity, yet he managed to behave courteously to Ms. Steene; even now the woman left his office reluctantly as if, despite the doctor's unambiguous words, he might change his mind and summon her back.

Chloe complained that Ms. Steene hadn't paid the consultation fee but had simply walked out of the office, rudely. Dr. Brede assured her it was all right, the consultation hadn't taken long—"Just expunge Ms. Steene from our records. As if she'd never been."

This season of dark-pelting rains! That seemed never to be ending except in patches of ferocious sunshine so blinding Dr. Brede had to wear dark glasses when he stepped outside, and was forced to drive his car—a silver Jaguar SL—with unusual concentration, for fear of having an accident. He was disturbed by frequent FOR SALE signs in the more affluent areas of Hazelton-on-Hudson; even at Weirlands, where once there'd been a waiting list for tenants, there were beginning to be vacated offices. It was a shock to see that the Hazleton Neck and Spine Clinic had departed with rude abruptness from its large suite in an adjoining building.

Yet more troubling, Dr. Brede's patients were canceling appointments, often failing to make new appointments, and failing to pay their bills. One of these patients had moved to Arizona—"No forwarding address!" Chloe lamented—and one was reputedly hospitalized after what might have been a suicide attempt. It wasn't likely that Dr. Brede would be paid what he was owed by these women—more than nineteen thousand dollars had accumulated in the past six months in unpaid patients' bills. Turning such delinquent accounts over to a collection agency was a desperate move Dr. Brede hesitated to make: even if the agency collected, he'd receive only a fraction of the money owed him.

Civilization is faces, "appearances": when these collapse, civilization collapses as well.

His last patient of the day. In fact, late Friday afternoon, Dr. Brede's last patient of the week.

"'Trepanning'—you've heard of it, Dr. Brede?"

The woman spoke in a thrilled, lowered voice. Her bright, fanatic eyes were fixed on Lucas's face.

"Doctor, I realize—it's a controversial procedure. It's—unorthodox."

Lucas stared at the woman, dismayed. Was this some sort of cruel joke? The image came to him of carrion burns circling a fallen creature not yet dead.

Irma Siegfried, the divorced wife of a rich Hazelton businessman, was a long-term patient of Lucas Brede. For the past decade she'd seen him faithfully—collagen injections, Botox and Restylane—face-lift, "eyelid lift"—liposuction; and now, unexpectedly, to Dr. Brede's chagrin it was a very different sort of procedure—*trepanning*—about which she'd come to consult with him.

Lucas knew that Irma Siegfried was devoted to him; yet he had reason to suspect that from time to time, especially when Irma spent part of the winter in Palm Beach or in the Caribbean, she'd had work done on her face by other cosmetic surgeons. The woman's fair, thin, dry skin—the skin of a natural, if now faded blond—was the sort of skin that aged prematurely despite the most diligent cosmetic precautions, so now Irma's naïve-girlish manner, a childlike sort of seductiveness that had been so effective only a few years before, was increasingly at odds with her appearance. In her eyes a hurt, wounded, reproachful glisten that touched Lucas Brede to the heart— *Help me, Doctor! You alone have the power.*

Initially Irma Siegfried pleaded the case for trepanning in a reasonable tone. She wasn't the sort of patient—like the contentious Ms. Steene—to bluntly confound her doctor's professional wisdom, still less his integrity. Irma told him that she'd reached a "spiritual impasse" in her life—she'd had "serious doubts" whether the Christian God existed during this seemingly endless winter, in the last months of the Bush administration—"And Mr. Bush was a man I voted for, Doctor—my family has always been Republican, but now"—in a tremulous voice telling Lucas that she'd come to the conclusion that only a "radical"—"revolutionary"—alteration of her spirit-consciousness could save her: *trepanning.*

Lucas asked what on earth she knew of *trepanning.* He did his best to disguise the astonishment and disapproval he felt.

Irma said that she'd learned through books and the Internet—"The New World Trepanation Order"—and had only just the previous week realized how essential it was for her to have the procedure. "It isn't for everyone, of course. But I know it's for *me.* I need to relieve the terrible stress of my nerves and certain 'noxious memories'—as *trepanning* has done for so many others."

"Really? What others?"

"On the Internet—they've given testimony. I've been corresponding with some of them—women like myself—'pilgrims.' I signed a pledge to establish an 'endowment'—at the New World Order—which is based in Geneva, Switzerland. The director is 'medically trained'—his teaching is that we are living in a debased 'Age of Lead' and radical measures are required for our salvation. And *trepanning* is very simple: a hole bored in the skull."

Lucas listened with disdain, disbelief. How casually the woman uttered these words—*a hole bored in the skull.*

"Doctor, I know it's 'dangerous'—of course! All that is courageous in our lives is 'dangerous'—even 'reckless.' I've come to you because I know you, and I trust you. All that you've done for me—which has been considerable, Dr. Brede—won't begin to compare with what I am asking you to do for me now, if you will find it in your heart to help me! If you can't, I will have to turn to a nonmedical practitioner of some sort—unless I fly to Geneva—there are *trepannists* who advertise on the Internet. The procedure is painless, it's said—or almost—but there is a risk of infection if amateurs perform it. And if the *dura mater* is penetrated in some way to cause hemorrhaging, that could be serious. But in recent dreams . . . "

Yet more bizarre, the matter-of-fact way in which the woman alluded to *dura mater*, as if she had the slightest idea what she was talking about, and how disabling, if not fatal, such a wound, carelessly executed, might be.

Bizarre too, that Lucas was listening courteously to her, and not bringing their conference to an abrupt close. If he insulted Irma Siegfried, he might never hear from her again; this was a risk he must take. His professional integrity! His common sense! Yet it was difficult to interrupt Irma, who spoke with such naïve hope of having a hole drilled in her head to release "toxic" thoughts, emotions, and memories that had been accumulating since her childhood—"Like a well that has been slowly poisoned."

It was touching that for her visit to Dr. Brede, Irma Siegfried was wearing elegant clothing—cream-colored cashmere, a strand of pearls around her neck, glittering but tasteful rings. Yet disconcerting when she began to speak more forcefully, like a balked child, charging that physicians like Dr. Brede made careers out of concentrating on the "physical" and neglecting the "spiritual"—the procedures she'd had on her face had been "stop-gaps" with no power to satisfy "spiritual yearnings."

And how did she know this?—she'd had "numinous dreams" since the New Year.

"Doctor, I'm not happy—not any longer—with just 'appearances.' The face-lifts, the injections—have created a 'false face'—what is necessary for us, to transcend our 'fallen' selves, is to return to the 'original face'—the 'original soul'—that is the child-soul, unblemished by the world. *Trepanation* has been a sacred ritual in many cultures, you know—as ancient as the Egyptians long before Christ—in prehistory, practiced by Neanderthals. There are 'trepanned' skulls to prove this—I've seen evidence on the Internet. It's believed that this is what poets mean by 'trailing wisps of glory'—'memory'—this return to the pure child-self. I remember my 'child-self,' Doctor—I was so happy then! Yet it hardly seems that that child was me, so many years have passed."

"That may be true, Irma—to a degree—"—but what was Lucas saying, did he believe this nonsense?—"but *trepanation* is not the solution. No reputable doctor would perform this 'sacred ritual' for you—I'm sure."

He felt a tug of emotion for the agitated woman, as for himself. It was so—so many years! His childhood in Camden, Maine, belonged now to a boy he no longer recalled, on the far side of an abyss.

"Doctor, if you, with your surgical skill, refuse me—I will have to turn to a stranger, on the Internet. I may have to fly to Geneva, alone—in secret since my family disapproves. Please say that you will help me, Dr. Brede!"

"I can't 'help' you! The procedure is dangerous, and useless—it can't possibly be of 'help.' It's true, radical and once-discredited procedures like lobotomies and electroshock treatment have been reexamined lately—but in very rare instances, and when other methods have failed. There is no medical justification for 'trepanning'—drilling holes into a healthy human head."

Whenever Lucas spoke, Irma Siegfried listened, or gave that impression, but in the way of a pilgrim whose fanatic faith can't be dampened by another's logic. "Dr. Brede, I would pay you, of course—twice the fee for a face-lift. This would be a 'spirit-lift'—it would save my life."

"Irma, I don't think we should discuss this any longer . . . "

Yet there was irresolution in Dr. Brede's voice—the faintest note, near-imperceptible. Like a dog sensing fear in a human voice however it's disguised, Irma Siegfried leaned forward, baring her small, porcelain-white teeth in a ghastly seductive smile. "Doctor, I would tell no one—of course! This would be our utter secret! I will pay you in advance of the procedure—you would not even need to bill me. Here, I've brought—a drawing—the 'sacred triangle'—"

Irma was smoothing out a sheet of paper. Here was a drawing of a triangle as a child might have drawn it, with a ruler. "Three very small holes, just above the hairline—here." Irma drew back her hair to suggest the positioning of the holes, in the area of what was called the frontal lobe—though she wouldn't have known this, still less what crucial functions the frontal lobe controlled. Sensing Lucas's reluctant interest, determined not to lose it, Irma was recounting how she'd dreamed the "sacred triangle"—which was, in fact, an ancient symbol predating even Egyptian history—out of the vast reservoir of the "collective unconscious" she'd dreamed this design which was fated for *her*.

Somberly Dr. Brede listened. The tight, affable smile had clamped the lower part of his face.

This is madness. You know the woman is mad.

Yes, but she has money. She will pay you.

Do I need money? How badly?

Such yearning in the woman's eyes! Lucas had seen that look of yearning in the eyes of countless others, that filled him with both repugnance and something like exhilaration, pride—so a priest might feel presiding over sacred rites, ritual confession, absolution, and blessing.

Or an execution, a sacrifice.

Lucas was thinking—would it matter? If he drilled, or pretended to drill, a few very small holes in this woman's scalp, barely penetrating the hard bone of the skull? It would be a kind of cosmetic treatment, above the hairline; he would take care not to penetrate the *dura mater*. The smile clamped tighter about his jaws.

"Dr. Brede? Will you—?"

Lucas hesitated. His heart clanged like a metronome. Yet hearing himself say, with infinite relief: "Irma, no. I think—no. I'm sorry."

Tears welled in the woman's eyes. Abruptly then the consultation ended.

Lucas stumbled into the adjoining lavatory. He ran cold water and splashed it on his burning face. How close he'd come to a terrible danger!—but he'd drawn back in time.

No. We can't. It would be a tragic mistake, we could never undo.

In the photos—you can see the child is brain-damaged. Some sort of birth-injury. The eyes aren't in focus. There's a look of cretinism . . .

We can't risk it. We can't get involved. We've been forewarned—the Russian "orphans" . . .

No. No. No. Absolutely no.

* * *

How was it his fault?—for years his wife had taken fertility drugs. A specialist had encouraged her, at enormous expense. Lucas had not been optimistic, though he'd wanted a child as badly as she did—of course. Soon he'd come to see that the powerful hormone supplements were adversely affecting her—her fixation upon a child, her emotional instability, mood swings. Her resentment of him, as a *man*. And when finally—almost unbelievably—she did become pregnant, at the age of thirty-nine, the sonogram had revealed serious heart and brain defects.

Audrey, please understand—there is no choice.

It is not infanticide! It is an act to prevent suffering. To put the fetus out of its misery before it is born.

Then, the desperation. Internet adoption agencies to which without Lucas's knowledge Audrey gave their credit card number. In a weak moment he'd promised her *Yes we can adopt we can try to adopt* but afterward he'd realized his error. Never had the woman forgiven him his error.

I. S.—these initials he penciled lightly on his personal appointment calendar. For Chloe wasn't to know.

The procedure was so simple, he wouldn't need an assistant.

She would be an outpatient, in his office. He would prep for the procedure himself.

The plan was: the patient would arrive at Dr. Brede's office soon after 7:00 P.M.—when it was certain that Chloe would have left for the day. She would have taken a tranquillizer at 6:00 and when she arrived, Lucas would give her a more powerful sedative; if needed, he could administer chloroform in very small doses.

Trepanation—so primitive a procedure, one would not have to practice beforehand.

Very carefully Dr. Brede would drill into the woman's scalp—very shallowly, into her skull. He believed he could do this. The diagram called for three minuscule holes to be opened into an equilateral triangle measuring a quarter-inch on each side. Irma had been adamant about paying Lucas beforehand, a check for $12,600.

Doctor, thank you, I am so grateful. Doctor, I will owe you my life—my new life.

Irma's teeth chattered slightly, she was so excited. As she lay back on the table in Dr. Brede's examining room, her eyelids that were blue-tinged as if with cold were shut tight and her thin hands were tight-clasped below her small, soft bosom. Though her skin was sallow beneath the harsh fluorescent lighting, and fine white lines puckered at the corners of her eyes, Irma was an attractive woman and it was touching to see that she'd shampooed her hair just recently and had creamed and powdered her face. Coral lipstick darkened her lips. On a thin gold chain around her neck she wore a small gold cross that slipped behind her neck when she lay back.

Doctor, thank you. I will adore you forever.

Soon then the patient was asleep. Her mouth drooped open, like an infant's. Determined to be cautious—Lucas didn't want the patient to wake up suddenly—he soaked a cloth in chloroform and held it beneath her nostrils for a count of three.

Lucas tugged on latex gloves. He was eager to begin. A sensation of elation, almost a kind of giddiness gripped him. *New life! Owe you my life my new life!* He parted the woman's fine, soft, sparrow-colored hair, clamped it aside. He dabbed her scalp with Betadine. The stinging sensation caused her to murmur faintly, querulously. With a small scalpel he made an incision in the skin—retracted the skin, less smoothly than he'd have wished—for his hands were shaky; he would have scraped the damp, exposed bone clean, but felt a wave of something like nausea sweep over him—he had to pause, to recover. Already the tiny wound was bleeding—this was distracting. And now—the drill!

If he'd have had time to prepare more thoroughly for this unorthodox office procedure, Lucas would have purchased a small dental drill from a dental supply store; but he'd been rushed, he'd made his decision overnight, and so the drill he'd acquired—at a hardware store at the North Hills Mall—was an eight-inch stainless-steel PowerLux. A handyman's tool, there was no disguising the fact. The sharp whirring of the motor, the eerie spin of the drill, the gleam of the stainless steel—Lucas's icy fingers trembled.

"Irma? Are you—asleep?" The woman's blue-tinged eyelids fluttered, though it was evident that she was soundly unconscious. Her breathing was slow, deep. Her breath smelled of something sweet—mouthwash, mint—and beneath a more acrid, slightly sour smell of animal apprehension, fear. *She knows!—her sleeping self knows. There is danger.*

Lightly he touched the drill against the woman's scalp—bright blood appeared at once, in a swift stream—this was more than he'd have expected, for such wounds don't commonly bleed quite so freely—he was prepared to sponge it away—yet, so rapidly the blood flowed, as the unconscious woman twitched and whimpered, immediately Lucas lifted the drill from her head. His heart was beating rapidly, the panic-chill rose into his throat. He waited until the woman quieted and resumed her deep breathing; he touched the drill to her scalp another time—again the bright blood startled him—and a smell of burning bone—distasteful, repugnant. This time the patient seemed on the verge of waking—her eyelids fluttered—her lips trembled—he could see the white of her eyeball, a glimpse of unfocused eyes that made him think of a zombie's eyes, or the eyes of one in a coma. *Tape her eyes shut. Her mouth. Secure her. To prevent hysteria.*

This advice seemed to come to Lucas from a source outside himself. He tried to identify the voice—one of the supervisors at the Institute—but could not.

These prudent steps he did. These precautions. This was not an emergency situation but you never knew—in an instant, in the OR, emergencies can erupt. This situation—the *trepanning*—seemed to be within control. The latex gloves were slippery with blood and the adhesive tape was slippery with blood, but he had no trouble taping the woman's eyes and her mouth and Lucas had no trouble strapping the patient to the table except the paper was badly torn already, and blood-stained—so quickly. And blood on the tile floor—the doctor's crepe-soled shoes would leave distinct footprints.

Lucas lifted the drill. Now!—he drew a deep breath. His blood-slick rubber gloves caused the drill to slip, just slightly. It was a heavy, crude instrument that belonged in a handyman's workshop, not in a surgeon's hands.

The *trepanation* would have gone far more smoothly except the doctor was nervous. He'd poured a shot glass of whiskey for himself after his nurse-receptionist left for the evening, and he'd swallowed two thirty-milligram tranquilizers of the kind he kept in his office for his skittish patients' short-term use. Immediately he'd felt better. Now in the stress of the moment he was considering a third tranquilizer but *No. Clarity is required. Clear-headedness. Courage.*

Like one leaning over a steep drop, Lucas leaned over the woman who lay limply on the examination table, unconscious, or comatose—the torn scalp bleeding profusely and the faded-girl's face now deathly white, contorted by the adhesive tape he'd wrapped tightly around her head. He'd covered her eyes and her mouth—but remembered to leave her nostrils free for breathing. And quickly, shallowly, and erratically the woman was breathing. Lucas lifted the drill, positioning the razor-sharp spiral borer against the bloody scalp. He saw that bloody clumps of hair and skin were stuck to the borer that would shake off, or fly off, when he began drilling. The revelation came to him as if from a great distance *This is not Lucas Brede, MD. This is another person who does trepanning.*

After several false starts he managed to finish the first of the tiny holes—*trepanation* was not so easy, as it was not quite so primitive, as the medical profession might think. Skill was involved here, in not penetrating the *dura mater.* The drill seemed steadier now in his hands—though still a clumsy, crude instrument—Lucas began the second hole, a quarter-inch from the first, as the whirring sound of the drill filled the room like an amplified scream. Still, the blood was a distraction— in the familiar quarters of his office he wasn't accustomed to such an excess—if a patient's face bled, Dr. Brede or Chloe wiped it away easily with a sponge. Now there was so much blood from the patient's head wounds that he couldn't sponge it away quickly enough. He was having difficulty seeing where the sharp point of the drill pierced the scalp—a fine mist of blood coated the lenses of his glasses—how to clean his glasses, in the midst of this procedure?—no choice but to remove them. Now, too, Lucas regretted not having taken time to mark the patient's scalp with orange ink—he'd reasoned that after all *trepanation* wasn't neurosurgery and didn't have to be so specifically directed. He wasn't "opening" the skull for brain surgery but only just perforating it, aerating it.

Like a well that has been slowly poisoned.

A new life.

The skeptics in his profession—the notoriously conservative "medical community"—would have little sympathy for Lucas Brede if he suggested to them that *trepanation* might not be so bizarre after all, as a kind of alternative medical procedure; since childhood Lucas himself had felt the slow leakage of his "soul"—his personality trapped and disfigured by the confinement of the bone-armor of the skull.

Of course Lucas had been skeptical also, and initially jeering—yet open-minded enough, after having sent Irma Seigfried away, to reconsider her request, and to summon her back.

He'd spent much of a night—one of his insomniac nights, which lately he'd come to welcome as a respite from heavy, stuporous, sedative-sleep—researching *trepanation* on the Internet. To his surprise he'd come to concede that the ancient custom was either beneficial or harmless if executed by a skilled practitioner. Through the centuries holes had been drilled in the skulls of myriad individuals and these holes showed evidence of having healed; there were skulls with several holes, suggesting that among some primitive people *trepanation* may have been a routine procedure, like removing infected teeth.

There was an ethical issue here, Lucas thought. As licensed surgeons are best equipped to perform abortions, so licensed surgeons are best equipped to perform *trepanations*. Refusing to serve desperate individuals for purely selfish reasons was as unconscionable in the one case as in the other.

You could argue that tattoos were much more dangerous than a skilled *trepanation* since needles are easily infected, and "tattoo-artists" were hardly licensed surgeons.

Maybe there was, as Internet testimonies suggested, a parallel world in counterpoise to Western medicine. It was just prejudice that valued Western medicine above all others.

The whirring of the drill was fierce in his ears, the weight of the drill increasingly heavy as he was obliged to hold it at an awkward angle, uplifted. Lucas was beginning to feel light-headed, dazed. The smell of singed hair and flesh, and the excessive blood, was making him ill. He was stuffing strips of gauze into the bleeding wounds but these soaked with blood immediately and were of no use. How tired he felt, required to maintain such a high degree of concentration, with no one to assist him or even to offer to wipe his face, or polish the lenses of his glasses; a surgeon isn't accustomed to working alone. Lucas was thinking he might pause for a few minutes—he should pause—to examine the patient's pulse—her heartbeat—for the patient no longer seemed to be breathing through her frantic widened nostrils—but a reckless sensation came over him, a sense of defiance—he would not turn back, now that he'd come so far.

Not many minutes had passed since Lucas had switched on the power tool, but these minutes had flown by swiftly as in an accelerated film.

He would clean out the wounds carefully, and dress them. He would caution the woman not to show anyone and not to speak of the *trepanning*. For this was a sacred ritual, and meant to remain private. When she woke the woman would feel some discomfort, he supposed—some pain—the brain didn't register pain but the scalp, the skull, and the *dura mater* registered pain—he would give her a prescription for Percodan—primarily she would feel an airiness, a strangeness—a floating sensation; almost, Lucas envied her; for it was enviable, to be so naïve, and trusting; it was enviable to be a child once again; as he, Lucas Brede, had never entirely been a child, but always confined, held captive by his elders' expectations of him. Thinking these resentful thoughts and holding the drill at a precarious angle, Lucas felt it begin to slip—the rubber fingers of his latex gloves were slippery with blood—or, what was more likely Lucas may have blacked out for a moment. And what happened, happened so fast he would have no clear comprehension of what it was—his hand slipped, the spinning borer must have penetrated the skull too deeply, and down, into the *dura mater*—in an instant this mishap had happened—the woman's body jerked, convulsed—her knees buckled, her legs flailed against the restraining straps—Lucas was grateful that her eyes were taped shut, he was spared locking his gaze with the gaze of the stricken woman—he heard a scream—a muffled scream—inside the adhesive gag.

But no, this wasn't possible. The woman had not regained consciousness. This was not possible, the scream had to be Lucas's feverish imagination.

Soon then the convulsing body lay limp. The struggle had ceased, the muffled screams had ceased. Dr. Brede staggered with exhaustion. He could not have been more drained if he'd performed an eight hour surgery before witnesses. His eyeglasses he groped for, couldn't remember where he'd dropped them, still the lenses were misted with blood and nearly opaque. The thought came to him as a consolation *You have put this one out of her mercy. That is—misery.*

The patient's remains, the sprawled and befouled female body, Dr. Brede would have to dispose of.

For he had no assistant. He was alone. It had always been so, Lucas Brede's soul.

The shrewdest stratagem was to begin cleaning up the premises as he waited for Weirlands to darken. A few scattered lights remained, at 8:28 P.M.

Forty minutes he'd labored to revive the patient.

Forty minutes he'd tried to breathe air into the patient's collapsed lungs; he'd thumped her chest and shouted at her, pleading and furious. His excellent medical training was of little use to him now, for a dead body will remain *dead*.

Awkwardly—impatiently—for he was unaccustomed to such a task—Lucas tore black trash bags into halves and wrapped the body in them, as best he could. The patient was partly dressed in the growing chill of death and on parts of the exposed body the torn and bloodied paper stuck. Lucas observed himself removing from the body's fingers the expensive glittering rings for *They would steal from her, whoever did this to her.*

His nostrils pinched. A pungent odor of singed flesh, singed hair, rank animal panic and terror. In her death throes the woman had soiled herself.

Chloe would know what to do. Chloe would cry *Oh Doctor—what has happened? I will help you.*

Relief swept over Lucas, that Chloe wasn't at the scene, that Chloe hadn't returned to the office wanting to check on him. *Oh Doctor—I saw the light still on here. I thought—I saw your car—*

His heart like a metronome. If he'd had to kill her, too. Poor Chloe who was in love with him.

Thinking *That, I have been spared. Thank God!*

He was a good man, a generous man. Chloe would testify on his behalf. Every female employee he'd ever had.

This was good to know—this was important to keep in mind—but he was beginning to feel anxious, seeing how much there was yet to be swathed clean in this befouled room with paper towels, hot water, and disinfectant.

No time now. He had to be practical. These mundane tasks he would perform *after.*

The urgent task was the disposal of the body. He envisioned a remote wooded area, or a river—the deep rushing Hudson River, by night—if the rain-clouds cleared, by moonlight—and then he would return to his office. And then he would clean what had to be cleaned.

Not a trace would remain. He would use several pairs of latex gloves if necessary. He would dump disinfectant, bleach on the floor.

There was the question—how exactly had the patient died?

Things are not always so evident as they seem.

Small holes drilled into the skull above the forehead could not explain death, for these were trivial wounds. Such wounds to the frontal lobe many an individual has sustained, and survived.

Violent blows to the head, bullets and shrapnel lodged in the very brain, fractured skulls causing the brain to swell like a maddened balloon—*These wounds are curious. But insufficient to explain death* the medical examiner would note.

Lucas Brede knew the medical examiner of Dutchess County. Not well, but the men knew and respected each other.

Only an autopsy can determine. This is common knowledge.

Cardiac arrest probable. Suddenly plummeting *blood-pressure, the consequence of shock.*

For it was not reasonable to think that Lucas had caused the patient's death by a sole act of *his.* When the *dura mater* had scarcely been penetrated.

He'd been careful. Obsessively so. The demanding woman had wanted "holes" drilled into her skull, but he would not drill "holes," of course, only small wounds.

The drill had failed him.

The drill was defective, was it?—surgical drills are set to shut off automatically when the skull is penetrated. But this drill purchased at a hardware store at the mall had failed to shut off.

He'd paid in cash. Hadn't given the sales clerk his credit card.

Calm in this terrible hour like one whose professional behavior—posture, even—"dignity"—was being preserved on tape, Lucas stooped to wrap the body in black plastic trash bags, kept in a storage closet in the corridor.

"Irma? Are you . . . "

Inside the mummy-wrapping of several trash bags he'd scissored to make a single large bag, the body had twitched. The body was heavier than you would expect, in its sprawling limbs a female slovenliness that suggested defiance, derision. Still around the ravaged head were strips of soiled adhesive tape covering the eyes that would be, Lucas knew, accusing eyes, and the mouth, that would accuse as well.

"Irma. My God—I am so sorry."

Was he?—this wasn't clear. His lips moved numbly in resentment, but by nature Dr. Brede was courteous.

His women patients adored him. His nurse-receptionist adored him. His wife had ceased to adore him, and the thought of Audrey filled him with such rage, he began to tremble anew.

How bizarre the body would appear when the slatternly trash bags were unwrapped! Around the head of graying, matted, bloodied hair the strips of soiled adhesive tape he'd wrapped carefully (he recalled), but the look of it was frantic, random. As if the deceased were a madwoman who had wrapped her own head for what crazed notion, whim, or expectation, who could say?

Recalling too: the latex gloves, that were surely torn; the blood-splattered surgeon-clothes, shoes, and even socks, that must be disposed of also. Thinking *It can all go in the same bag. And in the Dumpster. If they find one they may as well find the other.*

This logic he could not fully comprehend. Instinctively he felt this was a practical and sensible step.

He'd located the woman's purse also, which was an expensive purse of soft dark leather. He would take bills from the wallet, credit cards, keys—for whoever had done such a cruel thing to this woman would certainly take these items.

Drive some distance. Away from Weirlands. A far corner of Dutchess County deep in the country in the night.

If not a Dumpster, a rural dump. A landfill. Lucas would drag other trash bags over his, to hide it. The vision came to him of a vast open pit in the earth out of which steam lifted, a pit that opened into hell. But if he kept well back from the rim of the pit, he would be safe.

Thinking of this place somewhere in Dutchess County, he felt relief as if thinking were doing, and in an instant the arduous task was *done.*

Fortunately he had a change of clothes at the office, khaki pants and a flannel shirt, running shoes. Underwear, and socks.

After, he would return to the condominium overlooking the Hudson River. Possibly by then he'd be hungry, he would eat. In the refrigerator was a reserve of emergency meals, takeout from previous evenings, an excellent Brie from the Hazelton Bon Appétit, and those crisp Danish crackers.

No: this was wrong. This was not right. *After,* he would return to Weirlands. Hours of cleanup awaited him; he must not lose track of these crucial plans.

It was 9:19 P.M. Those lighted windows at Weirlands he'd been nervously eyeing were still lighted, so he thought *No one is there. Just lights on.* This was a relief. This meant freedom. Stooping, he pulled the body along the floor—along the corridor to the door at the rear—this, the delivery door and not the door that patients used. He was perspiring badly, though he was also shivering. Impulsively he left the body on the floor, wedged partly against a doorjamb, went to his office and dialed the number of his former home, and with the stoic resignation of one who knows beforehand that he will be disappointed, he waited for the phone to ring and was thus badly surprised, shaken by the failure of the phone even to ring and the smug, recorded, female voice *You have dialed a number no longer in service. This number has been disconnected.*

He would never forgive Audrey for abandoning him. For betraying him. He would never forgive any of them.

At last—Weirlands appeared to be deserted. Only three vehicles remained in the parking lot—Lucas's car, a car presumably belonging to his patient, and, at the far end of the lot, a commercial van. Out of his darkened doorway Lucas dragged the lifeless body in the trash bags, now heavy as a slab of concrete. His shoulders and upper spine were shot with pain. Belatedly he thought of the woman's coat—for surely this well-to-do woman would have worn a coat to his office—which was very likely hanging in the waiting room to be discovered by Chloe in the morning. This crucial thought, too, he filed *After.*

How chill the night air, how fresh and invigorating! Lucas felt a surge of hope. Too much was expected of cosmetic surgeons, he hadn't trained to be a holy priest after all . . . . The wisest stratagem would be to remove the woman's body from the premises as quickly as possible—he would drag it uphill through the parking lot and into the uncultivated area beyond the Weirlands property line, where no one ever went. A half mile to the east was the Hazelton Pike, a half mile to the north was the New York Thruway; in the interstices of smaller roads, a prestigious new residential development called Foxcroft Hills, and the new, artificial Foxcroft Lake were pockets of uncultivated land, less likely to be explored than the open countryside of previous decades.

No one will ever find it. Her.

Lucas had in mind a faint trail he'd noticed from the parking lot, through tall grasses—a shady area where someone had placed a single picnic table for Weirlands office workers—therapists, secretaries. Not once had Lucas ever seen anyone eating lunch at this table overlooking the asphalt parking lot nor could he have said exactly where the table was, or had once been, but it was in this direction he dragged the body, sweating now heavily inside his clothes. How annoying it was, the parking lot was littered at its periphery with fallen and shattered tree limbs; it was an effort to drag the body here, colliding with storm debris, making his task so much more arduous . . . .

Suddenly the thought came to him *Her car!*

Of course—*the woman's car*. Lucas would have to get rid of *her car*.

If he failed to remove the woman's car from the Weirlands lot, it would be discovered in the morning; the woman would be traced to Weirlands Medical Center, and to Dr. Lucas Brede. Rapidly his brain worked—of course, he would have to dispose not only of the woman's body but of her car as well.

Logically then, to save steps he might place the body *inside the car*.

In the trunk! He would place the body in the trunk—of course—and he would drive the woman's car some distance from Weirlands—twenty miles, thirty—across the George Washington Bridge and into New Jersey.

Once in a remote area of New Jersey off the turnpike he would abandon both the car and the body in the trunk of the car. He would drive the car to the edge of a steep precipice above the Hudson River, or another body of water, or some sort of quarry, or gravel pit. He seemed to know that New Jersey would be a safe territory, if he could but get there. He would jump out of the car at the last possible moment and the car would plummet down into oblivion as into a pit of hell . . . Lucas Brede would be safe then, for he would leave nothing of his own in the woman's car. And the car, and the body, would never be discovered.

Except: he would have no way of returning then to Weirlands. No way of returning to his expensive but mud-splattered Jaguar SL parked at the rear of Weirlands.

He hadn't thought of this. The thought was an obvious one like a tree root he'd just tripped over, nearly causing him to fall atop the tattered trash bags.

Quickly modifying his plan. For his brain worked swiftly, like the brain of a machine. As it wasn't practical to drag the woman's body into the woods above Weirlands, so it wasn't practical to drag the woman's body to her car and haul it to New Jersey: instead, he would have to drag the body to his own car and lift it into the trunk—panting and cursing as he struggled to lift the cumbersome thing that seemed to taunt him with its heaviness, and its smells that made him gag. And his arms ached, his body was faint with exhaustion. At last he managed to get the damned body into the trunk, to force its odd-angled limbs into the confining space beneath a spare tire and a tire iron. Horrible it seemed to him, that he had to stoop, to lift this so physical and obdurate *thing*; he had to grip it in his embrace, lift it into the trunk and slam the trunk lid down, but hastily and carelessly so that a torn part of a trash bag was visible, fluttering outside the trunk like a woman's black silk slip.

Doctor, I am so grateful. My new life.

He worried that some sort of inevitable moisture—blood, urine, liquid feces—was leaking through the plastic material into the trunk of his car that had been until now pristine-clean. The thought came to him *The trunk can be cleaned. At the car wash. Inside and out.*

If the car wash couldn't disinfect the trunk totally, he would dump disinfectant and bleach inside. The most virulent bacteria teeming in the bowels of the dead can be fatal to the touch of the living.

Next, he climbed into his car. This was strange! Because so ordinary, commonplace. He turned the key in the ignition—the Jaguar was sometimes slow to start—this time the motor came to life at once and the windshield wipers came on and the radio, which was tuned to WQRS. Nor did he have difficulty driving out of the Weirlands parking lot and along the private Weirlands Road to a busier street. He would follow this street until the intersection with Route 11, and he would turn south and continue for miles out of Hazelton-on-Hudson and through the suburban villages of Drummond, Sleepy Hollow, Riverdale; he would pass the exit for Fort Tyron Park; he would exit for the George Washington Bridge, and he would bring the body in the trunk into New Jersey as it was planned for him and there he would discard the body; he would know where when the exit loomed in his headlights. Again this thought was so vivid it was as if he'd already executed it, in the instant of thinking it. Then, he would turn the Jaguar around and return across the George Washington Bridge—he would take the lower level returning, if he took the higher level going—details like that were crucial. By midnight if he hadn't any delays, he would return to Weirlands and he would then drive the woman's car no more than two or three miles to the small Hazelton train depot where he'd park it unobtrusively and where often vehicles were parked overnight. This would attract no attention! This was a very practical idea. Once he left the woman's car in a safe, unobtrusive place he could wait on the train platform for a train to arrive; he would mingle with passengers, and hail a taxi at the foot of the stairs.

Where're you going, sir?

D'you know that new condominium complex on the river? There.

Just beyond the exit ramp for the George Washington Bridge traffic was being rerouted into a detour. Here were police cars, medical emergency vehicles, blinding lights. Traffic was backing up for miles. Lucas leaned out his window, sick with apprehension. He lowered his window and called out to a police officer directing traffic in the rain—what was wrong? why were they being held up? how long?—but the officer, a young man, rudely ignored him. In the roadway were fiery flares, sawhorses blocking the lanes. Farther he leaned out the window of his car calling out to another police officer, but smiling—remembering to smile—his strained, affable, doctor-smile—for Dr. Brede would want these law enforcement officers to see, if it came to giving testimony, or evidence, that he'd behaved calmly; Lucas Brede had been in a genial, rational, reasonable mood at this crucial time; somewhat edgy, of course, and impatient, as any driver would be in such circumstances.

Evidently there'd been an accident. Two vehicles—three vehicles. Giddily lights spun atop emergency vehicles. Sirens pierced his eardrums. Quickly Lucas lowered his car window. "Officer? Do you need any help? I'm an MD."

Politely Lucas was told no, told to remain in his car. Told no, his services as a doctor weren't needed, or weren't wanted, there was an ambulance at the scene. *Please remain in your car sir. Do not leave your car.* Seeing the wrecked vehicles on the roadway like broken bodies, piteous female bodies and glass glittering on pavement, confused by the piercing sirens, Lucas opened the Jaguar door and began to climb out into the roadway but another time was told, sternly this time, he was being shouted at, instructed *No.* Trying to remain pleasant, reasonable—"I don't think you heard me—I'm a doctor—a neurosurgeon. I can examine the victims—I can determine if there's dangerous hemorrhaging in the brain." An older police officer came to Lucas and asked for his driver's license. Lucas fumbled to comply. He was clearly not drunk nor even agitated. His hands shook badly—this might be palsy. This might be the onset of Parkinson's. There was blood on his khaki cuffs, but the flashing red lights did not detect blood. Smears of blood on the front of his coat, mysteriously—for he'd been careful with the trash bags which he'd tied with the unwieldy body inside, he was sure he hadn't brushed against them. Yet there it was, a smear of blood like a bird's wing. And on his hands. Unless this was older, long-dried blood from earlier in the day, that had been a very long day beginning with dark pelting rain before dawn.

"But I want to be of help, officer. Please let me help. I'm a doctor—this is my mission."

They had no time for him. His offer was rebuked. Rudely he was made to climb back into his Jaguar, and to wait like the other drivers. Eventually traffic bound for the bridge was rerouted. Eventually the stream of vehicles began to move. The terrible dark rain had lessened, now columns of mist lifted from the river far below like ectoplasm. Which river was this Lucas could not have immediately said, though he knew its name as he knew his own. He accelerated his vehicle onto the bridge. It was the upper level he chose. In the mist, the farther shore and the length of the great bridge were obscured. Lights shimmered uncertainly along the vast river, evidence of lives within. He started out, he would cross to that farther shore.

MICHAEL PATERNITI

■

The Suicide Catcher

FROM *GQ*

THE BRIDGE ROSE UP AND AWAY from the city's northwest quadrant, spanning the great Yangtze river. And yet, from the on-ramp where the taxi let me off that Saturday morning, it seemed more like a figment of the imagination, a ghostly ironwork extrusion vanishing in the monsoon murk, stretching to some otherworld. It was disorienting to look at, that latticed half-bridge leaving off in midair, like some sort of Surrealist painting. It gave off a foreboding aura, too, untethered and floating, and yet it couldn't have been more earthbound—and massive. Later I'd find out it was made from 500,000 tons of cement and 1 million tons of steel. Four miles long, with four lanes of car traffic on the upper deck and twin railroad tracks on the lower, it transferred thousands of people and goods to and from the city every day. But now the clouds clamped down, and a sharp scent of sulfur and putrid fish wafted on a dank puff of air. Rain slithered from the sky. There, before my eyes, the bridge shimmered and disappeared, as if it had never been visible in the first place.

Its formal name was the Nanjing Yangtze River Bridge, and it served one other purpose for the masses: At least once a week, someone jumped to his or her death here, but a total was hard to come by, in part because the Chinese authorities refused to count those who missed the river, the ones who'd leapt and had the misfortune of landing in the trees along the riverbank, or on the concrete apron beneath the bridge, or who were found impressed in the earth like mud angels, two feet from rushing water. Perhaps such strict bookkeeping came in response to the fact that China already posts the highest sheer numbers, about 200,000 "reported" suicide cases a year, constituting a fifth of all the world's suicides. For a long time, the Communist government simply ignored the problem, hoping it would go away, or maybe thinking in the most Darwinian terms of suicide as its own method of population control. One recent case highlighted just how the Chinese bureaucracy tended to deal with prevention. In the southern city of Guangzhou, workers had been ordered to smear butter over a steel bridge popular with jumpers, in order to make it too slippery to climb. "We tried employing guards at both ends," said a government official, "and we put up special fences and notices asking people not to commit suicide here. None of it worked—and so now we have put butter over the bridge, and it has worked very well."

In Nanjing, the bridge remained butterless, even as the city spit out its victims. Nanjing was now just another one of your typical 6-million-person Chinese metropolises, one of the famous "Three Furnaces" of China because of its unremitting summer heat. Daytime temperatures regularly topped ninety degrees here—due to hot air being trapped by the mountains at the lower end of the Yangtze River valley . . . and, oh yeah, because all the trees had been chopped down—and the sun rarely shone. Meanwhile, the city continued to explode in the noonday of the country's hungry expansion. The past was being abandoned at an astonishing rate, the new skyscrapers and apartment buildings replacing the old neighborhoods. Everything—and everyone—was disposable. Schisms formed. The bridge loomed. Loss led to despair, which, in turn, led to Mr. Chen.

I'd come through thirteen time zones just to see him. Once free of the taxi, I began trudging, a quarter mile or so, the bridge trembling under the weight of its traffic, piled with noisy green taxis and rackety buses, some without side panels or mufflers. Unlike the suspended wonder of Brooklyn or the quixotic *ponts* of Paris, this couldn't have been mistaken for anything but stolid Communist bulwark: At its apex, the bridge was about 130 feet above the water; was built with two twenty-story "forts," spaced one mile apart, that from a distance had the appearance of huge torches; and contained 200 inlaid reliefs that included such exhortations as *Our country is led by the working class* and *Long live the unity of the people.* A brochure claimed that the bridge was both the first of its kind designed solely by Chinese engineers, and also "ideal for bird-watching." People teemed in both directions. Umbrellas unfurled, poked, and were ripped from their rigging, leaving sharp spiders dangling overhead. As I registered the passersby—their eyes fixed downward—everyone seemed a candidate for jumping, marching in that mournful parade.

He was close now. I could tell by the banners and messages—some were flags, some were just scraps of paper—that fluttered earnestly from the bridge. *Value life every day*, read one. *Life is precious*, declared another. His cell-phone number was emblazoned everywhere, including little graffitied stamps he'd left on the sidewalk, ones I tried to decipher beneath the blur of so many passing feet. And then Mr. Chen came into view, conspicuous for being the only still point in that sea of motion . . . and the only one sporting a pair of clunky binoculars, the only one watching the watchers of the river.

He stood at full attention at the South Tower. Perched off one side of the tower was a concrete platform surrounded by Plexiglas, a capsule of sorts where yawning sentries did their own dubious monitoring of the bridge through a mounted spyglass, as if conducting a sociological study at a great remove. The sentries looked like kids, while Mr. Chen, who stood out front on the sidewalk, among the people, looked every bit of his forty years. He had a paunch, blackened teeth, and the raspy cough of an avid smoker, and he never stopped watching, even when he allowed himself a cigarette, smoking a cheap brand named after the city itself. He wore a baseball cap with a brim that poked out like an oversize duck's bill, like the Cyrano of duck bills, the crown of which read "They spy on you."

Six years earlier, working as a functionary for a transportation company, Mr. Chen had read a story about the bridge in the paper, about bodies raining to their end. Soon after, he quietly took his post at the South Tower. Ever since then, when not working his job, he'd been up on the bridge, pulling would-be's from the railing. According to a blog he kept, he'd saved 174 jumpers—and in the process had been hailed as one of China's great Good Samaritans. Of those he saved, some small number met near the bridge every year around Christmas to celebrate their new lives and ostensibly to offer their thanks. As part of the ceremony, they calculated their new ages from the date of their salvation. In this born-again world, no one was older than six.

Back home I'd stumbled on Mr. Chen's blog one day, reading it in jumbled Google translation, and became riveted by his blow-by-blow of life on the bridge. There'd been the husband and wife who'd jumped hand in hand. There'd been the man dressed in black, floating there on the water's surface as a boat tried to reach him, until the current finally sucked him away. Another fellow had been pulled off the railing, back onto the bridge, and in the fight that ensued—one during which Mr. Chen had to enlist the help of others—the man had bitten his tongue in half (good God!) and nearly bled to death on the sidewalk, leaving Mr. Chen covered in blood.

Mr. Chen's blog entries were sometimes their own desperate pleas: *Lovelorn girls of Henan, where are you?* read one. But more often they were a subdued, pointillistic chronicle of the day's dark news: . . . *middle-aged man jumped off bridge where the body fell to the flower bed: died on the spot . . . Speaking in northern accent, man gave me a cigarette, said: Alas! Wives and children . . . A woman in the southeast fort jumped in riverbed, dead on spot . . . Next to statue at southwest fort, man died jumping to concrete, one leg thrown from body, only blackened blood left behind. Meaningless life!*

And yet standing sentry among the hordes, Mr. Chen seemed a bit comical, or his mission seemed the ultimate act of absurdity. How could he possibly pick out the suicidal on a four-mile-long bridge? Were they marked somehow, glowing only for him? As no one seemed to pay him any attention, he was forced to take himself twice as seriously. And he was so engrossed in the Kabuki of his work that it occurred to me how easy a mark he might make for a practical joker tying shoelaces together. Had his heroics only been a figment of his imagination? Was he as unstable somehow as his jumpers? And was he serious with those binoculars, especially with visibility reduced to fifty yards or so in the murk? When I introduced myself, he waved me off. "Not now," he said gruffly. "I'm working."

Then his binoculars shot up to his eyes, sheltered by the bill of his cap, and he fumbled with the focus knob while gazing deep into the masses, searching, it would seem, for that fleeting infrared flare of despair, for the moment when he'd be called into action, ready for his hero moment.

One's reasons for being on the bridge belonged to the mysterious underworld in all of us, but to choose to die so publicly, so dramatically—turning languid flips or dropping straight as a pin—was something I couldn't quite understand. After all the humiliation one suffered, all the monotonies and losses, the erasures and disintegrations, after being constantly consumed by society, was it a small reclamation of the self? And what would it feel like to fly, to prove you could? The mere glimmer seemed almost too dangerous to consider. If you let it in, is that when you started to feel the pull of this other force? Could it be stopped?

There were the Stoics, who justified suicide, and the Christians, who condemned it. There was the honorable *seppuku* of samurai, and the cowardly cyanide of Nazis. And there were suicide's other famous practitioners: Virginia Woolf, entering the River Ouse with a heavy stone in her pocket; Walter Benjamin, overdosing on morphine in a hotel room in Spain in the belief that he was about to be turned over to the Nazis; Sylvia Plath, turning on the gas . . . and then, later, her son, too. Meriwether Lewis shot himself in the chest; Kurt Cobain, in the head. There were Spanish matadors and Congolese pygmies. Auntie Em from *The Wizard of Oz* and Tattoo from *Fantasy Island*. William James, the great humanist philosopher who, tilting dangerously close to self-annihilation, wrote his father, "Thoughts of the pistol, the dagger, and the bowl began to usurp an unduly large part of my attention," and later proclaimed, "I take it that no man is educated who has never dallied with the thought of suicide."

Those on the bridge weren't dallying anymore. They'd come, one after the other, to jump, their lives reduced to this single sliver. Beneath the hum and blare of traffic came that insidious sucking sound. How could just one man stop it?

Mr. Chen appeared to have a very strict routine on the bridge, no matter if it was snowing, blowing, or broiling heat. He stood at full attention at the South Tower, where a large percentage of his encounters came within the first one hundred meters past the fort, in that area of the bridge that spanned from the riverbank to the river itself. "In so much pain," he would tell me, "they jump the second they think they're over the mother river. And a lot of them miss the water."

His routine called for maintaining his station for about forty minutes out of every hour—then he fired up his moped, an unconvincing contraption on the verge of breakdown, and putted off down the sidewalk, weaving between walkers, a little like John Wayne astride a miniature Shetland pony. These were his rounds, up and down the bridge, motoring out one mile to the North Tower and then turning back. If he sniffed trouble out there, he might linger—in some cases might be gone hours—but today he reappeared a short time later, stitching deftly through the crowd, then kickstanding his Rocinante and resuming his same exact position, his same exact suspicious disposition, his same exact focused gruffness beneath the bill of his cap. He wore a collared shirt and dark slacks. Though he was stout, with plump hands, he held himself like a much bigger person. Like two of himself.

The sky roiled and spit, as if we were lost inside some potion. Again, the scent of diesel and fish. After fifteen minutes or so, I had a splitting headache, and yet Mr. Chen stood nearly stock-still, unfazed, scanning the crowd with binoculars. His life was a grand monotony, but in his stillness and stasis, the possibility for calamity existed in every moment, and that's what kept him coiled and at the ready.

Mr. Chen would later describe a recurring nightmare that went like this: Someone was up on the railing, and he was sprinting as fast as he could to save the jumper. Over and over, he would arrive too late, as the body pushed from the railing to the hungry ghost below. He said that he'd been visited on the bridge by a foreign psychiatrist who asked him if he might draw a picture of whatever came to mind. So he did: of a large mountain disappearing up into the clouds, which the psychiatrist interpreted as Mr. Chen trying to carry the weight of the weightless sky. Or something like that. Mr. Chen was fuzzy on the details and didn't have much time for this nonsense. The encounter smudged into the same colorlessness of every other colorless moment in the colorless flow of time on the bridge.

The rain had let off and the fog shifted a little, though the weekend traffic had worsened—the city dwellers heading out to the country, the country dwellers heading into the city. I meandered out on the bridge for a moment, away from the tower and the armed sentries and Mr. Chen, who didn't seem to care a whit about me unless I planned to jump. As I gazed downriver, in the easterly direction of Shanghai, a shipyard with an enormous crane appeared in the near distance while a temple loomed with its wooden pagoda on a hill. Skimming the river's brown, roiling surface came a steady, dirgelike stream of barges loaded with lumber, coal, containers, and sand. The view into its muddy waters was not for the faint of heart. There was one of two ways to die from here: on impact with the water's surface, which at sixty-five miles per hour is like hitting concrete, the shattering of bone and internal organs, the instant blackout and massive bleeding, the general pancaking and dismemberment of the body—or by drowning, by somehow surviving the impact and waking underwater, swept away in the current, unable to muster a frog kick given the various possible combinations of broken pelvis/femur/back/jaw, etc. Below, the waters eddied and swirled, etching a secret language on the surface. When a train passed, the whole bridge seemed to buckle and sway, causing me to clutch the railing.

One of Mr. Chen's blog entries was simply entitled "Girl's Tears." It told the tale of a girl from the country who'd come to the bridge, not far from this spot here, to end her life. It started with the observation that tears shed by girls were like tears of angels "that come from disappointment—or was it regret?" This was a runaway, said Mr. Chen, and she stood "tummy railing," looking down at the water, despondent. When Mr. Chen approached, he gave her three options: (1) leave the bridge, (2) call emergency services for help, or (3) let Mr. Chen take her to his house, where she could live for a time with him, his wife, and their daughter. Mr. Chen took her phone and called her belligerent boyfriend, and as he spoke to him, she climbed the railing to jump. He seized her hand; she pulled away, climbing higher on the railing, teetering for a second there. He tore her from the railing, but as the police arrived, she ran into traffic, then tried to disappear in the crowd. The police apprehended her and took her away. It was over just like that. One second he could feel her breath on him; the next she was gone, and Mr. Chen, tough as he was, claimed to have burst into tears.

"Next day called number," he wrote on his blog. "Always unanswered."

The reason Mr. Chen was in the business of saving lives now was that, as a boy, he'd always gone unanswered. There is a saying in Chinese he used, that he never possessed "mother's shoes." With those words, he threw back an oversize shot of a potent grain alcohol. "Getting drunk loosens the tongue," he declared empirically, then refilled our teacups as we sat together in a tight, crowded restaurant near the bridge. He clinked them in a toast and tossed another mini-bucketful into the back of his throat, where, according to my simultaneous research, everything caught fire and napalmed down the gullet to the stomach, where, in turn, it flickered and tasered a while, like rotgut lava. We had left the bridge for lunch, and he had insisted that I drink with him. Sensing we might be in the midst of a transitional relationship moment, I joined him in the first few rounds but then thought better of it—there was no doubt this guy was going to drink me under the table—and eased off. He laughed when I did, a disparaging laugh, wondering aloud at what kind of American I was.

Our party now included my translator, Susan—who was born in Nanjing but raised in the U.S.—and a wordless man who had suddenly appeared, ostensibly a close friend of Mr. Chen's, called Mr. Shi. We'd arrived at this "family restaurant" sometime after noon, after we'd all left the bridge together, Mr. Chen on his moped and the three of us on foot, taking endless flights of stairs down through the South Tower to the ground, where Mr. Chen was waiting to ferry us, one by one, on the back of his moped to the restaurant. I didn't know where to put my hands, so I grabbed the bulk of his shoulders.

We sat down to filmy glasses of beer and a clear, unmarked bottle of grain alcohol, and saucers of peppers and tripe, tofu soup, noodles, and fish stew. Mr. Chen and Mr. Shi began smoking Nanjings until we were wreathed in smoke. Overhead a fan lopped away off-kilter, on the verge of unscrewing itself from the ceiling. The walls of the restaurant were sepia colored, plastered with old posters, Buddha sharing the wall with a liquor ad. The hissing sound of the wok—onions and chicken and squirming mung beans—agitated beneath the clatter of plates and the gruff, rising voices of men (there were no families here, only workmen) huddled at the eight or so tables, heads sluicing with liquor, too.

Mr. Chen explicated his opening statement. See, in the old times, before "the Communist liberation," a great deal of pride was connected to these homemade textiles, for both parent and child. The shoes and socks were a declaration of individual love in a country obsessed with the self-effacing collective. His own mother had always been an erratic presence, but after his parents split when he was eight, she disappeared for the better part of a decade—and so, too, did his "mother's love," as he put it. That's when he went to live with his grandmother, in a village outside the city. Widowed at eighteen, his grandmother served an important function in the village: She was a peacemaker and therapist of sorts, if utterly unschooled. It was from her that Mr. Chen had learned the fine art of persuasion. It was from the incompleteness of his own family that he'd built this not-so-secret life as the defender of broken humanity. And the weight of the task had become its own burden.

"I've aged terribly in my six years on the bridge," he said, again clinking teacups with Mr. Shi. "To age!" He drank and then admitted that he had a lot of gray hair, due to the weather and stress—stress on the bridge, stress at work, stress at home. He caught me gazing at the thick, black, spiky forest matting his head. "I've been dyeing it for years," he said.

He sat back, removed his glasses, rubbed his eyes with the backs of his hands. He poured another glass, this time hesitating before drinking, and spoke again as he stabbed a piece of tripe, then began to chew. On the bridge, he said, there were three types of jumpers, and they had to be dealt with either by force or finesse, by blunt words or wraithlike verbiage fashioned into a lasso. Mostly they came peaceably, but sometimes it was a donnybrook. The first category included the mentally unstable or clinically insane. In the frenzy of letting go, these were the ones who might take you with them, grasping onto anyone as some proxy for "mother's love." So—Mr. Chen would charge them like a dangerous man himself, wrestling, punching, kicking, doing whatever was necessary. "I'm very confident in my physical strength," he said. "Since I have no psychological training, my job is to get that person off the bridge as quickly as possible." Whereupon he might take him or her to "the station," which, as it turned out, was an in-patient psych ward at the highly reputed Nanjing University, one of the few places in the city where the suicidal could receive professional care and treatment.

The second category was the emotionally fragile, the wilted flower, the person who had lost someone—a husband, a child, a wife, a parent—or suffered from some sort of abuse and saw no way to go on. If the potential jumper was a woman, Mr. Chen's strategy was to try to bring her to tears, for that often broke the tension, and once emotion poured forth, he might grab for her hand and huddle her away. Men, by contrast, were both simpler and trickier. You forked one of two ways. Either you told him bluntly that you were about to punch him in the nose if he didn't step away from the railing, or you did the exact opposite: You approached in a nonthreatening, even companionable, manner, offering a cigarette to the figure lingering too long by the railing, and from there steered him to a place like this restaurant, where together you could drink grain alcohol and really talk, something that wasn't so easy in a culture that still held fast to a Confucian ethic of stoicism.

The final category, he said, included the ones who "failed really hard, or too often." Usually men, these would-be jumpers had often lost a great deal of money and weren't feeling so wonderful about themselves anymore, especially when their failures were thrown into relief by those riding on the heady high seas of the new China, driving fancy cars, wearing designer clothes, smoking expensive American cigarettes. Mr. Chen then pointed to Mr. Shi and said, "He was one of those."

Mr. Shi, a thin man of thinning hair, blinked laconically through the smoke. Though the stage was set for him to unspool his tale, he showed no interest in taking up the story. "Later," barked Mr. Chen. It was strange, and not a little confusing, how gruff he could be while making himself, and those around him, so vulnerable. When more plates of food arrived, he shoveled beans and noodles, fish and broccoli onto his plate, then lit upon it all as if it were prey, gobbling and drinking, then gobbling some more.

I regarded him once more in this dim light. He was unabashed in his mannerisms, a man who seemed to live so fully inside this hexed world of suicide that he had little time for polish or polite chitchat or getting-to-know-you. When I asked if he had heard of the famous Hollywood film *It's a Wonderful Life*, in which Jimmy Stewart plans to end his life on a bridge until an angel named Clarence saves him, he cut me off by shaking his head. No; he didn't care about movies or my attempts to draw fatuous parallels. Nor were we kindred spirits: Simply showing up did not confer membership to the club. He barely bothered to look at me when responding to my questions.

In turn, I soon found myself growing anxious there in that restaurant—very anxious—watching Mr. Chen and Mr. Shi drain glass after glass. My mind suddenly seized upon the notion that this was a Saturday, the busiest day on the bridge, and here we sat. However absurd it had felt to be standing on a four-mile bridge, thronged by thousands, trying to pick out jumpers, I felt a sudden onrush of dread at not being there at all, as if the welfare of all humanity depended on our vigilance. Part of it had to do with the effect of the grain alcohol. And part of it was fatigue—the result of all those time zones to get here. In that loud, hot space, I felt simultaneously this desire to stand and leave and yet to lay my head down and rest. The irrefutable truth was that nothing—neither butter nor Mr. Chen—would dissuade the jumpers from coming: So what was the point of being here at all?

That was the question that occurred to me now in that mung-bean-and-hooch restaurant, that hole-in-the-wall, listening to the guttural rebukes of Mr. Chen: What was I doing here at all, in a place where people came to kill themselves, 7,000 miles from my home and family? This wasn't an assignment that had been given to me. I'd chosen it. I'd come as if there were some message for me here, some fragment to justify, or obliterate, that slow bloom of doubt. But now I could feel the pressure under the soles of my feet: The bridge ran under me, too.

If you dig deep enough into the past, every family has its suicide. My maternal grandmother had told me the story of a relative, dating from the nineteenth century: a young woman fresh from Ireland, a Catholic who'd married a Protestant. She was isolated, living with her husband's family in upstate New York, in the region known as the North Country, and her life became a slow torment from which there seemed to be no escape, even after bearing a child. Her beliefs were pilloried and belittled. She slowly unraveled. One day she put rocks in her pocket and stepped into a cistern, where she drowned.

But such events didn't just belong to the past—or to some mythic country, either. From my own suburban hometown, I remembered a sweet, shy kid, roughly my age, who seemed incapable of any sort of demonstrativeness, who drove himself to the Adirondacks in winter, purchased a coil of rope along the way, found a sturdy tree, and hanged himself. I had nightmares about that boy, shagged in ice until his father found him and cut him down.

And the neighbor down the street, found in the bathtub . . . And the kid who ran his motorcycle into a tree, an accident but for the note left behind saying that's exactly what he intended to do . . . And so on. Even in suburbia, suicide had seemed like its own opaque parable, the never-happened, glossed-over secret.

I came upon the story of a boy, a British art student named Christian Drane, who'd photographed suicide spots in England for a school project—including a bridge in Bristol, where he was approached by a stranger who wondered if he was all right—and then hanged himself in the Polygon woods of Southampton. No one could believe it. He'd made everyone laugh. He had a tattoo on his arm, representing his family. Afterward, his girlfriend told an inquest that Christian was the happiest person she knew, "cheeky, spontaneous, excitable." He whisked her to Paris for her birthday, wrapped her in "fairy lights" and took her portrait. He posted other photos from his project online: other bridges, subway stations, and Beachy Head, the chalk cliffs of Eastbourne, the most famous of English suicide spots. Each bore the moniker "Close Your Eyes and Say Goodbye."

The photograph of Christian that accompanied many of the news stories showed a boy with mussed-up hair and pierced ears with black plugs, looking impishly askance at the camera. Had the pretense of the project emboldened him, or was "the project" merely his eventual suicide? His final note, which no one claimed to understand, read: "To mum and anybody who cares. I have done something I can never forgive myself for. I am a bad person. I am sorry."

The Yangtze ever beckoned. And its pull was finally felt at the family restaurant by Mr. Chen, who abruptly stood, grunted a little, walked out the front door like a superhero summoned by dog whistle, then fired up his moped and went swerving off, his *They spy on you* double-bill back on his head, binoculars dangling around his neck. Left in his wake, we—Susan the translator, Mr. Shi, and I—straggled back to the bridge in a slow-motion amble. It felt good to be in the open air again, somehow cleansing after all the smoke and noise.

Bent like a harp, Mr. Shi was the kind of gentle man you instantly wanted to protect, to shield from life's bullies or from the falling monsoon rain that now switched on again. It seemed to pain him to have to speak. He was too slight for his somewhat dirty slacks and pale blue dress shirt—and carried himself with so little swagger he seemed resigned to the fact that he interested no one. Except I was interested. I wanted to know what Mr. Chen had meant when he'd identified Mr. Shi as one who'd failed really hard. Mr. Shi squinted at me as he lit a cigarette and then started to speak, hesitated, and started again. He said that several years back, his daughter had been diagnosed with leukemia. He'd borrowed money for her treatment and had fallen tens of thousands in debt, even making the desperate blunder of engaging with a local loan shark.

When he went to the bridge on that fateful day, he loitered by the railing long enough for Mr. Chen to lock in on him through his binoculars, and then this man was suddenly standing next to him, saying, "Brother, it's not worth it." After a while, Mr. Chen got Mr. Shi to smoke a cigarette and coaxed him off the bridge, down to the family restaurant to drink and talk, whereupon Mr. Shi's entire story poured forth. Mr. Chen listened closely, trying to understand as best as possible Mr. Shi's predicament, and then began to formulate a plan. Mr. Chen would speak with the loan shark and all the other vengeful parties in the matter. He'd negotiate a truce, a repayment plan, a job search. He insisted that Mr. Shi meet him the following day, at his workplace, at the transportation company, where he often welcomed the weekend's forlorn and misfit to his desk, a recurring gesture that had left his bosses exasperated and threatening to fire him. He'd given Mr. Shi hope and friendship (though details of the repayment plan were murky), and Mr. Shi had found a way to begin life anew.

In this moment of sheepish intimacy—Mr. Shi had a habit of making eye contact, then looking away as if embarrassed—he reminded me of something Mr. Chen had said: "The people I'm saving are very, very kind. They don't want to hurt anyone, so the only way they can vent is by hurting themselves. In that moment when they are deciding between life and death, they are much simpler, more innocent in their thoughts. They almost become blank, a white sheet."

In a way, Mr. Shi was human pathos writ large; in another, he was the smidgen of hope that caused the caesura before jumping.

It struck me as odd, however, that it required a moment like this, walking with him now, to realize that while the deeper, more ancient brain was at all times in dialogue with death, and while that dialogue asserted itself into one's conscious mind from time to time, the frontal lobe was a powerful combatant in self-denial. No matter what declivities I'd found in my own life, I'd always thought of suicide as something occurring over a divide, in the land of irrevocable people, when evidence suggested again and again—sweet Mr. Shi, right here in front of me!—that wasn't the case at all.

We climbed the South Tower stairwell back to the bridge and found Mr. Chen again, standing sentry, and he proffered us a slight if somewhat cool nod. He seemed so alone, standing there; even his wife and daughter knew little of his life on the bridge. They didn't know he'd once been stabbed in the leg; they didn't know the emotional storms he'd weathered on those days when he lost a jumper. ("I want to give them a clean piece of land," he said, using a turn of phrase. "I don't want them worrying.") Now the rain galloped harder; a sea of umbrellas popped open, moving south to north and north to south. Then, as quickly, the rain stopped, and a low-lying monster cloud filled with a muggy kind of light and a crowding heat blanketed everything. One wondered if there'd ever been blue sky in Nanjing. Below, the barges glided downriver in the same stream that carried fallen trees and clumps of earth in the direction of distant Shanghai. While Mr. Chen scoured the crowd, Mr. Shi crouched under the shelter of the fort and lit a cigarette. Cars and trucks and taxis came and went, honking horns, the taste of fuel and smog thick in the air.

Another reporter appeared on the bridge. Young and wearing a flouncy miniskirt and white high heels, she held a device that looked to be the size of a pen, which acted both as her tape recorder and camera. It seemed like secret-agent stuff, but she announced herself to be a student from Shanghai, here to do a big exposé on suicide. Softened a bit by alcohol and the spectral vision of youth itself, Mr. Chen intermittently answered her questions, allowing that the hours between 10 A.M. and 4 P.M. were the most likely for attempts and that his method on the bridge boiled down to intuition. "I'm looking for their spirit as much as their expression and posture," he said. Then he made a grand show of getting on his moped, kicking it to life, and put-putting off on patrol, John Wayne again on his Shetland pony.

We both stood watching him go, the young woman and I, until he disappeared behind tatters of sky-fog that had come loose. In his absence, I was buffeted again by a wave of ennui, this crescendoing sense of uselessness. But then the young student reporter turned to me, beaming with bright eyes, and blurted in broken English, "What angel is he!"

There are always two countercurrents running through the brain of someone contemplating suicide, much like the currents working at odds in the river itself: the desire to escape and the dim hope of being saved. The mind, having fixated on suicide as an option, might take signs of encouragement in everything: cloud formations or rough seas or a random conversation. In the failure of the mailman to arrive. Or the store sold out of a particular brand of cereal. As the mind vacuum-seals itself to its singular course of action, and as the body moves in concert—as suction takes hold and begins to claim its molecules—the only solution to the inevitable chain of unfolding events, the only possibility at being saved, is an intervention of some sort, a random occurrence or gesture. The hand on the shoulder. Then, the mind that has held so long and fast to the body's undoing might shift, and unburden, and de-aggregate, in some cases, almost instantly. Recidivism rates for those mulling suicide are low for all but the severely depressed. Help someone focus step by step across the bridge and he'll be less inclined to ever return.

In my reading, I kept coming back to William James, brother of Henry, journeying across the European continent in 1867, his despair at feeling a failure, the pull of ending it all. In his Norfolk coat, bright shirts, and flowing ties—"His clothes looked as if they had come freshly pressed from the cleaners," a contemporary once said, "and his mind seemed to have blown in on a storm"—he decamped to Berlin, and took the baths at Teplice, in what was then Bohemia. Later, plagued by intense back pain that had migrated to his neck, he took the hypnotic drug chloral hydrate as a sleep aid, and tried electric-shock therapy, which failed to provide relief. In his deepest depression, he felt he'd arrived at a terminus. And yet he withstood the urge of self-annihilation, never again contemplating suicide. A friend of his, a woman named Minny, who helped encourage him through his troubled time (then died herself at a young age), reminded him in a letter of the proposition ever at work: "Of course the question will always remain, What is one's true life—& we must each try & solve it for ourselves."

Now, in the country that brought the world twenty percent of its annual suicide victims, I stood awaiting Mr. Chen's return while breathing in the particulates and invisible lead chips of progress. Time came to a very still point in the late afternoon, and I ambled out onto the bridge with Susan, the translator, realizing that whatever vision of Mr. Chen's heroism had brought me here in the first place, it was folly to think I'd actually ever see him save someone.

Susan was telling me about a family acquaintance who, years back, had jumped from the bridge in winter (most suicides here occurred in the fall and spring). Bundled in many layers against the elements, she had gone to the bridge in distress, climbed the railing, and leapt. One hundred and thirty feet down, at the speed of sixty-five miles an hour, she had hit the river, but if it was the angle or the specifics of her swaddling, if it was will or fate, she had lived, survived not just the fall but also the currents and hypothermia and, most of all, the killer flotsam. Every once in a while, for whatever reason, someone was chosen—but what I wanted to know was this: Having returned from the river, was she happy now, had she found in the aftermath her true life, solved the thing that had first gone missing in her? Susan considered the question. "I think happy enough," she said, "but who knows?"

Just then a man lurched past us, a flash of green. We paid him no mind, really, until he was about twenty steps beyond us, out where the bridge first met water. He stopped, put both hands on the railing, and threw a leg up. The green man's body rose, and now he was hooking his ankle on the top bar, then levering himself from vertical to horizontal until he lay on top of the railing. People streamed by, apparently unaware, staring down. Now the green man began to push his way over the railing, at which point I knew that I was not dreaming and that he was going to kill himself. I shouted, and then burst toward him, sprinting past Mr. Chen's posters and flags.

The green man began shifting to the other side, listing as if on the curl of a wave, half of him letting go into space. Reaching him, I reflexively planted a foot against the concrete base of the railing, latched an arm up and over, then wrenched his body as hard as I could while I pushed back from the railing. Just like that, his body, which was as limp and resigned as if he'd been filled with sawdust, came tumbling back into the real world, where he assumed the full proportions of his humanness again. He had a very tan face and rough hands. He reeked of alcohol. Even before we'd hit the ground, he'd blurted something in Chinese, and then repeated it as I held him in a tight bear hug, readying for a struggle that never came.

"I'm just joking," he implored. He had the supplicant, bedraggled demeanor of a man at loose ends. "I'm okay, thank you."

Shocked back into the world of the living, the green man didn't wait for the question; he just began talking, in a fit of logomania. "The reason I tried to kill myself," he blurted, "is because my father was in the army . . . "

His story seemed disjointed, and more so because Susan was trying to do three things at once — translate, call Mr. Chen, who was not answering, and figure out how to get the attention of Mr. Shi, who was stationed back at the fort, casually smoking cigarettes. A crowd began to gather, an airless huddle. The man went on. "My father is 90 and very sick. We lost his documents in a fire, and we have no money to care for him. The government needs proof that he was in the army, but we are a family of soldiers. I was one, too. . . . "

Mr. Chen had said that people become innocent again on the bridge. They become simple and open in a way that they never otherwise were in real life. And here I was, bear-hugging a man in green coveralls named Fan Ping, trying to crush some spirit inside him that had opted to, in Mr. Chen's words, "dive downward." He was talking to me earnestly, though I didn't understand a word. He was a child, needing someone to understand. His eyes swelled, and two streams of water released over his smooth, rounded cheeks. I don't know, but it didn't seem like crying exactly. It was like something done less out of grief than reflex. With my arms around him, hands chained, I could feel his heart thudding into mine. His breath of stale spirits filled my lungs. When I looked down, my shoes were his, two terribly dirty, scuffed sheaths of cheap, disintegrating leather. We could barely stand as we swayed together.

Fan Ping said that he was thirty-seven years old and that his mother had died three years earlier. He worked for a gas station, Sinopec, and made four hundred dollars a month. He was one of those known as a *guang gun,* or "bare branch," unmarried, a victim of demographics in a country where 20 million men went without wives. "What am I supposed to do now?" he said.

The crowd of onlookers registered their concern and curiosity. Some in the back were laughing, unsure of what indeed was transpiring, or just made nervous by it. I had an irrational flash of hating those people in the back, of wanting to lash out, but all that really mattered was keeping my body between Fan Ping and the railing, in case he made another lunge. Eventually Mr. Chen appeared and dismounted from his moped. On cue, the crowd parted while Mr. Chen stepped forward, invested with the power and understanding of all the nuances at play here. Fan Ping started his story again—*army . . . sick father . . . dead mother . . . gas station . . . so sorry to try to kill self*—and Mr. Chen asked me to let go of the man, something I wasn't at all inclined to do. Then he pulled out a camera and took Fan Ping's picture, which seemed, at best, like an odd way to begin and, at worst, like a major violation of the man's privacy. Then, glaring straight at Fan Ping, who stood slumped and dirty, with bloodshot eyes, Mr. Chen spoke.

"I should punch you in the face," Mr. Chen said. "You call yourself a family man . . . A son . . . Chinese? If your father hadn't been in the army, and if you didn't try to kill yourself just now, I'd punch you. You're not thinking—or are you just shirking your responsibility? I really would like to punch you now. Hand over your ID . . . "

Fan Ping seemed utterly flummoxed, reaching into his pocket and fishing out his identification card. Mr. Chen made a show of studying it, then derisively handed it back—was this a diversion, part of a new therapeutic method?—and in the same brusque tone asked what in the world was he thinking, coming up here like this? Fan Ping replied that he wasn't thinking at all; he just didn't have the money necessary to care for his father—and that his life boiled down to this vast, sorrowful futility.

Mr. Chen sized him up again, with a withering look. I could see part of Fan Ping's blue sock poking through the worn leather of his shoe. "Yes," said Mr. Chen dismissively. "We all have our troubles."

Watching Mr. Chen face off with Fan Ping in that gray late afternoon was like watching twin sons of different mothers: They were both short and stout. Mr. Chen asked Fan Ping where he lived. A country village outside the city. Mr. Chen asked how he'd gotten to the bridge. By foot, from his job. The conversation went on like this for some time while slowly Mr. Chen's tone shifted from outrage and aggression to a more familiar, fraternal concern, even sweetness. "I promise you that there's nothing we can't fix," he said, "but first we have to get you off this bridge." Then later: "I'm here to help you." In his dishevelment, Fan Ping didn't seem capable of movement, as perhaps he hadn't entirely given up on the idea that had brought him here in the first place. And Mr. Chen intuited this. He moved in closer and clasped his hand, a special shake, a locking of pinkies that meant brotherhood, then didn't let go, dragging Fan Ping to the fort and a bus stop there while the crowd followed. He arranged for Fan Ping to meet him at his office first thing Monday morning. He wrote the address on a scrap of paper and stuffed it into Fan Ping's pocket. He punched the digits of Fan Ping's cell-phone number into his own.

"You promise you'll be there," Mr. Chen said.

"I will," said Fan Ping.

"Unless you try to jump off the bridge between now and then," Mr. Chen deadpanned. It wasn't quite a joke, but Fan Ping laughed, as did several in the crowd looking for some sort of release—and then Mr. Chen made it all okay by laughing, too.

Meanwhile, the student reporter from Shanghai grabbed me, tottering on high heels, and asked if she might conduct an interview. Not waiting for an answer, she began peppering me with questions, compensating for my lack of Chinese with her almost-English: "Do American engage in this so-called suicide event?" . . . "From bridges is always the favorite, no?" . . . "Does American—you—have fixes for problem?" . . . "Do you also enjoy *Sex and the City*?"

I couldn't even pretend. My hands, which rarely shake, were shaking. And I floated from my body, watching Mr. Chen and Fan Ping walk ahead, watched—from some high, hovering angle—as Mr. Chen placed the man on a bus and Fan Ping squished down the aisle in his disintegrating shoes and took his place by the window, looking straight ahead. The bus gurgled, backfired, then lurched forward, gone in a plume of gray smoke. That's when some part of me came tumbling back down to myself. I turned and strode back out on the bridge to the spot where Fan Ping had readied to die. I came to the railing, peered down once more to the dark, roiling waters, and felt as if I might regurgitate my lunch noodles.

There would have been no way to survive that fall. And for some reason, standing there, I felt a sharp pang of loss, though no one had been lost. I felt I'd been a step too late, though I'd been one step ahead. It wasn't Fan Ping I was thinking about; it was all the other lives—within me and disparate from me—that had been lost. Yanking Fan Ping from the railing hadn't offered a stay of any kind; instead, it brought death nearer. Mr. Chen wasn't a caricature but a bearer of so much imminent grief. I was bound to him by a feeling Mr. Chen had elucidated for me in one of our talks, a feeling of standing in a spot like this on the bridge, after an incident like this, hovering between heaven and earth, "heart hanging in air."

Back at home, the months passed, and so the day-to-day reasserted itself. And yet sometimes, randomly, Mr. Chen appeared in my mind, standing guard at his station at the South Tower, scanning the crowd. And on those few occasions when I found myself describing what happened on the bridge to friends, I could hear my voice retelling the story of Fan Ping, and it sounded preposterous, even delusional. It sounded as if I might be a man of comical self-importance or full of conspiracies, the sort who wears a hat that reads *They spy on you*. Soon I stopped mentioning it altogether. After Fan Ping pulled away on the bus that day, I had joked with Mr. Chen about catching up to him on the big scoreboard of lives saved.

"It's 174 to 1," I told him. "Watch your back."

He smirked dismissively and said: "You're only given a half point for that one."

As it turned out he was right again. He already knew what I'd later find out. That is, if I'd ever imagined saving someone from a bridge, it probably would have been a fantasy bathed in altruistic light, in which I . . . SAVED . . . A . . . HUMAN . . . LIFE! But then it slowly dawned on me: I'd tried to stop Fan Ping merely so I wouldn't have to live with the memory of having watched him fall. My worry now was that he would somehow succeed in trying again.

So I contact Mr. Chen. He tells me that on the Monday morning after Fan Ping tried to kill himself—the morning that the two men were supposed to meet at his office—Mr. Chen arrived at work and his boss promptly fired him. He left the office building immediately and went to his station at the bridge, not so much because he was despondent but because that was where he felt he belonged. All the while, he dialed Fan Ping's number over and over again, but the phone was out of order. And remained that way, all these months later.

There's nothing to do now, says Mr. Chen, but wait for him to come back. Rest assured, he'll stop Fan Ping. Even as he's recently saved a father, and a few students, and a woman with a psychiatric problem. He knows what Fan Ping looks like. In broiling heat and blowing monsoon, he's out there, ever vigilant, waiting in his double duck-bill, scanning the crowd for Fan Ping—and all the others, too, who might possess thoughts of a glorious demise. He assures me he'll be waiting for them all—and you and me, as well—binoculars trained on our murky faces, our eyes sucked downward, trying to read the glimmer off the surface of the river below.

The only question remains: Can he reach us in time?

■

Homing

FROM *Agni*

BEFORE, IT HAD ALWAYS BEEN a good road. Never big or busy, but alive, with an open feel despite the cul-de-sac. Ray and Nona's house took up one side, and opposite them was a sports field, ringed by shaggy eucalyptus trees. Unusual, fortunate, to have so much green space in the middle of town. People came past all the time: dog walkers, soccer players, domestic workers taking the shortcut down to the taxi rank. Somewhere among the houses on the far side of the field, a man kept homing pigeons. In the evenings you could hear his looping whistle and see the flock turning, specks against the blue of Table Mountain. Nona and Ray always listened for the birdman's call.

At the end of the road was the face-brick retirement home. "Look at the oldies," Ray said, watching through their kitchen window as a posse of ancient women—and one man—ventured out from the home. It was a short walk down to the shops on the main road.

"Don't laugh. That's us, all too soon," said Nona.

"Doesn't bother me," said Ray. "Potter down to the shops, read the newspaper, have a cup of tea. Looks all right."

This was pretty much their schedule anyway. Nona was in her early sixties, Ray five years older. She'd done secretarial work and he'd been a safety inspector, but that was all in the past now. Although they were both in good health, it was easy to imagine the years ahead, living where they did. One day she and Ray would pack a small overnight bag, close the door behind them and simply walk up the road, into old age. And he was right: it wouldn't be so bad. They'd stroll around the field in the evenings, arm in arm. She wasn't ready for it yet, but she was also not afraid.

So it was upsetting when the old-age home closed down. Ray and Nona read the news in the paper, but by then it was a done deal. Overnight, all the residents were bussed out to bigger institutions in the bleak northern suburbs, far from the old part of town. The place stood vacant for barely a week before the workmen arrived, throwing up hoardings across the facade and also, shockingly, around the perimeter of the field. A high wall rose at amazing speed and was painted a peachy pink, and behind it there reared the pink backside of a new hotel. The noise of construction, which went on for months, was unbearable, but the greatest affront was the size and fleshy colour of the thing. Set down like a giant Monopoly piece, fatly overflowing its Monopoly square, the hotel filled up the space where the old-age home had been, and then turned the corner in an L and filled the space directly opposite Ray and Nona's kitchen window too. Brash, three stories tall, and featureless except for a row of mirrored windows that faced them over the top of the new wall.

"Are they even allowed to do that?" asked Ray.

"They already did," said Nona.

And at a stroke, the road was mortally wounded. Nobody rode a bicycle past Nona's kitchen window any more, nobody walked a dog. The birdman fell silent: the sky in which his flock once stirred had turned into pink-painted plaster.

As the weeks wore on, the tar cracked and developed sunken patches. Dandelions grew up between the pavement edging stones. No council workers came to clean, to clear the drains or fix the potholes: it seemed the road had been erased entirely from the city maps. In dying, it gave off the sweetish, not unpleasant smell of living matter breaking down, like compost.

It had long been a habit of Nona's, a little game, to look around at the city and think, How long would it last, if people were to vanish overnight? How many months or years before the bush came back, before birds made nests in the office blocks and troops of baboons started lifting chunks of tar from the road?

Not long, she realised now. Not long at all.

The new wall remained flawless. The paint was good stuff: it did not flake or puff with damp. Everything else in the alley, however, was in decline.

What disturbed Ray and Nona most was the least material of

things: the light. The house was much darker than before, and the road almost always sunk in shade. They noticed it especially in the mornings, when bars of pale gold used to drop through the kitchen window, illuminating the cornflakes and coaxing the two of them into the day. The sunlight still came in, but at the wrong time, and from an unnatural direction—east in the evenings. The first time it happened, Ray went outside to investigate.

"It's the windows," he called back into the house.

Nona joined him. The alleyway was strangely lit, as if with several weak spotlights. Indeed, it was the mirror-glass windows of the hotel, three stories up, reflecting the evening light. The new hotel had not only stolen their sunrise, it had slipped them this phony sunset in exchange.

"Well, that takes the cake," she said, eyes stinging slightly from the glare. Ray said nothing, just fetched a stiff-bristled broom and started sweeping away the last of the sand left on the pavement by the builders.

"It would be baboons," Nona explained once again. "They're clever, and strong, and they've got fingers. Plus those teeth."

"I disagree. Dogs. Dogs would rule. The pack instinct would take over." Ray was almost horizontal on the deckchair as he spoke, staring at the sky, although there was less of it now than there had been. They'd taken to sitting in the alley in the oddly lit evenings, as if it were part of their property.

"Well. Maybe, for a while. But the baboons would win out in the end. One on one, I'd put my money on a big male baboon. Dogs are too soppy. Half of them would pine away for their owners. They'd just lie down and die. And they wouldn't be able to open tin cans and things."

Nona could picture this all quite clearly, and with a kind of satisfaction: the baboons roaming the aisles of the abandoned supermarkets, the ravening dogs locked outside. Baboon babies playing on her kitchen table.

"Okay," conceded Ray. "Maybe baboons—on the ground. But the pigeons would do fine too. They'd carry on as per normal."

This was true. She liked that about birds. How they were adaptable, and took advantage. Walls were no problem, they could use walls, but they could also coast right over them if need be.

The deckchairs were Ray's idea, his way of making peace with the new lie of the land. But for Nona, although she took her place next to him in the evenings, the resentment did not fade. Every glance at the bland pink wall was a small humiliation. She wondered if there were wealthy guests already in the rooms, behind the glare of the windows: German tourists, Brits, Americans. She stared at the panes quite frankly, confident that no one was looking back. Those windows were not watchful eyes. They were more like expensive sunglasses: whoever was behind them wouldn't care to gaze down on Nona and Ray.

"Miss those birds," said Ray, blinking up at what was left of the sky.

And then one evening the pigeons came, a cloud of them, nine or ten, settling and separating into a row on top of the boundary wall. Ray saw them first, as he and Nona were eating an early dinner at the kitchen table.

"Look who's here!"

"What? Who?"

"The birds, the birds! The birdman's birds."

"How can you tell?" Nona peered through the window. They looked like regular street pigeons to her. Or were they sleeker, with a pedigree shimmer to the wings, and especially finely sculpted heads and beaks?

Ray hurried outside with a couple of crusts. The birds seemed to have been waiting for him: when the bread hit the ground, they descended, cooing and beating the air.

"Hungry," said Ray.

"Nonsense. A pigeon will never starve." Although who could say, with these fancy racing birds?

"And lost. They don't know the way home with this blooming big wall here."

"They're homing pigeons. They know the way."

"No, they do get lost," said Ray. "I read about it. They have magnets in their heads, and they get . . . I don't know, depolarised." He brushed the last crumbs off his palms, thoughtful. "Poor little buggers."

Now, on schedule, came the light from above, that unnatural flash that hurt Nona's eyes. For a moment she saw a great bird settling over them, a firebird with its wings outstretched.

"That's what it is," Ray said. "The light, the reflections. It's confusing them."

"Well. They probably have lice. Or bird flu. They look a little off."

The next day, Ray went out and bought a sack of birdseed, and after that the pigeons came twice a day, which Nona thought was excessive. Mornings and evenings, they sat waiting for him in a row on the wall, raising their tails to defecate. At least, thought Nona, most of them faced the alleyway, shitting judiciously down onto hotel property.

They read in the "Tonight" section of the *Cape Argus* that the hotel was a luxurious place, patronised by politicians and celebrities, both local and international. Some evenings they could hear the revels: laughter, music. On one occasion, fireworks. But no gaiety spilled over the wall onto Ray and Nona. All they got was the coloured glaze of party lights reflected in the windows, and the vibrations of popular songs through the bricks.

Nona moaned about the noise going on till all hours. Ray didn't seem to mind so much, or even to notice. Twice a day the birds came to his feet, and he fed them. Nona, though, felt on edge, distracted by the flare of the evening sunlight and then the shadow that followed. Even as the hotel lit up for the evening, gloom gathered at the base of the wall and flooded the alley to its mouth.

What she did not confess to Ray was how the pulse of the music also excited her—even prone on the ratty deckchair, on the shady side of the wall, among the dandelions and pigeon crap. It made her shift and sit up, straining to decipher the noises. Shrieks of pleasure. Crashes, laughter. A girl pushed into the pool? A smashed champagne glass? Once, sitting there beside Ray, she heard the distinctive pop and fizz of a champagne bottle, and then—miraculous—a cork came flying over the wall and landed in her lap. She held it up to Ray, eyes wide, but he was half-asleep and hadn't seen.

* * *

Along with the field and the retirement home, several other properties had surrendered to the hotel grounds: Nona had to walk all the
way around a large and irregular block to get to the entrance. She followed the boundary wall as it crooked left and right, at times trailing
a hand on its high-quality matte surface, guessing at what it might
conceal. What was the meaning of each swell and dip? What palatial
amenities — indoor swimming pool, putting green, tropical glass-
house — could require these annexes and niches, this complex outline? It was impossible, now, to recall what had been there before.

She came out onto the main road, holding her small bag close,
and followed the wall along a last straight run to the entrance. It was
a grand, curlicued, wrought iron thing, painted glossy black. The
guard seemed surprised to see a human being on foot at the gates,
but opened them a crack to let her through.

From the entrance ran an avenue of palms. Ahead, the building
was indistinct: a shimmer of pink, a suggestion of steps ascending.
The palms had not been there before, nor could they have grown so
fast. They must've been transported whole from somewhere else, and
then stuck into the soil like candles on a birthday cake. Nona remembered seeing a fully grown palm tree travelling down the road some
months before, the bole laid flat on the truck bed like a giant's body
on a bier.

She proceeded up the avenue, glancing side to side at the tended
lawns, the cool greens and whites of the flowerbeds, the dappled
light. There were very few people around. A gardener stood motionless by a wheelbarrow, and a couple of tennis players patted a ball to
and fro on a clay court in the distance. The air felt expensive: grass-
scented and easy on the lungs. How could this all fit into what had
been a small field, a block of flats, a modest neighbourhood?

The avenue was long. By the time she reached the marble steps
leading up to the entrance, Nona's feet were aching, as if she'd jour-
neyed miles. Inside the high-ceilinged lobby, though, her progress
was marvellously eased. The light was subdued and soft music carried her to the front desk — a bank of smooth wood just the right
height for weary elbows. Behind it flitted red-coated shadows, attentive and discreet. A young woman with dark eyes, dark polished skin
and a red tuxedo jacket came forward, tilting her head.

"I called yesterday," Nona said. "I have a booking. Your special?"

The carpeted foyer damped her words and made them unconvincing. She fumbled in her purse for the newspaper cutting, for proof. But already the young woman had found her booking, received her payment with a smile—as if it happened every day, as if one did this all the time—and handed her a key card like a winning ticket. Number twenty-three.

Nona found herself smoothly transferred into the care of a slim youth with neatly braided hair, the male twin of the receptionist. Polite hands lifted her bag and conducted her through the cool embrace of the elevator doors, up, and out into a golden corridor. The young man held her bag, not her arm, but Nona felt intimately escorted, barely needing to lift her feet. Door 23 fell away to admit her. As soon as the bellhop had withdrawn, she kicked off her shoes and collapsed across a huge white bed—the sheets as crisp and cool, she imagined, as a drift of foreign snow.

Nona could not lie still for long, though. She rose and took a turn around her room, inspecting the surfaces, the knobs and drawers. She and Ray had only ever stayed in rundown country hotels, two-star affairs, or campsites. She fingered the fruit arrangement, peeked into the minibar and examined the bonbon on the pillow. It was all strange and extravagant: this lavish provisioning, so blindly generous. Rare gifts for anyone with a key.

Nona opened the window, but felt no change. The air outside was as cool and conditioned as the air within. She leaned out—and there it was. Three stories below, beyond a strip of garden and just visible over the boundary wall: the alleyway, the house.

From this unfamiliar angle, she saw that the windows of her home were too small, and unevenly placed. A couple were cracked. She could see the plumbing on the back wall, too, and a shameful stain spreading from one of the pipes. Nona felt a rush of resentment.

Down in the alley, the pigeons—diligent heads bent, tapping away—made variegated patterns on the tar. Black and grey and white and mauve, each bird unique. They seemed to feed in silence, their clicks and coos too delicate to reach her ears.

Now something else, a blunt grey knob, pushed into the frame. It was her husband's head, surprisingly thin on top, inclined towards the birds. His arm was extended in its frayed, familiar cardigan, and after a moment a bird hopped onto his wrist. An intimate view: she looked away.

Nona had never been deceitful in her marriage, but she'd lied to Ray about this weekend. She'd used money from her own small savings to pay for the room, and told him she was off to visit her sister. Now the cost seemed much greater than when she'd cut out the ad for the two-night special. These were pleasures owed to him.

But at the time of her decision—that champagne cork still slightly damp in her palm—some action had seemed urgently required. And perhaps he was glad that she'd gone, that she wasn't there to disquiet him with her sighs and carping, her impatient rustling of the newspaper.

Directly below her window, peppermint grass flowed thickly to the base of the wall. There were parasols and camellia bushes and white garden furniture. A guest might sit down there of an evening, sipping a chilled drink, and never guess at what lay an arm's length away, on the shabbier side of the wall.

Yet another attentive shadow in a red jacket appeared beside her garden chair, this one with a drinks menu. Everyone working here was young and unobtrusively attractive: eyes that took note but did not linger, voices low, manner deferential yet flirtatious to a finely judged degree. The waiter leaned forward, showing her the tops of his long eyelashes.

"Gin and tonic, why not?" she said.

All at once Nona felt happy again. The ease was back, the sense of smooth movement, although she was sitting quite still. She and Ray, she saw, lived backstage of a perfect piece of theatre. The lighting in the garden was impeccable: even and mellow, unaffected by the alleyway's brassy reversals of glare and gloom. The only sound was a precise ticking in the air—the piston spritz of unseen sprinklers, or perhaps it was the hushed beat of luxury itself. The gin appeared, in a tumbler chocked with ice. She sipped and felt the coolness spreading down into her belly.

Some things were not controlled, however. Nona noticed white and olive streaks on the battlements: sure enough, the pigeons had left their mark on this side of the wall as on the other. And across the tabletop, a line of ants negotiated the crevasses and cul-de-sacs of the lacy metal to a spill of sugar at its centre. She imagined their tiny amazement at this manna. They made her think of Ray: their earnest, uncomplaining labour, their focus on the small satisfactions before them. She bent down to trace the line of insects to its source. It disappeared into the lawn and emerged again to doodle up the corner of a flower planter, along its edge and through a tiny crack at the base of the wall. So—lowlife ants, smuggling out the loot. Again she wondered: how long? For ants and birds and grass roots to level this wall again, grain by grain, to break open the path it had blocked?

But she didn't really want the wall broken down. What she wanted was for it to draw open and enclose them all—Ray, herself and even the birds—within its charmed perimeter.

She drank steadily, watching the ants come and go. Her glass emptied, and was filled. The evening light dimmed, while high above, the windows of the hotel began to shine—the angle oblique, the light more forgiving than it was at home. Small globes flickered on in the shrubbery, bathing the wall in dapples of rose and amber. Between the lights, the dusk softened and expanded. Patio doors opened and walls dissolved, making way for music, trays of cocktails, waiters, guests—such guests! Their clothes were precious and their scent was rare. Women leaned at elegant angles, calves taut above high heels. Men shouted with laughter, gloriously assured. More red-coated servers danced from the shadows, carrying ice buckets and bottle after bottle of champagne.

Nona did not speak to anyone, content to let the crowd wash around her. She tickled her lip with the bubbles in her constantly refreshed glass; she smiled at the dark-eyed waiters. She kept half an eye on the wall, but in all the flow and movement it stayed where it was. Nona and the wall were still.

Ah, but it must've been the drink. Later she would barely remember leaving the party, finding her way inside and along the hushed corridor. But the feel of everything remained: the textures of wallpaper, wood, and carpet. (Had she stumbled?) All so rich and inviting, so lush to the touch: luxurious friction. Was there a young man by her side, red-coated, bright-eyed, holding her arm? Perhaps. Certainly she felt accompanied, but it might've been the scented air itself that took her weight, that guided her to the proper door and pressed the handle down.

Nona did not usually sleep naked or on her stomach, but that was how she awoke. She was in a cool, dark place. She detected the firmness of an unfamiliar mattress, and then—out of one eye—the grey field of a curtained window. Breaking the bed's hold, she turned onto her back, wedged herself up against the pillows and took stock. The room was bleary and ruffled. Against the habits of a lifetime, her clothes were strewn on the floor. And there were other shapes, small but troubling, in the dimness beyond the foot of the bed. A breeze belled the curtain and something pushed through with a rustle.

She took a moment to let the scene develop. The curtains sucked out against the open window, as if the air in the room were plumping up, and the grey light strengthened.

There were hunched figures on the sill, on the desk, on top of the standing lamp. Six, seven of them—a fidgeting crowd of small, dour spectators. At the foot of the bed, one shook out its wings impatiently, stepped side to side and ejected a splatter of white onto the duvet.

Nona leaned over to the bedside table, poured herself a glass of water and drank deeply. Next to the jug were two wrapped biscuits on a dish. Digestives—the kind that Ray enjoyed with his tea. She pulled the cellophane off one, but her stomach turned at the first whiff of its mealy sweetness. The pigeons cooed and shuffled, turning their heads this way and that to follow her movements. She'd never thought of birds' faces as expressive, or even as faces—those carved heads set with glass eyes. But these seemed somehow expectant.

Nona held the biscuit in her fingers. She broke it in two, in quarters, smaller, and offered the pieces in her palm. Black eyes observed her sidelong, but no bird moved. With a sigh she let the crumbs fall to the floor.

In an instant the boldest bird had hopped down from the minibar, legs outstretched and wings braking. The others piled in. They were shades of the same grey as the carpet, but the birds' colour was alive and various. Wings fanned; snaky heads jabbed at the crumbs. Nona broke up the second biscuit.

An extravagant thought came to her. Room service. The phone was to hand, right next to the bed. She ordered toast, coffee, aspirin. More toast. When the knock came, she went to the door in her dressing gown and opened it just enough to take the tray, ignoring the waiter's knowing smile. As soon as he was gone, she poked out a hand to slip the Do Not Disturb sign over the doorknob.

Crumbs on the carpet, the credenza, the TV cabinet, at the foot of the bed. Nona poured herself a strong coffee and settled against the pillows to watch.

More birds hustled in through the window, shouldering each other, flapping and squabbling. Their claws scraped and ticked on the veneer cabinets, snagged in the bedspread. Every now and then one lofted into the air, wings clapping, before rejoining the others. Nona found the coo and rustle strangely restful. There was a dusty, sweet smell of feathers and bird shit. Her eyelids dropped.

She dreamed herself walking through the hotel, down a long gold corridor, looking for an exit. But there were no clear routes. The birds were with her, and they were trapped: flying into dead ends, wings battering against glazed windows and tangling in elevator cables. Nona pushed at the walls with her hands, searching for secret doorways, but the hotel could not be unbuilt.

She roused herself to use the bathroom and drink more water, then crawled back under the duvet. The birds were dozing, perched on towel rack and headboard. She wanted to sleep with them forever, suspended three stories in the air.

It was late afternoon when she finally rose. The pigeons had gone, leaving only feathers and the blots of their droppings.

Already she could see that the room—despite the soiling, the smell, the feathers on the floor—was shrugging off this brief habitation. When the carpet shook its nylon pelt, all traces would be shed. Soon the room would be dreaming again in its pristine blankness: thoughtless, faithless, without memory.

Nona dressed quickly, packed her few things, put out a large tip for the cleaning lady and left the key in the door. Downstairs, crossing the lobby, she avoided the eyes of the concierge.

Then down the long avenue of rustling palms, each with its own tribe of birds lodged like seeds in the crevices between the fronds. The grounds did not seem so enormous to her now. In every direction—beyond the flickering mesh of the tennis-court fence, past the rose garden—a wedge of pink wall blocked her line of sight. By the time she passed through the gates, the sun was low.

A block away from home, she heard the whistling. High and looping—not the birdman's, but still familiar. Funny that you could recognise the voice in a whistle. When she turned the last corner, Ray was in the alley, head cocked to the sky, birdseed in his outstretched palm.

"Home early," he said.

She put down her bag. "Missed you, didn't I?"

"They didn't pitch up this morning." He let the seed fall to the ground and wiped his hand on his trousers. Fretful, like an old man. "Didn't come."

"They'll be back," she said, taking his arm. "Those birds, they know which side their bread is buttered."

She helped him into the deckchair and took her seat alongside. It was the time of evening when the sun's reflection cast its shadows at their feet.

And so they reclined, Nona and Ray, their backs to the new hotel, saying a few quiet words to each other off and on. They watched the road and then the sky, and then the road again. That old road: altered but familiar, stolen from them and yet still theirs. Waiting in that changing light for the birds to find their way.

■

Pleiades

FROM *Gulf Coast*

Del

My parents were geneticists. They had a firm belief in the power of science to fix everything, to create everything. This belief was their religion, and they liked to proselytize as much as any born-again Christians. When they decided to have children they saw the opportunity to share their faith in science with the world. They wanted to make miracle babies so unbelievable that people would stop and stare, their own organic equivalent of a billboard for Jesus. Their original idea was to develop an *in vitro* procedure that would create identical twins. But they decided twins weren't spectacular enough, not enough of a challenge. They settled on septuplets. One fertilized egg split into seven pieces made seven sisters, all of us identical. Pleiades, my father used to call us, after the constellation of seven stars.

All the major networks were shooting footage at the hospital the day we were born. Protestors traveled from around the country to Los Angeles so they could picket outside, with signs that said "Seven Deadly Sins" and "Frankenstein's Children." Even the doctors who delivered us expected us to come out with birth defects; half a dozen neonatal specialists were standing by. But they weren't needed. We were small—about two pounds each—but other than that, my mother says, we were perfect. Our lungs, our hearts, our brain activity were measured and found to be normal. We all had a wisp of dark hair at the front of our foreheads, and eyes that would turn from blue to brown. My parents didn't want rhyming names or alliterative names but they liked to show off their knowledge of Greek, and so we were Leda, Io, Zoe, Helen, Cassandra, Vesta, and me, Adelpha—called Del.

My mother and father, in the magazine photographs, glow with a mixture of parental pride and professional elation. Without scientific interference identical twins account for one in every 250 live births, identical triplets one in two million, fraternal septuplets one in every four million, and my sisters and I just couldn't exist. But science made us and there we were, pink-skinned and button-nosed, each swaddled in our own colored blanket—red, orange, yellow, green, blue, indigo, purple—a wriggling, blinking rainbow.

The tabloids ran headlines like "Forced Septuplets Really Alien Babies!" and "Test Tube Septs Share One Brain!" After our first birthday the publicity died down, although reporters came around now and then hoping to do follow-up stories. In the scientific community our celebrity never waned. Throughout our childhood we took trips to visit scientists whom our parents referred to as our aunts and uncles. These people smiled at us and sometimes gave us hugs like real relatives, but they also liked to look at our skin cells under microscopes, or watch us play together through two-way mirrors. My mother and father ran experiments, too, and by the time we were six we thought no more of giving a blood sample than we did of making our beds, picking up our toys, or any other chore.

Our parents never told us which of us was born first because they thought it would affect our psychology. We reached the age of eleven considering each other separate in body but not in anything else. I have heard that twins, even identical twins with a particularly close relationship, like to emphasize that they are still individuals, but we did not. There's an old home video of us on the beach, eight or nine years old and wearing matching gold-spangled swimsuits. We move across the sand like a flock of birds in flight, wheeling with each others' movements, each head turned only a fraction of a second before the next so that it's impossible to say where one motion ends and another begins.

Perhaps it was the circumstances of our creation. Perhaps we were not truly separate people but parts of a whole, as a thicket of aspen trees all grow from the same network of roots. And even now maybe it is no different.

"You were so easy, really," my mother said to me a few years ago in tearful nostalgia. "You all liked peas, you all hated carrots. No one would use the pink crayons."

Who knows what would have happened if we had reached high school together, been forced to deal with romances and social intrigues and the possibility of attending different colleges. Perhaps we would have simply refused to be parted, clung together like a ball of ladybugs in winter. Or maybe we would have adjusted, moved apart and away from each other. But I doubt it.

We were eleven years old, doing a jigsaw puzzle on the living room floor of our beach house in Santa Cruz. Vesta set a corner piece in its place, put her hand to the side of her head and said she had a headache. We all looked at her and groaned; headaches had a way of catching between us, even though our mother tried to tell us that was impossible. A few minutes later Vesta shook her head and complained again, and then she fainted, we thought. But we had a horrible clenched feeling in our stomachs. Leda put her hands on Vesta's cheeks and Vesta didn't even flinch. We all went screaming for my mother.

At the hospital they said my sister had had a brain aneurysm, that she was dead. We wanted to argue but we knew it was true. We could feel it. That night we all slept piled on the floor of our bedroom, holding onto each other's wrists and calves and hair, terrified of losing one another. For months after that we felt sick, but we thought it was *just* sadness. We didn't know yet that for us there was no such thing as just sadness, that our grief had a life of its own, an invisible mouth like a black hole that drew us inexorably closer.

We were twelve when Leda got pneumonia. She never recovered. The doctors put her on every antibiotic they had, but she was dead in three weeks. Again my sisters and I felt that same tautness in our bodies, that surge of poison in our veins, but we kept quiet about it. We didn't need to discuss it with each other, and our parents didn't understand anything. They were depressed, guilty, frantic for the solution they felt sure must be out there just beyond their reach, but that didn't touch what we felt. We were all thinking, without ever saying so, that one death might be a freak accident but two was not. That we were all going to die.

Reporters followed us everywhere. There were Internet betting pools about which of us would die next. We started exercising, eating organic food, taking vitamins as if that was going to help. Another year went by and we lost Io. Anti-genetics protestors swarmed her funeral, glowing with self-righteousness. One woman carried a sign that said "Science Giveth and The Lord Taketh Away." She wore a lime green sundress and stared at us through the wrought iron fence of the churchyard during the entire service, never making a sound.

The remaining four of us began developing bruises in places we couldn't remember bumping. We were flown to specialists around the country, circulatory doctors, immunologists, gene therapists; we gave countless samples of blood and urine and tissue, were prodded and analyzed without receiving any conclusive results. They thought we had a new form of AIDS, or had somehow developed hemophilia, but none of the tests supported these theories.

Eventually our parents moved us to New York City so they could set up camp at Mount Sinai Hospital and put all their energy into trying to cure us. They weren't medical doctors and didn't really belong there, but I believe there was a bargain struck, something to do with donating our coveted tissue samples, the kind of utterly calculated and logical deal I didn't want to know too much about. I've always believed that the move had as much to do with getting away from their colleagues in California as it did with saving us; my parents were not so gracious in their defeat as they had been in their glory.

When Zoe got sick the rest of us began to consider desperate solutions. The three deaths we had suffered through were horribly painful, to be sure, but in a way the most difficult, the most shocking and surprising and worst thing was finding ourselves still alive the next day. We felt mocked, being forced to face, time and again, this brutal proof of our distinctness. We decided to bring it to a neat end, for all of us, if Zoe didn't improve.

By then we were sixteen, old enough to be crafty, to filch chemicals from our parents' lab that were sure to be fatal, keep them in little vials in our pockets as we stood around the hospital bed. But at the crucial moment—heart monitor flatlining, alarms sounding, frantic nurses attempting resuscitation—we failed to act. Not one of us so much as moved a hand toward the poison. We still wanted to live in spite of it all.

The next time we didn't consider the plan again. We just sat silently by Cassie's bedside, kissed her tears, and watched her go. Then it was me and Helen, and we were terrified and sick all the time. We kept wondering which one of us would die next, wondering whether it was worse to be dead or alive and alone.

We dreamed about the others. Sitting down to dinner or choosing our clothes for the day, we sometimes hesitated, waiting for them without realizing what we were doing. Their breath filled the room, their fingertips were on our skin. Helen and I began to feel stretched, overfilled, oversensitive to everything. Loud noises frightened us beyond reason. The sound of our parents yelling or crying, both of which they did frequently, made us dizzy.

Helen started having trouble breathing. We were eighteen and it would have been the year of our high school graduation, but we'd long since quit school. For the next five years she was battered by a drawn-out illness, waves of health and sickness lifting her up and throwing her down again. My parents whisked in and out of our house like ghosts in their fluttering white lab coats, going back and forth to the hospital to examine cultures under the microscope, visit Helen, or meet with another doctor promising a cure. By then I could have told them exactly what was wrong: the emotion and sensation of seven people condensed into two bodies was too much for the bodies to bear. But that was an explanation that wouldn't satisfy the rigors of science, so I knew it wouldn't satisfy them. There was nothing they could do about it anyway.

Helen kept saying to me, "What will we do?" Her skin looked like it had shrunk, tight and shiny across her bones. There was nothing to say because we both knew the answer: "We" would not do anything. She would die, and I would stand in the damp grass of the cemetery with no one to squeeze my hand at the graveside. My parents were around of course, but I'd grown up without having to speak my mind, and I never knew what to say to them. Besides, I was finding them increasingly hard to love. I kept thinking about that protestor at the churchyard, years ago now, and an idea began tormenting me: maybe there was only meant to be one of us. Maybe all that splitting had been a bad idea. I missed my sisters, but it was more than that. I could feel enough for seven people, as if my sisters wanted me to live for them. I wondered if Nature, once she had pared us down to one body, would let me survive, or if it would just be worse for me in the end.

My parents were desperate by now. They began planning ways to cure me, clone me, freeze me if I died, plotting it in their bedroom at night, never thinking I might be listening from the hallway. Despite their collusion they hated each other. They both wanted me to love them, to forgive them for whatever mistake in their calculations had brought this on us, to forgive them on behalf of my sisters, too. Surely I could. Surely I was all of us in one.

But I couldn't, or maybe I just didn't want to. I felt my sisters in me and around me and I knew that, whatever pain awaited me, letting my parents decide my fate was the worst choice I could make.

"Go," said Helen, "Maybe you can outrun it. If one of us is left, that's enough."

Rob

A car comes down the road, an old blue hatchback covered in dust, and it slows down just when I've decided it's not going to stop. To my mind that always tells you the driver is struggling with himself, should he pick me up or shouldn't he.

I'm pretty good at choosing cars by now; I can almost tell by the way they roll down the window whether to trust the driver or not. But when I bend down to look inside it seems to me I judged wrong this time. The girl behind the wheel looks like a zombie, skin falling off her, patches of hair missing. She could be could be twenty, thirty, I don't know; she's so messed up it's hard to tell.

"Where are you going?" she says.

"L.A."

"I'll be passing near there."

It's something about the way she looks at me, not threatening but not afraid, that makes me get in. Besides, it's not often you find a ride that'll take you through ten states, and I'm in no position to be picky.

Two hours down the road we blow a tire and the spare's no good. We wait for a tow truck, eat supper at a diner in town while the tire gets patched. I order chicken fried steak and she eats a fruit salad. She saves all the grapes for last and slides each one over her tongue like a marble. "I can taste the sunshine," she says.

When she opens her wallet to pay the waitress it's stuffed thick with cash. She plucks off a hundred dollar bill to pay a twelve dollar tab, and there's another hundred underneath. It's enough to tempt even an honest man.

"You always carry money like that?" I say. "It's not safe."

She smiles a little, her lips full of cracks like old rubber ready to split. "Neither is picking up hitchhikers, but that didn't seem to bother you."

"Still."

She waves a hand at her blistered face. "Look at this," she says, "I'm past the point where I worry about something bad happening to me."

We pick up the car but it's late to be starting out, so we get a motel room for the night, two beds, cable TV. She falls asleep right away, and her breathing gets so quiet I worry a couple of times that she's dead, and lean over her bed to check. In the middle of the night, though, she begins to moan. She's still asleep, her eyes skittering back and forth underneath the lids, tears slipping between the lashes. I turn the bedside lamp on but it doesn't wake her, and I'm afraid to touch her now. I sit on my bed with my hands in my pockets, edge of the headboard cutting into the back of my neck along the sunburn, wondering how long is the walk to the next bit of civilization. Wondering whether you can really leave a girl to die alone in a motel room, or what do you do if you stay.

She wakes up just after sunrise looking worse than ever, which I wouldn't have thought was possible. She sits on the edge of the bed with her face in her hands.

"I don't know if I can do this by myself," she says.

"Let me drive for a while," I say.

When we get on the road we talk a little, but I can tell she doesn't like conversation much. She starts peeling the dead skin off her arms, piece by piece like she's stripping wallpaper, absent-minded the way that some people chew their fingernails.

"Stop that," I say, and she looks up and kind of smiles, sheepish, and folds her hands in her lap. "What's wrong with you, anyhow?"

"I'm sick," she says, like that's all there is to it. "Don't worry, you can't catch it."

"Does it hurt?"

"Usually."

"Don't you have a doctor or something?"

"Dozens of them," she says.

I look her up and down. "Well I guess they aren't worth a damn, are they?"

We both laugh. She looks different when she laughs, like there's a brightness spreading through her face, like the sound fills her whole self and not just her mouth.

"You should have flown, though. It would've been easier on you."

"It wouldn't," she says, "It makes me vomit these days. Besides, this was a last-minute decision, and now I get to see what's between New York and California."

"I guess I don't like flying much myself. What are you aiming to do when you get there?"

"Go to the beach," she says, as if she was just another sand bunny in a string bikini, a bored college girl on spring break with nothing else to do.

We drive and talk about the music on the radio, movies, the weather. She sleeps a lot, her head resting against the window, hands balled together in her lap, a pained look on her face the whole time. I wonder if her body hurts even in her sleep, if she's healthy or ravaged in her dreams.

Partway through Illinois we hit a nasty snarl of traffic, somebody sure enough dead up ahead judging by the number of cop cars and ambulances that go screaming past us along the berm. We're near an exit, though, so we escape after a few minutes, get ourselves onto 66 and stop for lunch at a roadside burger joint, one of those chains that used to cover the country but now only exists in a few God-forsaken outposts. They have a picnic table to the side, wood gone grey and full of splinters, on a patch of dead scrub grass and hard-packed red clay. We take our food out there. Del licks the salt off her fries but doesn't eat them, just watches me with my hamburger.

"What's the matter?"

"I don't eat meat anymore," she says.

"Maybe that's your problem."

She shakes her head, chews on the end of one fry while she stares at the ground between her feet.

"You can have these," she says, pushing the paper sleeve of french fries at me. She gets down on the ground and starts scratching at the dirt with her fingernails, and at first I think she's looking for something but then I see she's just making a pile of red dust. She scrapes some more, picks up a stone to do a better job, working with all her strength.

"What the hell are you doing?"

Instead of answering she takes her waxed paper cup from the table, dumps half the soda out of it and scoops the dirt in. She sits down again and I watch her stir the whole mess together with her straw until it's like pudding, and then she starts spooning that slop into her mouth.

"Stop it or you're gonna be sick for sure," I say, but she keeps going. I grab her arm and let it go again. Her skin is too hot. Her bones feel like they could crumble in my hand. The more time I spend with her the clearer it is to me that she should die, that dying would be good for her. When she can't eat any more she wipes her mouth on her sleeve and leans her elbows on the table.

"Sometimes I feel like I'm just going to fly apart. Like nothing in me is solid," she says. "Who's to say what fixes that?"

I throw the rest of my food away and help her back to the car, but I drive too slow, still picturing her in the hard prairie light with a mouthful of mud.

Del spins the radio dial, finds a rock song with a heavy bass line, and she taps her fingers on her thigh in time. Her eyes tick around in her face like they're trying to see everything at once, until she closes them. She rests the back of her hand on my knee and I can feel the heat right through my jeans. Her palm is unnaturally smooth, without the normal lines that hands always have, and I wonder if it's hard for her to hold things, if they slip off that skin like it was vinyl. Looking at her makes it hard to think. Death is in her and through her and all around her but she moves and breathes regardless.

By eight o'clock it's dark out. Del is asleep, and with no conversation and nothing but dark highway to look at I get tired quick. I find a motel and pull off. Del stirs, lifts her head and leans it down again.

"Why are we stopping?" she says.

"It's late. I'm too tired to drive any more."

"I'm in a hurry."

"A few hours won't make a difference."

She doesn't answer but closes her eyes. I check in, park the car near our room and help her inside.

"Do you want to take the first shower?" I ask her.

"No," she says, but then she looks down at her clothes, smeared with mud.

She goes into the bathroom and closes the door. I stand outside in the dark and listen to the sound of the water against the bathtub, against her body. She showers for a long time, half an hour maybe, so that I start to wonder if something's happened to her. At last the water stops, and I sit at the foot of one of the beds and pretend to watch television in the darkness. Del opens the door to the bathroom and steam and yellow light pour out around her like a magician's cloud of smoke. She is naked, standing up straight, and I see that she's taller than I thought, taller than I am. I look down at my feet and close my eyes to stop myself staring.

"It doesn't matter," she says. "I rinsed my clothes, and I wanted to let them dry."

She steps closer and I can smell her, mud and heat lightning, black pepper and rain, apples fermenting in the high grass, all of it compressed together. She pulls the covers off the other bed and crawls between the sheets. The darkness is filled with the smell of her.

Turning on her bedside lamp she says, "You can sleep here if you want."

She says it the way you might offer to lend someone five dollars, and somehow that makes it crueler to say no. I want her to keep that pride. Besides, I don't know anyone who wouldn't want a hand to hold on their way out of this world, myself included. It doesn't seem like the kind of thing you should have to beg for.

I sit beside her on her bed and she pulls my hand onto her forehead and closes her eyes. On her chest, over her heart, is a fist-sized bruise, dark purple. The flesh there looks like it would be soft and wet to the touch, like pulp. Her body is marked with blisters, scratches, bruises, veins that look like they're trying to come through the skin. The wholeness of my own body, even with all its wrinkles and scars, suddenly seems unfair; she's just a girl after all.

She slips a hand between the buttons of my shirt and moves her burning fingers across my chest. I stretch out on the bed, the two of us shoulder to shoulder, and we lie there for hours. Her body where it touches me is a razor. The hours of the night stretch and blend. I wake up next to her and find that I'm crying, that I'm clinging to her wasted body. She smoothes her palms along my back and whispers to me, and all it does is make everything hurt more. I want to chase the darkness out from under her eyes, breathe life back into her, fill her up with mud if that's what'll make it work. I've never known a woman more painful, but I want to touch her all the same.

I say, "Look, let me take you home. You're too sick to be doing this. We'll go together."

She shakes her head.

"Take a good rest then," I say, "how do you expect to get better moving around all the time? Stay in bed a couple of days, why don't you."

"I don't want to rest. Let's drive the whole way tomorrow."

"It's got to be another eighteen hours."

"Please. I'll pay you if you want, let's just go."

"For Christ's sake, don't get insulting."

She wakes me up at dawn, trailing her fingers along my cheeks, and I'd wager she didn't sleep the whole night. As soon as I'm dressed she walks outside and gets in the car, and I don't argue.

By dusk my eyes feel like they're made of glass, but we're near the coast. I shake Del awake and ask her where she wants to go. She presses her hands against the window and squints into the darkness. "It all looks different than I remember it."

Whenever we pass someone on the street she calls out to ask for directions, and the people point and wave us along, if they answer at all. We turn onto a bigger road with cars buzzing past, and as soon as we do I can smell the ocean. Del shivers in the seat beside me and grips my knee so hard it aches. It's dusk, and against the skyline you can see the lights of a carnival turning on, first the ferris wheel, then the booths, sending up a blaze of bulbs and neon to replace the fading sunset.

"This the place?"

"I don't know," she says. "I think so. It was just an empty board-walk last time I was here."

She leans against me as we walk down the midway, our arms looped together. Del looks all around her, gawking as if she never saw a carnival before, like she fell asleep in her bed at home and woke up here and can't figure out what the hell happened in between. We come to an amusement stand and the barker starts in on me, *Win a prize for the pretty lady!* He's got to notice how she looks, but I guess carnies have seen just about everything. He smiles at her like she was Miss America, and I give him five dollars for a stack of baseballs to pitch at the milk bottles. I hate this game—they weight the bottles so that it's almost impossible to win—but I do all right, two bottles down.

"Anything in the bottom row," says the barker.

"Pick what you want," I say to Del.

She gets one of those glow necklaces and puts it on her head like a crown. The strange light makes her look almost normal. We buy an ice cream and a funnel cake and eat them next to the roller coaster.

"This is almost like a date," she says.

"I learned better than to date young girls like you; it's always trouble."

"Do you date dead girls? I bet that's even worse." She smiles, but it's not a real smile, and she starts crying.

"Come on, now," I say, and I put my arms around her and hold her head against my chest, green light from her glowing crown climbing up into my eyes. The roller coaster swoops over us, the people scream. The merry go round stops and a bunch of kids climb off and run past, laughing as they go. Del looks up and wipes her eyes with the back of her hand.

"Sorry," she says.

"Nothing to be sorry for."

"I thought I was going to make it."

"Who says you aren't?"

"I want to go down to the beach."

We find the stairs that lead us to the sand, and as soon as we take five steps the light and the noise from the carnival start to fade. I put my hand around her waist to help her walk. The sand is white and fine and cool as Christmas, and it'll turn your ankles if you're not careful. We go down to the water's edge where the footing is better, where the waves sweep against our toes. Del takes her shoes off and throws them into the ocean before I can stop her.

She takes my hand and guides it in between the buttons of her shirt, over her breast, presses it against the bruised spot on her chest. The flesh is even softer than I'd imagined; my fingers sink into it until I can feel her bones through her skin, and below them the shuddering of her heart.

"This is what I feel all the time," she says, "only it's the whole world beating." She pushes my hand closer until I'm afraid my fingers will go right through the skin, and that heart sounds like it could devour me.

Del

For a moment, with Rob's hand against my chest, I can almost imagine a life all my own, almost understand how that could be fulfilling. He holds me to him and I am alive wherever his body touches mine. But ghosts with my face surround me, six other hearts beat in time with mine. There is nothing I can give him because nothing I have is mine.

I step away from him, across the sand. A moist breeze skims my shoulders and I feel myself dissolve, as if the salt air could unravel my genetic code like a piece of knitting. Nature won't have me, won't let me buy my life with their deaths. Aberrations, abominations, Nature wants us gone. Who knew the world was so unforgiving, so eager to cull?

There are shells, says Helen, *don't cut your feet*, and every shell touches the sole of my foot seven times. There is nothing strange in this anymore, that she can choke to death on her own blood while I sleep in a roadside motel, and yet still be with me days later, whispering in my ear. *Walk into the surf,* my sisters say, *the ground pulls out from underneath our toes*; the waves are sevenfold in their coldness, the salt air seven times as pungent.

The water sings between my fingers, surges around my knees and shins as they press into the sand. *Drink deep,* my sisters say. This is where things crumble irrevocably, where there is nowhere left to go. We'll become salt. We'll become storm clouds on the water. And then emptiness, one to seven to one to zero in the space of twenty-three years. Science will have nothing to do with us anymore, nor we with it. We will be just a void in the cosmos, a dark place in the sky where there was once starlight.

OLIVIER SCHRAUWEN

∎

The Imaginist

FROM *Mome*

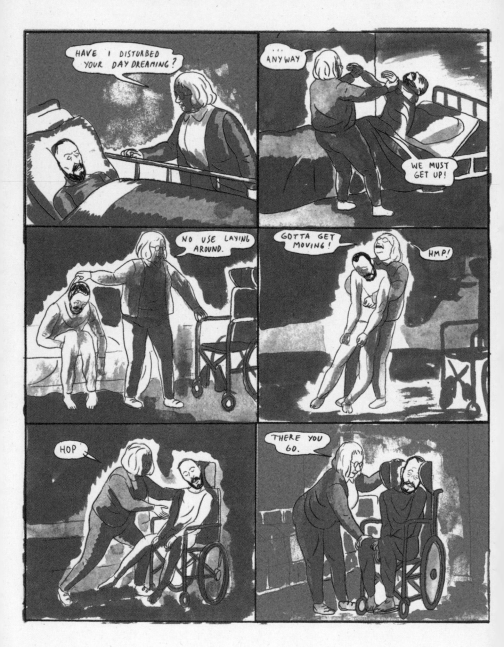

JAMES SPRING

■

Mid-Life Cowboy

FROM *This American Life*

AT THIRTY-NINE, I TOOK A LITTLE inventory of my life, and found myself to be unremarkable in almost every way.

For more than a decade I'd held a job writing ad copy and radio commercials in San Diego. I had a wife, two kids, two mortgages, Tivo, prescription reading glasses—and about twenty extra pounds that I no longer had the energy or ambition to lose. My fortieth birthday was only a couple of months away, in April.

My wife Kellie had a brighter attitude about it all. "We'll throw you a big party," she said. "It'll be fun."

"I don't think so," I said. I didn't want a party.

"It's your big four-oh," she said. "Think about what you want to do for it."

I did think about it, for a long time. And in the end, what I thought was . . . I'm going to do something . . . big . . . to help somebody else in a big way. It's going to be . . . a great big thing, and when it's done, I'm going to feel really, really good. And helpful.

"What do you mean help somebody?" my wife said.

"I don't know," I said. It was still pretty shapeless inside my head. I used to be a boat captain. I knew parts of Mexico better than pretty much anybody. Maybe that was a start.

"Who are you going to help?" my wife said. "Help them what?"

"I don't know," I said. "Something's going to come up. Maybe an earthquake will hit, and I'll help dig people out. Or maybe a helicopter will go down in Baja. I could help find it."

This was all met with the most epic of eye rolling. And sighing.

* * *

At least twice a week, this conversation continued to divide us. She'd talk about party planning, and I'd have to remind her that I might not even be around. I might be out. You know, rescuing people.

April arrived, and still no earthquakes or helicopters. So, one Friday, about five o'clock, right after work, I thought, maybe I should be a little more proactive. I did a Google search on two words that seemed to make the most sense for my plan: "Baja" and "missing."

It might be time to explain the "Baja" part.

In the late eighties, I worked in the area that the drug enforcement agency calls the western Mexico/Baja corridor. But I wasn't one of the good guys. It was over twenty years ago. I had just dropped out of college, and I was a little aimless, and I reconnected with a friend I'll call "Alex," back in San Diego. Alex had put together an enterprise moving methamphetamine along the west coast. Right about the time I arrived, a new law had been passed in the U.S. that made it tough to get the main ingredient—ephedrine . . . but I was pretty sure we could still get it in Mexico. The border was less than a half an hour away.

The ephedrine pipeline was easy to establish, and soon, it got filled with other stuff, too. Coke, marijuana. Personally, the drugs held no attraction for me, which made it easy to justify my actions. I mean, if these dirt bags wanted to ruin their lives with meth, let 'em.

It turned out I was really good at the job. I got to know my way around Mexico. Around the marinas and hidden ranchos and dirt airstrips. Around the cops and soldiers. I came to love the Baja peninsula. But during this time, the business was falling apart back on the U.S. side. Alex and his pals had developed bad drug habits, and they got really sloppy.

I'd been away in Mexico during two police raids on the house in San Diego. But I was there for the third one. I was arrested and taken to jail with the others. But the cops didn't have a warrant, and so they had to drop the charges.

I moved out of the house. A couple of weeks later, some bad guys came in the middle of the night. Black sweatshirts, black ski masks. They beat Alex into a coma, raped his girlfriend. They stole everything they could get their hands on.

After that, I packed up my red Jeep and I drove south to Baja. And I didn't come back for four years.

By the time I moved back to San Diego in 1993, I'd fashioned myself into an upstanding citizen. An ambitious and enthusiastic member of the workforce.

And life rolled along pretty much like I suppose it does for most people. An HMO, a 401k, a family. I kept waiting for the other shoe to drop. But life was really . . . steady. It was good—far better than I deserved.

And so, on the eve of my fortieth birthday, I brought up Google and typed the words "Baja" and "missing."

The top result was a day-old newspaper article about a fugitive couple wanted for kidnapping, and murder. The story, essentially, was that this couple, Richard Carelli and Michele Pinkerton, were a pair of chronic meth-heads who killed their landlord in San Francisco and then drove to Santa Cruz and kidnapped their own six-year-old daughter from the grandparents who had been given legal custody. And oh, yeah . . . also on the run with them—their two-month-old baby girl. With Down syndrome.

Clearly, these were not great parents. A year earlier, they were holed up in a motel when police raided their room and found them with a pile of stolen property and methamphetamines. Their daughter, Viana, then four years old, was found hiding under the motel bed. The newspaper picture of Viana showed a smiling little girl with blonde hair and blue eyes, and a dress with pink polka dots. She looked just like my daughter Addie.

Police had been searching for Viana and her parents for more than three months. This article said that a month earlier, a tourist might have spotted the family in a town called San Quintin, on Baja California's Pacific coast.

Methhead kidnapper murderers on the run. I was a former meth supplier. I absolutely do not believe in destiny. But Jesus Christ.

There was a link to a "missing" flyer with pictures and a phone number to call. I dialed, and a switchboard operator answered for the San Francisco police department. I realized I had no idea what to say.

"Hi," I said. "I'm calling about a flyer. For a missing girl. Viana Carelli."

"A flyer, sir?" the operator said.

"Or I guess, a poster?" I said. "Like a missing poster."

"Sir, do you know the whereabouts of a missing person?"

"No," I said. "I want to hel . . . I just need to talk to somebody in charge of the Viana Carelli case."

"Can you spell that, sir?"

I spelled the name. She put me on hold three times. Obviously I hadn't called the right person. I looked up other contact info for the San Francisco police department. I made a couple more calls, and quickly realized that I needed to fake a little more competence.

Here's what I was going to say: "Look, I'm certain that there is a team of officers and volunteers conducting canvassing and search parties. I would like to volunteer to join the effort."

But the conversation never got that far. Instead, each time, nobody knew what I was talking about. I finally convinced somebody to transfer me to the detectives' division. I got an answering machine message saying the office was closed until Monday morning.

The lack of information—the lack of interest—by the police department was surprising. Unbelievable, really. This whole story had become front page news because of the way the San Francisco police had already bungled it.

The newspapers said that after Carelli and Pinkerton's landlord was reported missing, the police didn't respond for a month. And when they did finally arrive at his building to look for him, they found his tenants, Carelli and Pinkerton, unwilling to let them search the property. A police dog keyed on Carelli's van in the driveway. There were bloodstains visible in the open garage. But the officers had no warrant. They allowed the couple to drive away in their beat-up, white Mercury sedan. The cops eventually towed Carelli's van, but then—incredibly—they didn't search it. On the impound lot, somebody finally looked inside and found the body of the landlord. He had been dead for six weeks. By this time, Carelli and Pinkerton were already hundreds of miles away. Cell phone records showed that they'd made it as far as Vegas. And then, for three months, nothing.

So maybe the San Francisco police were not the best resource here. I looked online for volunteer groups. Flyer passer-outers. Candlelight vigils.

Again, nothing.

All that was left, at this point, was the little girl's family—the grandparents, and an uncle that the newspaper had called the family spokesman. Probably every nut job in the world was calling them—the smarmy investigators and the psychics. Grifters, con men.

I found the uncle's phone number, and then just sort of dialed. It went exactly like you'd think it would. Which is to say, badly.

If your main objective in a conversation is to convince someone that you're not crazy, you've already lost.

Essentially, what the uncle said was: "Thank you for your concern. The police are doing everything they can. We appreciate the support."

And then the call was over.

I was on my own. To be honest, it felt sort of good. Sort of familiar. But better. Because I knew, without a doubt, that this was the right thing to do. I was going to Baja. Now I just had to go home and tell my wife.

She wasn't happy.

"You said you were going to help people in an earthquake," she said. "This isn't our problem. This isn't your fight." She was crying and yelling. "They're drug addicts! They're murderers!" She spent a long time listing reasons why I shouldn't go.

I understood why she was worried. Baja's rough. Every couple of weeks there's another string of beheadings, or a government official hung from a bridge—usually thanks to the drug cartels.

Last year a guy nicknamed El Pozolero—the stew maker—confessed to dissolving the bodies of more than three hundred of his victims in acid. These stories help keep Baja pristine. Free of tourists. Free of development. Free of laws. It is like the old Wild West. And like the old west, there's no cell phone service. So Kellie knew she couldn't even call me down there.

I kept repeating the one thing she couldn't argue with. "Nobody is looking for those little girls," I said. "If I don't go, who will?"

The next day—Saturday—I packed. Gas cans, topo maps, GPS, water jugs, Fix-A-Flat. I sent an e-mail to my boss saying that something sudden had come up, and that I would be taking a vacation week. Or maybe two. I took the lousy "missing" flyer that I had found online and redesigned it. I added a picture of the infant and a photo of a car in the *Autotrader* that matched Richard Carelli's white Mercury. I translated the flyer to Spanish, and changed the headline to read "*secuestrada*," which means "kidnapped." I went to Kinko's and printed twenty-five hundred copies.

Baja California itself is a dusty peninsula that begins near the San Diego/Tijuana border and ends a thousand miles later, in the resort town of Cabo San Lucas. There's only one road that runs from top to bottom, and at various points along the way, it passes tiny villages, and military checkpoints, and about two dozen of the state-run Pemex gas stations.

Without much to go on, this is what I chose to believe: Richard Carelli knew nothing of Baja. He spoke no Spanish and had no friends. He had no weapons at this point, and no money. The family was still traveling in the Mercury sedan. They would not willingly double back through military checkpoints or cross into areas where they would be required to show ID and register.

Between the beat-up sedan and the newborn, they had to be somewhere close to the highway.

I spent the first day passing out fliers—at gas stations, at police stations. At military checkpoints, where I also passed out old *Playboy* magazines I'd put in my truck to grease the skids with soldiers, a trick I resurrected from the old days. I made countless stops and starts. At every market and rancho near a dusty crossroads I told the story.

Not a single person had heard it before. But they were all titillated now, by the drama of the murderous couple and their poor children.

Just before dark I arrived in San Quintin, the town where the couple might have been spotted a month earlier. Taco stands, bars, hotels, campgrounds. Nobody had seen or heard of the family.

I went to bed sometime around midnight, but I couldn't fall sleep. I lay on the lumpy mattress and tried to envision every possibility. Were Carrelli and Pinkerton living in a village? Had they squatted at an abandoned ranch? Had they found a benefactor? Were they already dead? I wondered if maybe I was insane to be here. And sometime before I fell asleep, it hit me that they might not even have come to Mexico at all.

The next morning I woke to the sounds of roosters. Day Two. I got in my truck and headed south. I had my doubts, but I figured I had to keep going.

An hour later, I came to a tiny farming community called Santa Maria. I went into a market and left a stack of flyers. A small group of men was milling around a pot of coffee.

When I went back outside to the gas pumps, the guy who ran the market came out with one of the flyers in his hand.

"These people," he said. "They were here."

"Really?" I said. Somehow I doubted it.

He looked at the flyer again. "They bought water, milk, and potato chips. They asked if we sold diapers, but we don't."

His grocery list was so specific. They were here. They had to be.

"What vehicle were they driving?" I asked.

"This one." He pointed at the flyer.

"How long ago?" I asked.

"Three weeks."

The timing was exactly right.

"Did you see the children?" I asked.

"No," he said.

I thanked him and left, with a new plan. I would race straight down to the Baja Sur state line—the halfway point of the peninsula—where the family would be forced to register.

I would bribe the immigration officials for a peek at the book and confirm that Carelli and Pinkerton didn't sneak past. And then I'd double back, and I'd scoop them up like a net.

I was driving so fast now that the tires squealed on the turns. Before half an hour passed, I reached the village of El Rosario. The Pemex station there could be the last gas for two hundred miles.

I've probably filled my tank in El Rosario three hundred times. It was too important a place to not stop for a minute and hang some flyers. I jammed on the brakes and skidded across the lane into the gas station. I was posting a flyer near a gas pump when one of the attendants approached.

"Yo la vi," he said. "I saw her. The blonde."

"Where?" I asked.

"At pump number one," he said. "She asked me about a cheap place to eat."

"When?" I said.

"Three days ago."

"Three days?" I said. "Do you mean three weeks?"

"Days," he said. "Three days ago."

Next door to the gas station was a small motel. I showed the flyer to the two ladies working behind the reception desk, and when they saw it, they both shrieked and covered their mouths.

Yes, the family was here in El Rosario. They were living in a small house, just two doors away from the home of one of the receptionists. Yes, they were still driving the white car, but they had been trying to sell it in the village. And yes, the little girls were still with them, but the infant, whose name was Faith, was very sick. The blonde woman, they told me, was earning money by teaching dance lessons to children in the village for ten pesos an hour — a buck an hour.

The house was a hundred meters away. Less.

"What time are the classes?" I asked.

"Three o'clock," one of them said.

I looked at my watch. It was 2:45.

Carelli and Pinkerton were here. Now. A block away.

Things were moving so fast through my head that it felt like earth time had stopped. I could suddenly see everything that I needed to do next so clearly.

I told the women at the motel not to tell anyone about our conversation. I ran back to the gas station and ripped down the flyers and took back the stack I'd left. I needed to get my truck and its American license plates off the road. Fast. It was a tiny town. I had to assume that word would soon get back to Carelli and Pinkerton.

I drove a half-block to the town's small payphone office and hid my car behind the building. An operator connected me to the uncle in Santa Cruz.

"I found them," I said. I told him the story as quickly as I could. He gave me a phone number for a U.S. Marshal handling the case and I got him on the phone.

"I found them," I said. The U.S. Marshal seemed doubtful. Annoyed. I let him know that I could get together a team of local police and go get Carelli.

"Don't do anything," he said. "Call me back in one hour."

I looked at my watch again. It was now after three. Dance class was in session. If I called the U.S. Marshal back in an hour and he instructed me to contact the local cops — which was the only reasonable option — that whole process might take another hour. Maybe more. And it might be too late.

I went across the street to the cinderblock police station. Three cops were gathered around a small television, watching a movie with Chuck Norris and a midget. I later figured out the movie was *Lone Wolf McQuade*, the 1983 classic in which Chuck Norris's character makes an incursion into Mexico to take care of business.

Man: Hey Partner! Where you headed?
Chuck Norris: Mexico.
Man: Mexico!? What the hell for?
Chuck Norris: They got my daughter.
Man: Well hold on, I'm coming!
Chuck Norris: It's not your fight!
[motorcycle roars]

"I need to speak with the *comandante*," I said.

One of the cops leaned back in his chair. "I'm the comandante. What do you want?"

He was clearly irritated by the interruption, but he led me to a tiny room with a metal desk, and closed the door.

When I'd finished telling him the story, he radioed his off-duty cops and told them to report to the station immediately. They called for backup from San Quintin. The dance class was half over.

In the police station bulletproof vests were pulled from lockers. Weapons were loaded. One of the cops found an extra flak jacket that would fit me.

At the one hour mark, I dialed the U.S. Marshal from the telephone in the police station.

"It's no good," he said. "The paperwork is not in order." He told me we'd have to wait until tomorrow.

"There will be no tomorrow," I said. "There are two white men in this town. Richard Carelli, and me. And pretty soon he's going to know it—if he doesn't already. And then he's going to do whatever it takes to run again."

The Marshal exhaled sharply.

"Ugh," he said. "Call me again in a half an hour."

You've got to be kidding me, I thought.

I decided right then, I was not going to call the U.S. Marshal again.

The Mexican cops stood all around me, waiting for the word.

I told them that I needed to make one more phone call. I dialed the uncle in Santa Cruz.

"Look," I said. "The U.S Marshal says that we have to wait until tomorrow." I explained that it didn't have to be this way, that I didn't work for the U.S. Marshal. But this wasn't my decision. It was his family. Only he could decide.

He conferred for a few moments with the grandparents and then he said, "The paperwork will be ready by the time it's needed. Go do it."

Mexican federal cops arrived from San Quintin a few moments later—four unmarked truckloads full of guys with big mustaches and leather jackets. Most of them carried assault rifles.

One of the trucks was sent out to observe the house. They radioed back to the station that the children were out front with the mother. A few seconds later came the report that the father was now outside, too. The leader of the federal squad said "*Vamonos*." Then he put a hand on my chest and ordered me to stay put.

Ten minutes later they returned. Michele Pinkerton and the children were in the back of one truck. Carelli was handcuffed in another. They jerked him out of his seat and stood him in front of me, and when he saw me, the fight drained out of him. Any fantasy he might have held about the arrest being just a Mexican shakedown was dead.

He asked me why he was being arrested. I didn't respond. Viana stared out the door of the other truck wide-eyed and nervous. Michele Pinkerton was working hard to convince her daughter that everything was okay. She held the baby tightly in one arm and hugged Viana with the other, rocking them both gently against her.

We caravaned back to the federal headquarters, where a big group of cops whooped as Richard Carelli was pulled from the truck and led up to the station. Michele and the girls were taken out of the other truck, and Viana watched in horror as her father was led through the doors. She moved onto the sidewalk and stood next to me. She was really dirty, but she seemed healthy.

"Hi," I said.

"*Hola*," she said.

"Speaking Spanish now, huh?"

"*Si.*"

"You okay?"

"*Si.*"

The cops asked me to wait in one of the offices with Michele and the girls. Viana kept asking about her father. Michele assured her that he was fine. She was trying to find another blanket to wrap around Faith. The infant was so tiny, and her breathing was raspy. Michele did everything she could to not look at me. I sat for a long time, just watching her trying to stave off this new reality. Viana leaned over Faith and kissed her forehead. The baby cooed, and Viana laughed, and Michele draped her arms around her daughters and she smiled a smile so sad that I had to look away.

Carelli was next door in a jail cell. He called to me. "Sir. Excuse me. Sir. Can you please tell me why we're here? Sir, please . . . "

One of the cops entered the office where we sat and grabbed a leg shackle—this heavy, black, iron thing that looked like it belonged in a dungeon. He carried it to Carelli's cell. Viana started to cry.

"I have a daughter," I said to her. "She's four. She looks just like you. She likes to play princess. Do you play princess, too?"

Viana nodded.

Michele straightened up in her chair and asked me, "Are you from here?"

"No," I said. "I'm from California."

Her eyes teared up, and she nodded. "Yeah."

This was not what I signed up for. She just seemed like a mom. Where was the screaming? The blaming? The meth-head excuses? Where was all the horrible parenting? Had they all been cured by their time here?

Suddenly I didn't really feel like I was riding in on the white horse. I just felt like I was meddling with somebody's family. What right did I have to upend the lives of these two little girls?

"What does the baby need?" I asked. "Diapers?"

Michele nodded. "Yeah. And formula."

I drove into town, and bought way too many baby supplies, and some stuff for Viana, too. Then I stopped at a taco stand and bought three dozen *carne asada* tacos.

Viana lit up when she saw the food.

"Did you bring food for my daddy, too?"

I asked the cops if it was okay for her to deliver tacos to her father. I helped her make a plate and then followed her to the cell where her father was cuffed to the bars.

"Hi, honey," he said. "Are you okay?"

She nodded. He held her face in his hands and kissed the top of her head through the bars. They spoke softly for a few minutes. I tried to fade as far away as I could. Carelli fought to keep it together. He looked up at me. "Are you a bounty hunter?"

"No," I said.

"What are you?"

"I'm just a guy . . . trying to help."

He seemed to hold this for a long moment.

"Thank you," he said.

I looked down. "Yeah."

I called the uncle in Santa Cruz. Tried to explain what I'd seen. That the girls seemed well cared for. That they seemed loved. I told him that things were different than I had expected.

"Well," he said. "Viana loves her grandparents, too."

I drove home the next day. I didn't know it yet, but the media was already in a full frenzy. CNN and CBS and Fox were calling my office. All the news reports were pretty black and white.

Reporter: . . . and after a whole month, police had no luck finding the girls, but one guy did in just two days. James Spring . . .

They were calling me a hero. But I didn't feel like one. In a lot of ways, I felt like a home wrecker. I did a couple of interviews, but they went poorly.

Reporter: How in the world did you pull this off? You went to Mexico, and what did you do?

Spring: Basically I created a flyer in Spanish, and the thing about Baja . . . .

So I stopped.

The one bright spot in all the coverage, the one moment that made me feel like maybe I had done the right thing, was some video shot at the airport, when Viana got off the plane in the U.S.

Viana: Grandma!

[Viana sees her grandmother at the arrival gate, and yells "grandma," and runs into her arms. They're both crying.]

Grandmother: It's okay, you're home now.

I must have watched that video a hundred times.

All week, the phone calls didn't stop. Producers were trying to buy the movie rights. Long-lost relatives tried to reconnect. Everybody was calling. Except Viana's grandparents. I had been thinking of them a lot. I just wanted to know that the girls were happy—not happy, but, you know . . . that they were okay. That they were going to be okay. But the grandparents didn't call. I couldn't call them—I mean, they had to be overwhelmed. I felt like maybe I'd intruded into the girls' lives enough already.

But I needed to do something. I sent a huge box of presents to the kids, and a notebook for Viana so she could write letters to her parents. On the inside cover, I wrote her a note. I tried to make her understand why I'd done this. It was kind of an explanation, kind of an apology. Even though I knew she was way to young to comprehend any of it.

I got no response.

And then I started learning some odd things.

On one newspaper's website, I found a comment from a guy who said he was Michele Pinkerton's brother. He called her "white trash" and said that he hoped she was brought to justice for her crimes.

A reporter told me that he'd interviewed the grandfather, and that the guy had made some pretty hateful remarks about Richard Carelli—about hoping that Carelli would become some big black guy's girlfriend in prison.

And then there was a photographer who'd been sent to take pictures of the family, who gave an equally depressing report. He said he couldn't shoot any photos in the house because it didn't look like children even lived there. No toys, no kid stuff on the walls. But of course, that doesn't mean anything. That's just cosmetic. It didn't mean they weren't taking good care of them or didn't love them.

I didn't know what to believe. I was worried about those little girls. And nothing I'd heard since Baja was making me feel any better.

Eight months passed. A trial date was set. And then one day, in the middle of the week, I got a call from Viana's grandfather.

It wasn't a thank you, but it was like a "Man, that thing you did in Mexico was really something." And I said, "Yeah?" And then he reiterated his hopes that Viana's father be raped in prison every day for the rest of his life. He told me that the trial was about to begin, and that I might get some phone calls from prosecutors. And then, the call was over.

Carelli was charged with first degree murder. He admitted the landlord had died during a fight they had, but said it was unintentional. At trial, the details came out. The landlord's lip was busted open, his nose was broken. He was badly bruised, and had been stabbed with a small knife. His body was found wrapped in a sleeping bag, bound with duct tape, and buried under a pile of trash in the back of the van. The official cause of death was suffocation.

The defense argued that meth had given Carelli a condition called hypofrontality—meaning he couldn't think straight, so he made wacky decisions, like storing a corpse in his van. And kidnapping his daughter. And fleeing to Baja. In other words, the meth made him do it. Which, as a former meth smuggler, didn't make me feel so great.

The trial ended with a hung jury. Richard Carelli wasn't convicted of first degree murder. He'd have to be retried on a lesser charge.

At some point I got a phone call from a private investigator. Michele Pinkerton's public defender had hired the guy to track me down.

"Miss Pinkerton says that you spent a couple of days with her and the kids in Mexico," he said.

I told him that seemed a strange way to describe it.

"Did you see her," he asked, "interacting with the children?"

I told him that I did.

"Well, she was thinking you might have some good things to say about what you saw there . . . "

It took me a moment to understand that I'd just been asked to be the character witness for a convicted meth addict and accused murderer who'd taken her kids on the run. And in a way, I was really tempted. Because she did seem like a good mother on that day—a mother who loved her kids, anyway, and whose kids loved her. But I couldn't do it. None of this had really turned out like it was supposed to—not like I imagined it would. I was afraid to nudge the outcome again, one way or another. I did not want to put my thumb on the scale. I could think of too many ways my testimony might just make things worse.

This was none of my business when I went to Baja. And it wasn't my business now. Only now I knew it.

Editor's note: In the nearly two years since his fortieth birthday, dozens of people who heard about what happened have contacted James, asking him to help find their missing loved ones. He's decided to help out in a few cases. There was the paranoid schizophrenic in Laguna Harbor, the guy who's been missing for thirty years, the tow truck driver's missing wife, the father who stole his son and fled to Mexico. His current case is a missing family of four in Southern California. He says his wife is not too crazy about any of this.

JAMES STURM

■

Market Day

FROM *Market Day*

I WARD OFF FURTHER SINISTER THOUGHTS BY FOCUSING MY ATTENTION ON THE IMMEDIATE.

THE ROTE.

AS I HAVE DONE SINCE CHILDHOOD, I COMPULSIVELY COUNT MY FOOTSTEPS.

THREE HUNDRED ELEVEN, THREE HUNDRED TWELVE

IT IS NOT UNLIKE WEAVING— THE COUNTING, THE MEASURING

A REASSURING RHYTHM THAT PROTECTS FROM UNCERTAINTY.

IT IS IN THIS MANNER I PROCEED.

I IMMEDIATELY TRY TO THINK OF HOW I COULD REFLECT THIS MOMENT IN A RUG. A SMALL STREAK OF COLOR SLICING THROUGH A LARGE BLOCK OF GREY.

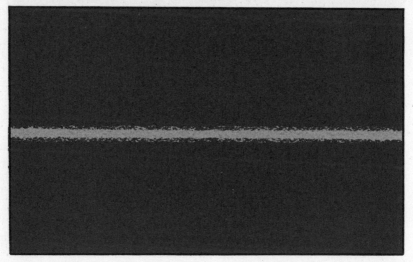

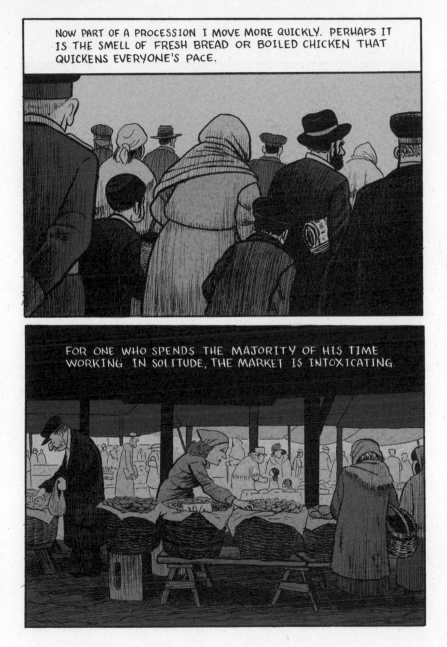

NOW PART OF A PROCESSION I MOVE MORE QUICKLY. PERHAPS IT IS THE SMELL OF FRESH BREAD OR BOILED CHICKEN THAT QUICKENS EVERYONE'S PACE.

FOR ONE WHO SPENDS THE MAJORITY OF HIS TIME WORKING IN SOLITUDE, THE MARKET IS INTOXICATING.

FIRST AND FOREMOST, I LOVE THE ABUNDANCE. IT MAKES YOU BELIEVE THE DAYS OF SCARCITY AND WANT WILL NEVER RETURN.

I LOVE THE CHILDREN, OBLIVIOUS TO EVERYTHING BUT THEIR OWN FUN...

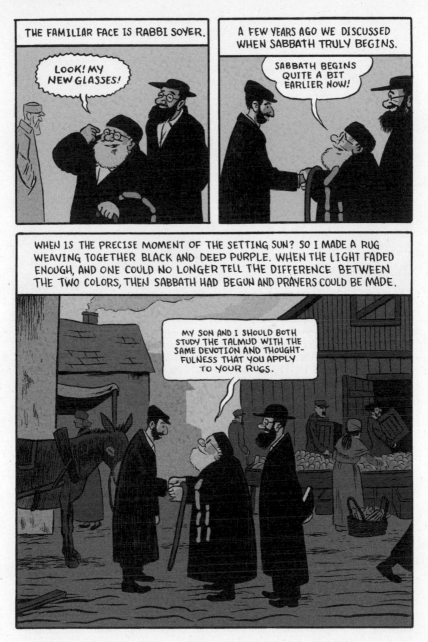

YES, A RUG SHOULD COVER YOUR FLOOR AND BE MADE STURDY AND SOUND AND LAST MANY YEARS. BUT GOD ALSO TELLS US IT IS OUR HOME THAT IS OUR MOST SACRED SPACE. THAT NEITHER THE HOLY NOR THE PROFANE CAN EXIST WITHOUT THE OTHER.

SOMETHING AS COMMON AS A RUG CAN INDEED EMBODY THE GIFTS AND MIRACLES OF GOD—THE FIRST STEPS OF ONE'S CHILD, THE MOMENT SABBATH BEGINS, OR THE GLORIOUS BUSTLE OF MARKET DAY.

HOW WOULD THIS ALL COME TOGETHER AS A SINGLE RUG?

JOAN WICKERSHAM

■

The Boys' School, or the News from Spain

FROM *Agni*

The Other Girl

She was small, sullen, dressed in a short skirt and white vinyl boots, wearing pale lip gloss.

She was the only other girl in the boys' school.

She didn't smile when you were introduced. "I'll show you where the ladies' room is," she said; and before you knew it you were standing inside it with her. It was the kind meant to be occupied by only one person. "I'll wait outside," you said, and she said, "Why?" and lifted her skirt and sat down.

She was your age, thirteen. She was rich, you saw when you went home with her one day after school. A young blond man, who worked for her mother, picked you both up after study hall and drove you to her house. A big new house, like a ranch on a TV show—new wood, a huge staircase with too many spindly banisters, lots of red plush. There were horses, and there was an indoor swimming pool, and a pantry full of sweet things. She ate half a bag of cookies, coolly, standing there. "Shouldn't we go easy?" you asked. "Won't they mind?"

"Who's they?" she said.

She and her mother were both named Lily. Everyone called the mother Big Lily, and the daughter was Lily Joyce.

Big Lily ran a factory, which was somewhere else on the property.

Big Lily owned so many acres that the factory was invisible; you never saw it. You never knew what it made, either—something invented by Lily Joyce's father. She didn't talk about him, except to tell you once that he had shot himself ten years ago and that's when her mother had taken over the company.

Later the two of you went swimming in the pool—you in one of Big Lily's bathing suits which, embarrassingly, fit you; Lily Joyce in a small white bikini. Chlorinated steam wafted up from the water; the air was hot and murky and stinging, and the light was thick and green. The young man came in and watched you and Lily Joyce swimming for awhile. Then he pulled off his shirt and jumped into the water. He teased Lily Joyce and chased her and picked her up and threw her toward the deep end. She came down screaming, splashing, flailing to get away from him. He threatened to pull down her bikini top, and she laughed and laughed.

The next year Big Lily married him. He was twenty-two; Big Lily was forty-seven.

"What's it like to have him as a stepfather?" you asked.

"It's okay," Lily Joyce said, with no expression on her face.

The Math Teacher

He was brusque, but also enthusiastic. He came to class every morning with wet hair, but it never dried, so maybe it was oiled. You could see the neat trails of the comb in it, like ski tracks in the snow. Sometimes in the winter, when you went for a walk in the afternoon—the boys were at sports, but there was nothing for the girls to do between lunch and afternoon study hall—you saw him skiing in the woods. He raised his ski pole to show he had seen you, a salute, and then went on, churning and sliding away under the fir trees.

He was German, or Scandinavian: pragmatic, blue-eyed. He had a crisp energetic encouraging way about him. You liked him but felt guilty around him; he seemed to think better of you than he should have.

In class, he—Mr. Sturm—wrote big columns of numbers on the blackboard, underlining the answers and the equal signs so hard that the chalk squeaked. Then "There!" he would say, turning away from the board toward the class. "Everybody get it?"

Nobody did, but no one said anything.

"Any questions?"

There weren't.

His Wife

She wore her black hair piled on top of her head, a lofty delicate structure composed of many soft, elaborate, little puffs. A *croquembouche*, you realized years later, coming upon a picture of one in a magazine and instantly thinking of her. All of her was like that—something confected in a bakery. She smelled sweet, her white skin was powdered, her nails were tapered and polished pale pink; when she raised her finger in the classroom, you could see the sun shining pinkly through her fingertip.

You were nervous around her at first, because you started in the school at mid-year and you had never studied a foreign language before. In class the first day she said something to you in Spanish which you didn't understand. Then she asked you in English to conjugate the verb "*decir*." You sat there while she smiled encouragingly, and finally you said that you didn't know what "*decir*" meant, and you didn't know what "conjugate" meant. The boys laughed. She swiftly told them, "You may not realize it, but you are being cruel and ignorant." You were grateful for, but embarrassed by, this; it felt like too fervent a defense, too much championing over too little a thing.

She started meeting with you in the afternoons to give you a crash course. Once you got the hang of it, you loved Spanish, memorizing lists of verbs, showing off to her what you'd learned since the last time. " . . . *viviremos, viviréis, vivirán,*" you would finish triumphantly, and she would say, "*Muy bien, Marisol!*" "Marisol" had nothing to do with your real name—a dull, one-syllable thud of a name, you thought—but you had chosen it from the list of Spanish girls' names she'd showed you on your first afternoon with her. "Don't I have to pick one that's sort of the Spanish version of my name?" you had asked.

"Why? Pick a name you wish your parents had given you," she said—and so became something else you'd always wished for, a kind of godmother. A woman who was not your mother, or an aunt, or one of your mother's vaguely impatient friends. A woman who paid attention to you as a *girl*. Your mother cared about different things: books, politics. "You can be anything," your mother told you fiercely; and you believed her—with an amendment, also fierce but too humiliating to be said aloud: You could be anything, except pretty. You didn't know how. Hair, skin, nails, clothes—yours were terrible, or at least inept. In those afternoons at Mrs. Sturm's house, you saw things—ruffles, rose-colored lipstick, a fur collar, a charm bracelet shifting and twinkling on a delicate wrist bone—that you didn't see at home, and certainly were not going to see anywhere else at the boys' school. You learned that prettiness was a possible thing to care about, even if you didn't have any idea how to achieve it.

Still, even as you yearned for it, you worried that it was, in fact, trivial—that she might be trivial. In class, she would write on the blackboard, in her big, airy script, *Las noticias de España*. You knew, from headlines on the front page of *New York Times*, which was always lying around in your house, that there was actually news from Spain that year: Franco's death, elections, uncertainty about the new king's allegiances. Mrs. Sturm's news was news of nothing, news of fluff. *Esta semana es Las Fallas*, she would write, and you would dutifully copy it down, imitating the curly tips of her capital "e" and the way she had of writing "a"s like the "a"s in printed books, fat little structures with curving roofs. She explained, glowing with gentle excitement, that the festival of Las Fallas involved the building and burning of large puppets! It was very festive! Perhaps someday you would all go to Valencia and see this for yourselves! Her news was full of festivals—this one was a mass-participation drum festival, that one was a reenactment of a battle between Moors and Christians, fought over a papier-mâché castle. Constant bullfights, lots of flamenco—but sometimes there were special bullfights and special dances—La Feria de Sevilla!

"Olé!" she said, standing at the blackboard, stamping her little heels, lifting her hands still holding the chalk in a graceful dancer's pose. The boys snickered, more than they would have dared to with a teacher who intimidated them but not as much as they would have with a teacher they disliked.

You didn't snicker, but you were embarrassed for her—the nakedness of her fantasy of herself as a fiery senorita. You wanted to protect her. Look at me! she seemed to be crowing, innocently, like a naked child darting into the living room during a dinner party. You wanted to wrap her in a blanket and gently lead her out of the room.

After a couple of months you didn't need extra help with Spanish anymore. You'd caught up with the boys, and you were doing well in class. But you kept going to Mrs. Sturm's house: she started having you and Lily Joyce over on Monday afternoons. "We women have to stick together," she said.

She gave you tea in translucent flowered cups, along with cookies that, like everything of Mrs. Sturm's, were small elusive feminine mysteries. What did they taste of? Lemon? Vanilla? Something pale and delicate. Something far removed from the hunky chocolate things you and Lily Joyce tore into together standing in Big Lily's crammed dark pantry.

The Boys

There were so many of them. All those heavy shoes clomping down the stairs and along the corridors between classes, all those tweed sport coats. During morning chapel, sitting there with your head bowed as the school chaplain said prayerful things in a stagey voice, you thought: There are two hundred and twenty-seven penises in this room.

Trying to Describe It

You couldn't. One weekend you were invited to a slumber party in the town you had moved away from earlier that year, where you'd gone to a regular public school. That night, when you were all sitting around in your pajamas, the girls — your old friends — asked you what it was like to go to school with all those boys.

"It's fine," you said.

"You must be so popular!"

"I guess," you said.

"Do you just kind of . . . have your pick?"

"Well," you said. "It doesn't really work that way." You tried to explain that being one of only two girls made you conspicuous. It made boys not want to be seen talking to you. They were afraid of being teased. They didn't want to stand out, to be different. In a way this was true. But in another way you knew, even as you were saying it, that it was wise-sounding bullshit. Nobody minded being seen talking to Lily Joyce. The boys kidded her, exchanged loud insults with her in the halls, grabbed her green book bag and tossed it to one another over her head as she ran back and forth with her arms waving, trying ineffectually to retrieve it; they imitated her shrieks — "Aaaaah! Aaaaah! Waaah. I'll tell! I'll *tell!"* — and she laughed at the imitations while continuing to shriek that she *would* tell.

Lily Joyce was a small, cute, flirty girl. You were tall, heavy, serious — somehow not a girl at all. You were conspicuous but invisible. The boys who spoke to you asked how you had done on the math test, or if you understood this whole diagramming sentences thing.

You couldn't tell this to your old friends. What's wrong with me? you thought, and tried not to think, all the time. You worried that there was some fundamental thing that might be missing, some difference between you and other girls that was just now starting to show itself but that would become more and more apparent as you grew up, like the progressive divergence of two nearly parallel, but not parallel, lines.

Von Bruyling

Once, though, a boy did say something to you.

"Any time you want it, I can give it to you."

He was older, a ninth grader (the school only went up through ninth grade), someone whose voice had changed, who shaved. He said it to you in a low voice, coming up behind you on the stairs and smoothly passing you before you were sure you'd actually heard him.

But you did hear him. His name was von Bruyling. You hadn't liked him, even before he muttered to you on the stairs — he wasn't nice, he wasn't smart. You got that what he'd said had been a joke. A mean joke. You, he was implying, were the last person who would ever want it, and the last person he'd ever want to give it to.

Still, sometimes after that when you were home lying on your bed, with the door shut and your hand between your legs, you thought of von Bruyling's stupid face, and his low voice growling those words over and over.

The Double Bass

Another embarrassment: To play an instrument that looked like you. They'd assigned it to you, or you to it, in your old public school, because you were tall and strong and could physically handle it. Now you were stuck with it. Double bass players were rare, so you'd won a scholarship to take lessons at a conservatory. Your mother, almost maniacally proud of what she had decided must be prodigious musical talent, drove you there every Saturday. The double bass lay across the back seat, its neck and scroll sticking out through the open car window; you wished for a tree growing a little too close to the road, or the sudden press of a tunnel wall. The bass decapitated; you and your mother safe; but your mother somehow knocked sensible, agreeing to let you quit.

Your bass teacher loathed you for loathing the instrument. Every lesson was the same: You would plunk out a few notes, and he would stop you. "Did you practice?"

"Some," you would say.

"You have to practice."

"I know."

Practicing was the most boring thing you had ever done. Plunk plunk plunk (rest). Plunk plunk plunk (rest). That was pretty much how the double bass part went in every piece of music your teacher assigned you. He was right, you never practiced.

Then one afternoon at school, a boy came up to you and said, "I hear you play the bass."

"Yeah," you said, wary. You weren't expecting another von Bruyling incident—this kid was younger, and he seemed nice—but you had found that in this school humiliation lurked everywhere and jumped out when you forgot to look for it.

"Because I'm putting together a rock band," the boy, whose name was Henderson, went on.

So then you were the bass player in a rock band.

During the whole time you were in it, the band played only one number, over and over, a song called "Groovin' With Mr. Bloe"—which, in turn, at least the way your band played it, had only one phrase of music, repeated over and over. The bass part went:

Plunk plunk-plunk-plunk, plunk-plunk-plunk, plunk-plunk-plunk plunk; and so could not claim to be much more interesting than the bass parts your conservatory teacher assigned you. But playing in a rock band felt strange and glamorous, out of character for you. Upstairs in your room you practiced "Groovin' With Mr. Bloe" with a diligence and fastidious musicality that would have made your conservatory teacher cry if he had ever had the chance to see it.

After a few weeks you made up your own words to "Mr. Bloe"—an incantation for Henderson to fall in love with you—and sang them softly in your room while you practiced, and silently whenever you played with the band.

Telling

Eventually you told Lily Joyce. "Huh," she said. "Henderson?" She'd been waiting a long time for you to start liking a boy. In the time you'd known her she'd liked Stewart, Cook, Childs, McDonald, Chesborough, Hilts, and Sperber. They were all boarders at the school; they would get off-campus permissions to go to her house on Saturdays, mostly one at a time but Chesborough and Hilts she invited together, because she liked them both.

"What do you do when they come over?" you had asked her once.

Lily Joyce shrugged. "Swim. Listen to records. Sometimes we make out." With Chesborough she had played something called Seven Minutes in Heaven. You didn't know what it was, and you didn't ask Lily Joyce to explain. But Chesborough was another one of those manlike, shaving ninth graders; and Lily Joyce's exact words were, "I let him play Seven Minutes in Heaven," so you sort of knew.

"Why Henderson?" she asked you.

You weren't going to give Lily Joyce a list of reasons. *He's so clean. I like how his eyes are blue and his eyelashes are dark. I even like how his glasses are held together on one side with tape. He's a very serious, not very good guitarist.* You didn't like him because of those things; it was more that you liked those things because you liked him. "He's cute," you told Lily Joyce.

This was a term she recognized and honored: it was valid currency with her. "What are you going to do?" she asked.

"Do?"

"*I* know. You need to get Mrs. Sturm to put you with him at the dance."

There are children who are too old to be children. It stops being a problem when they get older—they grow into themselves—but before that happens it's perpetually awkward. For you it was a mix of judgment and wistfulness. You thought all this stuff was stupid, but you also had no idea how to get it, and you wanted it.

"Oh, goody. Let's," you said to Lily Joyce. She laughed; she liked it when you were sarcastic. Egged on, you grabbed her hand and started skipping toward the Sturms' house. The two of you skipped along the colonnade, laughing, just as the boys were trailing out of their dorms to go down to the gym for sports. You felt wildly happy, bounding forward with the wind blowing against your face and hair, with all those boys watching. (Later, though, you'd use the memory to humiliate yourself: it had felt like two pretty girls skipping along a colonnade but it must have looked like big you galumphing along beside little Lily Joyce.)

Mrs. Sturm made tea and put out the mysterious pale cookies on a flowered plate. You sat in her living room, where she had always had a fire going on these winter afternoons. "Well, ladies," she said.

"Ask her," said Lily Joyce to you.

"No, that's okay," you said. You knew that Mrs. Sturm was in charge of organizing the upcoming dance, and that each boy from your school would be "put with" a girl bused in from some girls' school. But asking her to put you with Henderson seemed crass to you, dishonorable. She liked you; didn't you owe it to her not to take advantage of that fondness by asking for a special favor? Maybe you would end up with Henderson anyway, either accidentally or because Mrs. Sturm, with her almost magical delicacy, would somehow know without being told to put the two of you together.

Besides, you were afraid to tell her you liked a boy. You didn't want to bore her, or make yourself look silly.

But Lily Joyce was pointing at you. "Mrs. Sturm, she wants to be put with Henderson for the dance, and I want to be with Sperber."

Mrs. Sturm went over to her writing desk—a small, many-compartmented thing that she had told you was an old campaign chest from the time of the Napoleonic wars—and came back with a pad and a tiny pencil. "Lily Joyce, Jeff Sperber," she said, writing. She smiled at Lily Joyce, and then at you. "And Mark Henderson?"

You nodded, emboldened by her matter-of-fact feminine complicity: all right, you would throw yourself onto the conveyor belt and let it carry you toward the dance.

"Mark Henderson," she said in her light silvery voice as she wrote. "Very sweet boy." She smiled at you again. "*Muy bien, Marisol.*"

At the Dance

Your band played. You were up on a platform, grooving with Mr. Bloe. Then suddenly Henderson lifted his head and yelled out, "Drum solo!" and the kid on drums went crazy for a few minutes, banging out what sounded like a big collision of pots and pans and sandpaper all happening in a bowling alley. "Keyboard!" yelled Henderson, and you started to realize that you were going to be next. Shit. "Bass!" shouted Henderson, and the other instruments quieted down and there you were—the lighting didn't change but you felt like it had and that you were suddenly standing in a cone of merciless brightness—and you didn't know what to do but you settled for plunking out your usual sequence of notes with what you hoped was special emphasis, as loudly as possible, twice; and then you nodded at Henderson and he went into his own loud, squeally guitar solo which, you saw then, had been the whole reason why he'd accorded solos to the rest of you.

Seeing this—how badly he had wanted to play this energetic, incoherent solo, how transparently he'd tried to hide his desire to do it, how the tape on his glasses gleamed beneath the lights—made you tender toward him, and maybe a little less shy when Mr. Bloe finally came to an end and you laid down your instruments and joined the dance. Still, you were pretty shy.

"Mrs. Sturm put us together," Henderson said, leading you over to the punch table.

You shrugged. Mrs. Sturm winked at you from her seat by the refreshment tray.

You and Henderson fast-danced. Then you slow-danced. He held one of your hands and put his other arm around your waist, leaving six inches between you: mannerly, respectful, correct, a relief, disappointing. Everyone else was hugging, barely moving. All these strange girls had arrived on a bus, pretty, in pretty dresses, and had gone in straight for the kill. Their faces were buried in the shoulders of the boys from your school. They were letting themselves be touched, and kissed, forgetting or not caring about the teachers who were chaperoning. Sperber's hands were moving lower on Lily Joyce's back; her dress was hiked up and you could see the striped cotton of her underpants. Mr. Sturm came over and said something to them, and they moved apart a little. The Sturms danced: majestically. They looked like ice skaters. It would have been funny, if they had done it with any less grace or dignity.

In the last slow dance Henderson pulled you gently to his chest and you were one of the hugging couples. "I like you," he said, low against your ear. "You're my girl."

In Your Bed

You replayed it over and over. He holds you. "I like you," he says. "You're my girl."

You Are Normal

Or if not quite normal, then at least pretty close.

Your Godmother

"I'm so glad for you," Mrs. Sturm said. "Tell me everything."

You did. About how Henderson was getting off-campus permissions now and coming over to your house, often, on Saturday afternoons. How much he liked your parents, and how much they seemed to like him. How your mother cooked for him: pot roast, spaghetti and meatballs, rice pudding—he said her rice pudding was his favorite dessert ever. How he teased your little brother and sister (he introduced himself to them using an outlandish false name, and refused to back away from it even when they shrieked at him to tell them the truth), and how they teased him about his accent (he was from Kentucky). How gentle he was when he petted your old German Shepherd. How you and he went for long walks in the fields and woods behind your house, how the two of you never ran out of things to talk about.

"He's a nice boy," Mrs. Sturm said. "A real gentleman."

This was an afternoon when the two of you were alone in front of her fire, an afternoon when you'd just dropped by hoping to see her. Lily Joyce was home with a cold. You would not have talked this way if she'd been there. You wanted to tell Mrs. Sturm these things about Henderson: she would understand them. Lily Joyce was always trying to pry things out of you, but if you told her she would call it "the sappy stuff," and want more details about the kissing. "Has he tried to put his hand inside your shirt yet?" she would ask, in a voice that was impatient, excited, but also gruff and businesslike: if the answer had been "yes," she would have had an entire set of campaign plans ready to unfurl and explain to you in detail. "Of course not," you said, and you could see her rolling up the plans again and putting them away.

You had talked to Lily Joyce some about the kissing—you had technical questions that you knew she would be able to answer—but you didn't mention it to Mrs. Sturm. It was private; and your conversation with Mrs. Sturm was about something more. You didn't use the word—neither of you did—but you were talking about love.

"When I met my husband," she told you, "I knew right away. I was very young. Not as young as you are, but young. It was my junior year of college, I was spending it in Madrid. He'd finished graduate school—he studied mathematics at Göttingen, did you know that?—and he was backpacking around Europe with a couple of friends. We met standing in line to get into the Prado."

Suddenly you were nervous. You were moved that a grownup—this grownup—would talk to you so frankly. But you had never heard of Göttingen or the Prado; didn't want to interrupt to ask what they were; hoped she wouldn't quiz you on them later. And though you dreamed about marrying Henderson, you didn't expect to actually do it. You loved Mrs. Sturm for taking you seriously, but she was taking you too seriously.

"I was intimidated," she said. "He was older. So confident. He had so many languages—German, Spanish, Italian, French, even some Dutch. And so handsome! Unattainable, I thought when he spoke to me. But he did speak to me. Smitten, he told me later. Right away he was smitten. He told me I was beautiful." She smiled at you, and there was a silence. She wrapped her soft cream-colored shawl more tightly around her shoulders and crossed her arms, hugging herself.

For some reason you expected that now she would say something about children, about how sad it was that she and Mr. Sturm didn't have any. But what she said next surprised you.

"Marry for kindness."

The front door opened and Mr. Sturm walked in.

"Well," Mrs. Sturm said. "This is a surprise." She trailed a white forearm over the back of the sofa, and he came and took her hand.

"Darling," he said, and kissed her forehead. "A pleasant one, I hope."

"We were just talking about you."

"*Sturm und Drang*," he said, and she laughed and so did you. You had heard him make this joke in math class, after he'd assigned an especially tough problem to solve. You could tell from the way she laughed that she had heard the joke before, too, and that she was protecting him from knowing how many times he'd already told it.

Men

You were getting that men were strong and fragile, powerfully tempting and dangerous, gentle and mean, impressive and obtuse, in need of both placating and protection. Meanwhile the boys' school kept ticking away with its own peculiar, habitual brutality.

The day after spring vacation ended and all the boarders came back to school, a boy in your English class was crying. He was quietly but audibly sniffling, and his face was red and wet.

"What's the problem, Lederman?" the teacher asked. "*Homesick?*"

The boy didn't answer. The teacher stood up, came out swiftly from behind his desk, grabbed the back of Lederman's blazer, and lifted him into the air. He carried Lederman—a small boy, he dangled like a kitten—to the door, opened it, and threw him out into the hall.

"Stay there until you're ready to start acting like a man."

No one spoke to Lederman after class when the bell rang and he came back into the classroom with his head down to collect his book bag. So you didn't either.

There was a prayer you all said in morning chapel, right after the Lord's Prayer. It started with *Dear Lord in your wisdom guide my steps,* and it ended: *Make me strong and sound and more a man each day.*

The News

One morning in Spanish Mrs. Sturm fainted. She was in the middle of *Las noticias,* talking about one of her innocent, rustic, pinkly romantic festivals — something about bulls, as usual, bulls and flowers — when she suddenly said, "Oh," and then folded sideways and slid to the floor.

Several of the boys jumped up and ran to her. They stood around, they knelt, one boy very lightly patted her shoulder. "Mrs. Sturm," he said. "Um, Mrs. Sturm."

You got up and went over, too. "What should we do?" the boys were saying.

Her eyelids flickered and she made a series of soft, mewing little moans. "Oh . . . oh . . . oh." She tried to sit up. "Oh . . . " and her head sank down again.

You didn't try to help. You loved her, she'd been so good to you; but watching her lying on the floor, you felt no alarm, no sympathy. Only a cold disapproval at the whole performance. That's what it seemed like to you: a performance. The graceful slump to the floor, the bewildered fluttery coming-to amid a group of worried, gallant males — this was one of your own secret fantasies for yourself. You would faint, Henderson would catch you, bend over you, revive you. You had imagined it, but you would never actually permit it to happen. You felt, austerely, that she could have chosen not to faint. You thought this sort of thing was controllable. You recognized this scene and deplored it. She was a grownup; she should have known better.

Two of the boys helped her to sit up, supporting her shoulders with surprisingly competent and unafraid solicitude. Someone ran to get help from the front office. "I'm all right, I'm all right," she kept murmuring. You saw that her hair was coming down: the structure had toppled, not all the way but it was listing, and some of the little puffs were unwinding and sticking out in tufts from her head. That's when you recovered your tenderness for her, and your love; and you pitied her.

The next day the science teacher taught math; and the assistant headmaster sat in the classroom during Spanish while you all did exercises out of the textbook. Mrs. Sturm was sick, you thought, and Mr. Sturm must be taking care of her. You were coming down the stairs to go to lunch when Lily Joyce grabbed you by the arm and pulled you into the ladies' room. "Did you hear about the Sturms?"

"Are they having a baby?" you asked, with a sudden wild lift of joy. That would fix everything, you thought, without beginning to think yet about what it was that needed fixing.

"No, no," Lily Joyce panted, "she's been sleeping with the boys."

"What boys?" you asked stupidly. You honestly didn't understand what she meant.

Lily Joyce lifted her arm and made a big circling gesture that seemed to encompass the entire school. "*These* boys. I don't know who all of them are yet, but . . . " and she mentioned a few names, mostly boys you knew by sight but had never spoken to. Then: " . . . and von Bruyling," she said.

"That's disgusting," you said; but all of a sudden you believed her.

"She's fired," Lily Joyce whispered, unlocking the ladies' room door — you would both have to run, if you didn't want to be marked down in conduct for being late to lunch — "and he quit. They're leaving."

What You Saw

Early the next morning, when your mother drove you to school, the Sturms' pale blue station wagon was turning out of the main driveway as your car slowed to turn in. You saw that the car was packed full with their things. He must have been driving, but you didn't see him. What you saw, in the quick blur of their car turning away from yours, was her drooping head resting on her hand, and her pale forearm propped against the window.

The Rest of the Story

You never knew it. Not all of it. But you got some pieces, over the years. You heard more names, of more boys. Some were big muscled football players, some were small and childlike and scholarly. There was no pattern.

You heard that Mr. Sturm had hanged himself. You had no way of knowing if it was true. You remembered him coming home unexpectedly that afternoon when you and Mrs. Sturm had been talking, and you wondered if he'd been trying to catch her with a boy, or trying to prevent her from doing something she couldn't stop herself from doing.

You thought of her saying, "Marry for kindness."

You graduated from the boys' school and went on to another school, where you were happier.

You heard that Big Lily had come home from the factory one day and found the young blond man—her husband—in bed with some girl, had thrown him out, had cracked up and spent time in a sanitarium, had come home and gone back to running the factory and a number of local charities as well. You heard that Lily Joyce dropped out of high school and married a gas station attendant and moved out west.

You got a letter from Mark Henderson, followed by a visit. You were both seniors, at different boarding schools. He came to see you one Sunday and took you out for a drive. "I need to tell you something," he said. "I feel really bad about this. I need to get it off my chest. I used you."

You laughed. "For what?" Those careful little kisses?

"To get to a home," he said. "I was so homesick. I wanted to eat with a family, around a table."

"That's all right," you said. "You don't need to apologize."

"Yes I do," he said. "I shouldn't have done it. I shouldn't have acted like I really liked you when really I was just using you."

"It was years ago," you said. "You were a child. Don't worry about it."

Then he asked if you were seeing anyone. "Sort of," you hedged. You weren't, but you were afraid he might ask if you were interested in him.

"*I'm* seeing someone," he said. "A woman." Then he said, "She's a teacher. My dorm mistress, in fact. We joke about that."

So you wondered, then, though the idea of him and Mrs. Sturm had never occurred to you before.

Many years later you heard he was back in Kentucky, working as a high school teacher. You wondered about that, too.

The End

You went to Madrid with your husband. You were in your forties. You stood in line with him at the Prado, and for the first time in years you remembered the Sturms. You told your husband. "What a terrible story," he said. He was holding your hand.

While you waited you looked around at the people standing in line with you. Parents with children, nuns, old men, a group of students shoving one another and laughing, all wearing the same blue cap. You saw beautiful women and smitten men. You thought about how lovers, or any two who fascinate each other, choose in rapture and ignorance.

The line moved and you and your husband moved with it, slowly, toward the old building, where the people who'd waited longest were disappearing, being swallowed into its shadowy mouth.

CONTRIBUTORS' NOTES

Daniel Alarcón is the author of two story collections, a graphic novel, a book of interviews, and *Lost City Radio*, winner of the 2009 International Literature Prize given by the House of World Culture in Berlin. He was recently named one of *The New Yorker's* "Twenty under Forty," and is cofounder of *Radio Ambulante*, a series of monthly Spanish language audio documentaries debuting in early 2012.

Adama Bah is a twenty-three year old student living in East Harlem, New York. Her story is one of eighteen oral histories in the *Voice of Witness* book *Patriot Acts: Narratives of Post-9/11 Injustice*, edited by Alia Malek. *Voice of Witness* is a nonprofit book series that uses oral history to illuminate human rights crises. For more information, visit voiceofwitness.org.

Tom Barbash is the author of the novel, *The Last Good Chance*, and *New York Times* best-selling nonfiction book *On Top of the World*. He has held fellowships from the NEA, The MacDowell Colony, and Yaddo. His stories and articles have been published in *Tin House, One Story, The Virginia Quarterly Review, ESPN* the *Magazine*, the *New York Times, Bookforum*, the *Observer*, the *Missouri Review*, and other publications. He currently teaches in the MFA program at California College of the Arts.

Clare Beams's short stories have appeared or are forthcoming in *One Story*, *Willow Springs*, and *Inkwell*, among other places. She is a graduate of Columbia's MFA program in fiction. She and her husband now live in Massachusetts, where she teaches ninth-grade English. She's at work on more stories and is finishing up a novel.

Joshuah Bearman once wrote eight thousand words about the metaphysics of Ms. Pac Man for *Harper's*, compiled an entire volume of writing on the Yeti, and has spent a lot of time with aspiring Fabios, real life superheroes, international cat burglars, and the lone survivor of the Heaven's Gate cult. He has written for *Rolling Stone*, *Wired*, the *New York Times Magazine*, *Salon*, *Slate*, and is a contributor to *This American Life*. He is working on a memoir called *St. Croix*.

Sloane Crosley is the author of the *New York Times* bestsellers *I Was Told There'd Be Cake*, which was a finalist for the Thurber Prize, and *How Did You Get This Number*. She is a weekly columnist for the *Independent* and editor of *The Best American Travel Essays 2011*. She lives in Manhattan, where she's a regular contributor to *GQ*, the *New York Times*, and National Public Radio.

Tim Crothers is a former senior writer at *Sports Illustrated*, and has contributed to *ESPN the Magazine* and the *New York Times Magazine*. He is the author of *The Man Watching*, a biography of University of North Carolina (UNC) women's soccer coach Anson Dorrance, and coauthor of *Hard Work*, a biography of UNC basketball coach Roy Williams. He is currently writing a book about Phiona Mutesi, set to be published in 2012.

Don DeLillo was awarded the 2010 PEN/Saul Bellow Award for fiction. He was born in New York City in 1936, and his many novels include: *White Noise* (1985), winner of the American Book Award for fiction; *Mao II* (1991), winner of the PEN/Faulkner Award; and *Underworld* (1997), one of the best three novels of the last twenty-five years, according to the *New York Times* in 2006. His most recent novel, *Point Omega*, was published in 2010. DeLillo lives in Bronxville, New York, with his wife.

William Deresiewicz is a critic, essayist, and the author of *A Jane Austen Education: How Six Novels Taught Me About Love, Friendship, and the Things That Really Matter.* He is a contributing writer at *The Nation* and a contributing editor at the *New Republic.* His work has also been published in the *New York Times Book Review, Slate, Bookforum,* the *Chronicle of Higher Education,* and elsewhere. His work was nominated for a National Magazine Award in 2008, 2009, and 2011. His current book project is to be called *Excellent Sheep: The Disadvantages of an Elite Education.*

This past spring, **José Hernández Díaz** graduated from the University of California, Berkeley, with an English degree. Next, he plans to do an MFA in creative writing. His favorite poets are those of the Chicano Renaissance, as well as the Beats. Hernández has been published in *Bombay Gin, ABCtales, La Bloga,* and *The Peak.* He's an active member of the online group "Poets Responding to SB1070," where he has posted eight poems in an effort to resist the Arizona law.

Anthony Doerr lives in Boise, Idaho. He's the author of four books: *Memory Wall, The Shell Collector, About Grace,* and *Four Seasons in Rome,* and his writing has won three O. Henry Prizes, two Pushcart Prizes, the Rome Prize, the New York Public Library's Young Lions Award, and a Guggenheim Fellowship.

Neil Gaiman has written acclaimed books for both adults and younger readers, and has won many major awards, including the Hugo and the Nebula. His novel *The Graveyard Book* was the only book to win both the Newbery and Carnegie (UK) medals. His *New York Times* best-selling books include *Coraline* and *Stardust* (both adapted into films), *American Gods,* and *Anansi Boys.* His comics series *The Sandman* was described by the *Los Angeles Times* as "the greatest epic in the history of comic books."

Mohammed Hanif was born in Okara, Pakistan. A former head of the BBC Urdu Service, he is the author of *A Case of Exploding Mangoes,* which won the Commonwealth Prize for Best First Book in 2009. He lives in Karachi.

Ralph Haskins was born and raised in Monterrey, Mexico. His family moved to South Texas during the social turmoil of the 1960s. The new cultural challenges he experienced led him to express himself through poetry. Today, Ralph lives in McAllen, Texas, where he supplements his poet's income by moonlighting as a science teacher at a local high school.

Amy Hempel's *Collected Stories* won the Ambassador Award for best fiction of the year, and was one of the *New York Times'* Ten Best Books of the Year. She has won the REA Award for the Short Story, and the PEN/Malamud Award for Fiction. She teaches writing at Harvard and Bennington College.

Javier O. Huerta is the author of *Some Clarifications y otros poemas* (Arte Publico, 2007). He is currently studying for his Ph.D. in English Literature at the University of California, Berkeley.

Chris Jones writes for *Esquire* and is a contributor to www.grantland. com. He also keeps a blog about writing at www.sonofboldventure. blogspot.com. He lives in Port Hope, Ontario, with his wife and two sons. He doesn't get much sleep.

William Joyce has achieved worldwide recognition as an author, illustrator, and leader in the digital animation industry. He was named by *Newsweek* as one of the one hundred people to watch in the new millennium. He is also a cover artist for *The New Yorker* and a member of both the Producers and Writers Guilds of America. Projects based on his works have been successfully translated into feature films and television shows, including *Robots, Meet the Robinsons, Rolie Polie Olie,* and *George Shrinks.* Joyce is currently codirecting *The Guardians,* an animated feature for DreamWorks. More at moonbotstudios.com.

Charlie LeDuff is a Pulitzer Prize–winning writer, filmmaker, and multimedia reporter. He works for the *Detroit News,* and was previously a national correspondent for the *New York Times.*

J. Robert Lennon is the author of seven books, including *Mailman, Castle*, and *Pieces for the Left Hand*. His next novel, *Familiar*, will be published in 2012. He teaches writing at Cornell University.

Sylvia Maltzman grew up in Miami, a fact which is often reflected in her poetry. She has a bachelor's degree in English from Florida International University and she plans on tackling a master's as well. Her writing has appeared in various venues nationally and internationally, including the webzine *Arachneed* (India), and she has put out a self-published poetry collection, *Down to the Wire*. Tutor, teacher, and assistant are a few of the hats she wears daily, along with a blue straw fedora. She's in love with the ways that God gets our attention through nature; hence, her favorite quote is from Walt Whitman: "Look for me under your boot-soles."

Mac McClelland is the human rights reporter for *Mother Jones*, and has been described variously as "a total badass" by the *American Prospect* and "a profane young bisexual" by the *Wall Street Journal*. Her piece in this collection was nominated for a National Magazine Award, and was adapted from her 2010 book *For Us Surrender Is Out of the Question*.

Joyce Carol Oates is the author most recently of the story collection *Sourland* and the memoir, *A Widow's Story*. She is the 2010 recipient of the Ivan Sandrof Lifetime Award from the National Book Critics Circle and has been a member, since 1978, of the American Academy of Arts and Letters.

Michael Paterniti's stories have appeared in numerous publications, including the *New York Times Magazine, Harper's, Esquire*, and *GQ*, where he is a correspondent. He is the author of an upcoming book entitled *The Telling Room*, a true tale about cheese and revenge in a small Spanish village.

Padgett Powell is the author most recently of *The Interrogative Mood*. His book *You & I* is being published in England this fall.

Henrietta Rose-Innes is a South African writer based in Cape Town. Her latest novel, *Nineveh,* was published by Random House Struik in August 2011. She has also published a collection of short stories, *Homing*, and two previous novels, *Shark's Egg* and *The Rock Alphabet*. In 2008 she won the Caine Prize for African Writing, for which she was short-listed in 2007. She received the 2007 South African PEN Literary Award and was a runner-up for the 2010 Willesden Herald Short Story Prize.

Anjali Sachdeva likes to hike in the back country and ride the bus for days at a time. Her work has been published in *Northern Woman*, *Sonora Review*, *Alaska Quarterly Review*, and elsewhere. She lives in Pittsburgh and is an assistant editor at *Creative Nonfiction*.

Olivier Schrauwen was born in Belgium in 1977 and studied animation at the Academy of Art in Gent, and comics at the Saint Luc in Brussels. He currently lives in Berlin.

Gary Shteyngart was born in Leningrad, U.S.S.R., in 1972, and emigrated to the United States seven years later, settling with his family in New York. He is a graduate of Stuyvesant High School in New York City; Oberlin College in Ohio, where he earned a degree in politics; and Hunter College of the City University of New York, where he earned an MFA in Creative Writing. He is the author of two novels: *Absurdistan* and *Super Sad True Love Story*. Shteyngart now lives in the Lower East Side of Manhattan. He teaches writing at Columbia University and Princeton University.

James Spring's stories have been featured on various National Public Radio programs, including *Stories from the Heart of the Land* and *This American Life*. His hobbies include riding dirt bikes and locating people who have disappeared in Latin America. He lives in San Diego.

James Sturm is the cartoonist of *James Sturm's America, Satchel Paige: Striking Out Jim Crow, Adventures in Cartooning, The Fantastic Four: Unstable Molecules*, and *Market Day*. He is also the editor of *The Center for Cartoon Studies Presents*, a series of historical graphic novels about the lives of notable Americans. His comics, writing, and illustrations have appeared in scores of national and regional publications including the *Chronicle of Higher Education*, the *Onion*, the *New York Times*, and on the cover of *The New Yorker*.

Samuel Clemens, later known as **Mark Twain**, was born in 1835 in the small town of Florida, Missouri. The pseudonym came from his days as a river pilot: "mark twain" is a term that means "two fathoms," telling pilots the water is deep enough to navigate safely. Clemens/Twain grew up in Hannibal, Mississippi, and at thirteen left school to become a printer's apprentice. He soon became an editorial assistant, a river pilot, and later a newspaper reporter. He wrote twenty-eight books, including *The Adventures of Tom Sawyer* in 1876, and *The Adventures of Huckleberry Finn* in 1885. He died in 1910.

Joan Wickersham's *The Suicide Index* was a National Book Award finalist, and her short stories have appeared in various publications, including *The Best American Short Stories*. Her essays are published every other week in the *Boston Globe*'s op-ed section. "The Boys' School, or the News from Spain" is part of her new book of fiction, which is all about love.

THE *BEST AMERICAN*
NONREQUIRED READING
COMMITTEE

FOR ANOTHER YEAR, the student committee in San Francisco was joined from afar by a group of talented Michigan high schoolers. Based at 826michigan (in Ann Arbor) and led by Kendra Shaw, this contingent of the *Best American Nonrequired Reading* (*BANR*) committee, like the students in San Francisco, unearthed articles and stories, read them, sparred over their merits and flaws, and helped with the sprawling task of putting together this collection.

 Melanie Bahti is from Ann Arbor, and went to Greenhills High School while working on this book. She is currently living in Morocco and will be attending Bryn Mawr College in 2012. She likes to drink tea and look at maps. Her favorite piece in the collection is "We Show What We Have Learned." It makes her nervous.

Erin Baughn is a junior this fall at Community High School in Ann Arbor, Michigan, where she spends her Novembers furiously writing for National Novel Writing Month. She procrastinates writing novels by watching anime. Erin is a Facebook stalker, a regu- lar stalker, and is possibly being stalked herself. If you were to look in her window late at night, you would find her baking, or watching

Glee or *American Idol.* Erin is also an obsessive fangirl about: Scott Westerfeld novels, music by Tokio Hotel, and black holes.

 Hanel Baveja is a sophomore this fall at Huron High School in Ann Arbor, Michigan. Her favorite authors include J. D. Salinger, John Updike, and playwright Walter Wykes. She plays soccer and the clarinet, and enjoys reading, writing, and Tuesday night *Best American Nonrequired Reading* meetings at 826michigan. Her favorite story this year, if she had to choose just one, is "The Boys' School," by Joan Wickersham, because it's like a quiet storm that just keeps building and building and it's really quite glorious.

Ezra Brooks-Planck is a fan of Michael Crichton, Robert Jordan, and Ricky Gervais. He is a sophomore this fall at Chelsea High School in Ann Arbor. An avid anglophile, he sometimes speaks in an English accent, drinks British tea, and uses English vocabulary. He enjoys fighting dragons, goblins, and kobolds, and likes to raise his sword in the air and yell, "For Stormdine!" His favorite selection this year is "Art of the Steal," because he has always liked the idea of being very stealthy.

 Sophie Buchmueller is a senior this fall at Pioneer High School in Ann Arbor. She enjoys reading, traveling, and being outside in the sun. She can't stand the cold, and winter is her least favorite season. She plays lacrosse for school and club teams, and plays Ping-Pong for fun. Her favorite piece is "Art of the Steal," because it is too outrageous to be true, except that it is.

Claire Butz is a sophomore this fall at Pioneer High School in Ann Arbor. She loves playing field hockey, even if it means dribbling around her room before bed. Claire is a member of the Ann Arbor Area Community Foundation's Youth Council and helps to distribute grant money to organizations that work with youth.

By the time you read this, **Julia Butz** will be a freshman at Georgetown. A native of Ann Arbor, Michigan, Julia attended Greenhills High School while working on this book. Highlights over the years include: the Ann Arbor/San Francisco penpal exchange, scheming ways to procure free cupcakes from the shop across the street, and dissecting new stories to understand what makes "the best." Her favorite piece in the book this year is "Market Day."

Gabby Cabarloc is a senior this fall at Unity High School in Oakland, California. The things she likes to do most include changing her hair color based on the time of year, hanging out with her dog, and procrastinating on her homework. She also likes concerts and browsing antique stores. Her favorite story in this year's book was "Pleiades," because it felt so personal.

Sophie Chabon has been writing herself bios since the third grade, just waiting for one to be published. Now, as a junior in high school in San Francisco this fall, her sentence construction and diction are much better than when she was younger. As a result of her constant bio writing she has tired of listing her interests, and would instead like to provide the reader of her forty-five thousand nine hundred and thirty-seventh bio with a piece of advice, which she swears is the only advice the reader will ever need. Grow a mustache. (Her favorite story this year is "A Hole in the Head," because it is wonderfully written, and incredibly fun.)

Gabe Connor lives in San Francisco. Gabe only wears Grandma's leftover Christmas sweaters; flannel is overrated. His new band, the Dronettes, have been described as "Ronnie Spector with Robert Smith's hair, sprinkled with glitter by T. Rex and set on fire by

Dee Dee Ramone." Gabe daydreams. He is currently trying to get out of high school, but while he was working on this book, he was a junior at Gateway High School in San Francisco. Now he is a senior. His

favorite story in the book was "We Show What We Have Learned," because it made the classroom setting a lot less boring.

Kitania Folk was a junior while editing this book, and she is a senior now, at Lowell High School in San Francisco. She enjoys brioches, Japanese writers, walking all over San Francisco, and the moment when you know that an experience you've had is going to be a great story. She's been told she's a good storyteller. She believes that people should get to do what they want to. According to the people close to her, she drinks too much coffee, but what can she say, she likes the taste and she does what she wants to. Her favorite piece in this anthology is "Butt and Bhatti," because it shows how sprawling chaos can stem from one specific person's point of pain.

Sarah Gargaro is a sophomore this fall at Greenhills High School in Ann Arbor, Michigan. She enjoys sweaters, good books, Latin (but not the verbs), and consuming or concocting delicious food. She's a talented whistler and a Michigan football fan. She also has a birthmark on her back in the shape of a girl chasing a rabbit.

Evan Greenwald—what a guy. You've somehow already met Evan. He's there, at the back of your head. Think about it. You'll realize you're already in love. You're in love with him and now he's being whisked away to Sarah Lawrence College, eighteen years old, so soon, flashing you the kind of grin that burrows itself into your eye sockets and does a modest little jig. You're clawing after him with your hands, but he's gone. Your hands are hammier than you remember. Jesus. Is it unsettling? To be inexplicably heartbroken over someone in a matter of seconds? It's okay, it's okay. Evan's here. *[Editor's note: This bio was written by Paolo Yumol. Evan, a native of the Bay Area, went to Marin School of the Arts in Novato, California, while editing this book. He reports that his favorite story in this year's collection is "The Boys' School," because it "eerily reflected events of my childhood, which makes me feel instant and old."]*

Michelle Grifka is a freshman at the University of Chicago. While editing this collection, she went to high school in Ann Arbor (she doesn't want to say which one). She likes sweet over salty, classical over jazz, and prose over poetry. Her favorite piece is "Best American Adjectives, Nouns, and Verbs Used in Reporting on the Gulf Oil Spill of 2010" for two reasons: One, it shows the funny/interesting side of a serious issue, and second, it proves that journalism isn't boring after all, but colorful and worth reading.

Connor Haines is an unpleasantly stereotypical nerd. A native of Ann Arbor, he is now, as you read these words, attending Cornell College in Iowa. He attended a high school in Ann Arbor, and he refuses to name it. His hobbies include reading, writing, *Dungeons and Dragons*, video games, making snide comments, and being irritated. Among other eccentricities, Conner eats cake frosting on hamburgers. His favorite piece in the collection is "Market Day," because the quiet dignity and concerns of the protagonist make him very likeable, and the setting for the story is unusual.

Christian Hernandez is a senior this fall at Unity High School in Oakland. He was born and raised in Oakland. He is an Oaklander, though he would never actually refer to himself this way. He's a musician on the rise. He loves to write poetry, song lyrics, and play any instrument, but especially the guitar. His favorite story this year is "A Hole in the Head," because it's a thriller, and it makes the reader feel like he or she is right there in every scene.

Quinn Johns is a sophomore this fall at Huron High School in Ann Arbor. Quinn spends his free time reading a variety of both fiction and nonfiction. He enjoys writing quietly during Michigan summers. His favorite piece is "We Show What We Have Learned," because of the unexpected conclusion.

Althea James has spent her whole life growing up in the same house in San Francisco. While working on this book she went to the Urban School (in SF), and this fall she is a freshman at the University of California, Santa Cruz. She enjoys storytelling, drawing, and taking the bus. She recently read the Harry Potter books for the first time and now wishes she was a wizard. Her favorite piece in this year's collection is "Art of the Steal," because it makes her want to be rebellious yet respectful at the same time, which seems like a pretty good goal in life.

Dorrian "Lyric" Lewis is a sophomore at City College in San Francisco, studying music. While working on this book she completed her freshman year, and recorded music. She is a cancer survivor, but still keeps a smile on her face. She sings and writes poetry, and performs around the Bay Area. Dorrian loves to laugh. Her favorite story in this year's book was the oral history of Adama Bah.

Michelle Li, a native of San Francisco, was a sophomore at Mission High School while editing this book, and is now a junior. She enjoys watching documentaries and eating watermelon slices. She dreams of traveling the world, to every continent. So far, she's been to North America, Asia, and Africa. Her overall favorite story this year was "Art of the Steal," because it was unlike anything she'd read before.

Tenaya Nasser-Frederick, who attended high school at his home in San Francisco while editing this book, is starting at Bard College either this fall or in the fall of 2012. He likes spending time with his cat, Seymour. He remains a devoted student of Hindustani music and Swedish massage. Tenaya cannot get enough of Percee P. His favorite piece this year was "Second Lives," because it had so many layers.

JuJu Miao is a junior this fall at Huron High School in Ann Arbor, Michigan. When she's not stressing about schoolwork, she's listening to her iPod, reading comics, doodling, or goofing off with her friends. She loves to travel, but hates airplanes, and hopes that teleportation machines will be invented in her lifetime. This is her second year with *BANR* and she has enjoyed meeting all the goofy/funny/smart/just-plain-awesome editors. She has not changed a lot since last year. Her favorite piece in the book is "The Imaginist," because it really shows how a little imagination can change your life.

Theo Olesen grew up in Brooklyn and Berkeley. He was a senior at Berkeley High School while working on this book, and is now a freshman at a college in New York that he does not feel comfortable naming for various unexplainable reasons. His favorite colors are black, white, and gray. His favorite story this year is "A Hole in the Head," because it's the only one with a title that makes it sound like it could have been written by Ice Cube.

Viggy Parr attended Greenhills High School in Ann Arbor, Michigan, while working on this book, and is a freshman at Georgetown this fall. She enjoys volleyball, photography, creative writing, community service, and science. She loves to read novels, short stories, and poetry. She plans to double major in English and Biology, then earn a Ph.D. in microbiology. "Orange" is her favorite piece in this year's collection because it is quirky and funny.

Alia Phillips went to a high school (she won't name which one) in Ann Arbor while working on this book. She is a freshman at McGill University this fall. She enjoys photography, eating, and bios that don't sound like online dating profiles. Favorite things include: alliteration, summer, and www.stumbleupon.com, but she would also settle for a soft pretzel. Her favorite piece in the book is "The Imaginist," because of how the two story lines combine in the end.

Andrew Sanchez attended Oceana High School in Pacifica, California, while working on this collection. He is beginning his first year at City College in San Francisco this fall. Andrew enjoys nineties hip-hop, green apples, and anything that expands his mind. Don't ask him what his favorite color is. Andrew's favorite story this year was "The Deep." His mind was expanded whilst reading it, thus deepening the crevices in which brain worms live.

Rachel Shevrin attended high school in Ann Arbor, Michigan, while working on this anthology. This last was her third year on the committee. When she is not discussing stories in the basement of 826michigan, she is probably dancing, teaching middle school kids about social justice, or taking naps in sunbeams. She hopes you've enjoyed this book, and was wondering if you would be her friend. She's a freshman at the University of Washington this fall.

Nick Shiles is also a freshman at the University of Washington this fall. He attended Sacred Heart High School in San Francisco during his tenure with *The Best American Nonrequired Reading*. He enjoys eating grilled chicken sandwiches, and other types of sandwiches, too. Namely turkey, or even the occasional BLT. He also enjoys tango dancing and other Latin American cultural activities. His favorite sport is curling and he hopes to one day curl like a Canadian. His dislikes include (but are not limited to): avocados, rust, newly laid concrete, mayonnaise, communism, and capitalism. His favorite story in the book this year is "Mid-Life Cowboy," because he has a special affinity for *This American Life* and he is very happy to see a *TAL* story in the collection.

Carlos Reyes "The Hammer" Tambis was born in Puebla, Mexico. He lives in the Mission District in San Francisco and attends there the School of the Arts academy, where he is now a senior. (While working on the book you have in your hand he was, logically, a junior.) He has a dog named Chloe, and his interests include: video games, movies, hanging out with friends, homeland security, sports, and good food. He plans to go to college and would love to someday live in Tokyo. His favorite thing, above all, that he read this year was *Richard Yates* by Tao Lin, because he — Carlos — feels he is in a similar situation. He wishes an excerpt from it would have made it into this year's anthology.

 Chloe Villegas never finished that story about the lions. She was a senior at International High School in San Francisco while working on this book, and she went to her senior prom in a jaguar costume. She is a freshman at Bard College this fall. Her favorite story this year was "Weber's Head," for its suspense. Still, she wishes the story about the cat that died and got cremated (and whose ashes were then thrown all over two stunned adults by their strange child) would have gotten into *BANR* that one year.

By the time you read this, **Marley Walker** will be a freshman at Syracuse University, majoring in Journalism and Cultural Anthropology/Geography. A native of San Francisco, she attended the School of the Arts while working on this collection. Marley has been a lifelong vegetarian, and, as a vegetarian that did not eat a lot of vegetables in her youth, her proudest moment was succumbing to the deliciousness of tomatoes on May 17, 2010. Going Zorbing is the number one thing she would like to do in the near future. For now, though, she gets her thrills from spending excessive amounts of time outdoors. It is a great day when she can lie in the grass at the park on a beautiful afternoon, spread a map out in front of her, and plan a trip. Unfortunately, this also includes pondering what measly jobs she can hold down in order to save up enough money to go to Ukraine, India, Bangladesh, Burundi, Tobago, and many, many other places. Marley's favorite trip to date was a one thousand mile bike ride around Nova Scotia. Her favorite piece in the book this year is "For Us Surrender Is Out of the Question," because it's a travel narrative, but it's journalistic and reads like good fiction.

Elise Wander is a freshman at the University of Chicago this fall. She attended Community High School in Ann Arbor, Michigan, while editing this anthology. When she lived in Ann Arbor, Elise drove a truck named Sebastian. She likes pencils and the piano, and spends her time stringing words together.

Karen Yu attended Galileo High School in San Francisco while working on this book. She is a freshman at the University of California, Irvine, this fall. She plans to major in East Asian studies and psychology. In two years, she intends to study abroad in Korea.

She likes to listen to music and watch Korean dramas, and she also loves to sing opera. Her favorite story in the book this year is definitely "Art of the Steal," because it gives the audience a window into how a thief thinks.

Paolo Yumol is a sunshine kind of guy. He walks into a room and you just have to say, "There he is!" Then he says, "Here I am!" He is always wearing headphones, even in his sleep. He makes you want to eat yogurt. Really. You think that I am making that up, but one day you will meet him and you will say, "Oh, so that's what that bio was talking about!" As you read these words, he is beginning his senior year at Lick-Wilmerding High School in San Francisco, where he jumps on the walls and then jumps off the walls and says, "Surprise!" They love him over there. *[Editor's note: This bio was written by Evan Greenwald. Paolo reports that his favorite piece in this year's book was "The Deep." "The entire story," he says, "feels like swallowing a fat, salty taco."]*

Special thanks to assistant (to the) managing editor **Kendra Langford Shaw**, and to editorial assistants **Amanda Foushee**, **Jill Haberkern**, **Jennifer Howard**, **Jordan Karnes**, **Emily McLaughlin**, **Nicole Pfaff Moore**, **Ben Shattuck**, **Brian Short**, and **Michael Zelenko**. Thanks also to the following organizations, institutions, and citizens: 826

Valencia, 826michigan, Houghton Mifflin Harcourt, Nicole Angeloro, Mark Robinson, Walter Green (who, it should be noted, designed the cover), Jared Hawkley, Charley Locke, Brian McMullen, Adam Krefman, Eli Horowitz, Andrew Leland, Andi Mudd, Russell Quinn, Jordan Bass, Juliet Litman, Mimi Lok, Chris Ying, Michelle Quint, Sunra Copeland, Greg Larson, Laura Howard, Juliana Sloane, Gerald Richards, Nínive Caligari, Leigh Lehman, Erin Archuleta, Ryan Lewis, Mariama Lockington, Lauren Hall, Miel Alegre, Kelly Martin, Anne Farah, Raúl Alcantar, Valrie Sanders, Margaret McCarthy, María Inés Montes, Miranda Tsang, Vickie Vértiz, Justin Carder, Marisa Gedney, Emilie Coulson, Rebecca Power, Gina Gagliano, Amy Sumerton, Amanda Uhle, Catherine Calabro, Becca Pickhus, Megan Levad, Tao Lin, Daniel Gumbiner, Lauren LoPrete, Ian Huebert, Peggy Burns, Eric Reynolds, Paul Baresh, Trish Farnsworth-Smith, Merrilee Heifetz, Isaac Fitzgerald, Emily Condon, Courtney Moreno, Stephanie Long, E. G. Kaufman, Mrs. Gummidge, all the poets ever, Ibarra Brothers, Babylon Burning, and Golden Gate Copy Service. Also, William Tell.

NOTABLE
NONREQUIRED READING
OF 2010

BRYAN CHRISTY
  The Kingpin, *National Geographic*
STEVEN CHURCH
  All of a Dither, *Agni*
JOSHUA COHEN
  The Joshuas Cohen, 2010, *Puerto del Sol*
AUDREY COLOMBE
  White Horse, *Puerto del Sol*
R. CRUMB
  The Sweeter Side of R. Crumb, W. W. Norton
S. J. CULVER
  First-Order Differential Equations, *Puerto del Sol*

LAWRENCE-MINH BÙI DAVIS
  Like the Locked Antlers, *McSweeney's*
VANESSA DAVIS
  Big Fun, *Make Me a Woman*
ERICA JOHNSON DEBELJAK
  The Apple and Paradise Too, *The Pinch*
JANINE DI GIOVANNI
  The Book of the Dead, *Granta*
MARK DOSTERT
  Behavior Management, *Cimarron Review*
BRIAN DOYLE
  King of the Losers, *New Letters*
KATHERINE DUNN
  Rhonda Discovers Art, *The Paris Review*

SARA EDWARD-CORBETT
  The Bird, The Mouse, and the Sausage, *Mome*
JENNIFER EGAN
  Safari, *The New Yorker*
JOSH EMMONS
  Arising, *The American Scholar*
SUSAN ENGBERG
  A Clean Bowl, *Epoch*
BRECHT EVENS
  The Wrong Place, *Drawn & Quarterly*

B. H. FAIRCHILD
  Logophilia, *New Letters*
KALI FAJARDO-ANSTINE
  Remedies, *Bellevue Literary Review*
SEAN FLYNN
  Boom, *GQ*
JOHN FRANK
  Pink Suitcases, *The Sun*
THOMAS FRANK
  Bright Frenetic Mills, *Harper's*
ANDREW FRIEDMAN
  Alien Snow, *Ghost Town*

J. MALCOLM GARCIA
  Bed 18, www.guernicamag.com
DAGOBERTO GILB
  Shout, *The Barcelona Review*
ANNE GISLESON
  Rise off Your Knees, New Orleans, *Oxford American*
RACHEL B. GLASER
  The Jon Lennin Xperience, *Puerto del Sol*

MICHAEL HAEDERLE
  The Best Fiscal Stimulus: Trust, *Miller-McCune*
ANTHONY HAM
  Island in the Sand, *The Virginia Quarterly Review*
KAREN HAYS
  Clockwise Detorsion of Snails, *The Normal School*
JAMEY HECHT
  Tim the Immortal Giraffe: True Story, *American Short Fiction*
LACEY PRPIC HEDTKE
  Likes/Dislikes, self-published zine
AMY HEMPEL
  Greed, *Ploughshares*
SMITH HENDERSON
  Number Stations, *One Story*
PABLO HOLMBERG
  Eden, *Drawn & Quarterly*

SAMANTHA HUNT
  The Messenger, *A Public Space*
KIM HYESOON
  Seoul, Kora, *Azalea*
PYUN HYE-YOUNG
  The First Anniversary, *Azalea*

KRISTEN ISKANDRIAN
  Small Acts of Violence Leading Indirectly to the Wiring Issue that
  Caused the Duplex to Burn Down, *Mississippi Review*

MICHAEL JADA & DEREK VAN GIESON
  Devil Doll, *Mome*
PETER JAMISON
  Head Case, *SF Weekly*

DIMITER KENAROV
  It's Impossible to Leave Iraq, *Esquire*
ETGAR KERET
  Lieland, *Zoetrope: All-Story*
RACHEL KHONG
  Today Is a Fish, *Phoebe*
AIDAN KOCH
  Green House, *Mome*
TED KRITIKOS
  I Would Get to Try Life, *Noon*

MICHAEL LACEY
  What's Mom Worth?, *Phoenix New Times*
THOMAS LAKE
  Five-Year-Old Slugger, *Sports Illustrated*
REIF LARSEN
  The Puppet, *One Story*
YIYUN LI
  A Small Sacrifice, *The Threepenny Review*
TAO LIN
  Richard Yates, *Melville House Publishing*

DEB OLIN UNFERTH
Want, *Noon*

ANNE VALENTE
A Very Compassionate Baby, *Annalemma*
WILLIAM T. VOLLMANN
Too Late, *A Public Space*

JOY WILLIAMS
Baba Iaga and the Pelican Child, *Electric Literature*
GARY WOLF
The Data-Driven Life, *New York Times Magazine*
GRAEME WOOD
Limbo World, *Foreign Policy*
ANNIE JULIA WYMAN
A Glimpse of Unplumbed Depths, *The Believer*

JAMES YEH
9/16/10, *Swill Children*
RACHEL YODER
Deliver Me, www.therumpus.net
CHARLES YU
Designer Emotion 67, *Oxford American*

ABOUT 826 NATIONAL

Proceeds from this book benefit youth literacy.

A LARGE PERCENTAGE of the cover price of this book goes to 826 National, a network of tutoring, writing, and publishing centers for youth in eight cities around the country.

Since the birth of 826 National in 2002, our goal has been to assist students ages six through eighteen with their writing skills while helping teachers get their classes passionate about writing. We do this with a vast team of volunteers who donate their time so we can give as much one-on-one attention as possible to the students whose writing needs it. Our mission is based on the understanding that great leaps in learning can happen with one-on-one attention, and that strong writing skills are fundamental to future success.

Through volunteer support, each of the eight 826 chapters — in San Francisco, New York, Los Angeles, Ann Arbor, Chicago, Seattle, Boston, and Washington, DC — provides after-school tutoring, class field trips, writing workshops, and in-school programs, all free of charge, for students, classes, and schools. 826 centers are especially committed to supporting teachers, offering services and resources for English language learners, and publishing student work. Each of the 826 chapters works to produce professional-quality publications written entirely by young people, to forge relationships with teachers in order to create innovative workshops and lesson plans, to inspire students to write and appreciate the written word, and to rally thousands of enthusiastic volunteers to make it all happen. By offering all of our programming for free, we aim to serve families who cannot afford to pay for the level of personalized instruction their children receive through 826 chapters.

The demand for 826 National's services is tremendous. Last year we worked with more than 4,700 volunteers and nearly 24,000 students across the nation, hosting 469 field trips, completing 167 major in-school projects, offering 387 evening and weekend workshops, welcoming over 300 students per day for after-school tutoring, and producing over 850 student publications. At many of our centers, our field trips are fully booked almost a year in advance, teacher requests for in-school tutor support continue to rise, and the majority of our evening and weekend workshops have waitlists.

826 National volunteers are local community residents, professional writers, teachers, artists, college students, parents, bankers, lawyers, and retirees from a wide range of professions. These passionate individuals can be found at all of our centers after school, sitting side-by-side with our students, providing one-on-one attention. They can be found running our field trips, or helping an entire classroom of local students learn how to write a story, or assisting student writers during one of our Young Authors' Book Projects.

All day and in a variety of ways, our volunteers are actively connecting with youth from the communities we serve.

To learn more or get involved, please visit:

826 National: www.826national.org
826 in San Francisco: www.826valencia.org
826 in New York: www.826nyc.org
826 in Los Angeles: www.826la.org
826 in Chicago: www.826chi.org
826 in Ann Arbor: www.826michigan.org
826 in Seattle: www.826seattle.org
826 in Boston: www.826boston.org
826 in Washington, DC: www.826dc.org

826 VALENCIA

Named for the street address of the building it occupies in the heart of San Francisco's Mission District, 826 Valencia opened on April 8, 2002 and consists of a writing lab, a street-front, student-friendly retail pirate store that partially funds its programs, and satellite classrooms in two local middle schools. 826 Valencia has developed programs that reach students at every possible opportunity—in school, after school, in the evenings, or on the weekends. Since its doors opened, over fifteen hundred volunteers—including published authors, magazine founders, SAT course instructors, documentary filmmakers, and other professionals—have donated their time to work with thousands of students. These volunteers allow the center to offer all of its services for free.

826NYC

826NYC's writing center opened its doors in September 2004. Since then its programs have offered over one thousand students opportunities to improve their writing and to work side by side with hundreds of community volunteers. 826NYC has also built a satellite tutoring center, created in partnership with the Brooklyn Public Library, which has introduced library programs to an entirely new community of students. The center publishes a handful of books of student writing each year.

826LA

826LA benefits greatly from the wealth of cultural and artistic resources in the Los Angeles area. The center regularly presents a free workshop at the Armand Hammer Museum in which esteemed artists, writers, and performers teach their craft. 826LA has collaborated with the J. Paul Getty Museum to create Community Photoworks, a months-long program that taught seventh-graders the basics of photographic composition and analysis, sent them into Los Angeles with cameras, and then helped them polish artist statements. Since opening in March 2005, 826LA has provided thousands of hours of free one-on-one writing instruction, held summer camps for English language learners, given students sportswriting training in the Lakers' press room, and published love poems written from the perspectives of leopards.

826 CHICAGO

826 Chicago opened its writing lab and after-school tutoring center in the West Town community of Chicago, in the Wicker Park neighborhood. The setting is both culturally lively and teeming with schools: within one mile, there are fifteen public schools serving more than sixteen thousand students. The center opened in October 2005 and now has over five hundred volunteers. Its programs, like at all the 826 chapters, are designed to be both challenging and enjoyable. Ultimately, the goal is to strengthen each student's power to express ideas effectively, creatively, confidently, and in his or her individual voice.

826MICHIGAN

826michigan opened its doors on June 1, 2005, on South State Street in Ann Arbor. In October of 2007 the operation moved downtown, to a new and improved location on Liberty Street. This move enabled the opening of Liberty Street Robot Supply & Repair in May 2008. The shop carries everything the robot owner might need, from positronic brains to grasping appendages to solar cells. 826michigan is the only 826 not named after a city because it serves students all over southeastern Michigan, hosting in-school residencies in Ypsilanti schools, and providing workshops for students in Detroit, and Lincoln and Willow Run school districts. The center also has a packed workshop schedule on site every semester, with offerings on making pop-up books, writing sonnets, creating screenplays, producing infomercials, and more.

826 SEATTLE

826 Seattle began offering after-school tutoring after school in October 2005, followed shortly by evening and weekend writing workshops and, in December 2005, the first field trip to 826 Seattle by a public school class (Ms. Dunker's fifth graders from Greenwood Elementary). The center is in Greenwood, one of the most diverse neighborhoods in the city. And, thankfully, enough space travelers stop by the Greenwood Space Travel Supply Company at 826 Seattle on their way back from the Space Needle. Revenue from the store, like from all 826 storefronts, helps to support the writing programs, along with the generous outpouring from community members.

826 BOSTON

826 Boston kicked off its programming in the spring of 2007 by inviting authors Junot Díaz, Steve Almond, Holly Black, and Kelly Link to lead writing workshops at the English High School. The visiting writers challenged students to modernize fairy tales, invent their ideal school, and tell their own stories. Afterward, a handful of dedicated volunteers followed up with weekly visits to help students develop their writing craft. These days, the center has thrown open its doors in Roxbury's Egleston Square—a culturally diverse community south of downtown that stretches into Jamaica Plain, Roxbury, and Dorchester. 826 Boston neighbors more than twenty Boston schools, a dance studio, and the Boston Neighborhood Network (a public-access television station).

826DC

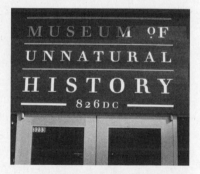

826 National's newest chapter, 826DC, opened its doors to the city's Columbia Heights neighborhood in September 2010. Like all the 826s, 826DC provides after-school tutoring, field trips, after-school workshops, in-school tutoring, help for English language learners, and assistance with the publication of student work. It also offers free admission to the Museum of Unnatural History, the center's unique storefront. 826DC volunteers recently helped the students of two nearby high schools publish *Get Used to the Seats: A Survival Guide for Freshmen*, a book of advice for incoming high schoolers. 826DC's students have also already read poetry for President and First Lady Obama, participating in the 2011 White House Poetry Student Workshop.

SCHOLARMATCH

ScholarMatch, a project of 826 National, is a nonprofit website launched in April 2010 committed to helping students pursue a college education, no matter what their financial status. At the website ScholarMatch.org, students create online profiles that reflect their commitment to their academic future. Potential donors learn about the students in their community through these profiles. Donations to students are then made and the funds are allocated toward a student's scholarship goal. Donor-student relationships grow out of the process, and the student heads to college with the support and motivation to succeed.

Along with the website, ScholarMatch is also a college resource center. Modeled after the 826 National network, it emphasizes one-on-one attention with students. At its office space at 849 Valencia Street in San Francisco's Mission District, it holds workshops and offers drop-in guidance to families and students on their paths to higher education. Whether it's understanding the language of financial aid or personal essay assistance, ScholarMatch provides students with the space and the people to help.

Learn more at: www.scholarmatch.org